THE FORCED LOAN AND ENGLISH POLITICS 1626–1628

FOR MY MOTHER AND FATHER

THE FORCED LOAN AND ENGLISH POLITICS 1626–1628

RICHARD CUST

CLARENDON PRESS · OXFORD
1987

Oxford University Press, Walton Street, Oxford OX2 6DP
Oxford New York Toronto Melbourne Auckland
Delhi Bombay Calcutta Madras Karachi
Petaling Jaya Singapore Hong Kong Tokyo
Nairobi Dar es Salaam Cape Town
Associated companies in Beirut Berlin Ibadan Nicosia

Published in the United States
by Oxford University Press, New York

British Library Cataloguing in Publication Data
Cust, Richard
The forced loan and English politics:
1626–1628.
1. Great Britain—Politics and government
—1603–1714
I. Title
320.942 JN191
ISBN 0–19–822951–8

Library of Congress Cataloging-in-Publication Data
Cust, Richard
The forced loan and English politics, 1626–1628.
Bibliography: p.
Includes index.
1. Finance, Public—Great Britain—To 1688. 2. Intergovernmental fiscal relations—Great Britain—History—17th century. 3. Great Britain—Politics and government—1625–1649. I. Title.
HJ1012.C87 1987 336.42 87–7977
ISBN 0–19–822951–8

Set by Hope Services, Abingdon, Oxon
Printed and bound in Great Britain by
Biddles Ltd, Guildford and King's Lynn

Acknowledgements

I WISH to thank all those who have contributed to the preparation of this book. It began life as a University of London Ph.D. thesis and I am grateful to the Social Science Research Council and the University of Birmingham for funding my research. I also owe thanks to the staffs of all the local record offices and research libraries which I have visited, and to the Duke of Westminster and Mr F. H. T. Jervoise for permission to cite the manuscripts in their possession. All have been unfailingly patient and helpful in answering my numerous fiddly enquiries. In particular, I owe a very considerable debt to the staff and students at the Institute of Historical Research in London. This has long been the friendliest and pleasantest of environments in which to carry out research; and its Tudor and Stuart seminars have provided the best possible opportunity to exchange information and discuss ideas.

I am extremely grateful to the many individuals who have helped in particular ways. Ann Hughes, Tom Cogswell, Peter Lake, and Christopher Thompson all read drafts of the typescript and have contributed immeasurably through their comments. Pene Corfield, Patricia Croot, Norah Fuidge, Jeff Goodman, David Hebb, Jacqueline Levy, Brendan Mannion, Stephen Roberts, Elizabeth Russell, Alan Thomas, David Thomas, Nigel Wood, and Diana Young have always taken an interest and given much help and encouragement. Anthony Fletcher, Mark Kishlansky, John Morrill, Brian Quintrell, Ian Roy, and Nicholas Tyacke have been extremely generous in providing advice and guidance. Johann Sommerville and John Reeve kindly allowed me to make use of their work before publication. Meryl Neale and Sue Offley have patiently deciphered my handwriting and typed the manuscript.

My greatest debt is to Conrad Russell. It should be evident that without his seminal work on the early seventeenth century this study could not have been written; and it was he who first introduced me to the excitements of historical research, and who ever since has guided me and encouraged me with thoughtful, generous, and unfailingly open-minded criticism.

Finally, I wish to thank Ann and Alice Hughes who have given me support, encouragement, and much else besides.

RICHARD CUST

Birmingham,
August 1986

Contents

List of Maps

Abbreviations

Place of publication is London unless otherwise stated.

Add. MS	Additional Manuscript, British Library
APC	*Acts of the Privy Council*
BIHR	*Bulletin of the Institute of Historical Research*
BL	British Library
Bodl. L.	Bodleian Library, Oxford
BRL	Birmingham Reference Library
C. and T.	*Court and Times of Charles I*, 2 vols. ed. T. Birch (1848)
CD 1625	*Debates in the House of Commons in 1625*, ed. S. R. Gardiner (Camden Soc., New Ser. vi, 1873)
CD 1628	*Commons Debates 1628*, 4 vols., ed. R. C. Johnson, M. F. Keeler, M. J. Cole, and W. B. Bidwell (New Haven, 1977–8)
CD 1629	*Commons Debates for 1629*, ed. W. Notestein and F. H. Relf (Minneapolis, 1921)
Chamberlain	*The Letters of John Chamberlain*, 2 vols., ed. N. E. McLure (Philadelphia, 1939)
CJ	*Commons' Journals*
CSPD	*Calendar of State Papers Domestic*
CSP Ven.	*Calendar of State Papers Venetian*
A Declaration	*A declaration of the true causes which moved His Majestie to assemble and after forced him to dissolve the two last meetings in Parliament (1626)*
DNB	*Dictionary of National Biography*
Eg. MS	Egerton Manuscript, British Library
EH	Eaton Hall, Cheshire
EHR	*English Historical Review*
ERO	Essex Record Office
FSL	Folger Shakespeare Library
GEC	G. E. Cockayne, *The Complete Peerage*, 13 vols. (1910–59)
GRO	Gloucestershire Record Office
Harg. MS	Hargrave Manuscript, British Library
Harl. MS	Harleian Manuscript, British Library
Hist.	*History*
HJ	*Historical Journal*
HLRO	House of Lords Record Office
HMC	Historical Manuscripts Commission
Holles	*The Letters of John Holles 1587–1637*, 2 vols., ed. P. R. Seddon (Thoroton Soc., Rec. Ser. xxxi, xxxv, 1975–83).

HRO	Hampshire Record Office
JBS	*Journal of British Studies*
JCAS	*Journal of the Chester Archaeological Society*
JEH	*Journal of Ecclesiastical History*
JMH	*Journal of Modern History*
KAO	Kent Archives Office
Lansd. MS	Lansdowne Manuscript, British Library
Laud	W. Laud, *The Works*, 6 vols. (Oxford, 1853)
LJ	*Lords' Journals*
LP 1628	*Lords Proceedings 1628*, ed. M. F. Keeler, M. J. Cole, W. B. Bidwell (New Haven, 1983)
Melb. H.	Melbourne Hall, Derbyshire
NA	*Norfolk Archaeology*
NH	*Northern History*
NLW	National Library of Wales
NNRO	Norfolk and Norwich Record Office
NRO	Northamptonshire Record Office
NUL	Nottingham University Library
P. and P.	*Past and Present*
P. in P. 1628	*Proceedings in Parliament 1628. Appendices and Index*, ed. M. F. Keeler, M. J. Cole and W. B. Bidwell (New Haven, 1983)
PRO	Public Record Office
Proclamations	*Stuart Royal Proclamations*, 2 vols., ed. P. L. Hughes and J. F. Larkin (Oxford 1973–83)
Rous	*The Diary of John Rous*, ed. M. A. Everett Green (Camden Soc., 1st Ser. lxvi, 1856)
Rushworth	J. Rushworth, *Historical Collections*, 7 vols. (1659–1701)
Rymer	T. Rymer, *Foedera*, 20 vols. (1704–35)
SP	State Papers
SRO	Somerset Record Office
Strafforde Letters	*The Earl of Strafforde's Letters and Dispatches* 2 vols., ed. W. Knowler (1729)
TCC	Trinity College Library, Cambridge
TEAS	*Transactions of the Essex Archaeological Society*
TRHS	*Transactions of the Royal Historical Society*
VCH	*Victoria County History*
Wentworth Papers	*The Wentworth Papers 1597–1628*, ed. J. P. Cooper (Camden Soc., 4th Ser. xii, 1973)
Yonge	*The Diary of Walter Yonge*, ed. G. Roberts (Camden Soc., 1st Ser. xli, 1848)
YRO	Yarmouth Record Office

Dates are old style unless otherwise stated, except that the year is taken to begin on 1 January.

Introduction

It has recently been remarked by a leading parliamentary historian that 'In England in the 1620s the majority of important political events took place outside Parliament . . . Major political decisions were usually taken at Court, and other major political events tended to take place in the country, well away from the Palace of Westminster.'[1] In spite of this, research and writing on the period, with the exception of a number of local studies, has continued to concentate on the events and personalities of the Parliaments. We are still much better informed about parliamentary politics and legislation than the workings of the Court or the main institutions of central government, such as the Privy Council and the Exchequer. And, whilst the careers and attitudes of leading MPs have been thoroughly studied, comparatively little is known about the views of the King or his leading advisers. This is perhaps understandable, given the relative wealth of sources for investigating Parliament and the continuing debate over its role before the English Civil War; however, as Professor Russell's remarks, cited above, indicate, it has led to a very real imbalance in our understanding of the period. If, as has been argued, a meeting of Parliament was an occasional, in some senses 'abnormal' event, it follows that we need to have a better understanding of the periods between Parliaments, when politics returned to relative 'normality'. And if the crucial decisions were being arrived at outside Parliament, often far away from Westminster, then a knowledge of these is essential to setting the Parliaments themselves in their proper context.[2] It is in response to such considerations that this study has been undertaken.

The beginnings of the Forced Loan can be traced back to the fiscal crisis facing the Crown in the aftermath of the 1626 Parliament. At the time it was more or less committed to fighting a war on two fronts, against both France and Spain; and with the cost of this accelerating to upwards of £1,000,000 a year it was in

[1] C. S. R. Russell, *Parliaments and English Politics 1621–1629* (Oxford, 1979), p. 1.

[2] Ibid., pp. 1–8; C. S. R. Russell, 'The nature of a Parliament in early-stuart England', in *Before the English Civil War*, ed. H. Tomlinson (1983), pp. 123–50.

desperate need of additional revenue. This the Parliament had failed to provide. After voting in principle to give the King four subsidies, the Commons had brought charges against the Duke of Buckingham, thus causing Charles to terminate the proceedings. Following this the Council made an abortive attempt to raise money through a direct appeal to the taxpayer. In July 1626 letters were dispatched to the shires, outlining the King's needs and asking that the equivalent of the four subsidies be paid in the form of a benevolence. This scheme was poorly conceived and inadequately supported; however the main reason for its failure was the widespread feeling that it threatened the principle of requiring parliamentary consent for national taxes. Benevolences had been condemned by statute in the past, and this provided the justification for most shires to reply that they would give, but only if the money was voted in the proper manner.[3]

It was to get around this objection that the Council's next scheme took the form of a loan. It was based on earlier Privy Seal Loans which had generally been regarded as a legitimate means of extra-parliamentary supply; however there were important differences. Privy Seal Loans were levied by personal letters sent out to selected individuals, whereas this loan was to be raised from the subsidymen *en masse*, with each being assessed at the equivalent of five subsidies. And whilst the privy seal letters contained specific promises of repayment, these were now left extremely vague.[4] Such differences indicated that what was being proposed more nearly resembled a tax than a loan; and what made this particularly objectionable was the context in which it was being levied and the severity of the measures taken to enforce it.

When the Forced Loan was adopted by the Council in mid-September 1626 this was done in the face of general expectation of a Parliament. The immediate cause of the levy was a new foreign policy crisis, precipitated by the defeat of Charles's ally, Christian of Denmark, at the Battle of Lutter. But the decision to raise money in this particular way was also very obviously shaped by the legacy of the previous Parliament. Fears that a fresh summons would lead to renewed attacks on the Duke persuaded both King and Council to put this off and make another direct request to the taxpayer. In these circumstances the loan inevitably came to be

[3] Russell, *Parliaments and English Politics*, Chs. 5–6; S. R. Gardiner, *History of England*, 10 vols. (1883–4), vi. 125, 131.

[4] Gardiner, *History*, vi. 143, 158; F. C. Dietz, *English Public Finance 1485–1641*, 2 vols. (2nd edn., 1964), ii. 25–6, 62–3, 115; PRO SP 16/36/42–3.

seen as akin to a benevolence. In spite of the King's assurances that it would not be repeated, it was regarded by many as yet another threat to the traditional method of raising supply. To add to this when the Council began to collect the loan it resorted to the most forceful measures at its disposal. The first efforts to raise money were made in October 1626, with Privy Councillors holding meetings with commissioners for the shires around London. Here they extracted promises of payment and bound over leading refusers, who were then either committed to prison or pressed in readiness for service abroad.[5]

In these early stages the service proceeded relatively smoothly. At the end of October, however, it received an unexpected setback when the bench of Judges, led by the Lord Chief Justice, refused to subscribe to the loan's legality; and this resistance was reinforced two weeks later when a group of fifteen leading peers also refused to subscribe and expressed their open opposition. As a result for much of November the fate of the levy hung in the balance, and the Council seriously considered abandoning it. In the event they decided to proceed, but only after a lengthy series of discussions and a firm lead by the King.[6]

During December the Councillors once again resumed their meetings in the shires, this time in delegations of two or three, often accompanied by courtiers or peers who supported the service. The counties visited before the end of the year—Berkshire, Cambridgeshire, Hampshire, Sussex, and Suffolk—were by and large co-operative, and the Council helped to ensure this by offering them concessions over the repayment of billeting charges. It was not until the middle of the following January that the service again ran into serious opposition. Then, in successive meetings in Northamptonshire, Lincolnshire, and Gloucestershire, groups of leading gentry commissioners not only refused to co-operate, but openly resisted. Once again the Council responded forcefully. The ringleaders were summoned to London, and from February onwards large numbers were detained there under virtual house arrest, whilst the lesser refusers were once more threatened with pressing. The effects of this severity, however, were less beneficial than before. Resistance in these shires was widely reported and this seems to have stimulated opposition elsewhere. Thus in Essex for the first time large numbers of ordinary subsidymen, below the level of the gentry,

[5] See below, Ch. 1, ii.

[6] Gardiner, *History*, vi. 143–4, 148–9; see below, Ch. 1, ii.

became openly obstructive towards the local commissioners.[7]

From March 1627 onwards the struggle to collect the money became a process of attrition. The Privy Council in London continued to summon refusers, and provide support and encouragement; but the main burden of work fell on local commissioners and collectors. It was they who had the task of knocking on doors, chasing up defaulters and cajoling those who were reluctant to pay. During the summer months the money came in steadily, and by the end of November the total received by the Exchequer had reached £161,532, which, added to the £82,244 granted in various forms of concessions, meant that £243,776 had been accounted for. This compared very favourably with the £275,000 raised on the five subsidies granted by Parliament in 1628, and indicated that in financial terms the loan had already been a considerable success.[8] The cost of this politically, however, was extremely high.

The presence in London of large numbers of gentry refusers continually directed public attention to the severity of measures taken to enforce the loan; and the pronouncements of some of the levy's more aggressive supporters—such as Robert Sibthorpe and Roger Manwaring, who preached in favour of regarding all taxes, from whatever source, as due to the King by divine right—raised disquieting questions about the extent of royal power. Concern over these issues came to a head with the Five Knights Case of November 1627. Since the previous April a group of leading refusers had been seeking a public trial in which the basis of the loan, together with the grounds of their confinement, could be tested at law. The Council finally acceded to this, but in the event any discussion of the loan's legality was avoided, and what was at issue was simply the King's power to imprison without showing cause. In spite of this, however, the decision against the Five Knights provoked a public outcry, and ultimately became the central issue in the 1628 Parliament.[9]

In the longer term the impact of the loan was reflected in the Petition of Right. The first five clauses of this each referred to it in one way or another, and the document as a whole was intended to prevent a return to the methods adopted whilst it was being

[7] Gardiner, *History*, vi. 154–8; see below, Ch. 2, iii; Ch. 5, ii.

[8] PRO SP 16/85/76; R. Ashton, *The Crown and the Money Market* (Oxford, 1960), pp. 29, 41.

[9] Gardiner, *History*, vi. 205–17; Russell, *Parliaments and English Politics*, Ch. 6; J. Guy, 'The origins of the Petition of Right reconsidered', *HJ* xxv (1982), 289–312.

collected.[10] Because of this the loan has often been seen as one of the most significant episodes in pre-Civil War politics. For S. R. Gardiner it was the product of 'new counsels' by which Charles came increasingly to rely on the prerogative; and the resistance to it was inspired by a high-minded regard for principle: 'the list of those who were willing to suffer persecution for their rights as Englishmen is a thing not to be forgotten. . . . The cause concerned rich and poor alike, and rich and poor stepped forward to suffer for it—each class in its own way. The day would come if they were pressed hard when rich and poor would step forward to fight for it.'[11] This view of the loan, as a staging-post on the 'High Road to Civil War', has also been echoed by later historians writing in the same, broadly Whig, tradition as Gardiner. T. G. Barnes, reviewing the situation in Somerset, argued that it marked 'the end of the justices as officers above the constitutional struggle that had disrupted the relations of the King and Parliament . . . opposition and pressure were so considerable that the issue could not be avoided as, time and again, the justices had avoided it before'; and Perez Zagorin has presented opposition to the loan as 'the first outbreak of large scale disobedience to the royal government', heralding the climax to a first stage of struggle between 'Court' and 'Country'.[12]

Latterly, however, this verdict has come into question. With the work of local historians and so-called 'revisionists' we have come to appreciate more clearly the extent of attachment to the local community and the continual striving towards consensus in relations between King and subject. This has led to a general revaluation of what have traditionally been seen as conflicts of principle. Local historians have stressed that opposition to national taxes generally owed far more to backsliding and a dislike of the disruption and inconvenience caused, than to any concern for constitutional propriety; and a greater understanding of the problems of administration—particularly in wartime—have led to a recognition that governmental decision-making was often a reflex action, prompted by the necessity to make ends meet.[13]

[10] J. P. Kenyon, *The Stuart Constitution 1603–1688* (Cambridge, 1966), pp. 82–5.

[11] Gardiner, *History*, vi. 122–33, 156–7.

[12] T. G. Barnes, *Somerset 1625–1640* (Oxford, 1961), pp. 167–8; P. Zagorin *The Court and the Country* (1969), pp. 109–10.

[13] J. S. Morrill, *The Revolt of the Provinces* (1976), pp. 13–30; A. Fletcher, *A County Community in Peace and War: Sussex 1600–1660* (1975), pp. 202–15;

These insights have been incorporated into the work of Professor Russell, and have led him to downgrade considerably the importance of the loan. Instead of regarding it as an attempt to undermine the position of Parliament and introduce prerogative rule, he has argued that it arose simply out of the Crown's immediate financial needs and that, once these had been met, the King was then quite prepared to return to more traditional methods. Similarly, far from being regarded as an issue of principle he has emphasized that for many 'the Forced Loan appears to have often been just another disagreeable and in the end inevitable demand for money'.[14]

As this verdict indicates, the precise significance of the loan is open to considerable debate; and in this debate are encapsulated many of the issues which have recently divided historians of the early seventeenth century. It raises questions about the importance of ideological principle in shaping political action; the impact of warfare on government and administration; the effects of a so called 'crisis of counsel'; and the political significance of social groups below the gentry.[15] A detailed study of the sort being attempted here should throw light on these matters and others besides. Before embarking on this, however, it is appropriate to say something about the source materials.

Sources for the loan fall into four main groups: the records of central government such as the council registers, the financial accounts of the Exchequer and the correspondence and working papers of the Secretaries of State (known as the State Papers); the records of local government to be found in quarter sessions papers, the collections of letters kept by Deputy Lieutenants and the minute-books of Corporations; the personal correspondence, newsletters and diaries produced by country gentlemen and various individuals around the Court, such as the Venetian ambassador; and finally a series of tracts, sermons, and proclama-

D. M. Hirst, 'The Privy Council and problems of enforcement in the 1620s', *JBS* xviii (1978), 46–66.

[14] Russell, *Parliaments and English Politics*, pp. 330–4, 337–40, 394–6.

[15] Ibid., Ch. I; T. K. Rabb and D. M. Hirst 'Revisionism Revised: two perspectives on early stuart parliamentary history', *P. and P.* 92 (1981), 55–99; K. Sharpe, 'Parliamentary history 1603–1629: in or out of perspective?' in *Faction and Parliament*, ed. K. Sharpe (Oxford, 1978), pp. 1–42; C. Hill, 'Parliament and People in seventeenth-century England', *P. and P.* 92 (1981), 100–24; A. Fletcher and C. Hill, 'Debate: Parliament and People in seventeenth-century England', *P. and P.* 98 (1983), 151–8.

tions relating to the loan, some of them printed and some in manuscript. This collection has certain specific strengths, and one particular weakness, which must be taken into account.

The most impressive aspect of the sources is the amount of information which they provide on links between local and central government. The financial records give details of every payment made into the Exchequer by the loan's collectors, and also a good deal of material on the way in which this process of collection was organized locally. The council registers contain a record of most of the defaulters who were summoned and dealt with for non-payment. And the State Papers, used in conjunction with these registers and local government records, give almost complete runs of the correspondence between local commissioners and Privy Councillors. One can therefore reconstruct the administrative processes by which the money was raised in considerable detail, and this has been done for the shires of Norfolk and Essex. It is also possible to go a good deal further and analyse the attitudes of those involved in government. The loan was in many ways as much a political as an administrative exercise. This means that the correspondence which it generated often reveals much about the political assumptions which governed relations between the centre and the localities. It tells us, for example, about the way in which the Council viewed the coercive powers at its disposal; about the extent to which it appreciated its own limitations; and about the things that Loan Commissioners were prepared to tell it, and thought it wanted to hear. Above all it reveals the subtle bargaining processes which normally accompanied dealings between central and local governors, and shows the way in which pledges of support were extracted in return for offers of patronage, promises of concessions, and threats of disfavour.[16] All this is very fully illustrated.

So too are the arguments which the Crown put forward to justify the levy. These appeared in a variety of guises: formal statements and proclamations, often made with the direct approval of the King; letters, memoranda and council speeches produced for the purpose of discussing the levy; and printed sermons and less formal statements produced as exercises in propaganda. These, of course, tell us a good deal about the way in which councillors, and others, felt that the levy could be made acceptable to the subject.

[16] See below, Ch. 2, iii.

However they also reveal an interesting division of opinion over its implications and significance, which suggests that there were fundamental differences of attitude between the King and many of his advisers.[17] Again this is well documented.

A third area which is relatively fully covered is the impact of the Duke of Buckingham's patronage, at least in so far as it affected some of the shires. Amongst the State Papers, there survives a good deal of correspondence belonging to Edward Nicholas who at this time was handling many of the Duke's requests for favour. His papers therefore illustrate the effects of Buckingham's interventions at a time when these were particularly significant. After the parliamentary attack of 1626, he had decided to trust only those who had demonstrated their absolute loyalty and take revenge on those who could be identified as his enemies. This had important consequences in that it brought about a purge of the Commissions of the Peace which upset the balance of power in several shires and caused local gentry to be drawn increasingly into court politics and discussions about the future of Parliament. It also led the Duke's adherents—finding that their position depended more than ever on his favour—to disregard the obligations of neighbourliness and turn informer against their fellow gentry. As a result the letters of clients like Sir James Bagg or John Poulett came to be filled with a series of unusually frank and detailed statements about the behind-the-scenes manœuvring of local politicians. Some of their assertions obviously need to be taken with large handfuls of salt, particularly the more vitriolic allegations of Bagg. But even when this is done, enough remains to provide some fascinating glimpses of the way in which court rivalries and parliamentary conflicts translated into local politics, and how this in turn influenced the broader political attitudes of county governors.[18] Once again the sources for this are comparatively full.

Where they are much less informative—and present considerable problems for the researcher—is in reflecting the extent of conflict and opposition. There are several reasons for this. In part it has to do with a tendency for some institutional sources to minimize evidence of disagreement and convey an impression of routine and continuity. A good example is the council register. If one examines the copies of letters and orders—signed by all the councillors present—which this contains one gets the very strong

[17] See below, Ch. 1, ii.
[18] See below, Ch. 4, ii.

impression that council decisions were arrived at by consensus. There is no evidence of debate and no sign of division.[19] However, this appearance is deceptive. A series of council regulations for 1625 make it quite clear that debate and discussion were a normal part of the Council's procedure:

When anie thinge is propounded at the Boarde it falleth consequently into debate, every man speakinge to it as hee findeth cause. If it bee apparent and cleere, resolution is taken accordingly, but if difficult and perplexed they take further time of consideration, desire a full Boarde, and appoint a seconde and sometimes a thirde or fourth meetinge. When all is sayd that wilbe spoken, they settle it by vote, beginning with the lowest and soe ascendinge upwarde. The major parte ordereth the matter.[20]

It was noted that 'this voteinge or opininge falleth out but seldom'; however significantly it was also remarked that when it did it was usually in 'causes of great consequence or in Arduis Regni'. The absence of any regular record of such debates was also explained, by the fact that they were normally conducted in secret, without the attendance of the Council Clerk. The final record produced by the Council, then, often belied the real extent of the divisions accompanying its proceedings.

Much the same point can also be made about local records, in particular the reports sent in by local commissioners. Here, however, the deception had less to do with institutional arrangements than with the conventions governing their exercise of office. In matters involving the Council a majority of local governors adopted the maxim of the Northamptonshire JP, Sir Rowland St John: 'It is observed to be a rule of discreet policy in general businesses to make a general answer, lest by descending too far into particulars something should be fastened upon which may produce an unexpected prejudice.'[21] A combination of neighbourliness, concern to minimise political division and unwillingness to invite conciliar intervention generally inhibited local governors from revealing the 'real' situation in their shires. This tendency has been revealed with regard to subsidy assessment or the reports sent in by ship money sheriffs, and it is equally apparent in the case of the loan. Commissioners usually tried to present their neighbours' responses as favourably as possible, and

[19] *APC 1625–1628, passim.*

[20] PRO SP 16/8/79.

[21] Cited by K. Sharpe, 'The personal rule of Charles I' in *Before the English Civil War*, pp. 67–8. For an example of this approach see St John's studiously vague account of the fate of the 1626 Benevolence in the eastern division of Northamptonshire: below p. 98.

the Council's lack of information on what was happening locally often allowed them to get away with this.[22] In consequence really frank and explicit records were only sent in when local governors had some specific reason for seeking favour or support from the Council; and this generally happened either because they were involved in a local power struggle or because the situation was getting beyond their control and they wished to avoid being held responsible. All this meant that again the official sources could underplay the extent of conflict and opposition.

To get around this problem it is generally necessary to look to unofficial sources. These come in a variety of forms. Occasionally we have sets of notes taken during council debates—often in the Council of War from which Clerks were apparently not excluded;[23] sometimes diaries and memoranda survive which reveal what individuals thought about contemporary politics; and, most useful of all, we have a considerable number of diplomatic dispatches and newsletters, covering incidents and episodes which often went unmentioned in official records. These latter sources were used a good deal by Gardiner, and clearly influenced his impression of the extent of political conflict; however more recently they have been treated with suspicion by 'revisionist' historians such as Russell.[24] It is therefore appropriate to say something about their reliability.

Most of Russell's specific reservations relate to the reports made by the Venetian ambassador. As he quite rightly stresses these reveal an extremely crude and ill-informed view of the nature of political divisions in England; one therefore has to discount their repeated references to a 'Puritan opposition' or their vague assertions about the nature of opinion in the country. However this does not mean that all the information they provided was valueless. As Russell himself has pointed out, when ambassadors were dealing with the rise and fall of court factions or speculation about policy-making and the future of Parliament—matters in

[22] Fletcher, *A County Community*, pp. 203–4; P. G. Lake, 'The collection of Ship Money in Cheshire during the 1630s: a case study in relations between local and central government', *NH* xvii (1981), 63–5; Hirst, 'Privy Council and enforcement', 52 n. See for example the efforts of the Notts. Loan Commissioners to excuse Sir Thomas Hutchinson after he had opposed the service or Lord Maynard's reluctance to certify refusers from Essex: PRO SP 16/55/1, 1 ii; *APC 1627*, pp. 74, 123; PRO SP 16/72/44.

[23] Berks. RO Trumbull MS, bdl. 48 (Sir Wm. Trumbull's notes on the Council of War, June 1626); PRO SP 16/28.

[24] Gardiner, *History*, vi. 149–50, 155–7 n.; Russell, *Parliaments and English Politics*, pp. xviii, 25–6.

which their masters expected them to take a professional interest—they were likely to be as reliable as any other source. Alvise Contarini, the Venetian envoy between 1626 and 1628, had developed close personal contacts with Councillors like Sir Dudley Carleton and the Earl of Pembroke; and once his reports have been checked against other accounts, and allowance made for the views of his informants, they can yield much valuable information.[25]

A similar point can be made about domestic newsletters. If one tries to use these to gauge the response of the majority then one is likely to get a distorted and exaggerated view, simply because they tended to focus on headline material and events which were out of the ordinary. However if one is using them for evidence on specific incidents, and the way these were being reported and discussed, then they are much more dependable. By the 1620s news-gathering had become a relatively sophisticated process, centring on St Paul's Walk and the Exchange in London. Here rumour and gossip were collected and exchanged each day, and surprisingly detailed information could be obtained about matters as diverse as the conduct of a county election or the latest deliberations of the King's advisers.[26] Francis Osborne, writing some years later, explained the origins of many of these reports:

> in regard of the universal commerce there happened little that did not first and last arrive here. And those news mongers . . . did not only take the boldness to weigh the public, but intrinsic actions of the state, which some courtier or other did betray to this society. Amongst whom divers, being very rich, had great sums owing them by such as stood next the throne who by this means were rendered in a manner their pensioners. . . . I have found since little reason to question the truth of what I heard then but much to confirm me in it.[27]

Where it is possible to test the accuracy of reports against other sources they generally bear out Osborne's verdict: for example two accounts of interviews with loan refusers before the Privy Council can be corroborated almost verbatim from the council registers.[28] All this, then, suggests that newsletters, when used in the right way, are a valuable supplement to official accounts and help to correct some of the distortions inherent in these. However

[25] *CSP Ven. 1625–6*, pp. 370–1, 528; ibid., 1626–8, pp. 101–2, 144, 434, 572.

[26] R. P. Cust, 'News and politics in early seventeenth century England', *P. and P.* 112 (1986), 60–90.

[27] Cited by W. Notestein, *Four Worthies* (1956), p. 31 n.

[28] *C. and T.* i. 193–4, 198; *APC* 1627, pp. 42, 62.

it should be recognized that even newsletters can sometimes underplay the extent of conflict.

As with reports of local governors this may have had something to do with a general concern to preserve harmony and avoid appearing to harp on division. However a more obvious reason was the widespread fear of letters falling into the wrong hands. The occasions on which this happened were relatively widely publicized, and this tended to make contemporaries extremely wary of discussing sensitive issues on paper; in particular news relating to the Duke was an area to be avoided.[29] It is therefore no surprise to discover Owen Wynn, in a letter to his father in North Wales, referring to the events of the 1626 Parliament as 'such as you may heare at the second hand with greater safetie then may be written'.[30] It was this sort of caution which also prompted the Earl of Clare to reprimand his son, after an indiscreet letter to Sir Thomas Wentworth: 'what you writt, you might better have spoken . . . for though I presume you may safely open your pack there, yet why should you putt your self into any man's curtesy, under the wittnes of your owne hand, espetially to be a critike in state matters'.[31] Fortunately Clare himself was sufficiently disgruntled with the Court to ignore his own advice and, as a result, his newsletters contain some remarkably frank and revealing comments. However most of his contemporaries were much more reticent, and the injunction which one sometimes finds to 'burne . . . this letter' reflects the considerable degree of caution when it came to discussing the issues of the day.[32] This must be allowed for when it comes to assessing the degree of public interest aroused by the loan and the contemporary view of its political significance. In particular it means that we should be very cautious about using arguments from silence to suggest a lack of concern or familiarity with the issues at stake; and where we have evidence of conflict, or principled opposition, we should give it due weight.

[29] *C. and T.* i. 167–8; I. Morgan, *Prince Charles's Puritan Chaplain* (1957), pp. 164–6.

[30] NLW Wynn of Gwydir MS 1389, 1391.

[31] *Holles*, ii. 314.

[32] BL Add. MS 11,044, fos. 11–12 (I am grateful to Christopher Thompson for this reference); W. S. Powell, *John Pory 1572–1636* (Chapel Hill, NC, 1977), p. 58.

I

The Privy Council, Parliament and Prerogative Finance, 1626–1628

I. THE LEGACY OF THE 1626 PARLIAMENT

ON the morning of 15 June 1626 the Lord Keeper, Thomas Coventry, delivered a message to the House of Lords announcing the King's intention to dissolve the Parliament. Earlier in the day he was reported to have been 'earnest with the King, upon his knees, to have it continued', but Charles was adamant and forced him to deliver the message by threatening him with dismissal.[1] When the announcement was made 'a general murmur sounded through the House' and Lord Montague, an old and respected parliamentary speaker and brother to the Lord President of the Council, rose to his feet and proposed that the Lords, 'should move His Majesty to think again before he carried out the dissolution by reason of the inconvenience that might arise both to the religious honour of His Majesty and the safety of the Kingdom'.[2] This motion was warmly applauded and the House immediately appointed a deputation, consisting of four senior Privy Councillors—the Earls of Manchester, Pembroke, Carlisle, and Holland—to attend the King and petition him 'to continue this Parliament by which these great and apparent dangers, both at home and abroad may be prevented, and your Majesty made happy in the duty and love of your people, which we hold to be the greatest safety and security of a King'.[3] They met with Charles in St James's Park, later in the morning, but in spite of their pleas he remained unmoved. He told them the 'wound is not from your Lordships but from the House of Commons' and insisted that the dissolution should proceed.[4]

Outside Parliament news of this was greeted with a mixture of

[1] *Rous*, p. 3; *CSP Ven. 1625–6*, p. 462.

[2] HMC *Buccleuch*, iii. 302; *CSP Ven. 1625–6*, pp. 452–3; Russell, *Parliaments and English Politics*, p. 321.

[3] *LJ* iii. 682.

[4] *CSP Ven. 1625–6*, p. 453; Russell, *Parliaments and English Politics*, p. 321.

dismay and apprehension. Londoners noted the disturbing portent of a whirlwind which suddenly appeared on the day of dissolution, swept up the Thames and beat against the walls of Buckingham's residence at York House, where it knocked down a set of steps which the Duke had recently constructed.[5] The secretary to the Venetian ambassador anticipated the problems that it would cause for England's affairs abroad: 'Everybody is astonished at this unexpected step of the King. Wise men think he has acted too precipitately and they foretell disturbances in the Kingdom and discredit abroad with the total ruin of everything, especially the affairs of Germany, since without a Parliament they do not know where to turn to find money'.[6] And Sir John Scudamore, at his country residence in Herefordshire, greeted the news with some gloomy, but perceptive, predictions of difficulties at home: 'It is good for no party. It looseth the King 500,000 besides his reputation abroade and at home. It sharpneth hatred against the Duke, who being twice Parliament blasted will bee hardly acceptable to the third. It is ill for the people, for they have gotten the King's displeasure and may feare the effects'.[7] The only group to welcome the dissolution were the dependants of the Duke who, again according to the Venetian's secretary, 'outwardly display the joy they feel, as they believe and say that by the dissolution the King has resolved to repress the hardihood and arrogance of his subjects, as His Majesty means to rule as a King and not to be ruled. They call for punishment against those who have spoken loudly against Buckingham and display great animosity towards Bristol'.[8]

This episode is interesting in several respects. It showed the King's determination and firmness of purpose once he had resolved on a particular course of action. It demonstrated the interest taken in Parliament by foreign observers, who looked to it for signs of how united the English nation was. It illustrated the concern of informed opinion that a Parliament should produce harmony and co-operation. And it brought to the surface the vindictiveness of Buckingham's supporters, which was to be a feature of the following months. However, perhaps its most revealing aspect was the indication of divisions within the Privy Council over the best means of governing the country. There were apparently senior ministers who, in spite of all the recent difficulties and the King's clear intentions, remained committed

[5] *C. and T.* i. 113–14, 117.

[6] *CSP Ven. 1625–6*, p. 453.

[7] BL Add. MS 11, 044, fos. 11–12.

[8] *CSP Ven. 1625–6*, p. 453.

to pursuing a dialogue between Crown and subject. Their motives were complex and involved; but they are worth exploring as an insight into some of the central assumptions which determined policy.

On a pragmatic level Parliament was still seen as the obvious means of raising extraordinary supply. This was so in spite of the declining value of subsidies which, since the 1590s, had come to appear increasingly inadequate as a means of financing modern warfare. During this decade Elizabeth had received an unprecedented twelve subsidies and twenty fifteenths, but had still accumulated debts of around £400,000. And in 1625 the costs of the conflict with Spain were estimated at well over £1,000,000 of which less than a third was met by parliamentary grants.[9] Yet these remained more valuable than figures alone would indicate because, unlike most other sources of royal revenue—including customs, loans and benevolences—they had not been pledged in advance and their yield was reasonably predictable. This made them, in the words of Philip Burlamachi, the Crown's leading creditor, 'a perfect security', and loans could therefore be raised on the 1625 and 1628 subsidies almost as soon as these had been granted. They constituted the ideal 'windfall revenue' which, as the Spanish experience with treasure fleets had shown, made them particularly valuable when it came to financing military expeditions.[10] Councillors, then, evidently had good financial reasons for persevering with the Parliament.

None the less this was probably not their principal motive. Of at least as much importance was Parliament's value as an exercise in public relations. In part this was directed towards foreign observers, whose attention to Parliaments was widely acknowledged.[11] However, as the terms of the councillors' petition indicated, the main object was to nurture the love of the people at home, and at the same time strengthen the monarchy. It was widely accepted that this could best be done through a meeting of Parliament, where, in return for listening to the subjects' grievances and providing the statutes and orders necessary to remedy them, the King could

[9] C. S. R. Russell, 'Parliament and the King's finance', in C. S. R. Russell (ed.), *The Origins of the English Civil War* (1973), pp. 97–8; Dietz, *English Public Finance*, ii. 219–22.

[10] PRO SP 16/8/26; Ashton, *Crown and Money Market*, p. 32; G. Parker, *The Army of Flanders and the Spanish Road 1567–1659* (Cambridge, 1972), pp. 152–6, 239.

[11] C. S. R. Russell, 'Parliamentary history in perspective 1604–29', *Hist.* 201 (1976), 17.

expect to be given a freewill offering of the subjects' personal property, to help him meet his own needs. This exchange of gifts was seen as symbolizing the English nation's consent to a system of limited royal government, the *dominium politicum et regale* of Sir John Fortescue. In many people's eyes, it was the meeting of a Parliament which gave to the Crown its peculiar strength and stability, and it is this above all which explains why councillors were so committed to persevering with it.[12]

Given this attitude, perhaps the most surprising aspect of the episode was not the behaviour of the councillors, but rather Charles's insistence on a dissolution. On the face of it this can be explained by the Commons' vote on 12 June to go ahead with presenting their Remonstrance against the Duke. Once this had happened then dissolution became the surest way of saving him. However the intention to press charges had been obvious for some time and one therefore has to ask why Charles had delayed dissolution until this stage instead of proceeding with it in April or May. The most plausible answer would appear to be the one offered by Russell, that this reflected the King's adherence to the ideals of his senior councillors. In support of this, it would seem that for much of the Parliament strenuous efforts were made to accommodate the Duke's critics; and the timing of the final dissolution probably related to a deadlock over the Bristol case in the Lords rather than to any action by the Commons. One might conclude, therefore, that Charles continued with the Parliament as long as there was any likelihood that this would produce results, and only abandoned it when it finally became clear that he could obtain neither supply nor a judgement against Bristol.[13] However, this would be to miss an important element in the story. Just as crucial to the King's final decision was his developing concern for his royal honour.

From the early stages of the Parliament Charles had adopted the dangerous tactic of trying to forestall criticism of his ministers by taking responsibility for their actions on himself. During the St Peter case in March he had claimed that the ship had been seized on his personal orders; and thereafter insisted that he alone was

[12] M. A. Judson, *The Crisis of the Constitution* (New Jersey, 1949), pp. 41–3, 68–106; Russell, *Parliaments and English Politics*, pp. 53–4, 338–9: G. L. Harriss, 'Medieval doctrines in the debates on supply, 1610–1629', in *Faction and Parliament*, pp. 76–8.

[13] Russell, *Parliaments and English Politics*, Ch. 5.

accountable for his servants' actions.[14] In the short term this yielded advantages in that it deflected the charge that Buckingham had been acting without royal knowledge or consent. However, as the Commons continued to voice their complaints, it threatened to bring them into direct conflict with the King's person. This was not something they wished for, or found in the least congenial, but it was predictable given Charles's approach.

The consequences were becoming apparent by the middle of March. The Venetian ambassador reported a council debate, apparently taking place on the 19th, at which the King had proposed a dissolution only to be talked out of it by Manchester and Sir Humphrey May, who emphasized 'the impossibility of subsisting unless the King were at one with his people'.[15] Thereafter, the suggestion was revived at intervals, with Buckingham and his dependants strongly in favour of dissolution—at least in the latter stages—whilst the more moderate councillors opposed it and the King oscillated between the two.[16]

In the statements made at the time Charles's doubts about Parliament were generally linked with a threat to his honour and authority seen as emanating from the Commons. On 29 March the Lord Keeper told the House that 'His Majesty cannot believe that the aim is at the Duke of Buckingham, but your proceedings do expressly wound the honour and government of himself and his father'.[17] In May this theme was further developed when the King declared to the Lords that their honour, as well as his, was now at stake.[18] And in the same month, the French ambassador, Bishop Mende, warned Charles to his face that unless he stood up to his subjects, and showed that he could protect the Duke, he would be humiliated in the eyes of Europe and his authority would be accounted no more than that of a Doge of Venice.[19]

Similar arguments were advanced at the time of the dissolution in mid-June. The secretary to the Venetian ambassador reported that 'from the King and the dependants of the Duke of Buckingham one hears complaints that the parliamentarians are too audacious and that His Majesty ought not to suffer his dignity and reputation

[14] Gardiner, *History*, vi. 67, 74–5, 107–8; *CSP Ven. 1625–6*, pp. 344, 351–2, 365–6.

[15] *CSP Ven. 1625–6*, p. 380; PRO C.115, N.5/8633.

[16] *CSP Ven. 1625–6*, pp. 380, 427, 432; PRO 31/3/63, fos. 87–9.

[17] Russell, *Parliaments and English Politics*, pp. 291–2.

[18] Gardiner, *History*, vi. 107–8.

[19] PRO 31/3/63, fos. 81–3.

to be taken away from him by his subjects'.[20] A proclamation issued on the 16th denounced the Commons' Remonstrance as containing 'manie things which tende much to the dishonour of his nowe majestie and of his late majestie . . . whereby through the sides of a peere of this realme they wounde the honour of the soveraigne'. Another for raising a benevolence, which reached only the drafting stage, referred to the 'malicious practises of wikked spiritts indeavoring to cross all propositions which we shall make'.[21] And the warrant, in which Charles authorized further investigation of Bristol and his accomplices, accused them of bringing before Parliament 'divers things tendinge much to our dishonoure and to the stirring up of the disaffection of divers of the members of both houses for the furtherance of their private ends'.[22] These views were incorporated, in a less strident form, in *A Declaration of the true causes which moved His Majestie to assemble and after inforced him to dissolve the two last meetings in Parliament*, published on 30 June. Here Charles accounted for his actions by describing how a few factious MPs had undermined the proceedings of the Commons so that instead of expressing their natural love and desire to co-operate with the Crown, they had mounted an 'intemperate' and 'disordered' assault on the royal favourite.[23] In such circumstances, he maintained he had no choice but to dissolve.

The King's actions, then, were consistently justified in terms of the misbehaviour of his subjects, and the sources of disruption were traced back to an 'ill-affected' element within the Commons. This was to have important implications for the making of policy over the following months, not least with regard to raising supply. Before exploring this, however, it is worth spending a little more time on the perception of a threat to royal authority. This had been heightened by recent events, but it was by no means new. Similar concerns can be traced into the reign of Charles's father

[20] *CSP Ven. 1625–6*, pp. 461–2. The Duke's dependants are not named, but there is evidence elsewhere to indicate who some of them might have been. Both Secretary Conway and Bishop Laud wrote letters at the time expressing views on Parliament similar to those cited above and the French ambassador identified the Earl of Holland as Buckingham's most consistent supporter in Council: PRO SP 104/167, p. 82; H. R. Trevor-Roper, *Archbishop Laud 1573–1645* (1962), pp. 444–6; PRO 31/3/63, fos. 74–6, 79–80.

[21] *Proclamations*, ii. 93–5; PRO SP 16/30/2.

[22] BL Eg. MS 2978, fo. 18^{r}.

[23] *A Declaration of the true cause which moved His Majestie to assemble and after inforced him to dissolve the two last meetings in Parliament* (1626), pp. 19–20.

and beyond and it is significant that in this context they were often linked with the dangers of 'popularity'.

For James the main threat to royal authority came from presbyterianism. From his early experiences in Scotland during the 1580s he recognized a link between the removal of bishops from the church and the destruction of hierarchy and royal authority within the state. So when he came to England he took steps to uphold their position and made it clear that, whilst he would accept some of the moderate puritan reforms, he would never countenance the 'imagined democracy' of the presbyterians.[24] A similar approach characterized his relations with Parliament. He was prepared to take steps towards moderate reform, but whenever the Commons overstepped the mark he tended to interpret their actions as part of a broad challenge to royal authority. Thus, for example, in the last stages of the 1610 Parliament he wrote of how they had 'perilled and annoyed our health, wounded our reputation, embouldened an ill-natured people, encroached on many of our privileges and plagued our purse . . .'; and in 1621 he complained that 'some fiery and popular spirits of some of the House of Commons . . . argue and debate publicly of matters far above their reach and capacity tending to our high dishonour and breach of prerogative royal'.[25] From statements like these it is apparent that elements in Charles's outlook were already well established; and an explanation of how they fitted together had been provided in a memorandum by Lord Keeper Ellesmere, composed soon after the dissolution in 1610.[26]

Ellesmere saw the maintenance of the political order as depending on a balance in which '1. The King is to have his regality and supreme prerogative and sovereignty inviolable preserved. 2. The nobles, prelates and lords to have their honor and dignity maintained. 3. The Commons to have their ancient liberties and privileges kept without breach or prejudice'. If any of these elements tried to extend its power then the balance of the whole would be upset and chaos would ensue. Ellesmere was

[24] M. J. Mendle, *Dangerous Positions* (Alabama, 1985), pp. 63–113. K. Fincham and P. G. Lake, 'The ecclesiastical policy of James I', *JBS* xxiv (1985), 169–207.

[25] HMC, *Salisbury*, xii. 266; J. R. Tanner, *Constitutional Documents of the Reign of James I* (1930), p. 279.

[26] This tract, entitled 'Special observations touching all the sessions of the last Parliament, anno 7 Regis and etc.', is printed in L. B. Knafla, *Law and Politics in Jacobean England* (Cambridge, 1977), pp. 254–62. For the background: ibid., p. 186.

therefore greatly concerned that 'the popular state ever since the beginning of His Majesty's gracious and sweet government hath grown big and audacious, and in every session of Parliament hath swelled more and more'. He outlined the ways in which the Commons had made a series of 'breaches . . . upon the regality and supreme prerogative of the Crown, under pretext of lawful liberty and ancient privileges' and cited instances where 'some particular persons have presumed to use in the lower house publicly very audacious and contemptuous speeches against the King's regal prerogative and power'. Finally he warned of the consequences of allowing this to happen: 'if . . . the liberties and privileges of the Commons be suffered to usurp and encroach too far upon the regality, it will not cease until it break out into democracy'.

Ellesmere was putting forward the conventional view that political stability could best be achieved by balancing the rights of Crown and subject; and in keeping with this he urged elsewhere that James should rule in co-operation with Parliament.[27] His analysis, however, revealed that, in spite of the emphasis on consensus, within such a view there was considerable scope for division. This was particularly the case when it came to considering who was responsible for upsetting the balance. For those critical of crown policy the blame could often be laid on corrupt courtiers and favourites close to the seat of power, whereas for those who identified more closely with royal authority this could be attached to popular, anti-monarchical elements amongst the Commons. Depending on the explanation adopted different remedies became appropriate. If one accepted—as on this occasion Ellesmere did—that the popular threat emanated from a few individuals, taking advantage of a particular set of circumstances, then Parliament could be dissolved and re-summoned as soon as suitable preparations had been made. However, if it was decided that the problems were a consequence of something more deeply rooted, a subversive tendency working away within society, then any re-summoning of Parliament could only be dangerous since it would give that tendency an opportunity to organize.

Precisely such an explanation was adopted in a document drawn up in the latter stages of the 1626 Parliament and addressed to the King.[28] The main premiss of this was one which Charles accepted

[27] Ibid., pp. 77–104.

[28] 'To his sacred majesty, Ab Ignoto' printed in *Cabala Sive Scrinia Sacra* (3rd edn., 1691); pp. 255–7. Rushworth noted of this that 'upon the impeachment of the Duke a paper was privately conveyed to the King

in his proclamation banning the Remonstrance, namely that the attack on Buckingham was really an assault on the power and honour of the monarchy: 'This great opposition against the Duke of Buckingham is stirred up and maintained by those who either maliciously, or ignorantly and concurrently, seek the debasing of this free monarchy, which because they fynd not yet ripe to attempt against the King himself, they endeavour it through the Duke's sides'. The author then went on to explain how the origins of this assault could be traced to a series of disaffected minorities, including outlawed debtors, East India Company merchants, common lawyers, and discourted peers, as well as more familiar opponents of the established order such as Puritans, Papists, and enclosing landlords. The first signs of their activity could be detected in the presbyterian programme of the 1584–5 Parliament, described as 'against the King's government, which they would have extinguished in matters ecclesiastical and limited in temporal'. And their cause had been strengthened in the last years of Elizabeth when, amongst 'Innovators, Plebicolae and King-haters', it had become the fashion to pray for the State as well as the Queen, 'this word . . . learned by our neighbourhood and commerce with the Low Countries, as if we were or affected to be governed by States'. James had faced the consequences in his first Parliament when lawyers, Puritans and 'free speakers' . . . 'stood strong against him under colour of Parliaments and Parliamentary Priviledges', even though 'since the time of H.6 these Parliamentary discoursings were never suffered as being the certain symptoms of subsequent Rebellions, Civil Wars and the dethroning of our Kings'. The King 'therefore strengthened himself ever with some Favourite, whom he might better trust than many of the Nobility tainted with this desire of Oligarchy'. However the lawyers and other groups had recently turned on this royal bulwark against republicanism and supported 'any complaint against both Church and King and all his servants, with their Cases, Antiquities, Records, Statutes, Precedents and Stories'. In the present Parliament, the author concluded, the struggle had reached a critical stage, so that if the King allowed the Duke to 'be but decourted it will be the cornerstone on which

importing thus . . .'. It can be ascribed to some date after 8 May, when the charges against Buckingham were delivered; however the identity of the author has remained a mystery. All that can be said with certainty is that he was someone close to the Duke who had a first hand knowledge of events at Court and in Parliament: Rushworth, i. 356–7.

the demolishing of his Monarchy will be builded. For if they prevail with this they have hatched a thousand other demands to pull the feathers of Royalty; they will appoint him Councillors, Servants, Alliances, limits on expence, Accounts of his Revenue'.

This was similar to Ellesmere's address in that it identified a threat to royal authority coming from below. However, whereas Ellesmere saw the threat as existing only in one Parliament, the author of this address saw it as something which could be traced back continuously into Elizabeth's reign and which had simply reached a new peak with the attack on Buckingham. Once the threat was viewed in these terms then the dissolution of the present Parliament and summoning of a new one was unlikely to be enough. Such a policy had been tried after the 1625 meeting—when those members who had attacked Buckingham were purged—but the result had been even more forceful attacks on him in 1626[29] The obvious conclusion was that disruptive elements had established such a firm hold that it was unlikely a Parliament could be held without their mounting some sort of assault. Given this a re-summons would become very unattractive to the King and, indeed, something to be avoided at all costs.

How far Charles went along with this line of reasoning is uncertain. When speaking in public he was a man of few words, and privately he was notorious for keeping his opinions to himself. What little we have suggests that he still regarded the enemy as a small, unrepresentative group of the 'ill-affected', pursuing their designs against the Duke for 'private ends'. He had probably not quite taken the crucial step of believing that this group was sufficiently influential to undermine the loyalty of the majority.[30] But this could not be far off. It was, after all, but a short

[29] Gardiner, *History*, vi. 33–4.

[30] Russell, *Parliaments and English Politics*, pp. 392–4; C. S. R. Russell, 'Why did Charles I call the Long Parliament'?, *Hist.* 227 (1984), 375–7; R. P. Cust, 'Charles I and a draft declaration for the 1628 Parliament' (unpublished paper). Of the statements discussed above the draft proclamation for raising a benevolence went furthest in this direction, suggesting that the 'wikked spirittes' already exerted sufficient influence to disrupt collection of taxes and that it was necessary for the people to give proof of their affection to the King before another Parliament could be summoned: PRO SP 16/30/2. There is also a clear indication of concern about a different, but related threat, in the Proclamation for settling the peace of the church published on 14 June. As originally drafted by Attorney-General Heath this was intended to silence Montague and the Arminians; but it was altered by Laud and Charles to apply in general against all those who 'stirre or move any new opinions . . . differing from the sound and orthodoxall grounds of true religion' and in

distance from attacking the favourite to attacking the King. As Charles was reported to have said during the Parliament 'If the Duke is Sejanus, I must be Tiberius.'[31] And he was certainly prepared to follow the logic of his anonymous adviser's conclusions. During the succeeding months he remained adamantly opposed to re-summoning Parliament even when circumstances seemed to make such an action inevitable.

If the King was determined to run the war without a Parliament, however, he had to persuade those councillors who had opposed the dissolution to accept such a policy. The absence of evidence of disagreement—in either newsletters or ambassadors' reports—suggests that, in the months following the 1626 Parliament, he achieved this without much difficulty. There were several circumstances working in his favour.

First of all it had become evident, as it had not been before, that Charles would stand by the Duke no matter what happened. Now that this was clearly established it left councillors with little alternative to acknowledging Buckingham's position and doing their best to co-operate with him; and this, in turn, meant accepting that Parliament could not be re-summoned for the time being as the merest suggestion of this would be construed as disloyalty. This development was accompanied by a narrowing in the range of the Duke's patronage which crucially affected the climate of opinion at Court.

Russell has recently stressed how very broad and catholic Buckingham's patronage had been in the early 1620s;[32] but what

practice it was used to silence puritans. It included the observation that 'in all ages great disturbances both to Church and State, have ensued out of small beginnings when the seedes of contention were not timely prevented': *Proclamations*, ii. 90–3; PRO SP 16/28/78, 79; 540/404; N. R. N. Tyacke 'Puritanism, Arminianism and Counter Revolution' in *Origins of the English Civil War*, p. 133.

31 Gardiner, *History*, vi. 107–8.

32 Russell, *Parliaments and English Politics*, pp. 9–12.

33 The distinction is between clients such as Sir George Goring, Sir John Savile and the 4th Earl of Dorset, who at various times were identified as the Duke's men before anything else, and the Earl of Manchester, Sir Thomas Coventry, and Sir John Coke who in this period, on the issue of whether or not to summon Parliament, appear to have disagreed with the Duke. The fact that they were able to do this, and still retain his favour, reflected the extent to which he was keeping his options open and maintaining a line which was deliberately ambiguous: *CSP Ven. 1625–6*, pp. 147, 449; R. Lockyer, *Buckingham* (1981), pp. 67–8, 108–11, 277, 324; D. H. Willson, *The Privy Councillors in the House of Commons 1604–1629* (Minnesota, 1940), pp. 148–9, 172, 195. For

has perhaps not been sufficiently emphasized was the way in which this contracted after 1625. There had long existed amongst the Duke's clients an inner and an outer circle. The former consisted of what were called his 'privados' or 'creatures', those clients who were prepared to defend his interests and support his line, almost regardless of the issues involved. The latter contained those who owed their initial advancement to Buckingham but who thereafter were to take a more detached and impartial view, often responding to the dictates of principle or the responsibilities of their office.[33] For much of the 1620s, of course, these two circles overlapped and the distinctions between them were frequently blurred. In our period, however, they tended to separate as the Duke came to rely more and more on his closest advisers.

The reasons for this are not hard to discern. The hostility of attacks on the Duke in the 1625 and 1626 Parliaments could hardly be disguised and they produced a strong reaction on the part of the favourite. As several contemporaries noted he had a very unforgiving side to his nature and an almost obsessive concern with identifying and punishing his enemies.[34] In the aftermath of the Parliaments these characteristics were vented to the full. MPs who crossed his designs were pricked as sheriffs and later removed from the Commission of the Peace; and those who had opposed him from within the Court were either turned out of their offices or made to pay a heavy price for remaining.[35] At the same time the Duke became far more selective in conferring his favours and increasingly demanding when it came to exacting pledges of loyalty and obedience.

This was reflected in the distribution of patronage. Grants of peerages, which had previously been available to almost anyone who was able to meet the asking price—and which often went to later opponents such as the Earl of Clare[36]—now became confined almost entirely to those who owed him an individual loyalty. These included two groups of peers created immediately before the 1626 and 1628 Parliaments—described by Sir Benjamin Rudyerd as 'Cardinals to carry the consistory'—as well as a number of clients who had served him loyally in the shires and

Coke's success in performing both sorts of role at various stages during the 1620s see: Willson, *Privy Councillors*, pp. 66–7, 95–7, 199–200.

[34] PRO 31/3/63 fo. 82; *Holles*, ii. 311; *Strafforde Letters*, i. 28.

[35] See below, pp. 187–90.

[36] L. Stone, *The Crisis of the Aristocracy 1558–1641* (Oxford, 1965), pp. 111–13; *Holles*, i. liv-v.

several crypto-catholics who were coming to play an increasingly conspicuous role in the life of the Court.[37] A parallel approach can be discerned in the nominations to Court office. When the Queen's household was reformed in August 1626—thereby removing a previous focus of opposition to the Duke—the key positions went to his more intimate adherents. His mother, wife, and sister were admitted to the Queen's bedchamber, where, according to the Venetian, they kept a constant watch on her; his father-in-law, the Earl of Rutland, became Lord Chamberlain; two of his long-standing followers, Sir George Goring and Thomas, Viscount Savage, became Vice-Chamberlain and Chancellor; Lord Percy, who had taken charge of one of Buckingham's proxy votes during the previous Parliament, became Master of the Horse; the Earl of Holland, described at the time as his 'only privado' became Lord Steward; and the Earl of Totnes who was ready to express his admiration of the Duke in the sycophantic terms which were becoming the order of the day, was made Receiver.[38] It was much the same story in appointments to Lord Lieutenancies: between 1626 and 1628 these generally went to obvious Buckingham clients such as Lord Percy, Viscount Mansfield and the 2nd Earl of Suffolk.[39] And, most significantly of all, the new Privy Councillors created in the period were all—with one exception—loyal supporters of the Duke. The Earls of Dorset and Bridgewater, appointed in July 1626, had demonstrated their adherence during the previous Parliament, as had Sir John Savile, promoted in November. The Earls of Suffolk and Exeter, appointed during December showed their fidelity during the following months. And Bishops Laud and Neile, who became councillors in April 1627, had been closely linked in religious matters for some time before

[37] *Dep. Keepers Rept.*, App. 47, pp. 111–14; PRO SP 16/20/23; *LJ* iii. 394–5; Rushworth, i. 392. The loyal local clients included, John Lord Poulett, William Lord Maynard, and Nicholas Lord Tufton; the crypto-catholics, Thomas Viscount Savage, Thomas Earl Rivers, Thomas Lord Brudenell, and John Earl of Peterborough: PRO SP 16/53/88, 524/100; P. Clark, *English Provincial Society from the Reformation to the Revolution: Religion, Politics and Society in Kent 1500–1640* (Hassocks, 1977), pp. 337, 344–5; Lockyer, *Buckingham*, p. 59; B. W. Quintrell, 'Gentry factions and the Witham affray, 1628', *Essex Archaeology and History*, 10 (1978), 121; J. Wake, *The Brudenells of Deene* (1953), pp. 114–21; HMC *Buccleuch*, iii. 321.

[38] *CSP Ven. 1625–6*, pp. 129, 494, 515, 542; *C. and T.* i. 140–3; Russell, *Parliaments and English Politics*, pp. 263–6; Lockyer, *Buckingham*, pp. 58–60, 108, 138; HLRO Proxy Book, 1626; SRO Phelips MS 219/35; PRO SP 16/42/15.

[39] J. C. Sainty, *Lieutenants of the Counties 1585–1642* (BIHR supplement 8. 1970), pp. 13, 16, 19, 29; HLRO Proxy Book, 1626; *C. and T.* i. 324.

this; indeed Laud had been one of the Duke's closer confidants since 1622.[40] The only appointee whom he does not appear to have supported was the Earl of Salisbury, who probably owed his advancement, in July 1626, to the favour of the King.[41]

These shifts helped to tip the balance against a policy of working with Parliament. The more experienced councillors who had defied Buckingham in the past—and who might have been expected to advocate traditional courses even in this situation—were either dismissed or forced to take a back seat. Williams and Abbot, both of whom had spoken out against a dissolution in 1625, were driven into exile.[42] The Earl of Arundel, the leading representative of the old aristocracy, was barred from Court and dismissed from the Council.[43] And the Earl of Pembroke, perhaps the most influential voice outside Buckingham's entourage, was obliged to maintain a low profile. By dint of a marriage contract with the Duke, in June 1626, he was able to hold on to his court offices in spite of being implicated in the opposition proceedings. But the price of forgiveness was to sacrifice much of his scope for taking independent political initiatives. He yielded up most of his patronage in Somerset and Cornwall and allowed Buckingham to make the nominations to key posts, such as the vice-wardenship of the Stannaries. He also appears to have withdrawn from involvement in the making of foreign policy, no longer forming part of the King's inner ring of advisers or being consulted by the Venetian on England's future intentions.[44] Pembroke's eclipse was

[40] *APC 1626, 1627, passim*; Russell, *Parliaments and English Politics*, pp. 286 n, 306 n., 317; PRO SP 16/33/30; Tyacke, 'Puritanism, Arminianism and Counter Revolution', pp. 130–3; Lockyer, *Buckingham*, p. 325; Laud, iii. 139–209.

[41] L. Stone, *Family and Fortune* (Oxford, 1973), pp. 115–17.

[42] *CSP Ven. 1625–6*, pp. 146–7; Gardiner, *History*, vi. 30–2, 206–7; Rushworth, i. 434–58, 'Archbishop Abbot his narrative'. This last document was a vindication of Abbot's actions in the period leading up to his sequestration from office in October 1627. It is undated, but from the references to his continuing exile in Kent it was clearly composed soon after this and before the Parliament of 1628. The narrative indicates that already by the summer of 1626 Abbot's authority in the church was being bypassed and his attendance at Council had been reduced by illness.

[43] K. Sharpe, 'The Earl of Arundel, his circle and opposition to the Duke of Buckingham, 1618–1628', in *Faction and Parliament*, pp. 231–5. Bishop Harsnett, an Arundel client also found himself 'deepe in their blacke books' during this period: BL Add. MS 39, 948, fo. 187. (I am grateful to Ken Fincham for this reference).

[44] Russell, *Parliaments and English Politics*, pp. 13, 326–7; V. Rowe, 'The influence of the Earls of Pembroke on parliamentary elections, 1625–1649', EHR l (1935), 242–56; PRO SP 16/1/43, 37/91; *CSP Ven. 1625–6*, pp. 126, 486.

a sign of the times. For those who were not prepared to accommodate themselves to the wishes of the Duke, the choice was either to shut up or get out; and this remained the case, at least until after the disaster at the Isle of Rhé.

In the meantime the voices heard most often in circles around the King were those insisting on the need for 'new counsels'. Most of this advice emanated from Buckingham's inner circle. As we have seen, it was his dependants who had pressed for the dissolution in 1626; and they remained of the same opinion during the following months, intervening at critical moments to divert discussion away from a Parliament.[45] The principal reason for this was, of course, the risk of another attack on the Duke; but this was not all. There is also evidence that they linked impeachment and the continuation of Parliament with a wider concern for the dangers posed by 'popularity'.

This had been the principal theme of a sermon delivered by Laud at the opening of the 1626 Parliament. Discoursing on the various elements endangering stability in both church and state he placed particular emphasis on the threat from 'parity':

> I know there are some that think the Church is not yet far enough beside the cushion: that their 'seats' are too easy yet and too high too. A 'parity' they would have: no Bishop, no Governor, but a parochial Consistory, and that should be lay enough too . . . And . . . they, whoever they be, that would overthrow sedes Ecclesiae . . . will not spare if ever they get power to have a pluck at the 'throne of David'. And there is not a man that is for 'parity'—all fellows in the Church—but he is not for monarchy in the State. And certainly either he is but half-headed to his own principles, or he can be but half-hearted to the 'house of David'.[46]

This was hardly calculated to appeal to MPs; however Laud was not alone in voicing such opinions. In a letter which was intended to attract Buckingham's favour, and which might therefore be presumed to reflect what were thought to be his opinions, James Howell discussed a different aspect of the theme. Writing in February 1626, he offered suggestions about various ways of negotiating the Parliament; but then stressed that 'I know your Grace doth not (nor needs not) . . . affect popularity . . . for he that pulleth off his hat to the people giveth his head to the Prince: and it is remarkable what was said of a late infortunate Earl, who a little before Queen Elizabeth's death had drawn the ax upon his

[45] *CSP Ven. 1626–8*, p. 342.

[46] Laud, i. 82–3; Tyacke, 'Puritanism, Aminianism and Counter-Revolution', p. 134.

own neck. That he was growen so popular that he was too dangerous for the times and the times for him'.[47] In similar vein, Sir John Lowther, who represented the Duke's interests loyally in Parliament, and was knighted for his services, in June 1626, recorded his impression that 'Few or none did labour in the generall good or generall favour, but for private bills, factions about elections and labour to pull doune great officers for the private splene of some leaders, the multitude glorieing in distruction . . .'[48]

All three of these spokesmen, then, shared with the author of the advice to the King cited earlier, a recognition of the dangers presented by 'popularity' and 'the multitude'. This suggests that such notions were becoming relatively widespread in the circles around the Duke during 1626; and this helps to account for the move away from traditional policies.[49] For, as Russell has remarked—in comparing Laud's ideas with those of John Pym—the rhetoric of 'popularity' represented a virtual mirror image of the more familiar rhetoric of 'anti-popery'. Both provided extremely powerful visions of subversive and disruptive forces which threatened to overthrow the existing order in society and the state. Both also provided strong incentives for political action; but in completely different directions. Whereas fear of popery tended to lead to calls for more parliamentary participation in government and the denunciation of evil counsellors,[50] a fear of 'popularity' implied the opposite way, towards limiting the opportunities for parliamentary interference and restricting power and influence to a select few. The rhetoric of 'popularity' therefore provided a real obstacle to the future summoning of Parliament.

The immediate result of this was a recognition—at least

[47] James, Howell, *Epistolae Ho Elianae: Familiar Letters*, ed. J. Jacobs (1890), pp. 232–4. For Howell's connections with several of Buckingham's friends, including catholics: ibid., pp. 114–15, 132–5, 228–30, 240–1, 251–4.

[48] *Lowther Family Estate Books 1617–1675* (ed.), C. B. Phillips (Surtees Soc. cxci. 1979), p. 229.

[49] Another of Buckingham's clients who evidently shared such concerns was the Attorney-General, Sir Robert Heath. See the discussion of his views in Cust 'Charles I and a draft declaration', partly based on his private meditations in BL Eg. MS 2982 fos. 81–4, 88.

[50] C. S. R. Russell, 'The parliamentary career of John Pym, 1621–1629' in P. Clark, A. G. R. Smith and N. R. N. Tyacke, ed., *The English Commonwealth* (Leicester, 1979), pp. 163–5. R. P. Cust and P. G. Lake, 'Sir Richard Grosvenor and the rhetoric of magistracy', *BIHR* liv (1981), 42–8; P. G. Lake, 'Constitutional consensus and puritan opposition in the 1620s: Thomas Scott and the Spanish match', *HJ* xxv (1982), 810–23.

amongst the Duke's adherents—that new means would have to be found for supplying the King's necessities. This resulted in a whole series of suggestions for ways of raising revenue, some more practical than others, but all infringing the spirit of traditional methods. Sir Edwin Sandys—who by this stage had abandoned his oppositionist stance of the early 1620s and thrown in his lot wholly with the Duke—came up with proposals for simply collecting subsidies 'without asking any leave'.[51] Henry, Lord Clifford—another ally of the favourite—urged that since 'To hope any longer for remedy from Parliament is to expect a Phisitian after Death', the King should simply help himself to the 'buried treasures of 2 or 3 hundred overgrowne members'.[52] Sir John Savile—with an eye to his own profit, as well as the King's—offered a bewildering variety of schemes which included compounding with those who held land by feudal tenure, raising money from recusants in return for discharging them from their fines and raising impositions on internal trade.[53] And the Earl of Dorset—who had advised Charles to dissolve Parliament in 1625 and remained one of the most 'hawkish' of the councillors—advocated a drastic use of force:

> the King's distress is at its height more from the necessity of having recourse to some violent remedy against his subjects than from any other reason . . . war must be maintained with the property of the subject, all being bound to contribute where it is just, and if in the last Parliament the people had agreed to the promised contribution they would have paid much less than the King will eventually compel them to disburse . . . at any rate there was no fear of insurrection in this Kingdom as it contained no fortresses, neither could foreign powers foment revolution from lack of large armies.[54]

The Venetian ambassador, to whom these remarks were addressed, in August 1626, was predictably shocked at their radical tone. However in substance they represented no more than the logical consequence of running the war without a Parliament. If Charles

[51] *C. and T.* i. 117, 131–2; Russell, *Parliaments and the English Politics*, p. 143; *Chamberlain*, ii. 549, 613; PRO SP 16/18/28.

[52] PRO SP 16/44/3. This memorandum is undated, but the reference to Parliament and the absence of any reference to the benevolence or Forced Loan imply that it was composed in June or early July 1626.

[53] BRL Coventry MSS, Commissions 1625–40, no. 8. (I am grateful to Conrad Russell for this reference.); J. T. Cliffe, *The Yorkshire Gentry* (1969), pp. 200–1; HMC *Buccleuch*, iii. 315; Rymer, xviii. 912; *C. and T.* i, 234, 249: *APC 1627*, p. 312.

[54] *CSP Ven. 1625–6*, p. 147, 528.

and Buckingham were to insist on this then in the end they would have to gird themselves for some extremely forceful measures.

A second circumstance strengthening the King's resolution to adopt 'new counsels' was the threat of a Spanish invasion. From April 1626 onwards reports had been reaching England that the Spanish were building broad-bottomed troop-ships and recruiting channel pilots from Flanders. On 6 June the King informed councillors that, according to reliable information, they had 200 ships and 4,000 men ready to invade; and throughout the remainder of June and July the Council of War discussed ways of meeting this danger. They debated whether the fleet should be sent to the Spanish coast or kept in the Channel; how it could best be enlarged; how the coastal towns could be fortified; and what preparations the militia should make to meet an invasion.[55] There can be no doubt that the threat of invasion was taken seriously; but, in spite of this, the Council's initial reaction was very clumsy and uncertain. During the final month of the 1626 Parliament it met in full session only four times, and this made discussion and co-ordination of policy very difficult.[56] Some councillors no doubt still clung to the hope that if Parliament could be made aware of the gravity of the situation, it would grant the necessary supplies. Others, however, were coming to recognize that this was unlikely; and in the process of doing so became more amenable to accepting the King's line.[57]

One of those was Secretary Conway, who throughout 1624 and 1625 had clung faithfully to a vision of the nation united in a war against Spain. By the end of the 1626 Parliament, however, he had become bitterly disillusioned and this was expressed in a letter to the Earl of Carlisle, dated 5 June:

> I have spoken with three or fowre of the parlement, the wisest of my acquaintance, and finde so little grounde to builde any hope upon as if I did not defy despaire it would take uppe every corner of me. I was of opinion that the worst of malice had spente itselfe, but every occasion multiplies it so much as certainly the thinges require the last triall, that his majesty should once more lay before them his necessities, and lay of

[55] Melb. H. Cowper MSS, bdl. 27, 12 Apr. 1626; Berks RO, Trumbull MSS, bdl. 48: PRO SP 16/27/41, 28/p. 23. This evidence runs contrary to Gardiner's view that the Council deliberately exaggerated the threat to prepare the country for a benevolence: Gardiner, *History*, vi. 124.

[56] *APC 1625–6*, pp. 480–98; *APC 1626*, pp. 1–7.

[57] Russell, *Parliaments and English Politics*, p. 321 n.

from himselfe and putt upon them the mischiefs and inconveniences that the publike affaires may runne into by forraine attempt or the home relief of necessities . . . I cannot see any helpe then that which they used to say in the plague time, every man to himself, Lorde have mercy upon us.[58]

One can see reflected here some of the main considerations which must have been weighing with councillors at this time. As they had repeatedly insisted, in speeches on the floor of the two Houses, it was Parliament that had got the King into a war and it was therefore Parliament which bore the responsibility for meeting his expenses.[59] If, in spite of this, it failed to do so then the King's overriding responsibility for defending the realm would make some other resort almost inevitable. In these circumstances, then, others, besides Conway, must have felt a strong inclination to take their cue from the King.

Charles responded by providing a clear lead, which probably did a good deal to reinforce his authority within Council. Between the dissolution and 30 June he appears to have been largely responsible for laying the foundations of a new policy which was to lead to the request for a benevolence in July. The first surviving mention of this appears in a memorandum of 17 June, drafted by Conway, presumably at Charles's behest. It suggested 'giving satisfaction to the people' by issuing a declaration of the causes for dissolution, proclaiming a public fast and setting up committees to consider methods of raising revenue and making economies. At the same time the King set a personal example, attending several full council meetings—which was very unusual for him at the time—and proposing a series of drastic cuts in his own royal 'Bounty'.[60] After the confusion and uncertainty of recent weeks this was precisely what was needed to restore morale and it must have disposed councillors to accept the broader royal initiative.

Perhaps the most important circumstance operating in this direction, however, was the relative ease with which Charles's wishes could be accommodated within accepted notions of constitutional propriety. Amongst the medieval doctrines which still governed the way councillors thought about supply, there

[58] Ibid., pp. 168, 185, 241, 263; PRO SP 78/79/64 (I am grateful to Tom Cogswell for this reference).

[59] *Debates in the House of Commons in 1625*, ed. S. R. Gardiner (Camden Soc., NS vi, 1873), pp. 1–2, 56–9, 79, 107; Russell, *Parliaments and English Politics*, pp. 291–2.

[60] PRO SP 16/30/18; *APC 1626*, pp. 37–9.

were numerous precedents enabling the King to tax his subjects outside Parliament.[61] Therefore, in the short term at least, running the war without Parliament did not require any dramatic shift of attitude. Doctrines governing supply, like so many other political ideas in the 1620s, were ambiguous, facing in two directions at once. They both encouraged the King to rule in consultation with the subject and justified him in extensive use of his prerogative power, something which can be illustrated in the arguments relating to the first of the Council's measures to raise supply outside Parliament, the benevolence of 1626.[62]

The main justification for a benevolence was the tradition which had developed since the thirteenth century whereby a monarch was entitled to demand extra aid from his subjects when there was a threat to the security of the realm. The method of raising this was governed by a series of conventions declaring that the King must first consult his Council and then refrain from coercion in collecting the levy; however where these were observed the subject was deemed to be under an inevitable obligation to pay, and on this basis benevolences had been raised as an alternative to parliamentary supply up to the mid-sixteenth century.[63] Against this tradition, however, there stood another, gathering weight in the early seventeenth century, which stated that even in cases of emergency the property of the subject could only be taken with the consent of Parliament. This principle had been maintained whenever Parliament had felt strong enough to stand up to the Crown, and this had resulted in a series of statutes condemning benevolences as illegal.[64] There were thus two separate and apparently contradictory sets of precedents, and it was open to councillors and others to draw on whichever supported their cause.

A similar ambiguity was evident in the case put forward by the King to justify the levy. This was outlined in three documents with which he was associated: the printed *Declaration* of the causes of dissolution, a draft Proclamation asking the people for a spontaneous grant of supply and the letters sent out to launch the benevolence in July.[65] In the *Declaration* he set out his case on the

[61] Harriss, 'Medieval doctrines in debates on supply', pp. 73–103.

[62] J. P. Sommerville, *Politics and Ideology in England 1603–1640* (1986), pp. 9–111.

[63] G. L. Harriss, 'Aids, loans and benevolences', *HJ* v (1963), 1–19.

[64] Gardiner, *History*, vi. 125, 131; Sommerville, *Politics and Ideology*, pp. 149, 157, 159.

[65] *A Declaration*; PRO SP 16/30/2, 31/30.

grounds that he was fighting a just war which he had been invited to undertake by Parliament. He had followed convention by consulting the Council and summoning a Parliament, where he had done his utmost to explain his needs. In spite of this, however, supply had been refused and his warnings about the risk of invasion and the necessity for emergency measures had been ignored. He therefore felt fully justified in resorting to the prerogative: 'This strange, unexpected and undeserved case, yea we suppose unexampled in this our Realme, enforcing us to new courses for the necessary defence of ourself and people, in which though we should use our sole royall prerogative, given unto us by God for the publique good of this great charge committed unto us, we could not but be justified in all right understanding'.[66] Having established this, however, he drew back, acknowledging that use of the prerogative was likely to cause friction between Crown and subject, and declaring that he wished, 'out of our naturall and constant resolucon, to treade in the steppes of lawe as much as we possibly may . . . to avoyde all shadow of just cause of griefe to any of our loving subjects'. He therefore announced that he was giving his people a last chance, 'in a case of this unavoydable necessitye, to be a law unto themselves and lovinglye, freelye and voluntarilye to performe that which by law if it had passed formerlye by act they had been compellable unto'.[67] If they responded favourably to this request he assured them that this 'will not onlye give us an ample testimonye of the dutifull and good affections of our people in generall but will give us just encouragement the more speedelye to meet in Parliament'. However if they refused it was implied that this would show that the 'malicious practises of wikked spiritts' were also at work in the counties and would leave the King no alternative but to resort more firmly to the prerogative.[68]

These arguments no doubt represented an approximate balance between the views of the King and the Privy Councillors who would like to have gone on ruling with Parliament. Secretary Coke, who was a consistent advocate of co-operation with the subject, hailed the benevolence, with some relief, as infinitely preferable to the straightforward coercion which had seemed likely once Parliament was dissolved. 'His Majestie', he declared to his ageing patron, Lord Brooke, was resolved 'to take no violent

[66] *A Declaration*, pp. 4–5, 15–16, 19–20, 22–3; Harriss, 'Medieval doctrines in debates on supply', pp. 75–8; PRO SP 16/30/2.

[67] PRO SP 16/31/30.

[68] PRO SP 16/30/2.

or extraordinary way to levie monies but in a common danger to rely uppon a common case and affection, that al men must have that wil not wilfully bee guiltie of abandoning there religion, Prince and Countrie to the enemie's power'.[69]

These arguments, however, also demonstrated the way in which traditional and conventional political ideas, intended to secure consensus and co-operation between King and subject, could be developed in a direction wholly contrary to this design. There was much in the King's statements to appeal to a moderate councillor like Coke. They incorporated a good many of the constitutional commonplaces of the period, setting out the Crown's case for supply in traditional terms and emphasizing the need to promote harmony and unity between King and subject; and by blaming the disruption of Parliament on a small fringe element, they held out the prospect of future meetings once this element had been purged. However there were also ideas which could be employed to strengthen royal authority at the expense of the subject. The notion of the prerogative as something which gave the King undefined powers to act in an emergency could be used to justify continual resort to unparliamentary taxation; the idea that co-operation by Parliament was being destroyed by disruptive elements could justify not re-summoning Parliament until there was clear evidence that these elements could do no more damage; and the promise that the King would call a Parliament if the subject showed himself to be dutiful and obedient could be taken to imply that a meeting of Parliament was something which the subject had to earn from the King as a concession. These notions, then, could all be used to justify a shift in the direction of prerogative rule. Much depended on the spirit in which they were interpreted and here, already, a certain tension could be detected. The emphasis on repudiating any 'violent or extraordinary way' in Coke's statement, was clearly at a variance with Charles's harping on 'new courses' and 'unavoydable necessity'.[70]

For the time being, however, such conflicts lay below the surface and the Council was content to clothe its actions in the rhetoric of consensus. This was perhaps the best way of ensuring continuing stability; for there could be little doubt that, without a constant stress on the love and harmony between King and subject, many of the tensions and ambiguities inherent in the

[69] Melb. H. Cowper MSS, bdl. 47, 2 July 1626.

[70] I am grateful to Christopher Thompson for emphasizing this point to me.

political ideas of the early seventeenth century would be brought out into the open and forced to the point of resolution.[71] The stage at which this was likely to happen was still some way off; but, as Privy Councillors and other contemporaries were only too well aware, if it were ever reached the resulting confrontation could be disastrous.

During the months immediately following the dissolution of 1626 a serious constitutional crisis became increasingly likely. Initially this was due to the fact that in facing war and the threat of invasion without parliamentary help the Council was required to contemplate practical measures which made some resort to the prerogative inevitable.[72] However it is also noticeable that in this period a new climate of opinion was developing at the centre within which councillors' responses became markedly cruder and less sensitive to the interests of the subject. The nature of this can best be appreciated by comparing the policies of these months with the measures implemented after the dissolution of 1625.

Then the King had explained the dissolution as the result of an unfortunate conjunction of circumstances, with the spread of the plague to Oxford accompanying the reluctance of a few MPs to grant supply speedily.[73] Consequently, in the following months, the government had continued to assume that it could raise supply from the next Parliament and had tailored its policy accordingly. In response to the Commons' petition of 1625, it issued a series of proclamations and orders requiring the full rigour of the law to be applied against recusants. It also tried as far as possible to raise revenue by methods which would avoid giving offence to the next Parliament, such as pawning the crown jewels and devoting recusancy fines to paying for defence.[74] And, when it did resort to levying money from the taxpayer, it deliberately chose the least controversial means of doing so. This was by sending out Privy Seal letters, requesting loans from prominent subjects in the counties. Such a scheme was usually very slow to operate and only provided a low yield of revenue—largely because it was open to lenders to furnish endless excuses—but it had the

[71] Judson, *Crisis of the Constitution*, pp. 41–3; Russell, *Parliaments and English Politics*, pp. 6–7; Sommerville, *Politics and Ideology*, pp. 145–88.

[72] Russell, *Parliaments and English Politics*, pp. 321–40.

[73] *A Declaration*, pp. 10–11.

[74] T. E. Cogswell, 'Foreign policy and Parliament: the case of La Rochelle, 1625–1626', *EHR* xciv (1984), 246–9; Dietz, *English Public Finance*, ii. 228.

advantage of being politically 'safe'. Both Elizabeth and James had used it without arousing any of the hostility which accompanied benevolences; and later opponents of the loan—such as the Earl of Clare and William Coryton—acknowledged it to be legitimate. The Council also took care to apply the scheme as moderately as possible. On previous occasions it had sometimes resorted to summoning defaulters to appear before it and browbeaten them into making payments by threats of imprisonment. But in 1625/6 no defaulters were summoned or punished, and on several occasions the Council listened respectfully as local gentry pleaded the poverty of their shires, and then allowed enormous reductions in their assessments. Some councillors even considered abandoning the scheme altogether once a Parliament had been decided on, presumably to avoid giving offence to MPs who were also being asked to provide subsidies.[75] In the event the scheme continued, but significantly it aroused no discernible complaint in Parliament.

In contrast to all this, after the 1626 dissolution the Crown began to act as if it would never have to face Parliament again. Early in July a council order was issued authorizing the collection of Tonnage and Poundage by letters patent under the Great Seal, and at the same time ordering the imprisonment of anyone refusing to pay. This was a sharp departure from the policy of the previous year—which had been simply to collect the unapproved Tonnage and Poundage without making an issue of it—and not suprisingly Parliament treated this as a major grievance when it met again in 1628.[76] The Council also seriously considered debasing the coinage, which could have had a disastrous effect on trade and caused a storm of protest in Parliament. This was discussed throughout the summer of 1626 and was only rejected when the King, after advice from Sir Robert Cotton, overruled the Duke.[77] Finally a suggestion was canvassed whereby recusants would be released from their fines in return for a fixed payment to the Crown. This was introduced by Charles himself and may well have reflected a recognition on his part that if he was to rule without Parliament he needed to find allies from outside the

[75] Dietz, *English Public Finance*, ii. 17, 62–3, 94, 115, 149; *Holles*, ii. 346–7; BL Harl. MS 39, fo. 452–7; G. R. Elton, *The Tudor Constitution* (Cambridge, 1960), pp. 57–8; *APC 1625–6*, pp. 421–32, 445, 453–4; Bodl. L., Firth MS c.4, p. 192; *CSP D 1625–6*, p. 192.

[76] *APC 1626*, pp. 63–5; Russell, *Parliaments and English Politics*, pp. 344, 386–7.

[77] PRO SP 16/23/75; *C. and T.* i. 142–6; *APC 1626*, pp. 247–8.

traditional protestant ruling class. During a council meeting on 1 July he 'spoke of the Catholics as the children of the Crown, like the rest, and proposed a compromise instead of violently taking away two thirds of their goods'. This was promptly supported by Buckingham and, more surprisingly, the Earl of Pembroke who was evidently under pressure to be on his best behaviour. As the Venetian observed, it seemed calculated not only to bring in 'a considerable sum of money', but 'also to win the good will of the Catholics'.[78] In spite of this, however, nothing came of it, apart from the commission issued to Savile in the north during 1627.[79] Whether this was because the Council had its mind on other things or because of resistance from the more moderate and protestant councillors is unclear; but the very fact that it was discussed again indicates that the Council was moving away from thinking about ways to accommodate a future Parliament.

The Crown's main concern at this time, of course, was to find a new way of taxing the subject directly. The original Privy Seal loan had been too slow and unproductive to meet its needs and therefore, in July 1626, it had opted for the speedier method of raising a benevolence. This again proved unsuccessful—largely because its dubious legality led to widespread opposition in the counties[80]—and in consequence, by August, the Council was preparing to try another scheme. This was a curious modification of the earlier Privy Seal loan and it is well worth investigating because once more it shows the direction of the Council's thinking.

On the 5 August 1626 collectors were appointed for a new loan and on the 14th the King wrote to the Council authorizing it to draw up a list of those fit to pay, based on the Lord Lieutenants' returns of 1625. However, it had already begun to issue Privy Seals on a very different basis. Whereas in 1625 it had compiled lists of between thirty and fifty gentry in each county, to lend sums ranging from £10 to £50, under the new scheme it selected much smaller numbers and gave them assessments of between £100 and £2,000.[81] The intention of this exercise appears to have been to combine revenue raising with the punishment of those who had defied the Court. The lists of assessments contained judges, office-holders and some particularly wealthy country gentlemen. However, they also included a cross-section of less wealthy

[78] *CSP Ven. 1625–6*, p. 480. [79] *C. and T.* i. 234; Rymer, xviii. 912.

[80] See below, Ch. 2, pt. ii.

[81] PRO E.401/2586, pp. 1–81, 459–77.

gentry, apparently selected on a much more random basis. Some—notably those from Northamptonshire, Leicestershire, and Rutland—were probably chosen from the lists supplied to the Council in 1625; but others were almost certainly included because they had crossed the Duke.

This was in keeping with the vindictive mood of Buckingham and his dependants. Their hostility towards the Commons' proceedings in 1626 has already been noted, and this found expression in the removal of seventeen JPs from the Commission of the Peace.[82] However, such an action could make no more than a small impression on the total numbers of those who could be regarded as the Duke's enemies. Reports suggested that several hundred MPs had voted in favour of presenting the Remonstrance before granting supply on 12 June and clearly it was out of the question to remove all of these. An alternative therefore was to punish them by imposing crushing Privy Seal loans, rated at between five and ten times the normal subsidy assessment. This had already been suggested in July as a way of punishing those London citizens who had refused to lend the King £100,000; now in August it appeared that it was actually being implemented, against selected MPs and local governors.[83] In Cheshire these comprised the two county members, Sir Richard Grosvenor and Peter Daniell esq., who were struck off the Commission of the Peace soon after. In Yorkshire it included those MPs who were enemies of Buckingham's clients, Savile and the Earl of Dunbar: Christopher Wandesford, Sir William Constable, Sir John Hotham, Sir John Jackson, Sir Francis Foljambe, and Sir Thomas Hoby. And in Essex it consisted of the clients of the Earl of Warwick, who had recently become estranged from the Duke: Sir Nathaniel Rich, Sir Francis Barrington, Sir William Masham, Sir Harbottle Grimstone, and Sir Thomas Cheeke.[84]

This essentially punitive Privy Seal loan, however, does not appear to have got very far. Some of the letters reached their destinations: Sir Rowland St John, Deputy Lieutenant of Northamptonshire received sixteen for distribution within the county on 2 September, and in Sussex Sir Walter Covert and Sir Henry Compton took the trouble to obtain discharges from their loans on 16 September. But very little money was received into the Exchequer, and on 22 September the loan was suspended by

[82] See below, pp. 188–9.
[83] *C. and T.* i. 111; *APC 1626*, p. 66.
[84] See below, pp. 189, 193–9.

Proclamation.[85] This prevented any real opposition from developing and saved the Council from taking the harsh coercive measures which would undoubtedly have been needed to enforce collection. Nevertheless the scheme still marked a significant progression from the benevolence. All appearance of promoting unity between Crown and subject was cast aside and instead the Council was putting itself into a position where extensive use of the prerogative was accepted as virtually inevitable. Moreover in saddling certain individuals with heavy payments, it was turning what had originally been a scheme for raising money into a device to punish the Duke's enemies. This was particularly disturbing. Not only did it demonstrate the control exercised by Buckingham over such matters; but it also reflected the way in which the preoccupations of his entourage were coming to influence what were basically administrative measures, and furnish these with a much harder political edge. This approach became even more marked during the levying of the Forced Loan.

II THE COUNCIL AND THE FORCED LOAN

The Privy Seal loan had been suspended because during September 1626 the Council decided on another method of taxing the subject, by what later became known as the Forced Loan. In origin this scheme was a response to the emergency created by Christian of Denmark's defeat at the Battle of Lutter. However, as we shall see, it was shaped in several crucial respects by the suspicion of Parliament and hard line attitudes which were becoming apparent during the summer.

News of Christian's defeat reached England on 11 September and caused the King to act immediately. He cut short his summer progress and hurried back to London, where, with tears standing in his eyes, he assured the Danish ambassador 'that he would render his uncle every assistance, even at the risk of his own crown and hazarding his life'. He then attended a four-hour council meeting at which he asked ministers to consider how he could supply the King of Denmark with aid.[1] For Charles this was very much a matter of personal honour. As well as being a close

[85] Beds. RO St John MSS 1297; PRO, E.401/2586, pp. 541–8; *Proclamations*, ii. 108. See also Christopher Wandesforde's Privy Seal for £100: Bodl. L. Carte MS 103, fo. 660.

[1] *CSP Ven. 1625–6*, pp. 547–8.

relative, Christian was also his main continental ally, dependent on English subsidies which had rarely been paid. He was determined to make amends and during the following weeks was driven forward by a sense of obligation akin to that which he appears to have felt towards the French Huguenots.[2] Meanwhile the Council had responded promptly. It sat twice a day to discuss the matter and on 14 September came up with a proposal to send 4,000 troops to Denmark, financed by a loan from the subject.[3]

The Forced Loan was thus, ultimately, born out of a foreign policy crisis, and the urgent need for funds which this had created. However, there was more to it than simply this. The official reason given for another extra-parliamentary levy—'tyme not admitting the way of a Parliament'—implied that the Council had no choice in the matter.[4] But closer examination reveals that this was not in fact the case.

The immediate response of informed observers was that this emergency made a re-summons of Parliament almost inevitable. One of Joseph Mead's London correspondents predicted that since 'Privy Seals do fail and contributions are but mockeries so there is no way left but a Parliament'; and Clare noted that the way had been opened for this by the reconciliation between Buckingham and Pembroke, which, it was hoped, would 'assure an amnestia of the last'. So confident were some of the gentry in Somerset and Cornwall that by the end of the month they had started canvassing amongst the freeholders.[5] However all these hopes were to be disappointed, largely because of the attitude of the King.

The indications are that after the dissolution of 1626 Charles's resolve to do without Parliament became more and more firmly established. The Venetian ambassador had noted hints of this throughout the summer months and recorded a particularly significant conversation with the Bishop of Mende in which the King had 'spoken . . . of the means used by the Kings of France to rid themselves of Parliament'.[6] This inclination resurfaced in the course of the Council's discussions in September. It appears that during the crucial debate on the 14th—at which the loan was

[2] Gardiner, *History*, vi. 140; Russell, *Parliaments and English Politics*, pp. 264–5, 323, 391, 397–8.

[3] *CSP Ven. 1625–6*, p. 548; *APC 1626*, p. 268.

[4] *APC 1626*, p. 268.

[5] *C. and T.* i. 148; *Holles*, ii. 334–5; PRO SP 16/37/5, 52.

[6] *CSP Ven. 1625–6*, pp. 462, 508.

eventually adopted—there was an attempt by moderate councillors to test out the water: when 'the King pressed the Lords much to devise how more money may come in by Privy Seals . . . the Lord Mandeville moved that by way of motive he would insert into the letters that they should be paid the next Parliament'.[7] This was calculated to raise the issue of a re-summons in a manner which was relatively inoffensive and uncontroversial; nevertheless the suggestion was quickly squashed by the King. He was reported to have 'disliked it utterly', warned that 'he would not take him for his friend that should advise thereunto', and stated uncompromisingly that 'they might pledge his word and crown, but there was to be no question of Parliament'.[8]

This declaration carried the day and was for Charles an important tactical victory. Not only did he manage to persuade councillors to commit themselves to using the prerogative in the short term, but he also succeeded in laying the foundation for a policy of running the war without Parliament which lasted nearly eighteen months. During this period the moderates who favoured more traditional courses were occasionally able to get this policy discussed—for example in the course of an extraordinary council meeting at Windsor, in August 1627, when 'someone ventured to say that without a Parliament they could not obtain adequate funds'—but they were unable to make much headway towards actually getting it changed.[9] This was largely due to the King himself who guided the Council's deliberations with a good deal of firmness and resolution. He was sometimes circumvented on specific matters as we shall see; but in general he managed to get his way and the overall direction of policy up to the end of 1627 owed more to his wishes than to anything else. For a shy young man of no more than twenty-seven, surrounded by mature and experienced councillors, this was a considerable achievement and it is therefore worth investigating what it was based on.

Charles's technique for managing Council was a simple one. He attended its meetings relatively rarely, and seems to have regarded it as essential to his royal dignity that he remain aloof from day-

[7] *C. and T.* i. 149. This presumably refers to the Earl of Manchester who originally held the title of Lord Mandeville and had been created Earl as recently as February 1626. His son Edward Lord Mandeville was not a member of the Privy Council. (I am grateful to Christopher Thompson for drawing my attention to this letter and its implications.)

[8] *C. and T.* i. 149; *Proclamations*, ii. 110 n.; *CSP Ven. 1625–6*, p. 558.

[9] *CSP Ven. 1626–8*, p. 342. For discussion of the subject on other occasions: BL Harl. MS 390, fo. 132; *C. and T.*, i. 224.

to-day administration.[10] However when he did intervene, it was in such a way as to stamp his authority on the proceedings. The meetings he attended were usually those involving discussions of basic policy and Charles left his councillors in no doubt as to his views on this. On one occasion, late in September 1626, when the word 'Parliament' was mentioned in Council debate, 'the King who was present said he did abominate that name'. In another instance he was reported as declaring that he would only call a meeting 'if reduced to extremity and pulled by the hairs of his head'. And, after the Windsor sitting in August 1627 had failed to produced the expected summons, Clare remarked that 'the King is so adverse as it is laesa maiestas to name it'.[11] As usual he had the measure of the situation. The King's unequivocal attitude—usually voiced in the bluntest of language—made life very difficult for those who wished him to rule with Parliament, and helped ensure that for the time being they kept their heads down.

But the King's wishes alone, however clearly stated, were not enough to ensure a particular line of policy. In this sense Charles was some way from being the autocratic absolutist that some have depicted. On the one hand he was constrained by the sheer physical impossibility of taking all matters of government into his own hands and was forced to refer much of the day-to-day business to his ministers;[12] and on the other he remained extremely respectful of the tradition whereby English monarchs took the advice of their Council before embarking on particular policies, often deferring to their judgement even where he had shown every sign of committing himself in another direction.[13]

[10] The Council Register records Charles as attending on ten occasions between September 1626 and July 1627: 14 Sept., 25 Oct., 10, 16, 21, 22 Dec., 4, 28 Jan., 16 Mar., 4 May: *APC 1626*, pp. 268, 328, 399, 414, 430, 431; *APC 1627*, pp. 2, 36, 140. However it seems that his actual attendance was more frequent than this since some appearances mentioned in other sources went unrecorded in the register: 12 Sept., 28 Nov. 1626: *CSP Ven. 1625–6*, p. 548; *C. and T.* i. 177. For his attitude towards day-to-day administration see the reasons he gave for not considering certain petitions: PRO SP 16/73/94. This should not be taken to imply that Charles was idle when it came to the work of government. Where a particular matter engaged his attention, such as the loan, he displayed considerable energy in pushing his councillors to greater efforts: see below, pp. 112, 137.

[11] BL Harl. MS 390, fo. 132; HMC, *Report on the MSS of H. D. Skrine* (1887), p. 84; *Holles*, ii. 366–8; BL Eg. MS 784, p. 128.

[12] PRO SP 16/68/28; 70/45, 96; 71/44; 72/28. For a general discussion of the problems facing monarchs at this time see, G. Parker, *Europe in Crisis, 1598–1648* (Glasgow, 1979), pp. 54–9.

[13] Harriss, 'Aids, loans and benevolences', 6. The Council's approval of

The consequence of this was that the shaping of domestic policy remained at all times very much a political process, dependent on debate and tactical manœuvring within the Council itself. In order to get his way, then, Charles needed more than just firmness; he also required the backing of at least a section of the Council and circumstances which he could use to his advantage.

The main support for the King appears to have come from Buckingham and his 'partisans'. Because the danger of some sort of attack on him remained, the Duke's first instinct was probably to shy away from a Parliament; however his precise role is one of the more elusive aspects of this period, obscured by the fact that he was largely content to take a back seat and allow Charles to make the running. He attended council meetings regularly enough—at the rate of one a week or more between September 1626 and June 1627, when he departed for Rhé—but he is rarely mentioned as having spoken up over important matters of domestic policy.[14] This was probably deliberate, part of a strategy designed to repair his public image and avoid funishing hostages to fortune in the event of a future Parliament; and in keeping with this, on occasion he went out of his way to foster the impression that he favoured a re-summons. In September 1626 the Venetian noted that 'reports get abroad from Buckingham's house that he and his partisans desire it', but then added significantly that, 'all this is supposed to be a collusive artifice designed with the King to regain popularity for the Duke if possible'.[15] If this was indeed the case it would suggest that Buckingham was trying, by a series of characteristically tortuous manœuvres, to keep a foot in both camps.[16]

Over the loan he followed a similar line. Several observers around the Court maintained that it was he, rather than Charles,

crucial decisions was carefully invoked in his Declarations of the reasons for dissolving Parliaments in the late 1620s: *A Declaration*, pp. 15, 18; PRO SP 16/138/45; *His Majestie's Declaration to all his loving subjects of the causes which moved him to dissolve the last Parliament, 10 March 1628/9* printed in Rushworth, i. app., p. 2. For examples of his readiness to defer to the majority see below: pp. 56, 82–5.

[14] *APC 1626; APC 1627, passim.*

[15] *CSP Ven. 1625–6*, p. 558. This 'collusive artifice' was apparently first practised in March 1626, when the Duke was reported to have begged the King in public for a continuation of the parliament, whilst petitioning in private for it to be dissolved: *CSP Ven. 1625–6*, p. 380.

[16] This was reminiscent of Buckingham's attempts to appeal both to Puritans and Arminians in the period 1624–5: Tyacke, 'Puritanism, Arminianism and counter-revolution', pp. 131–2.

who was the real architect of the levy, but this seems questionable.[17] Allowance has to be made for the tendency—particularly strong in commentators such as Abbot and Clare who were opposed to the Duke anyway—to blame him for all the most divisive policies. Furthermore it is clear that once he had departed for Rhé, far from there being a relaxation of pressure against loan refusers, as some had predicted, this was in fact increased.[18] If Buckingham was playing the decisive role in policy-making, then, it must have been a very shadowy and private role indeed. Perhaps the safest conclusion one can draw is that the King and the favourite were acting extremely closely together and that final responsibility was shared between them. It seems likely that, as on other occasions, it was the King who pressed ahead first with a new initiative whilst the Duke tried to anticipate his wishes and move to meet them.[19]

We are on firmer ground if we turn to the Duke's 'partisans', whose actions provide a much less ambiguous pointer to their master's basic line. In a sense of course all members of the Council were 'partisans' of Buckingham in this period, since this had become one of the conditions of remaining in office; however, as has been argued, within this basically loyal body there were different shades of opinion and different degrees of commitment. Several members of the Council's 'old guard' who owed little to the Duke—men like Pembroke, Abbot, Sir Humphrey May, and Sir Thomas Edmondes—remained firmly wedded to traditional policies; and they were joined by a number of Buckingham's protégés—Manchester, Coventry, Coke, and Sir Richard Weston. Whenever these councillors were given the opportunity to speak out on matters of basic policy they demonstrated a commitment to rule with Parliament along the lines indicated by Abbot, when commenting on the meeting in 1626: 'I saw on the one side the King's necessity for money; and especially it being resolved that the war should be pursued. And on the other side I could not forget that in Parliament great sums were offered if the Petitions of the Commons might be hearkened unto. It still ran in my mind that the old and usual way was best; that in Kingdoms the harmony

[17] *Holles*, ii. 338–9; Rushworth, i. 435–6, 439, 445–6, 455–6.

[18] *The Life and Original Correspondence of Sir George Radcliffe*, ed. T. D. Whitaker (1810), pp. 142, 144, 150, 152; *APC 1627*, pp. 387, 492–4; PRO SP 16/71/28.

[19] Tyacke, 'Puritanism, Arminianism and counter-revolution', pp. 132–3.

was sweetest where the Prince and people tuned well together'.[20] This coalition of moderates formed the basis of a majority within the Council who in the last resort, and on this specific issue, were prepared to oppose the apparent wishes of the favourite. This was not as hazardous as might appear because of the ambiguity of Buckingham's own position; and Sir Thomas Coventry was able to set himself up as a relatively outspoken proponent of a Parliament and still remain in favour.[21] In consequence a good deal depended on the minority within Council who were prepared to turn against a policy of rule with Parliament.

These consisted of two sorts of politicians. There were the ideologues for whom the threat from puritans and 'factious spirits' made any resort to Parliament potentially hazardous. Laud and Neile were the clearest, and perhaps the only, examples within the Council.[22] There were also the 'creatures', who felt a particularly strong dependence on the Duke and in the circumstances were prepared to abandon moderate policies. These included Sir Edward Conway who appeared to have lost faith in Parliament when it failed to meet the King's needs in June; Sir John Savile who was to be vehemently opposed to a re-summons as late as February 1628; and perhaps the most 'hawkish' of all Privy Councillors in this period, the Earl of Dorset. It was this group within the Council which appears to have provided the positive backing the King needed.[23] As we have seen, during the summer of 1626, several of

[20] For May, Edmonds and Weston see, Willson, *Privy Councillors*, pp. 90–5. For the remainder see above, pp. 55, 57, 68–70. Rushwroth, i. 454.

[21] At times Coventry was walking something of a tightrope and there were several rumours of his impending dismissal; however he had a shrewd instinct for the compromises needed to survive and by March 1628 was apparently in favour with both Buckingham and Pembroke, who acted as godparents to his grandson: HMC *Buccleuch*, iii. 312, 318; *Holles*, ii. 345; *C. and T.* i. 328.

[22] PRO SP 16/94/88. Neile's views have generally to be inferred from his willingness to align himself with Laud: see below, pp. 61, 63.

[23] PRO SP 78/79/64; *Holles*, ii. 375–6; *CSP Ven. 1625–6*, p. 528. Of the leading councillors Sir Dudley Carleton and the Earl of Holland are the hardest to pin down. At heart Carleton seems to have supported a summons of Parliament, and, in August 1627 confided to his friend Sir Thomas Roe his hopes that a successful meeting 'may rectifie all our domestique disorders'. However he was also, according to the Venetian, particularly dependant on the Duke, not least to save him from financial embarrassment; and this may help to explain the 'hard line' which he took on other matters relating to the loan: Trinity College, Dublin, MS 708, vol. 1, fos. 292–3 (I am grateful to Tom Cogswell for this reference.) *CSP Ven. 1625–6*, p. 560; see below, pp. 58, 63. In Holland's case the comments of the French ambassador during the 1626 Parliament and of Nathaniel Tomkins—a well informed court contact of Sir Robert Phelips—in November 1626, suggest that he was extremely close to the

them were coming forward with proposals for raising money, posited on the assumption that Parliament would not be required again; and they appear to have continued to follow this line in the subsequent months. Evidence of this is scanty before the discussions in the winter of 1627–8; but one occasion on which we do get a glimpse of their activities—during the August council meeting at Windsor—suggests that their attitude was consistent. The Venetian reported that as soon as mention of a Parliament was made 'the Duke's partisans tabooed this as dishonourable to the King. The same partisans proposed a public thanksgiving in all the churches for the auspicious landing at Isle of Rhé. All the members did not approve of this as being premature and unbecoming with the King's brother-in-law concerned, but flatterers who want to propitiate the favourite are not so squeamish'.[24] This sort of support was important in enabling the King to pursue rule without Parliament during 1626 and 1627; but it was not enough to prevent a re-summons in 1628. It is therefore necessary also to take account of the political situation, prevailing until after the return from Rhé, which helped to tip the balance in Charles's favour.

The Council's deliberations in this period were still heavily overshadowed by Parliament's refusal to grant supply in 1626. The emergency that this had created—and the sense of despair felt in June when it seemed that an invasion was likely—had inclined the Council towards accepting a benevolence; and similar circumstances prevailed again in September.[25] The country was facing a foreign policy crisis with no guarantee that if Parliament was re-summoned it would actually provide the money. In this situation it was not unreasonable to regard a new extra-parliamentary levy as the most appropriate course of action. The fact that it was now being called a loan rather than a benevolence avoided the obvious objection that it constituted an infringement of statute; and if it

Duke and one of those councillors most committed to seeing the loan go through. On the other hand he had been a member of the Lords' deputation opposing a dissolution in June; and the readiness of Tomkins to approach him, together with his later efforts to get Sir Francis Barrington out of a London prison, imply that he was regarded as sympathetic to those who had qualms about the loan. Perhaps what both these examples show is that even in these straitened circumstances a good deal of flexibility was still possible: PRO 31/3/63, fos. 74–6, 79–80; SRO Phelips MS 219/35; *LJ* iii. 682; PRO SP 16/60/10.

[24] *CSP Ven. 1626–8*, p. 342.

[25] *CD 1628*, iii. 396.

were collected in the right spirit it could be hoped that it would not be divisive.[26] This seems to have been the councillors' line of reasoning at the time; and certainly it was the approach implied in the initial steps towards the levy.

The loan was, strictly speaking, to be regarded as a general aid and so was subject to the same conventions as governed the benevolence.[27] These were carefully observed by the Council, both in devising the levy and presenting it to the subject. Some brief notes of their discussion on 13 September—which preceded the decision to adopt the loan—show that it was conceived out of a very traditional view of the subject's obligations:

1. That the commons and lords persuaded and put the King into this war. 2. That warres were never borne by the Kinge's charge without the great assistance of his subjects. 3. That to the maintenance of this war they have promised to assist the King with goods and persons.

The Council also determined the amount to be raised by considering what the subject had thought sufficient to satisfy the King's needs:

4. That themselves have in open Parliament declared their opinion of the charge to be worthie of 4 subsidies and 3/15th and 1/10th, that they gave the same in the Common House by a generall vote. 5. That the gathering of the value of the said subsidies and 1/15th shall not differ from them in substance, but in manner only £320,000.[28]

And when it came to defending the loan publicly the arguments used were again traditional. The two most comprehensive statements supporting it—a set of instructions to preachers, dated 20 September, [29] and the commission for levying the loan, dated 20 October[30]—presented a case very similar to that used to justify the benevolence. They set out the nature of the necessity—recounting how the King of Denmark had entered the war to aid the Queen of Bohemia to recover her inheritance and had now suffered a defeat which threatened the whole protestant cause—and explained that

[26] Gardiner, *History*, vi. 143.

[27] Harriss, 'Aids, loans and benevolences', 5–9.

[28] BL Add. MS 34, 324, fo. 256. These notes were probably made by Sir Julius Caesar, Master of the Rolls, who attended this discussion and amongst whose papers they have survived.

[29] *Instructions directed from the King's most excellent Majestie unto all the Bishops of this Kingdom and fit to be put in execution agreeable to the necessitie of the time* (1626). BL 1609/1081 also contains a copy of a letter from the Bishop of Peterborough to his clergy, requiring them to preach accordingly.

[30] PRO SP 16/36/42.

in such circumstances the King was entitled tc supply from Parliament. However Parliament, having been called, had refused to make a grant and so it was now open to the King to request an aid by way of a general loan. In terms of the precedents which favoured extra-parliamentary levies this case was extremely strong; and to make it even more watertight the loan commission closed off a large loophole in the arguments for the benevolence—the lack of any explanation as to why Parliament could not be re-summoned—by stating that 'the emergency cannot endure soe longe a time as the calling of a Parliament'.

These statements, however, as well as showing the traditional nature of the Crown's rhetoric, also disclosed a significant shift in its attitude towards the subject, reflecting the way in which 'new counsels' were coming to seem more appropriate at this time. This was probably due in large part to the failure of the benevolence. It has already been suggested that this levy was set up as a test of the subjects' loyalty and readiness to co-operate with the Crown. If it had succeeded, then, in the terms set out by the King, this would have demonstrated that the opposition in 1626 was no more than a small faction, unrepresentative of the country as a whole. However, if, as happened, the benevolence failed then this could be taken to imply that the disloyalty apparent in Parliament went much deeper and affected the whole nation.

A similar attitude can be seen in the case of the loan and the consequences for the subject were more clearly revealed. Evidence is provided in a Proclamation issued on 7 October 1626 in which the King gave his assurance that the loan would not be used as a precedent, but at the same time appeared to attach certain conditions.[31] It explained that

> this course which at this time is thus enforced upon us by that necessitie to which noe ordinarie course can give the lawe, shall not in any wise be drawne into example nor made a president for after tyme . . . we are fully prepared to call a Parliament soe soone as conveniently wee maie and as often as the Commonwealth's and state occasions shall require it, and by our people's affection nowe shewed unto us in this waie of necessitie, they shall the sooner invite us to the frequent use of Parliament, beinge confident in the hartes of our people.

For those who advocated policies of moderation this offered valuable reassurance, and the proclamation was repeatedly invoked

[31] *Proclamations*, ii. 110–112.

by councillors when they attended meetings with loan commissioners in the shires.[32] However viewed from another perspective it could appear profoundly disturbing since the later phrases seemed to imply that a meeting of Parliament should be earned through a demonstration of loyalty. In other words what was seen by many as a basic right, to which the subject was naturally entitled, was now being presented as a favour granted at the discretion of the monarch.

What was implied in this proclamation was to be clearly spelt out in February 1628 when Charles attempted to raise extra-parliamentary supply again, on this occasion through a levy of ship money. The letters announcing this established an explicit link between a display of loyalty and the summons of a Parliament.[33] After outlining the King's necessity, and referring to the imminence of a Parliament for which the writs had already been sent out, it continued: 'Now this wee must lett you knowe that if you make this present supplie wee will then goe on with our Parliament, if not then wee must thinke of a more speedie way . . . And wee further recommend unto you . . . that as our last divisions did us more harme than the Common Enemie so our present union testified in this foregoing signe of preparing the fleets may be the happie forerunner of future happinesse.' This was probably very close to being Charles's own personal view of the situation. It was not that he was opposed to summoning Parliament in any circumstances—after all the 1628 Parliament did eventually meet—but rather that he insisted on a summons on his own terms; and these included strong assurances that the subject would be docile and co-operative. This was perhaps the most distinctive new element in the situation since the Parliament of 1626; and it was this suspicion of the subject's loyalty which provided the motive force behind 'new counsels'.

Evidence for this at the time of the loan is relatively plentiful. It can be seen for example in the instructions to preachers drawn up by Bishop Laud in the name of the King.[34] These pointed to the cause of failure in the 1626 Parliament, and unreadiness to co-operate in the present emergency, as 'the breach of unity . . . growne too great and common amongst men of all sorts . . . wee know their loyall hartes and therefore wonder the more what should cause distracted affections'. In Laud's view the remedy for

[32] PRO SP 16/49/8; 55/1; *C. and T.* i. 325.

[33] R. J. W. Swales, 'The ship money levy of 1628', *BIHR* l (1977), 174–6.

[34] *Instructions . . . unto all the Bishops*, B-B2.

this lay not with the traditional means of a summons of Parliament—since this had been the root of the trouble—but in the provision of preaching, which would bring home the extent of the emergency and the King's necessity. These instructions received 'a very favourable acceptation' when they were read over to the King and Buckingham;[35] and the concerns which they reflected evidently influenced the Council's preparations.

This was particularly the case with the instructions to Loan Commissioners, the most significant of which were intended to counter the expected opposition.[36] Commissioners were told that 'if any shall object and whisper that if this way of raysinge monye take place then noe Parliament shall hereafter be called' they were to point out that time did not allow for a summons and to reiterate the promise that the loan would not be used as a precedent. When collecting the money they were enjoined to set an example by first subscribing to the loan themselves and then calling on those of their neighbours who were thought most likely to lend. The subsidymen were to be treated with individually, out of earshot of their fellows so that they could not be influenced by protests. Finally there were detailed instructions on how to deal with defaulters. Commissioners who failed to turn up to the service were to be certified to the Council; and subsidymen who refused were to be threatened with the same fate, then, if they remained obstinate, were to be examined on oath to find out 'whether any publikely or underhand be workers or perswaders of others to dissent or dislike from the course'. Such measures were needed after the earlier failures, and had been employed with medieval and sixteenth-century aids, but this did not make them any the less harsh or coercive, and they clearly illustrated the distance the Council had come since the benevolence.[37] The approach employed then of holding large meetings and simply stating to 'the country' the nature of the emergency was no longer considered sufficient.[38] It had to be supported by a series of measures which employed to the full the threat of punishment and force.

All this was likely to appear profoundly disturbing to councillors who clung to the belief that government in England was based on the co-operation and voluntary consent of the subject; but it was a

[35] P. Heylyn, *Cyprianus Anglicus or The History of the Life and Death of William by Divine Providence Lord Archbishop of Canterbury* (1671), p. 153.

[36] PRO SP 16/36/43.

[37] Harriss, 'Aids, loans and benevolences', 14–15.

[38] PRO SP 16/31/30–1.

measure of the way in which the situation worked against them that they were able to do little to prevent it. They were hamstrung by the logic of the case put forward at the time of the benevolence. As has been suggested, this was presented as a basic test of Englishmen's fidelity to their King which they had failed to pass. In these circumstances it was extremely difficult to justify a re-summoning of Parliament, or even a lenient line towards the taxpayer, since for councillors to be able to present a case for this, they had to provide some evidence of the subject's loyalty; and the discussion had been set up in such a way that the only evidence which was acceptable was co-operation over the loan. The moderates therefore had to allow such measures to go ahead, and do all they could to ensure their success, before they could convincingly argue for abandoning the policy. They were, in effect, trapped by a Catch-22 which forced them to hold back and unite behind the King's line.

During the period when the loan was being collected the loyalty and unity displayed by councillors was exemplary. In October and November 1626 large numbers of them attended meetings in Westminster and the home counties to launch the service.[39] From December to the following March they journeyed far afield to promote the levy in more distant shires, in spite of the miseries of winter travel.[40] And when the local commissioners looked like flagging, during July and August 1627, they sent out letters urging greater activity and backed these up by sitting almost daily to deal with refusers.[41] This constituted a remarkably unified response from a body which had apparently been divided in its initial attitude to the levy; and it was a measure both of the strength of the Council's collective loyalty and the extent to which, for the time being, the King had won the debate over policy. However in spite of this agreement over backing the loan, the differences that it had exposed still remained.

Whatever the Councillors' stance in public, in private it seems that some still entertained misgivings. These were voiced by Archbisop Abbot who had been called out of retirement at the King's request, to help promote the service.[42] He later explained how he had attended the council meetings around London and

[39] *C. and T.* i. 154, 157, 164; *CSP Ven. 1625–6*, p. 576.
[40] HMC *Buccleuch*, i. 264; *CSP Ven. 1626–8*, pp. 107–8.
[41] *APC 1627*, pp. 387, 492–4; PRO SP 16/71/28.
[42] Rushworth, i. 444, 455.

'neither did ever discourage any man from lending, nor encourage any man to hold back'. However at the same time he had continued to harbour doubts about the levy: 'It ran in my mind that this new device for money could not long hold out, that then we must return into the highway, whither it were best to retire ourselves betimes, the shortest errors being best. But these thoughts I suppressed within my soul . . . swallowed my own spittle and spake nothing of it to any man.' Abbot's views on politics and the constitution were basically those of councillors like Pembroke, Manchester, Coventry, and Coke and it seems probable that if he was concerned then so were they. Such concern, however, was hardly likely to produce public denunciations of the service, for all the reasons already discussed. Instead it seems to have led to differences of approach, and disagreements over emphasis, when it came to justifying and enforcing the levy; and these differences appear to have played on, and exacerbated, divisions within the Council, ensuring that, in spite of the display of public unity, the split increasingly widened.

The first issue on which differences arose was the size of the county loan commissions. Originally the Council had taken a decision to limit these to 'gentlemen well affected to the state, of greatest love and power in the country . . . and a fewe, and not above 6'. However at a meeting on 16 October several much larger commissions were adopted—comprising all the existing JPs and several others—and this remained the practice throughout the service.[43] We have no explanation for this change, and it is not entirely clear why it should have occurred; however it is possible to offer some suggestions which point to a division of opinion.

In part it probably came about as a result of practical necessity. Councillors may well have realized, on reflection, that the 'powers, favours and creditts' of local gentry—by which they set such store in their instructions to commissioners—were often only effective over a limited area. In consequence one finds a good many additions which appear to have been intended to fill gaps in the territorial influence of the commission.[44] However this was not the only consideration. There were others which were more overtly political.

It seems probable that the original decision to limit commissions

[43] BL Add. MS 34, 324, fo. 256; BRL Coventry MS, Commissions for the loan, no. 12; R. P. Cust, 'A list of commissioners for the forced loan 1626/7', *BIHR* li (1978), 203–6.

[44] Cust, 'A list of commissioners', 203–6.

was influenced by the Duke and his adherents. In the months leading up to the loan there was vigorous lobbying from some of Buckingham's supporters in the shires for the Council to extend its purges of the bench and 'make choise of men known to be well affectioned to His Majestie's service in every county and sparing of others not well disposed'.[45] This culminated in a memorandum, submitted to the Duke, just as the loan was being launched, in which, amongst other things, it was suggested that 'the Booke of the Commission of the Peace be looked into and out of it Commissioners chosen in each Countrye such as in Parliament or otherwise have made demonstracon of their good affection to His Majestie's service'.[46] Such a policy had obvious attractions to those who stood to gain from its implementation. It also chimed in with the notion becoming increasingly prevalent at Court, that the nation was divided between those who were loyal and those who were disloyal. However it was self-evidently not the way to reunite the nation and it was probably for this reason, above all, that the smaller commissions were abandoned.

For those councillors who continued to adhere to traditional ideals the whole notion of setting apart and distinguishing the 'well affectioned' must have been deeply offensive. They had already assented to measures which tended in this direction and they must have been coming to feel that enough was enough. If the divisions between King and subject were to be healed then the best way of doing this was not to exclude suspect gentry, but to give as many of them as possible the chance to display their fundamental loyalty. Nathaniel Tomkins, the London informant of Sir Robert Phelips, seems to have detected such an attitude as he fished around the fringes of the Court in November. He formed the impression that councillors wished 'to putt in those into the commission whose backwardnesse hath bin most doubted'; and this was borne out by the pattern of appointments. With a few exceptions all the most likely opponents of the levy were

[45] PRO SP 16/37/5, 91.

[46] PRO SP 16/526/10. The author of this is unknown, but he was clearly someone with staunchly Protestant leanings as he also suggested 'giving the people infinite content' by enforcing the recusancy laws and encouraging 'the most zealous preacher and the most resorted to' in each county to preach in favour of the levy. This serves as a useful reminder that Buckingham's immediate entourage did not simply consist of crypto-Catholics and high churchmen; it still included staunch Calvinists such as Attorney-General Heath: Russell, *Parliaments and English Politics*, pp. 233, 238; Cust, 'Charles I and a draft declaration'.

nominated, including several gentry summoned before it in the summer for obstructing the benevolence and those peers who refused to subscribe to the loan during November. This clearly suggested that a majority favoured reconciliation rather than punishment, and seems to have constituted a defeat for the more 'hawkish' element within the Council. However the moderates did not have everything their own way. Those who favoured reuniting the nation around traditional Protestant principles suffered a setback when—probably at the King's behest—a number of leading Catholics were also included in the commissions.[47]

Similar divisions emerged with a series of disagreements over how far to press the use of coercion. The first of these occurred in November 1626, following a refusal by the judges and some of the peers to sign their names to a declaration of the loan's legality. Subscription had been introduced in the original loan instructions to ensure that the commissioners and others set an example to those below them.[48] Therefore when the judges refused it on 28 October—in spite of the fact that most of them had already paid—this represented a significant setback to the service, particularly as they were joined some three weeks later by a group of about fifteen peers.[49] Several observers believed that this would force the Council to abandon the levy and summon a Parliament; and the uncertainty was sufficient to persuade councillors to abort a series of excursions into the shires, planned for mid-November.[50] In the event the loan did continue, but only after an extended discussion within the Council which again brought to the surface differences and divisions.

Disagreement focused on the issue of how to proceed with the non-subscribers. In some respects this was a practical question, hinging on the problem of whether a strict punishment was more likely to deter resisters or create martyrs. But it also raised a number of ideological issues and reflected fundamental differences of philosophy when it came to dealing with the relationship between King and subject. Leading the hard-liners was Charles himself, who was said to have vowed that in response to the

[47] SRO Phelips MS 219/35; Cust, 'A list of commissioners', 203–4.

[48] PRO SP 16/36/43.

[49] Gardiner, *History*, vi. 149; *C. and T.* i. 172; PRO SP 16/41/3; HMC *Buccleuch*, iii. 307–8.

[50] HMC *Buccleuch*, iii. 312–5; PRO SP 16/39/55.

judges refusal 'he will sweep all their benches'.[51] For him the issue was probably more than just a matter of compelling obedience. From the start he had become closely involved with the loan, representing it as the performance of his obligations towards Christian of Denmark and staking a considerable amount of personal credit on its success. Apart from the proclamation of 7 October—containing what amounted to a royal promise that the levy would not be made a precedent—the King had written individual letters to each member of the nobility, urging them to set an example by prompt payment, and had let it be known about the Court that he regarded the loan as a crucial test of loyalty to his person.[52] In the short term these measures were to prove effective, especially in 'whipping' the peerage into line; but it was a course of action which carried a high degree of risk.[53] If Charles's personal initiative was resisted or slighted then this would threaten what was arguably the Crown's greatest political asset, the sense of trust and obligation felt towards it by its leading subjects. As the Earl of Holland commented to Nathaniel Tomkins, 'the King's honor was really at the stake'.[54]

In these circumstances Charles was disinclined to compromise. However, there were those amongst his councillors who viewed the situation differently; and two of the members with long legal experience—Coventry and Lord Treasurer Marlborough—were reluctant to press the judges. They advised the King 'not to urge them to that which they held contrary to law and against their oath, nor yet to enforce them to deliver the reason of their refusal'.[55] Presumably they felt that as the legal status of the loan was somewhat dubious, it was better to sidestep the issue and avoid the impression of infringing the subject's liberties. However this was clearly not a line of reasoning which appealed to Charles; he promptly threatened to sack the two ministers.[56]

These differences came to a head on 27 November when the Council debated, before the King, the question of 'whether those stubborn lords that refused to pay the loan shall be committed or not'.[57] The case for the prosecution was put most forcibly by the Earl of Dorset, who, in line with the view he had expressed to the

51 HMC *Buccleuch*, iii. 312.

52 *Instructions . . . unto all the Bishops*, B-B2; HMC *Buccleuch*, i. 264: *C. and T.* i. 177.

53 See below, pp. 105–11.

54 SRO Phelips MS 219/35.

55 *C. and T.* i. 164.

56 HMC *Buccleuch*, iii. 312; *Holles*, ii. 337–8.

57 *C. and T.* i. 177.

Venetian ambassador, argued for the use of coercion, citing '1st, the general conformity of Essex, both to subscribe and pay upon the commitment of Sir Francis Barrington and Sir William Masham. And 2nd because if these lords were not also made examples of they would infect the rest of the Kingdom'. However in spite of this, and the evident preference of the King, the proposal for commitment was defeated, by two votes. This victory for the moderates was followed up two days later with a council letter declaring that subscription was not to be compulsory. The reason given was that it was unnecessary—'being to noe other end then that the collectors mought the more readily knowe what to demand of them'[58]—but again the decision clearly implied that the Council wished to avoid pressing commissioners to search their consciences and decide on the legality of the levy; and this marked a significant step away from confrontation.

The question of how far to push coercion was raised again when the Council considered the use of pressing for service abroad. The legality of this sort of punishment had long been considered dubious and it was to cause controversy again in the Parliament of 1628.[59] As was so often the case it appears to have been the King himself who initially suggested its employment. The first recorded mention of it was during the discussion of the Privy Seal loan on 14 September when Charles urged the Council 'to send those to Denmark who denied to pay'. This proposal was taken up in early October when the Council threatened some of Westminster refusers with compulsory service either in the fleet or the army; and a formal vindication of this course of action was provided by the King in a letter to the Council dispatched on the 20th:

> our intention is not to have the Boord trobled with everie ordinary person, but those only who in your judgments are fitt to bee called thither for the advancement of our service. And for the rest which shal refuse to assist with theire purses for the common defence our will and pleasure is that they performe it in their persons, and to that end . . . to bee inrouled amongst the companies of soldiers which are now to bee levied and imployed for our service.[60]

This statement—combining both practical arguments and arguments from necessity—should have provided all the justification councillors needed for employing pressing as a punishment; and yet they remained reluctant to use it. It has been possible to trace

[58] *APC 1626*, p. 388. [59] *CD 1628*, ii. 279–81.
[60] *C. and T.* i. 149; *CSP Ven. 1625–6*, p. 576; PRO SP 16/38/23.

its application in only two instances, and on two other occasions when it had been contemplated it was withdrawn.[61]

One of these episodes occurred in March 1627 when the pressing of Gloucestershire refusers was prevented by the scruples of Manchester and Conway. A signet letter had been prepared in the King's name which stated, in forceful terms, that the pressing was to be a specific punishment for refusing the loan. The two councillors, however, after consulting over this letter, decided that it was 'not fitt to be sent from the King as it is, in regard that it menconed the pressing of disaffected persons. His Lordship would have it absolute for the pressing of 150 men without menconing any such person'.[62] Precisely why they decided to make these alterations—after the original had been approved by the King—is not clear; but the change in wording implied an awareness that the use of pressing over the loan was a charged and emotive issue, and one which was better avoided.

Something of the arguments behind such a response could be seen in the council debate over the Chelmsford refusers, held on 16 March. These men had been offered press money, on the instructions of the Council, but had refused to accept it.[63] This, then, again raised the sorts of issues debated the previous November, questions about how far to press the use of coercion in a situation where the legality of the Council's actions was highly dubious. The hard-liners, in the presence of the King, proposed that these refusers should be punished 'by martial law and hanged up in the next tree to their dwellings for an example and terror to others'. However this was fiercely resisted by Lord Keeper Coventry, using similar sorts of arguments to those he had deployed previously. He pointed out firstly that 'as far as he understood the law none were liable to martial law but martial men' and secondly that 'he thought a subsidy new by law could not be pressed against his will for a foreign service [*sic*], it being supposed in law the service of his purse excused that of his person, unless his own country were in danger'. He then 'appealed to my lord treasurer and my lord president whether it were not so, who both assented it was so, though some of them faintly as unwilling to have been urged to such an answer.' The outcome of this was that the original proposal was dropped in favour of dealing with

[61] The two occasions when it was used were London, in October 1626, and Northamptonshire, in January 1627; *APC 1626*, p. 313; PRO SP 16/49/8.

[62] PRO SP 16/56/100; 89/4.

[63] PRO SP 16/57/1; *APC 1627*, p. 102.

the refusers in Star Chamber.[64] Once more, then, this represented a victory for the moderates, but again at the price of confirming the rift within Council.

Another area where this was apparent was the question of whether loan refusers should have soldiers billeted on them. The Venetian ambassador outlined the way most councillors felt about this when he reported in February 1627: 'There was an idea of quartering those troops in the counties most opposed to the subsidies so as to intimidate them to obedience and secure the government, but on reflecting that both soldiers and the populace were disaffected and discontented, and might create rather than suppress disturbances, they witheld their decision'.[65] Accordingly the use of punitive billeting appears to have been eschewed, at least until most of the money had been safely collected.[66] However, not all councillors felt the same way. The Earl of Dorset was prepared to use the threat of billeting to persuade Sussex commissioners to hasten collection of the loan; and Dudley Carleton remarked menacingly that if the expected opposition materialized in north Oxfordshire then 'Berkshire soldiers will be well content to be removed to eate Banburie cakes'.[67] Neither of these threats were carried out, but the readiness of councillors to utter them does indicate that some were prepared to be seen to be pressing coercion to its limits; and once more this brought out differences of attitude which played on the divisions already in existence.

The implications of all this, in political terms, were spelt out in the events leading up to the famous Five Knights Case of November 1627. This had its origins in the problems of dealing with the gentlemen refusers who had been summoned to London. To start with, most of these had been confined to prison as soon as they arrived.[68] By the end of February 1627, however, it was

[64] *C. and T.* i. 208. Mead is the only source I have found for this debate, although the council register confirms that the matter was discussed and that all those mentioned as speaking were present. It also records the final outcome of the discussion: *APC 1627*, p. 140.

[65] *CSP Ven. 1626–8*, p. 126.

[66] I have not found any direct evidence of councillors deliberately using billeting as a punishment against loan refusers before February 1628 when Nicolas suggested this as a consideration for billeting in Essex: PRO SP 16/92/86; Quintrell, 'Gentry factions and the Witham affray', 118–25. Nevertheless some MPs in the 1628 Parliament believed that such a policy had been pursued: *CD 1628*, ii. 367.

[67] Fletcher, *A County Community*, p. 196; PRO SP 16/50/36.

[68] *APC 1626*, p. 328; *APC 1627*, pp. 39–40.

becoming evident that the prisons simply could not cope with the numbers and this prompted a change of approach on the part of the Council. Instead of confining refusers, they punished them by compulsory attendance before the Council, every three days or so.[69] This was tedious and expensive for the individuals involved and had the added advantage of being less controversial than outright confinement. For some three months, then, most of those summoned were dealt with in this way. However, by the end of April the Council was again preparing to change tack; and at this point differences in attitude once more began to come to the surface.

Two contradictory sets of rumours started to circulate: one suggesting that all refusers were about to be released; the other talking of new humiliations to be heaped upon them, such as the creation of 'a running army to be in the land and that the King's standard shall be fetched out of the Tower, and that the gentlemen which refuse to pay the loans to march after it wherever it goes'.[70] These were precipitated by the Duke's impending departure for the fleet at Portsmouth, which seems to have sparked off a struggle to gain the initiative in handling refusers. Hard-liners, like Sir John Savile, were said to be determined to stick by the use of confinement in order to deter defaulters and punish the disloyal; whilst the moderates were thought to favour a less onerous punishment, in the form of house arrest out in the shires.[71] This latter policy was eventually adopted, and it seems to have been justified on both pragmatic and political grounds. As summer approached, and conditions in London worsened, the health of the prisoners was starting to cause concern and there was a very real prospect that if they were left in confinement some would die.[72] At the same time it was becoming apparent that the presence of all the leading refusers, gathered together in the capital, was providing a focus for continuing opposition and controversy.[73] Both these were circumstances which the Council was anxious to avoid. So by the end of June, under the supervision of Lord President Manchester—who had gained something of a reputation as the 'prisoners' friend'—it started to send refusers away to the counties, in the custody of local sheriffs, 'imagining them', as

[69] *Radcliffe Correspondence*, pp. 137–8; HMC *Skrine*, p. 110; *Holles*, ii. 345–6.

[70] *Radcliffe Correspondence*, pp. 142, 150, 152; *C. and T.* i. 220.

[71] *Radcliffe Correspondence*, p. 144; *Strafforde Letters*, p. 37.

[72] PRO SP 16/60/10; 66/17; 67/87.

[73] See below, pp. 232–4.

Clare noted perceptively, 'peradventure by dividing them more malleable hereafter, everyone as he is affected made better or made worse by company'.[74] This again appears to have been a success for the moderates; however it was not an end to the differences.

There was also the separate, but related, issue of how far the law courts should be used against these refusers. The moderates appear to have adhered to the view—put forward by Coventry and Marlborough in November 1626—that anything which raised the issue of the loan's ultimate legality was better avoided. They therefore tended to adopt a softly-softly approach, side-stepping various attempts by opponents of the levy to get the whole matter discussed in open court. Thus several groups of refusers about to face trial found themselves reprieved at the last minute. These included the Chelmsford refusers, who were supposed to appear in Star Chamber in March 1627, but were confined instead; the Northamptonshire defaulters, who were said to have been granted a hearing in Exchequer during April, but never obtained it; and the Earl of Lincoln, who was again expected to face the Star Chamber, but for the time being was simply kept in the Tower.[75] By these delays the moderate councillors successfully avoided a pronouncement which could only have stirred up further controversy; however, theirs was not the only approach to the situation.

There was also a strong lobby within the Council which favoured a public trial to demonstrate the Crown's firm resolve and to deter other refusers. This appears to have been the intention behind Attorney General Heath's investigation of charges against a Yorkshire loan refuser, Sir John Jackson. As he confided to Secretary Conway, 'these are very foule . . . if they can be made goode it would be very advantageous to the King's service to have a publik hearing of some cause of this nature, which may be fully proved'.[76] It also seems to have played some part in the King's insistence—against the advice of most of his Council—that an elderly Gloucestershire minister, John Burgoyne, should face trial in Star Chamber over various utterances he had made.[77] And it encouraged some to go even further and use the law courts to confirm the distinction between the loyal and disloyal. The most

[74] *C. and T.* i. 241; *Holles*, ii. 359–61.

[75] PRO SP 16/60/10; *C. and T.* i. 195. Lincoln was finally indicted in Star Chamber in September 1627 and sentence was passed against him in November: *Proclamations*, ii. 139 n.

[76] PRO SP 16/55/29.

[77] PRO SP 16/71/46, 78.

public example was an attempt by Laud and Neile to get the author of an anonymous pamphlet attacking the loan indicted for treason. Their argument—'that this soweing of division and setting of discention betweene the King and his people was treason in him that contrived the letter'—was clearly aimed at the Earl of Lincoln, whose servant was on trial in Star Chamber at the time and who was widely suspected of having written the pamphlet.[78] But such an open confrontation with a leading peer was clearly not to the taste of most of those present. As the reporter noted, 'the two Bishopps can espie treason in a case which concernes the King's prerogative when the judges that spake before could not see it, nor any of the Lords which spake after'.

The most significant consequence of this division was the trial of the Five Knights, which arose out of the Council's attempts to deal with a group of refusers who, from July 1627 onwards, obstinately resisted any attempt to make them leave London. The members of this group—led by William Coryton and George Catesby—recognized that their removal was a ploy to make opposition less effective and they tried to turn the tables by challenging the Council to declare the reasons for their confinement. The councillors response, however, was simply to side-step the issue, and separate the two ringleaders by placing them under close confinement in the Fleet.[79] There matters rested until the end of October, when the whole business was suddenly taken out of their hands. A group of five of the gentry remaining in London petitioned the Lord Chief Justice 'that counsel might be assigned them to plead for their relief out of prison'. The Judges responded by acknowledging that this was a just request and consulting the King, who had just returned from his summer progress. Charles listened to the plea and was said to be 'much moved thereat, but appeased by the reasons they alleged'. He therefore overturned the Council's policy and decided to allow the hearing to proceed.[80] In the event any questioning of the loan's legality was carefully avoided, by the Council making it clear that imprisonment was 'by his majesty's special commandment'. However the public outcry prompted by the verdict against the Five Knights

[78] FSL V. b. 70, fo. 73v.

[79] *The Fairfax Correspondence. Memoirs of the Reign of Charles I*, 2 vols., ed. G. W. Johnson (1848), i. 68; PRO SP 16/72/28; *APC 1627–8*, p. 58.

[80] *C. and T.* i. 280; PRO SP 16/85/53.

represented precisely the reaction that the moderates had been struggling to avoid.[81]

By the end of this case, November 1627, the debate on policy within the Council was progressing into a new phase which was to lead to the re-summoning of Parliament. This will be discussed in the next section. Before moving on to this, however, it is appropriate to say something more about the ideological division within the Council. What had begun as a disagreement over policy—rapidly subsumed in the emergency faced during the summer of 1626—had, by late 1627, hardened into a clearly defined rift, a struggle between political groupings in which was at stake not only the balance of power and the careers of individuals, but also fundamentally different views of the relationship between King and subject. The nature of this divergence can best be appreciated if we examine the assumptions underlying each set of opinions; and to do this it is necessary to look outside the Council, to the views being expressed by those linked to each side.

The fullest evidence relating to the attitudes of hard-liners is provided by a series of sermons preached between February and July 1627 by Matthew Wren, Robert Sibthorpe, Isaac Bargrave, and Roger Manwaring.[82] These were delivered in response to Laud's instructions to the clergy and followed a theme which Laud had suggested, that of reminding subjects of their duty of obedience. Wren, Bargrave and Manwaring's sermons were delivered directly to the King, and Manwaring's appears to have earned him royal favour and protection. Furthermore both the King and Laud displayed a very direct interest in securing the licensing of Sibthorpe and Manwaring's sermons. In Sibthorpe's case Charles took the unusual step of insisting that the Archbishop of Canterbury should approve the sermon, and then used Laud to provide written answers to Abbot's objections; whilst with Manwaring he overrode Laud's cautious advice 'to think better of it for that there were many things therein which will be very distasteful to the people', and insisted that it should be printed,

[81] Guy, 'Origins of the Petition of Right', 291; Russell, *Parliaments and English Politics*, pp. 334–7.

[82] Matthew Wren, *A Sermon Preached Before The King's Majestie on Sunday, 17th of February last, at Whitehall* (Cambridge, 1627). (I am grateful to Johann Sommerville for drawing my attention to this.); Robert Sibthorpe, *Apostolike Obedience* (1627); Isaac Bargrave, *A Sermon Preached Before King Charles, March 27th 1627; Being the Anniversary of His Majestie's Inauguration* (1627); Roger Manwaring, *Religion and Allegiance* (1627).

bearing the inscription 'by His Majestie's special command'.[83] It seems reasonable, therefore, to take the sermons as expressing views which had a strong positive appeal for Charles. How far other members of the Council would have subscribed to these is less clear. Laud—in spite of his reservations over the publication of Manwaring—and Neile would probably have found them broadly acceptable since they themselves stated similar views elsewhere.[84] But other councillors are unlikely to have been enthusiastic about arguments which constituted such a clear break with tradition. The decision to license Manwaring's sermon was taken when Charles was removed from the Council's presence, on his summer progress, and it is significant that only Sir Dudley Carleton, who was abroad for much of the period, appears to have offered any defence of Manwaring in the 1628 Parliament.[85] Given the King's clearly expressed intentions and the circumstances prevailing in 1627 some councillors were prepared to act in the spirit of the sermons, but they may not have felt comfortable in doing so.

The four sermons took as their central proposition the notion that the King's power was divinely ordained. From this they advanced to the idea that as the King was placed in authority by God, his conduct could only be judged and condemned by God. Therefore the subject had no right to resist the King, but had a divinely ordained duty to obey his commands. This duty of obedience was essential to the maintenance of hierarchy and an ordered social structure, which Manwaring demonstrated by comparing the King's position to that of the patriarch within the household.[86] There was, of course, nothing particularly novel about these propositions. They were all commonplaces which commanded widespread acceptance at the time and could be incorporated into a view of the constitution which also assigned a central position to Parliament.[87] Where the preachers departed

[83] *DNB*: Manwaring, Roger; Rushworth, i. 436, 438–9; *LP 1628*, p. 642.

[84] T. L. Moir, *The Addled Parliament of 1614* (Oxford, 1958), pp. 117–18; PRO SP 16/94/88. For the links between Laud and Neile and Wren: *Parentalia, or Memoirs of the Family of the Wrens*, ed. S. Wren (1760), pp. 45–7.

[85] *LP 1628*, 638–9. It is perhaps significant that Clare seemed to assume that his distaste for Sibthorpe's sermon was shared by his old friend the Earl of Exeter, a minor figure on the Council but one who probably aligned himself with the Duke: *Holles*, ii. 357–8; PRO SP 16/84/16.

[86] Wren, *A Sermon*, pp. 27–31; Sibthorpe, *Apostolike Obedience*, pp. 13, 16–18; Bargrave, *A Sermon*, p. 20; Manwaring, *Religion and Allegiance*, pp. 1–15.

[87] Judson, *Crisis of the Constitution*, pp. 176–88.

from the norm was in denying that the subject had any significant role to play and suggesting that the King was the only binding and cohesive force within society.

This point of view was stated most clearly and unambiguously by Manwaring: 'The sublime Power therefore . . . resides in earthly *Potentates* which hee never did communicate to any multitudes of men in the world, but onely and immediately to his owne *Viceregents*'.[88] The implication of this for the subject's role in government were worked out in relation to the functions of Parliament, both in making laws and granting taxes. In the case of laws Manwaring argued that they 'take their binding force from the supreme will of the liege lord', and Sibthorpe insisted that it was 'The King's duty . . . to direct and make laws', which, as Abbot pointed out, gave the impression that Parliament had no part to play in the process.[89] With regard to the granting of taxation, Manwaring was quite clear that the subject had no power to withold it, but was consulted simply to decide on the best means of distributing the burden. He described Parliaments as 'the highest and greatest representatives of the Kingdom . . . most sacred and honourable and necessary for those ends to which they were at first instituted: yet know we must that they were not to this end, to contribute any right to Kings, whereby to challenge tributary aydes and subsidiary helpes, but for the more equal imposing and more easie exacting of Originall Law and Justice'. Since the subject had a subordinate role in the government of the realm, any rights he possessed under the law were insignificant when compared with the royal will and authority, and Manwaring pointed out that the King's actions were not in any way restricted by statute:

> If any King shall command that which stands not in any opposition to the originall lawe of God, nature, Nations and the Gospell (though it be not correspondent in every circumstance to laws Nationall and Municipall) no subject may without hazard of his own damnation in rebelling against God, question or disobey the will and pleasure of his soveraigne. For as the father of his country he commands what his pleasure is out of counsell and judgement.[90]

Similarly Sibthorpe suggested that the idea of standing on the rights of the subject was derived from the Jesuits and resistance

[88] Manwaring, *Religion and Allegiance*, p. 11.
[89] Ibid., p. 9; Rushworth, i. 439.
[90] Manwaring, *Religion and Allegiance*, pp. 19–20.

theorists like Knox and Goodman, 'the one which makes the Church above the King, and the Pope above the Church . . . the other make the law above the King, and the people above the law, and so depose Princes by their tumults and insurrections'.[91]

Both Sibthorpe and Manwaring, therefore, viewed the subject's freedom of property under the law as insignificant and necessarily subordinate to the authority of the Crown, and it was this notion which underpinned their statements relating to the loan. When discussing this, both took pains to demonstrate that the King's demand was supported by a justifiable necessity, but then went on to argue that, even if it had not been, the subject was still obliged to render tribute to his monarch whenever it was demanded. Sibthorpe saw taxes as the rightful due of monarchs 'by the law of God as a sign of our subjection; by the law of nature as a reward of their paines and protection; by the law of nations as the sinews of a states preservation'. He therefore argued that 'Tribute may always be justly and with good conscience paid by the subject, although it be sometimes unjustly imposed and exacted by the ruler'. Similarly Manwaring maintained that taxes must be paid on every occasion that the King chose to demand them:

> To Kings therefore . . . nothing can be denyed that may answer the royall state and excellency, that may further the supply of their urgent necessities, that may be for the security of their Royal persons (whose lives are worth millions of others) that may serve for the protection of their Kingdome's territories and dominions, that may inable them to yeelde reliefe, ayde and succor to their deere and royal confederates and allyes, or that may be for the defence and propagation of that sacred and pretious truth.[92]

Having established this, the preachers could then proceed to argue that payment of the loan was also a basic test of the subject's loyalty and readiness to accept royal authority. Hence Sibthorpe pointed out that 'if a prince impose an immoderate, yea an unjust tax, yet the subject may not thereupon withdraw his obedience and dutie. Nay hee is bound in conscience to submitt'.[93] If this was the case then those who refused the loan could be regarded as the equivalent of rebels, and this was basically the theme of both Wren and Bargrave's sermons. Wren took as his text 'Feare God, my sonne, and the King' and used it to demonstrate how those at

[91] Sibthorpe, *Apostolike Obedience*, pp. 22–3.
[92] Ibid., pp. 15–17; Manwaring, *Religion and Allegiance*, pp. 18–21, 27–30.
[93] Sibthorpe, *Apostolike Obedience*, p. 16.

fault for their 'wilfull refusings' in secular matters were at the same time guilty of 'Atheism' and 'prophanation' in their relationship with God. This was a charge which he levelled particularly at 'The Great Professors of this religion, they that take upon themselves above others to be this God's chiefest sonnes and servants' who

> if any man dare be so true to God and the King as to shew them the dutie of better devotion they besmeare him presently with a coale of dangerous superstition; if of better allegiance they brand him soundly with the slaunder of ambitious flattery; and by all meanes they reckon them that stand least upon pointes with God in worshipping him the godliest men and best christians . . . them that stand most with the King against obeying of him the best subjects or (as now it goes currant in their own coyn) good patriots.[94]

Bargrave developed this theme further, basing his sermon on the more provocative text, 'Rebellion is the sin of witchcraft and stubbornnesse as the wickednesse of idolatry'. He drew parallels between the disobedience of Saul and the Israelites—in refusing to destroy the Amalekites—and the backwardness of his own day: 'I would to God that Saul and his people were only guilty of this sinne, but I feere that I have beene all this while but telling our own tale . . . I professe . . . that my conscience apprehends nothing so likely to provoke yet God's heavier judgements upon this land than our wilfulness and disobedience, our stubbornesse and contumacy first against God in heaven, secondly against his deputy on earth.' This 'wilfulness' was not however only the result of sinfulness. According to Bargrave it was also rooted in the familiar threats posed by 'popularity' and 'resistance theory'. Thus he was able to present opposition to the loan as a part of the puritanical and popular conspiracy to undermine the monarchy:

> Though the earth swallowed up Core and his complices, yet too many of this generation remains still; men whose purity consists in parity, whose conscience in disobedience . . . I know there is a generation who think themselves bound by their holy profession to quit subjects from their obedience, to authorise the deposition nay murther of Kings . . . The Gospell cannot suffer us to swell to this height of rebellion. Yet that wee may not too much over-valew our selves give me leave to wish . . . there were none amongst us who place their conscience too much in their will; who are all for faith and the first table, nothing for obedience and the second table. I would there were none to tell us that to obey our Prince, is

[94] Wren, *A Sermon*, pp. 34–8.

to betray our Countrey; none who stampe it as a maine brande upon the Clergy that they preach obedience.[95]

For Bargrave and the others this was the real crux of the matter. Obedience was the keystone in the arch of political order and in challenging the King's right to levy the loan, the resisters had inevitably raised the spectre of rebellion. In such circumstances there could be no room for compromise and—just as the godly tended to argue with popery—any sign of weakness could be seen as fatally selling the pass. Hence Sibthorpe could argue forcefully for the severest possible punishment: 'there was that saying of Solon which affirmed that commonwealths consist of reward and punishment, and that when these be taken away the whole discipline of cities faileth and is dissolved . . . neither can the wilfulnesse of wicked men be restrained but by severity and chastisement of paines'.[96]

With this statement he was of course touching directly on one of the problems facing councillors over the loan and the arguments he had put forward help to explain the readiness of some to resort to the extremes of coercion. This was perhaps the most significant aspect of these four sermons. The basic ideas had been voiced before—in the works of 'royalist divines' and others described by Professor Judson, Professor Mendle, and Dr Sommerville—but they had rarely been applied so directly to a political situation, and certainly not to one as highly charged as the loan.[97] Their appearance in this context was bound to be profoundly alarming. Not only did it make explicit a very worrying interpretation of the Council's actions; it also implied a growing gulf between the views of the King and most of his subjects.

For those councillors who favoured more traditional ideals in relations between King and subject the opportunities to put their point of view were more restricted. They were placed in something of a cleft stick by the need to maintain a united front in public and the King's insistence that there should be no talk of a Parliament. They were therefore unable to challenge the loan openly or even offer a convincing argument against it in Council. However their viewpoint did not go entirely by the board. As we have seen they took every opportunity to play down the existence of division by

95 Bargrave, *A Sermon*, pp. 4–5, 14.

96 Sibthorpe, *Apostolike Obedience*, p. 1.

97 Judson, *Crisis of the Constitution*, pp. 171–217; Mendle, *Dangerous Positions*, pp. 104–6, 108–9; Sommerville, *Politics and Ideology*, pp. 9–50, 117–41.

advocating a more lenient treatment of refusers and avoiding confrontation with the liberties of the subject. They also attempted to prepare the ground for a reconciliation by offering repeated reassurances that the loan was a one-off and no more than a response to an immediate emergency.

This was the theme of the speeches made by the Earl of Manchester and his brother Lord Montagu when they addressed the Northamptonshire subsidymen in January 1627. It also seems to have been the intention behind the Lord Keeper's charge in February, in which, according to Clare, 'the Judges ar commanded to give thanks at the assizes to the cuntry for their forwardness in this most royall subsidy . . . and ar promised (wittnes the proclamation) that the like shall be never putt upon them agayn'.[98] And it certainly emerged from the speeches made by Coventry, Coke and Weston during the Star Chamber trial of Thomas Perkins in May 1627.[99] Perkins, a groom to the Earl of Lincoln, had been convicted of distributing a pamphlet attacking the loan as an attempt to create a new method of taxation and obviate the need for Parliament. As we have seen, this encouraged Laud and Neile to try to extend the definition of treason. However it also gave moderate councillors an opportunity to discuss the justification for the levy, on a very public stage and at just about the time when the King was sponsoring publication of the sermons on obedience.

The clearest distinction between the views of the moderates and those of the preachers of the four sermons related to the grounds on which each justified the loan. Whereas the preachers had suggested it could be levied by the King's will, as his absolute right, both Coke and Weston took great pains to show that it rested on justifiable necessity, respectable precedent and something approaching the consent of the subject. Coke pointed out that the practice of levying loans was 'not newe but presented in all tymes of necessitie from King Wm. to King Charles the first'; whilst Weston argued—against Perkins's allegation that the judges had refused to subscribe to the loan—that 'it is well knowne they were the next men to the councell that lente as in a body to the King'.[100] More surprisingly—in view of his behaviour in November 1626—

[98] PRO SP 16/49/8; *C. and T.* i. 198; HMC *Buccleuch*, i. 265; *Holles*, ii. 345–6. This was also the theme of an anonymous speech prepared by a Privy Councillor for a meeting with Loan Commissioners in the shires: PRO SP 16/52/75.

[99] PRO SP 16/527/55; BL Harg. MS 321, fos. 135–8; FSL, V. b. 70, fos. 73–4.

[100] BL Harg. MS 321, fos. 136–7.

Coventry made much the same point, claiming 'that all the Judges in England gave voluntarilie to this loane and that there was none towards the lawe that held it to bee against the law but one . . .'.[101] As the Star Chamber reporter noted, this was not, strictly speaking, true; however the fact that Coventry and Weston took such pains to claim a judicial sanction illustrates the importance they attached to accommodating the levy within the law, and this in turn suggested that they recognized law as something which limited the demands a King could make on his subjects.

This point of view came out most strongly in Coke's speech. He pointed out that, although in this case the King had the full force of necessity supporting his claims, he was still obliged to make every attempt to gain the subject's consent and co-operation, as he was in fact doing:

> Tho some have done it by waye and uppon occasions which are worthie to bee forgotten, but the best Kinges have done it in cases of necessitie, and by such waies as came nearest to consent. And in both theis His Majesty hath proceeded with royal care and moderation . . . And in this necessitie His Majesty considered not the next way, but the fairest and which his predecessors had taken with out offence. For the contention it is cleared by proclamation, by instruction, by commission, by acts uppon record, by experience.[102]

A similar view was provided by Weston in dismissing Perkins's argument that the subject could give money only in Parliament. He pointed out that on the contrary it was permissible for subjects to display their love and loyalty just as clearly by giving extra-parliamentary grants. However he also made it clear that parliamentary consent was to be regarded as the normal basis for raising taxes. It was therefore desirable that Parliament meet as soon as possible:

> The false chardge of the Parliament; give noe way but by Parliament as if there were noe obligacon of love and duty betwixt King and people but joyntly in Parliament; yet it is both joint and severall in Parliament and out of Parliament . . . for in Parliament all agreed to give; as one said the clocks differed, one went faster the other went slower, but all slacke uppon giveing—and I doubt not but the affection of the people in this loane will invite the Kinge shortly to call a Parliament.[103]

This last statement, in particular, illustrated the way in which a respect for the rights of the subject led to an emphasis on

[101] FSL, V. b. 70, fos. 73–4.
[102] PRO SP 16/527/55.
[103] BL Harg. MS 321, fos. 137–8.

government as a partnership between King and subject, a process of bargaining and co-operation summed up in Weston's vision of 'the affection of the people' inviting 'the King shortly to call a Parliament'. This same stress was also shown in his efforts to play down the extent of division caused by the loan. Whereas the four preachers had condemned all refusal to pay as rebellion, and Laud and Neile had introduced the charges of treason, Weston was careful to draw a distinction. Those who, like Perkins, 'must censure the power, not excuse themselves but to accuse the state, it is tyme to punish such: for the advise it is most contemptuous against the King and State: contempt of a King is worse than hatred, for to destroy the life and soule of a monarchy if you suffer contempt of authoritie'. Those who were simply 'content to deny' on the other hand, and who accepted their punishment gracefully, were by implication to be treated much more charitably.[104]

By this sort of argument, then, councillors of Weston's persuasion could hope to salvage something from the loan. They could never be entirely at ease with such a policy since it obviously constituted an attempt to levy money without Parliament. However they could take some comfort from the legal precedents and the assurances that it was a one-off; and it is significant that these seem to have allowed Coventry—who had expressed misgivings about the loan's legality elsewhere—to defend it in Star Chamber. What was probably a good deal more alarming to these moderates were the coercive measures taken in support of the levy and the doctrines put forward by the four divines to justify it. Unfortunately there is little direct evidence as to what they thought about these. A certain amount can be read into their reluctance to use some of the powers available to them; but for a more detailed understanding of their concern it is necessary to use statements from others who shared their constitutional attitudes and were also involved with the levy.

The first of these comes from a letter written by Sir Robert Pye, Auditor of the Receipt, to Buckingham in September 1627.[105] Pye drew attention to the disastrous effects of the loan, complaining that

> We are upon the third years anticipation beforehand: land much sold of the principal, credit lost, and at the utmost shift with the commonwealth. Deputy Lieutenants are not active, and Justices of Peace of better sort are willing to be put out of commission, every man doubting and providing

[104] Loc. cit. [105] PRO SP 16/79/2.

for the worst, so that all our fears increase at home . . . I know no way to advise but by some speedy accomodation of this loan, for nothing pleaseth so long as this is on foot, and of late no money or little, hath been paid thereupon.

This letter is an interesting illustration of the desperation felt by a financial official facing up to the necessity of paying for a war which the country could no longer afford; but its real importance was in the remedy Pye propounded for this problem. His main concern was with the ideological tone of the government's measures, with restoring the will of local governors to co-operate by reassuring them that the Council's approach was based on moderate ideals; and he saw the key to doing this as removing the doubts which had been raised by the loan. Perhaps the most significant aspect of all this was that the letter was written by Pye at all, since he was normally regarded as subservient to the wishes of his master, the Duke. This suggests that he felt that there was strong support for his views within the Council, possibly from his other court patrons, Pembroke and Montgomery, or else from Coventry, Coke, and Weston, whose service he particularly commended to Buckingham.[106]

The second statement is more substantial and revealing, coming from Abbot's 'Narrative' of his reasons for refusing to license Sibthorpe's sermon. Abbot was unusual in that his exile from Council had given him the opportunity and incentive to set down some particularly outspoken opinions. However in most other respects—except perhaps his continuing hatred of Buckingham—he can be taken as typical of the moderate, traditionalist councillor. As we have seen he harboured misgivings over the loan, but had kept these to himself and loyally supported the initial council meetings in October 1626.

For Abbot the most disturbing development was not the levy itself, but the measures, and in particular the doctrines, put forward to support it. He described the tendering of oaths as 'somewhat of a new world'; he was worried by what he saw as high-handed use of the prerogative to imprison loan refusers, and on learning that some of these were to be pressed 'began to remember Uriah that was sent in the forefront of the battle'.[107] Above all, however, he was deeply concerned about the doctrine of absolute obedience advanced by Sibthorpe since this threatened to

[106] G. E. Aylmer, *The King's Servants* (1961), pp. 355–6; Sheffield City Library, Elmhirst MSS 1351–62; PRO SP 16/79/2.

[107] Rushworth, i. 439, 454–5.

destroy the rule of law which he saw as the foundation of the political order. In support of such a view he was able to cite no less an authority than James I, and he recalled how the King had passed judgement on a sermon by Bishop Harsnet—on the text 'Give unto Caesar the things that be Caesar's'—by declaring that 'the Bishop only failed in this, when he said *The goods were Caesars*, he did not add *They were his according to the Laws and Customs of the Country wherein they did live*'. It was this principle that Abbot saw as under direct threat from Sibthorpe's sermon. As he said 'the words extend so far and are so absolutely delivered that by this Divinity if the King should send to the City of London, and the inhabitants thereof, commanding them to give unto him all the wealth which they have, they are bound to do it'. The effects of this doctrine were liable to be so cataclysmic that he could only suppose it was part of a plot by Buckingham to overturn the constitution: 'I had some reason out of the grounds of that sermon to fear that the Duke had a purpose to turn upside down the Laws, and the whole fundamental courses and liberties of the subject: and to leave us not under the statutes and customs which our progenitors enjoyed, but to the pleasure of Princes, of whom, as some are gentle and benign, so some other to ingreat themselves, might strain more than the string will bear'.[108]

If Abbot felt such a profound unease, then, it seems likely that other councillors were also concerned. One can perhaps detect echoes of this in the comments of Pye or of those who spoke up in the Star Chamber; however undoubtedly the clearest evidence of a real concern was the vigour and determination with which they fought for a re-summons of Parliament, after November 1627.

III. THE COUNCIL AND THE SUMMONING OF THE 1628 PARLIAMENT

The Council debate which preceded the summoning of the 1628 Parliament was probably the bitterest and most divisive of the entire 1620s. It was conducted between groups of politicians who felt that not only were fundamental political beliefs at stake, but, in some cases, their careers as well; it lasted for nearly three months—from December 1627 to February 1628—and involved the participants in a series of increasingly devious tactical

[108] Ibid. 442–3, 455.

manœuvrings; and it resulted in the unusual occurrence of the King being forced to back down over the main feature of his domestic policy. How did this come about? How did Charles come to lose the initiative which he had preserved so successfully during the period of the loan?

Part of the answer lies in the changed situation which councillors faced at the end of 1627. The success of the loan, the removal of an immediate threat of invasion and, above all, the failure of the Rhé expedition, all served to create a new climate more favourable to the moderates.

Paradoxically one of the main circumstances working in this direction was the widespread payment of the loan. As we have seen, at the time of the benevolence the King had set up discussion in such a way that it was difficult to argue convincingly for a Parliament until the subject had given a demonstration of his basic loyalty; and the only demonstration which would satisfy was co-operation over the loan. In the event the King would try to insist that the subject needed to do still more to earn a re-summons. But the very fact that the levy had been paid gave the moderates valuable ammunition when it came to arguing for the subject's readiness to meet his wishes; and councillors like Coke and Weston took every opportunity to remind him of this.

Another crucial circumstance was the defeat of the Rhé expedition. Whilst this was being prepared and mounted the Council had had little option but to support it; and had it succeeded this might well have been enough to restore the Crown's credit and ensure that the initiative remained with Charles and the Duke. As it was a policy which was clearly their responsibility had failed dismally and for the first time since before the 1626 Parliament this brought into the open disagreements over foreign affairs. By the beginning of 1628 the Venetian could identify three groups within Council, each with distinct opinions. The first, led by Charles, Buckingham, and Conway, favoured the continuation of the war much as before, with the main effort being directed against the French; the second, in which the old Francophile Pembroke was probably playing a leading role, wanted peace with France and a concentration on the war against Spain; whilst a third, in which Weston seems to have figured prominently, favoured the abandonment of the war altogether.[1] In the event their deliberations produced no real

[1] *CSP Ven. 1626–8* p. 584; Gardiner, *History*, vi. 225.

change; but the discussion of alternatives inevitably led to a reconsideration of domestic policy and allowed the moderates scope to suggest new approaches to maintaining the war effort.

Alongside this there were hints of a new direction in religious affairs. Ever since the York House Conference of February 1626 the initiative had been held by a group of Arminians, led by Laud and Neile. With the support of the King and Buckingham, they had controlled appointments to bishoprics, set the tone for sermons preached at Court, and brought about the disgrace of Archbishop Abbot.[2] Once the Duke had departed for Rhé, however, their control began to show signs of weakening. In August 1627 Henry Lesley, one of the royal chaplains, was able to preach a sermon before Charles which contained an uncompromising assertion of the Calvinist view of predestination, and this was immediately published at the behest of Montgomery, brother to the Earl of Pembroke.[3] In October another royal chaplain, John Preston, preached his most celebrated court sermon on the theme of England's failure to fulfil its covenant with the Lord and the judgements which would follow. This was delivered a few days before news arrived of the defeat at Rhé and inevitably many saw Preston's words as prophetic. Through Laud's influence he was silenced before he could preach a sequel, but the first sermon had been widely publicized and came to be seen as a public condemnation of the 'idolatry' of the Court.[4] Then in November Joseph Hall was appointed Bishop of Exeter, the first acknowledged Calvinist to be preferred to a bishopric since before York House. It is uncertain who secured his advancement—probably his court patrons, who included Carlisle, Norwich, Pembroke, and Montgomery—but it is significant that this was opposed by Buckingham. As Hall himself later admitted if the Duke's letters, 'he being then in France, had arrived but some hours sooners, I had been defeated'.[5] Individually none of these

[2] Tyacke, 'Puritanism, Arminianism and counter-revolution', pp. 133–4; Rushworth, i. 434–57.

[3] Henry Lesley, *A Sermon Preached Before His Majestie at Wokin 28 August 1627* (1627), pp. A2-A3, 3–12. (I am grateful to Nicholas Tyacke for this reference.)

[4] Morgan, *Prince Charles's Puritan Chaplain*, pp. 189–90; *The Life of the Renowned Dr. Preston Writ by his pupil Thomas Ball*, ed. E. W. Harcourt (1885), pp. 156–62; BL Eg. MS 784, p. 131.

[5] *The Works of Joseph Hall D.D.*, 12 vols (Oxford, 1837), i, xxiv-v, xxix-x, 361; v. 150, 366; *CSPD 1627–8*, p. 451. Laud later claimed that he had supported Hall's preferment, which was perhaps another indication that the climate had improved for the Calvinists: Laud, iv. 297; PRO 16/525/21, 23. For

episodes was particularly significant; but taken together—and set alongside evidence of some 'liftings' against Laud at Court, inspired by Sir John Coke, and Laud's own fears recorded in his diary, that he would be made scapegoat for the Rhé disaster in a coming Parliament[6]—they indicate an important change in the political climate. It was now seen to be feasible to challenge a particular line of policy, even when it had the backing of King and favourite.

Perhaps the clearest sign of this shift was the re-emergence of Pembroke. The Earl was by nature an extremely cautious politician, reluctant to act unless he felt the situation to be in his favour. Presumably he had been encouraged by the setbacks to Buckingham's reputation, the prospects of an Anglo-French *entente* and the renewed talk of a Parliament; hence the hints of his involvement in foreign policy and religious affairs and a renewed readiness to confront the Duke in public. After the return from Rhé his client Dr Turner was reported to have been spreading derogatory tales about Buckingham's generalship, and Pembroke himself took this even further, reportedly engaging in 'a great contestation about the loss . . . in the King's presence, when the King also acknowledged that Sir Sackville Crow had written to him of a far greater (*sic*) than the Duke would acknowledge'. With the Earl prepared to assert himself once more the moderates had gained a powerful figurehead since he continued to enjoy the King's favour and was probably the one person on Council with sufficient influence to intimidate Buckingham.[7]

The most important circumstance working in favour of a re-summons, however, was the Crown's desperate financial plight. An estimate produced in December 1627 showed that £600,000 was urgently needed for the army and the navy, to counter the threat of invasion and prepare another fleet for Rhé. To meet this expenditure the Crown had raised £120,000 from the City, secured loans from its normal creditors, Burlamachi and Russell, and continued to sell crown lands, disposing of £143,000 worth between Michaelmas 1627 and Easter 1628. But these solutions could not be employed indefinitely. The revenue for the coming year was already anticipated by two-thirds and the Crown was

evidence of Carlisle and Norwich's dislike of Arminianism see: PRO SP 16/116/11.

[6] Heylyn, *Cyprianus Anglicus*, p. 168; Laud, iii. 206.

[7] *C. and T.* i. 280, 291; Rowe, 'Influence of the Earls of Pembroke', 248; C. S. R. Russell, *The Reign of Charles I, 1625–1642* (1974), pp. 24–5.

running out of securities to provide for its creditors.[8] It became essential to find some method of raising money from the subject and therefore from the beginning of December 1627 to the end of February 1628 the Council debated the problem almost daily, often in the presence of the King.[9]

In the course of these debates a wide variety of expedients was discussed, ranging from indirect taxes on consumer products, such as salt or beer, to direct taxes on those who held government offices or posts in the professions.[10] The problem with most of these proposals, however, was finding a way to enforce them. Given the unpopularity of their previous policies it seemed unlikely that any new project could be made to work without the use of extreme coercion. This was illustrated in a debate over collecting a *6d.* excise on beer during which the Council concluded that 'Perswasions . . . would not gaine it, and in Judiciall Courts it not hold against the subjecte, that would stand upon the right of his owne propertie and against the fundamentall constitutions of the Kingdome. The last resorte was to a Proclamacon, for in Starre Chamber it might be punisheable, and thereupon it rested'.[11] Once councillors found themselves being backed into adopting such extreme courses, this inevitably raised the issue of whether it would not be better to re-summon Parliament.

For some this was clearly the preferred solution. A memorandum drawn up by Sir John Coke—which envisaged raising money through a Bond of Association to which individuals would subscribe—suggested that it was essential for the King to 'lay aside al jealosies and occasions of distraction' by issuing a declaration of his 'resolution to cale a Parliament this sommer'.[12] Much the same concern was also apparent in an anonymous council speech from this period, in which the author considerd how Charles's revenues might be increased to a level comparable to that of the Kings of France:

> I was ledd to thinke that this might be donne by some generall easie course to make it amount to a good somme to the King: and yett with noe

[8] BL Harg. MS 321, fo. 141; Gardiner, *History*, vi. 220; Ashton, *Crown and Money Market*, pp. 40, 132–5.

[9] *CSP Ven. 1626–8*, pp. 530, 558–9, 575; BL Harl. MS 7010, fo. 67v; *APC 1627–8, passim*.

[10] PRO SP 16/126/47.

[11] BL Harg. MS 321, fos. 139–40.

[12] PRO SP 16/88/78. This is probably the proposal referred to by the Venetian ambassador which would date it at sometime in December, 1627: *CSP Ven. 1626–8*, p. 530.

great prejudice to the people then to increase and improve their industrie. I am still of the same mynd and affection, especiallie in regard of the urgent and pressing necessities of this tyme. But I nowe fynd by what hath ben discussed at this Board that it is dangerous to putt anie of these thinges in practice without eyther the consent of a Parliament or the hope of gayning the conformitie and submission of the people thereunto.[13]

With its emphasis on balancing the interests of the Crown and the subject this was a classic statement of the moderates' case, and there can be little doubt that, during the weeks of the council debate, this sort of argument was advanced on several occasions.

As with other council debates the details of precisely what took place remain obscure. However enough evidence has survived to show who were the principal participants on either side and what arguments they employed. As before at the head of the anti-Parliament group stood the King and Buckingham, supported by Dorset, Laud, Conway, Savile, and probably others. The King made his position clear at the beginning of the debate on financial expedients by declaring that 'to call a Parliament the occasion will not let me tarry soe longe'; and Dorset and Laud immediately spoke up to pledge their support for whatever alternative the King might favour.[14] Conway argued for extra-parliamentary supply in a lengthy memorandum on foreign policy; and Buckingham again felt confident enough of the King's opposition to Parliament to engage in the sort of posturing noted in October 1926. Reports were spread that 'the Duke himself proposed in Council to assemble Parliament as the ordinary and most expeditious way, but the King rejected it entirely'; also of the unlikely scenario of 'the Duke . . . twice upon his knees before the King for that end, saying that if himself were found worthy of death let them not spare him'. However, informed observers were not taken in. The Venetian again described these efforts as 'a collusion between the King and the Duke'; and Ralph Starkey, a London antiquarian and newsletter writer, observed gleefully that the whole charade eventually backfired:

My Lord Duke hath importuned the Kinge for this Parliament both publiquely and privately, ever since his returne. Tis thought his importunitye was the greater in regard he was persuaded the Kinge would never yield unto it. Yett in his absence, uppon others motion, the Kinge both

[13] PRO 16/126/44. The editor of *State Papers Domestic* suggests that the author was Sir Thomas Edmonds, but there is no evidence for this beyond the speaker's obvious familiarity with French affairs.

[14] BL Harg. MS 321, fo. 140.

yielded and signed the warrant and sent it awaye without acquainteing the Duke therewith. That when it came to the Duke's knowledge he would not believe it.[15]

There were two principal strands running through the case against a summons. The first of these was the familiar argument—based on precedent and used to justify the loan—that extraordinary necessity entitled the King to levy extra-parliamentary taxation, provided that he presented his request in the proper manner. The second was less common, and seems to have owed a good deal both to the King's experience of being refused taxation by his subjects and the doctrines of obedience promoted by the royalist divines. This was the view that, in order to secure suitable obedience from the subject, it was necessary to make him accept yet another unparliamentary levy, lest an immediate re-summons be seen as countenancing the sort of defiance met with over the loan.

This idea was expressed on several occasions by the King: for example when he declared in Council that rather than re-summon Parliament 'he would first of all find money so that the present necessities may not render more audacious those who opposed him before'. It was also subscribed to by Buckingham who argued that a new Privy Seal Loan should go ahead 'lest refractories thereby might be encurraged'. And it clearly influenced the terms in which the Crown presented a request for Ship Money, in letters sent out in February 1628.[16] As we have seen these insisted that money be paid before a Parliament could meet as a specific pledge of the subject's loyalty.[17] Some of the notions which underpinned this requirement were evident in a series of arguments drawn up by Laud, opposing the summons of Parliament.[18]

[15] PRO SP 16/91/20; *CSP Ven. 1626–8*, pp. 558–9; *C. and T.* i. 305; PRO C.115/N4, 2 Feb. 1627/8. Lockyer has argued on the basis of Sir John Coke's statement in the 1628 Parliament—that 'All of us at the Council can tell he was the first mover and persuader of this assembly of Parliament to the King'—that Buckingham sincerely wished for a summons. But this should surely be read as the attempt of a council moderate, and loyal client, to make the most of the Duke's ambiguous behaviour: Lockyer, *Buckingham*, p. 425; Rushworth, i. 472.

[16] *CSP Ven. 1626–8*, p. 559; *Holles*, ii. 375–6; Swales 'The Ship Money Levy of 1628', 174–6.

[17] See above, p. 49.

[18] PRO SP 16/94/88. At his trial in 1644 Laud acknowledged having written this document, but claimed rather obscurely, 'I was not the author of these fears and hopes, but an amanuensis to higher powers': Laud, iv. 357. It will be evident that my reading of this important document differs from that of

Like the royalist divines he saw royal authority as something conferred almost exclusively from above, owing little to the consent of the subject. This came out most clearly in his statement on the authority by which taxes were to be levied: 'subsidyes are due by the laws of God, nature and nations, and Parliament have but their deliberations and consents for the manner of givinge'. Parliament thus had little say in the granting of taxes, and there was no sense in which a parliamentary subsidy was seen as a gift or display of affection on the part of the subject. Laud took a similar view of Parliament's relationship to the church: 'That House, one or both, can by [*sic*] no competent judge in any poynt of Doctrine . . . The King suffers by this as much or more then the Church, for in the statute of submission of the clergy the King and convocacon ar judge of all Ecclesiasticall causes. And why should Parliament take this from ether?'

Given such a concept of royal authority it was hardly surprising that he should see every concession made to Parliament as a reduction of the Crown's power and resources. In particular he explained the way in which offers of subsidies had to be traded for grants which were often of greater monetary value: 'theise [*sic*] is first to sell subsidyes and not to give them. (The last Parliament of King James they gave 3 subsidyes and had that from the King that was worth 6 if not 10, to be bought and sold).' This was reinforced with reminders that Parliament was unlikely to provide money quickly or give more than three subsidies which was not nearly enough; and that should they fail, and the meeting 'breake againe in discontente', this would make alternative means of supply less accessible. These were telling points which touched on some of the main practical problems facing the Crown; however it is important to note that they were not the main theme of Laud's argument. They were included largely in order to illustrate what he evidently saw as a more important consideration, the disruptive influence of 'factious spirits'.

The memorandum was couched in the form of a list of 'feares' which Laud associated with the prospect of a Parliament. The first three of these were probably those uppermost in his own mind: '1. That they will begin where they left. 2. At least they will looke to sacrifice somebody. 3. The men restreined about the loane will studdy revenge, at least unquiet?' However, they were clearly linked to a perception of a wider threat. Laud discussed the

Conrad Russell: nevertheless I am extremely grateful to him for suggestions on this: Russell, *Parliaments and English Politics*, p. 338.

likelihood that 'they will fall uppon church busines' and related the Church's preservation to the more secular concerns being voiced at the time of the loan: 'The Church is to weake already. If it had more power the Kinge might have more both obedience and service.' He also recalled the damage which concessions in Parliament inflicted on the basic means of exercising royal authority: 'by theis Bills of Grace the flowers of the Crowne are parted with and the prerogative soe decreased as I dare not speake of the consequence'. And finally, in an observation calculated to trigger one of Charles's most sensitive reflexes, he returned to the need to compel obedience: 'factious spirits will take hart if they see the Kinge yeeld to them without any submission of theirs, as some were seene to laugh outright in the last Parliament when they gott their ends upon the Kinge'. In several important respects, then, Laud's memorandum reflected the increasingly familiar fears of a 'popular'/'puritan' conspiracy against the Crown; and these led him to the predictable conclusion that the best policy was to avoid a summons altogether. MPs should 'sitt less time that they may not understand one another too well'; and the King should adhere to the principle that 'where publique necessities presse, extraordinarie wayes are to be admitted'.

Laud's view of the situation was, of course, an extreme one; and perhaps only the King and Neile, amongst the other members of the Council, would have subscribed to it wholeheartedly. Nevertheless some aspects of it had clearly struck home and helped to delay the re-summons. The fear of disruption by the loan refusers was recognized as a major obstacle and caused several of the moderates to involve themselves in attempts to exclude these at the county elections.[19] Similarly worries of a renewed attack on the Duke prompted assurances that councillors would not countenance such action.[20] All this was an indication of the extent to which the loan had shifted the climate of opinion and made 'new counsels' much more acceptable. It was also a measure of the problems still faced by the moderates.

The supporters of a return to traditional policies were a much less clearly defined group than their opponents and it is more difficult to pick up their individual contributions. It seems likely that Pembroke played a more prominent role than previously; and he was probably backed most vociferously by the previous advocates of moderation: Coventry, Manchester, Coke, and

[19] See below, pp. 311–13.

[20] *CSP Ven. 1626–8*, p. 584.

Weston. The arguments they used followed broadly familiar themes, with the main points being mentioned by Laud whilst preparing his statement:

> 1. That the Kinge and the people maye peece againe and the Kingdome not bee indangered by this disunion.
> 2. That upon sight of their former errour they will leave personall prosecutions and give.
> 3. That perhapps they may give 3 subsedyes for the first yeare and though they will not doe all that is necessarye, yett it will be a good help.
> 4. That the sight of this *Union* at home will doe much good to the affaires abroad. That the very conveninge them will take of the former humour of some men, that thinke nothing can be well without it.[21]

For a clearer indication of the attitudes and assumptions which lay behind these arguments it is necessary to look at another memorandum, drawn up by Sir Robert Cotton in January 1628 and entitled 'The Danger Wherein the Kingdom Standeth and the Remedy thereof'.[22]

This was addressed to the Council and was almost certainly—as Rushworth suggested—drawn up at the request of some of its members, since they had employed Cotton in the past to advise on historical precedent.[23] It took the form of a defence of the moderate ideal of co-operation between King and subject which the author saw as coming under threat as a result of the loan. He described the levy as 'unknown and untrodden ways', and emphasized the fears raised in peoples' minds by

> the late pressures they supposed to have been done upon the publicke liberty and freedom of the subject, in commoning their goods without assent by Parliament, imprisoning and confining their persons without special cause declared, and that made good against them by the judges lately, and pretending a writ to command their attendances in foreign war: all which they are like to enforce as repugnant to any positive laws, institutions and customary immunities of this commonwealth.

In these circumstances Cotton considered it necessary to outline the fundamental importance of achieving a balance between the rights of the subject and the rights of the Crown, and to restate the notions and assumptions on which this idea of balance rested. For

21 PRO SP 16/94/88.

22 Rushworth, i. 467–72. A manuscript copy of this exists dated 27 Jan. 1627–8: BL Lansd. MS, fos. 258–69.

23 *C. and T.* i. 145–7; BL Cotton MS, Julius III, fo. 192^{r}.

this he looked to the lessons of history, and described how, in the years following the Armada, Queen Elizabeth had taken care to moderate the demands on her subjects, following a maxim attributed to Lord Burghley, 'Win hearts and you have their hands and purses'. He also urged the need to encourage the 'better sort' to feel that they had a stake in the nation, something which could best be done through a meeting of Parliament. Measures involving coercion and the excessive use of the prerogative could only discourage this, and lead to discontents which Cotton described as 'a more fatal enemie than any foreign forces'. Finally he recalled some conventional wisdom for the benefit of the King: 'that by Parliament, resteth principally on the royal person who may with ease and safety mould them to his fit designs by a gracious yielding to their just desires and petitions'.

There was, of course, nothing unusual in such views. What is interesting is the fact they then were presented at all, that some councillors—in the context of a major policy debate—felt that it was necessary to restate the principles which had normally been taken as read by the advisers of Elizabeth and James. Once again this indicated the extent to which the climate had altered and the middle ground had shifted. And this meant that in spite of their advantages, the moderates still had a good deal to do in convincing the King.

Charles appears to have recognized, from the start, that he would be under considerable pressure to re-summon Parliament. Therefore, at an early stage, he obtained from councillors what looks very like a commitment to follow whatever line he laid down. They were required to acknowledge that 'the question was of obeying the King, not of counselling . . .'. He also attended council meetings with what was, for him, a quite remarkable frequency, and on these occasions took the chair, thus enabling him to direct debate away from a re-summons.[24] This gave an initial advantage to the opponents of Parliament; however, as has been suggested, the moderates found ways of introducing the subject into discussion of financial measures, and on 26 December they seemed to have made some headway by securing, in the King's presence, a decision to release the loan refusers. Another stage was reached in mid-January when a group of councillors, probably led by Pembroke, undertook to prevent any proceedings against Buckingham. And Laud's list of points made in favour of a

[24] BL Harg. MS 321, fo. 139; BL Harl. MS 7010, fo. 69^{v}.

summons, along with Cotton's advice, showed that the moderates' views were being openly aired. Finally on 29 January, after an all night debate conducted in great secrecy and with the Duke absent, it was decided to send out the writs, for 17 March.[25]

This appeared to signal victory for the pro-Parliament lobby. However their success was limited by various considerations which made it doubtful whether the two houses would actually meet. First of all the Council had already decided—in response to a letter from the King—to levy a Privy Seal Loan worth £200,000 in which the heaviest demands would fall on former loan refusers.[26] Secondly—by 6 February—it had also agreed to send out the letters for the Ship Money levy, which postponed the meeting of Parliament until 28 April and specifically stated that no assembly was to be permitted until the money had been paid.[27] Quite how a measure like this was pushed through a Council containing a pro-parliamentary majority is something of a puzzle; but it seems likely that Charles and Buckingham took advantage of an invasion threat from both France and Spain to persuade their colleagues that emergency measures could not wait on the meeting.

The passage of these measures threw the onus back on the supporters of the assembly, and in the following two weeks the debate over a summons became more intense than ever. Reports of clashes between the Duke and other councillors filtered through to the newsletter writers, and in a new set of Council regulations, issued on 20 February, members had to be warned of the need to 'speake with respect one to the other, and no offence to be taken for any unfitting advice delivered'.[28] In their efforts to get the Ship Money levy revoked the moderates were clearly helped by the Mantuan crisis and the passing of the invasion scare which, as Dr Swales has stressed, removed the immediate need for supply.[29] However this alone was not enough to ensure their success. They still had to persuade the King to call in the Privy Seals and restore the Parliament to its original date; and in order to do this some councillors seemed prepared to appeal for support and invite pressure from outside the Council, even to the extent of

[25] *Wentworth Papers*, pp. 282–3; *CSP Ven. 1626–8*, pp. 588–9; Laud, iii. 207.

[26] *C. and T.* i. 321; *Holles*, ii. 375–6; PRO SP 16/540/35.

[27] Swales, 'The Ship Money levy of 1628', 167, 174–6.

[28] *Holles*, ii. 375–6; PRO SP 16/93/83.

[29] Swales, 'The Ship Money levy of 1628', 172–4.

encouraging resistance to the two levies. This obviously had to be done discreetly and proof that it happened is hard to come by. However a good deal of circumstantial evidence does point in this direction.

The first stage was to inform the public that a summons of Parliament was in the balance. This was done through circulating manuscript copies of Cotton's 'Advice', which sold for 2*s*. apiece, and probably also through deliberate 'leaks' to newsletter writers and ambassadors.[30] The second stage was to encourage non-payment of Ship Money and Privy Seals, and to ensure that these were met with requests for a summons of Parliament. It is here that one can perhaps see an element of collusion. The two leading refusers of the Privy Seal loan, the Earl of Bedford and the Earl of Devonshire, were close allies and well-connected at Court, with Devonshire a particular intimate of the Earl of Pembroke.[31] This was suspicious particularly as those counties which were to the fore in resisting Ship Money, Devon and Wiltshire, were also the counties where Bedford and Pembroke acted as Lords Lieutenant. In both cases the local bench drew up a list of reasons for refusing the levy which was then widely circulated. This would surely have been unlikely had they not expected a sympathetic hearing from the Council.[32] There were also hints of official prompting elsewhere. In Warwickshire the Earl of Northampton, who was Lord Warden of the Marches, allowed the local gentry to remind him of his previous undertaking 'that they should be paid the last loan at the next Parliament, and would he now draw them to a new one before the Parliament?' And in Berkshire the Earl of Banbury, newly appointed to the Council, 'having promised the county there that in case they would, as they did, come roundly off with the late five subsidies, he would never move them to anything unparliamentary again, . . . nobly performed his promise

[30] K. Sharpe, *Sir Robert Cotton 1586–1631* (Oxford, 1979), p. 183; *CSP Ven. 1626–8*, pp. 584, 588, 605; *CSP Ven. 1628–9*, p. 10. Council 'leaks' in this period are discussed more fully in Cust, 'News and Politics', 71–3.

[31] *Holles*, ii. 375–6; *CD 1628*, iii. 10 n; Russell 'Parliament and the King's finances', pp. 110–13; Russell, *Parliaments and English Politics*, pp. 280, 289 n.

[32] Sainty, *Lieutenants of the Counties*, pp. 18, 36–7; *Cabala*, p. 258; Longleat House, Thynne Papers, vol. 8, fo. 133. (I am grateful to Alison Wall for this reference.) There are copies of the Devon reply in BL Add. MS 30, 926, fos. 8–9, Sloane MS 1775, fo. 72. (I am grateful to Ian Palfrey for this reference), and Grays Inn MS No. 31, pp. 115–17 (I am grateful to Caroline Barron for this reference); and of Wiltshire's in HMC *Various*, iv. 172.

in this, refusing and sending back the letter directed to him, alleging his promise as reason thereof'.[33]

All this provided valuable ammunition for the moderates in enabling them to argue that any alternative to Parliament was not only undesirable, but also impracticable. This probably helped to tip the scales in the decisive debate on 20 February, described by the Earl of Clare:

> Those that would have contnued the distance between the King and the people have adjourned the Parlement to the 28th April, counselling in the meantime, the sending forth of privy seales . . . but my Lords of Bedford and Devonshire making answer that they would not lend, consultation was taken whether the Privy Seales and Commissions should proceede or no: and, after much dispute, my Lord of Buckingham and his Controwler argewing (lest refractories thereby might be encouraged) a necessity to leave the Privy Seales uppon all those that refused, at the last vicit pars melior, which coveted to smoothe the way that Parlement might boggle at nothing.[34]

Even this, however, was not a complete victory. The King required the Council to go on considering 'alternatives to parliamentary supply, which brought forth the notorious excise commission, condemned in the 1628 Parliament; and the Venetian recorded an undertaking by the moderates that 'unless the Commons grant the money immediately and without further debate, the King will be justified in exercising his prerogative, burdening them with taxes and compelling them'.[35]

News of the final decision to hold a Parliament as originally intended was greeted with widespread relief, which mirrored the despair at the dissolution of 1626. Clare's comment that 'at the last vicit pars melior' was echoed, for example, by Rowland Woodward, a Signet Office Clerk, who gratefully acknowledged

[33] *C. and T.* i. 325; *APC 1627–8*; pp. 286, 330. Swales has taken some pains to demonstrate that this report was mistaken, arguing that Banbury had previously signed the letter for the ship money levy, and that anyway there was not time for popular protest to have made itself felt. Against this it can be pointed out firstly that Banbury was required by council regulations to sign the letter once a majority decision had been reached, regardless of his personal view; and secondly that the Devon and Wiltshire letters show there was time for protests to be expressed. Mead is usually a reliable reporter of council events and there seems no reason to doubt him in this instance: Swales, 'The Ship Money levy of 1628', 171–2.

[34] *Holles*, ii. 375–6. Sir John Savile had been made Controller of the Household after suit to Buckingham: PRO SP 16/59/35.

[35] *CD 1628*, iv. 241–2; PRO SP, 16/94/67; *CSP Ven. 1628–9*, p. 10.

that 'The Parliament holds according to the first report, and the fearfull prœludium of Privy Seals and letters not to be represented upon the stage, so that there is more hope of better harmony in the Lower House'. The sense of deliverance felt by the moderates in the Council was expressed in Lord Keeper Coventry's opening address to the two houses 'Consider . . . the means which his Majesty useth to attain these purposes. It is by Parliament, a way most pleasing to the English which brings forth many pardons, and causes good Kings to refrain their prerogatives, and this way best suits his Majesty's own disposition'.[36] At last it must have seemed as if the doubts and differences of the previous eighteen months could be buried, and the traditional balance between King and subject restored. But why had the search for this taken so long? If the wish for unity was so widespread why had it not produced results sooner?

The most recent interpretation of these events—provided by Professor Russell—has stressed the impact of financial difficulties created by the Parliament's refusal to provide subsidies and the overwhelming pressure of necessity whilst the country faced two foreign enemies.[37] As we have seen there is a good deal to support this reading. The sense of despair felt by Conway in June 1626, the Council's readiness to unite behind the King when invasion threatened and the use of arguments drawn from necessity to justify both the benevolence and the loan all suggest that the situation the Council faced was a crucial factor in determining policy. But was it the only one? There was evidently a powerful lobby within Council which felt that in spite of all the problems—with the past evidence of Parliament's unreliability and the likelihood that they would not give enough to cover the King's needs—it was still important to persevere with efforts at co-operation. More than anything they seem to have feared a breakdown of the 'union at home' which could follow from the King failing to consult his subjects. They therefore took every opportunity to push for a re-summons, sending a deputation to talk with Charles when dissolution threatened in June 1626, attempting to raise the issue at the time when the loan was launched and finally persuading the King of their case in February 1628. This pressure from within the inner circles of government indicates that the policy eventually adopted was far from being just the inevitable outcome of a particular set of circumstances. Instead,

[36] PRO SP 16/93/87; *CD 1628*, ii. 9–10.

[37] Russell, *Parliaments and English Politics*, pp. 321, 330–1, 338–40.

its inception can ultimately be traced back to the tactical and political battles fought around the council table.

The balance of advantage in these was, of course, to some extent determined by circumstance. The original decision to levy the loan was taken when something had to be done quickly and it seemed too soon to rely on the subject's goodwill, particularly after the failure of the benevolence. Similarly the decision to re-summon Parliament in 1628 was greatly helped by the catastrophic failure of the policy towards France. However it was also the result of political factors. One of these was the balance of influence at Court. The Duke's success in surviving the 1626 Parliament gave him an aura of impregnability which seems to have ensured a dedicated following and persuaded his enemies to lie low. This was only diminished after the defeat at Rhé, which encouraged individuals like Pembroke to come out and challenge him again openly. In the meantime, however, Buckingham had succeeded in promoting a group of particularly devoted clients to positions of trust, both at Court and in Council, and they provided a powerful lobby in favour of alternatives to Parliament. Another was the way in which certain spokesmen—most notably the royalist divines—interpreted the events of the period. Their constant emphasis on the dangers posed by 'popularity' and the need for obedience helped to create a climate in which 'new counsels' appeared much more acceptable. But most significant of all was the attitude of the King himself. It was Charles's insistence, voiced time and time again, that under no circumstances would he allow a Parliament, which did more than anything to carry along the reluctant moderates. Only when he was finally dissuaded from this, by a clear majority of councillors, was a re-summons possible.

The precise reasons for Charles's determination to carry on without Parliament are not easy to discern. Part of it undoubtedly had to do with the despair he felt at its treatment of him in the past. As he protested it was Parliament that had got him into a war in the first place and therefore Parliament that should pay for it. If it was not prepared to do so what alternative had he but to look elsewhere? Again, however, this was not the whole story. The comments picked up by the Venetian ambassador and his own oft-stated determination to protect and uphold his personal honour suggest that he was not just concerned with Parliament's failure to grant supply, but was also coming to see it as spearheading a 'popular' assault on the very foundation of monarchy. The attack on Buckingham in 1626 and the past history of challenges to the prerogative seem to have convinced Charles that a disloyal and subversive faction was gaining the upper hand. In these circumstances the very idea of a Parliament was coming to appear unpalatable. Ultimately he was still prepared to summon it because tradition and the weight of opinion within the Council favoured such a course of action. But he was also coming to insist that it provide guarantees of loyalty and good behaviour which it was unrealistic to expect it to fulfil and which made its future continuance less and less likely.

The fears which attached to Parliament also seem to have influenced Charles's view of his own subjects. The King, in this period, appears to have been in the grip of something approaching paranoia whenever he contemplated the question of whether his people were loyal and obedient. This emerges from the way in which he tried to treat the whole issue of prerogative taxation in terms of a test of allegiance and a vote of confidence.[38] His letters over the loan and Ship Money, his use of oaths and his assumption that there would be resistance, his insistence on publishing the sermons by Sibthorpe and Manwaring, and above all the vindictiveness with which he pursued those who resisted the loan—as if they had affronted him personally—all indicated a lack of trust reminiscent of Richard II in his latter days.[39] This could not but be extremely damaging when so much depended on goodwill and a readiness to co-operate.

The consequences are not hard to discern. Charles's curtness and inflexibility when addressing his Council—typical of which was his insistence that it was a question of 'obeying . . . not of counselling'—made him a difficult man to advise, particularly if the advice was unwelcome. The treatment he meted out to an individual like Abbot, who—in being forced to read Sibthorpe's sermon and then being told by his avowed enemy, Laud, that his criticisms were unacceptable—faced something approaching a ritual humiliation, was hardly calculated to encourage others to serve him. And his determination to offer a precise justification for his actions—to hammer out the point that 'noe ordinary rules can prescribe a law to necessitye'—made the reassurances of moderate councillors far more difficult to sustain. Most damaging

[38] A similar insistence on Charles's part was evident during the discussions over the Petition of Right: Guy, 'Origins of the Petition of Right', 306–7. (I am grateful to John Guy for drawing my attention to this tendency.)

[39] C. Barron, 'The tyranny of Richard II', *BIHR* xli. 102 (1968), 1–18.

of all, however, was his absolute refusal to lay the blame for disruptive policies on 'evil counsellors'. This was crucial to sustaining the subjects' faith in the basic soundness of their monarch and both Elizabeth and James had managed it with considerable adeptness. Charles, however, stubbornly refused to play the game. He seems to have felt that the potency of the royal word was such that he had only to pronounce for that to be the end of the matter. This was revealed most strikingly in the 'collusive artifice' which he engaged in to rescue the Duke's popular credit. Instead of allowing Buckingham to shoulder the blame for not summoning Parliament, Charles deliberately contrived that everyone should know that it was he who principally opposed it and who stood in its way. Hardly anything could have been more calculated to alarm the sensibilities of ordinary Englishmen and upset the delicate balance of faith and trust on which the constitution rested.

In these circumstances—with the King's authority being seen in unusually high profile and repeated stress on the need for loyalty and obedience—it was hardly surprising that 'new counsels' came to flourish. The King's attitude helped to promote a climate of opinion which carried along a former advocate of tradition, such as Conway, and saw the beginnings of a displacement of the pro-Protestant/pro-Parliamentary ideals which hitherto had been the keynote in policy-making.[40] It was no accident that at this time Catholic peers and high-church clerics were starting to assume a much more prominent role in the life of the Court and the circles around the King. The 'new counsels' can be seen in a very real sense as the secular counterpart of the rise of Arminianism.[41] Both were in some degree responses to the perception of a 'popular'/

[40] It is evident from D. H. Willson's description of earlier debates within the Privy Council that this was the first time during the early seventeenth century that the principle of ruling in partnership with Parliament had been seriously questioned. In previous discussions councillors had raised objections to particular Parliaments, but these had usually been based on the practical consideration of whether or not Parliament could deliver on supply. The crucial new element between 1626 and 1628 was the doubt over the subject's fundamental loyalty: Willson, *Privy Councillors in the House of Commons*, Ch. 2.

[41] Mendle, *Dangerous Positions*, pp. 63–113; Lake and Fincham, 'The ecclesiastical policy of James I', 169–207; Russell, *Parliaments and English Politics*, pp. 404–5. This is not to argue for an inevitable link between Arminian theology and absolutist ideas. As Dr Sommerville and Dr Tyacke have demonstrated such ideas were also characteristic of some Calvinist authors: Sommerville, *Politics and Ideology*, pp. 9–50; Tyacke 'Puritanism Arminianism and counter-revolution', p. 140.

'puritan' threat. And both constituted challenges to the broad based agreement which had linked together the Privy Council and the ruling classes since the time of Elizabeth. Just as Arminianism undermined the doctrinal consensus, so the loan and the measures accompanying it struck at a cental belief in the rule of law and the principal of seeking the subject's consent; and just as Charles's backing for the new divinity raised disquieting and subversive doubts in the mind of an individual like John Pym, so his well publicized opposition to the summons of Parliament was to draw others of his subjects into contemplating overt challenges to royal authority.[42]

[42] Russell, 'John Pym', pp. 160–4.

2

The Collection of the Loan: A Study in Relations Between Central and Local Government

I. INTRODUCTION

BETWEEN the Parliaments of 1626 and 1628 the Council tried to finance England's war effort by a variety of expedients, ranging from the traditional stopgaps of selling crown lands and prize goods to more ambitious attempts at reforming the royal revenues and extending the scope of impositions. However, as we have seen, its main emphasis throughout was on raising supply by direct taxation, and in particular on the benevolence and the forced loan. These two schemes absorbed much of the time and energy of the Council, apart from a brief period in the early summer of 1627 when it was overwhelmed with the preparations for the Rhé expedition. They also received first priority as far as the King was concerned and prompted him to intervene with uncharacteristic directness in the running of domestic affairs. However, in spite of this, the fate of the two schemes was markedly different.

The benevolence was a very obvious failure, even by the not very exacting standard of seventeenth century levies. The total amount paid into the Exchequer was £948. 16*s*. 4*d*. from just four counties;[1] and although several of the remainder were forestalled from making their contribution by a royal proclamation, in most cases the sums they were prepared to give were minimal. The evidence surviving in the State Papers suggests that only Cumberland and Rutland came anywhere near offering the four subsidies requested by the King, and far more typical of the country as a whole was the £111 raised in Derbyshire or the £70 in Nottinghamshire.[2]

[1] PRO E.401/2442, unpaginated (but see under 'Contribuco versus tutela et defencon huius Regni'). The four counties were Middlesex, Surrey, Warwickshire, and Carmarthen.

[2] HMC, *Cowper*, i. 280; PRO SP 16/35/10, 90; 36 /34.

In contrast the forced loan was strikingly successful. Exchequer accounts show that £184,820. 0*s.* 10*d.* was finally paid into the Receipt, whilst a further £82,244. 15*s.* 1d. was estimated to have been paid in the shires and spent on billeting, coat and conduct, and purveyance. On the most optimistic calculation, then, it is possible that it yielded as much as £267,064. 15*s.* 11*d.*, which compared very favourably with the £275,000 raised on the five parliamentary subsidies of 1628.[3]

In the light of recent interpretations of the early seventeenth century, the failure of the benevolence is readily understandable. It has become something of a commonplace that much of the politics of this period can be read in terms of a continual friction and conflict between the centre and localities. The centre was usually making demands and imposing burdens which the localities were doing their best to withstand and resist. In these circumstances the interests of the Privy Council and their agents in the counties are seen to have diverged markedly. Councillors were forever trying to squeeze more out of local inhabitants, whilst local governors—spurred on by a mixture of self-interest and the expectations of their neighbours—attempted to obstruct the process, particularly over taxation. This situation has been highlighted in the work of a number of local historians and has recently been described by Russell as the crucial weakness of the governmental system, bringing it towards the point of breakdown between 1626 and 1628[4]

Given this sort of analysis the benevolence can be seen as yet another victim of the obstructiveness and backsliding which regularly undermined the Council's efforts. However such an explanation makes it difficult to understand why, a few months later and in response to a levy which in many respects was perceived as similar, taxpayers were agreeable to

[3] PRO E.401 / 2322–5 (these volumes are unpaginated, but see the weekly totals given under the heading 'Mutuum', 'Mutuum de magnatibus', 'Collectoribus mutuum a communalitat'); SP 16/85/76, 77; Ashton, *Crown and Money Market*, pp. 29, 41. The figures for billeting, coat and conduct, and purveyance are a maximum, based on the assumption—made in the Exchequer summary account—that all this money was received in the counties where it was employed. This seems unlikely, but I have been unable to find accounts which would make it possible to estimate what the shortfall might have been.

[4] A. M. Everitt, *The Local Community and The Great Rebellion* (Historical Association, 1969), pp. 5–10; Morrill, *Revolt of the Provinces*, pp. 13–14, 22–9; Fletcher, *A County Community*, pp. 202–15; Russell, 'Perspectives in parliamentary history', 25–7; Russell, *Parliaments and English Politics*, pp. 64–70, 323–6.

contributing and local governors were persuaded to co-operate.

The explanation generally given has been that this was a result of remorseless pressure and coercion. Gardiner argued that it was the risk of pressing and imprisonment which caused unwilling subsidymen to pay; Barnes, examining the situation in Somerset, stressed the importance of the Council's continual prodding of local commissioners; and more recently Professor Holmes has argued that 'the general success enjoyed by the loan was because it was forced, because the government dedicated itself . . . to crushing opposition'.[5] As we shall see there is plenty of evidence to support such verdicts and it cannot seriously be doubted that enforcement was an important reason for the high yield of the loan. However certain problems still remain which suggest that this was perhaps not the only, or even the main reason.

One still has to explain, for example, how the Council overcame its chronic inefficiency and inconsistency, limitations which—as Professor Hirst has demonstrated—habitually crippled its attempts at enforcement during the 1620s. Was it simply that it applied itself more diligently than usual; or were there other inducements available to persuade local inhabitants to co-operate? One also has to account for the surprisingly positive response of some local governors. As we shall see quite a substantial number of them were prepared to expend their energies and expose their local credit to an extent that went far beyond what one could have expected in response to the simple threat of punishment—which in any case was extremely hard to carry out where more than a few were involved.[6] This again would seem to indicate an extra dimension to the relationship with central government. Hence it will be argued that co-operation over the loan and the raising of money was the result of something much more complex than undiluted enforcement. It will be attributed to what Dr Lake has described, in a similar context, as a 'unitary process of political management and the balance of interest groups'.[7] The main theme of this chapter, then, will be an examination of the collection of the loan as a case study in this sort of process. First of all, however, it is necessary to look at the benevolence.

[5] Gardiner, *History*, vi. 154–5; Barnes, *Somerset*, pp. 166–7; C. Holmes, 'The County Community in Stuart Historiography', *JBS* xix (1980), 67. See also the discussion by Hirst on which Holmes bases his conclusion: Hirst, 'Privy Council and enforcement', 52, 59.

[6] Hirst, 'Privy Council and enforcement', 45–66.

[7] Lake, 'Ship money in Cheshire', 70.

II. THE BENEVOLENCE

The main burden of collecting the benevolence of 1626, as with previous schemes, fell on the local governors. In the initial letters from the King and Council on 7 July they were instructed to meet the local subsidymen and, after persuading them of the need to contribute, collect in the money.[1] However this was not a service they could perform single-handed. In the absence of statutory backing they had no powers to punish resisters and needed the support of the Council. They also needed to be able to offer the subsidymen something more than a bald statement of the King's necessities, and for this were again dependent on the Council. The benevolence was therefore in several senses an exercise in co-operation between central and local governors, and the causes of its failure can be ascribed as much to the Council as to the local JPs.

In the first place it failed to provide any adequate incentive to pay the money. Most national levies in the early seventeenth century contained some of the elements of a bargain to make them more palatable. Privy Seal loans were paid on the understanding that they were personal gifts to the monarch which would be duly acknowledged and ultimately repaid; subsidies were usually presented as an exchange of gifts between king and subject; and even the ship money levy in the 1630s could offer local interest groups the opportunity to win important rating and jurisdictional disputes.[2] The benefits not only provided a direct encouragement to the taxpayer, but also eased the position of the local governor, enabling him to present himself as the means by which his neighbours had secured various concessions and advantages. With the benevolence however all such benefits were absent. The 1626 Parliament had been dissolved with its main task of removing the Duke uncompleted; and because the benevolence did not take the form of a fixed levy the possibility of ratings disputes or concessions did not arise. The only positive inducement to pay was an emergency which was being invoked for the third year in succession and which most Englishmen had ceased to believe in.[3]

[1] PRO SP 16/31/30, 31.

[2] Lake, 'Ship money in Cheshire', 51–2.

[3] *CSPD* 1623–5, pp. 205–7; Russell, *Parliaments and English Politics*, pp. 8, 326.

This was the threat of a Spanish invasion which the Council publicized widely during the summer months. In July proclamations were issued for a public fast and for coastal inhabitants to repair to their counties, and these were followed up with orders to carry out musters, provide shipping and repair fortifications.[4] Much of this activity seems to have been intended to persuade taxpayers to repeat the sacrifices they had made in 1588; but in this sense it was largely a failure. From about mid-July contemporary commentators ceased to pay much heed to the rumour of invasion, and JPs who tried to encourage contributions by stressing the emergency got little response. Richard Taylor who was chosen to perform this task in Bedfordshire found that in spite of his comparisons between 1626 and the Armada year the 'vote of every Hundred' was 'not to give to His Majesty in this way'. And the Nottinghamshire JPs reported that even though they had emphasized 'The imminent dangers unto the King's majesty, his Kingdom and subjects by a mighty and provoked enemye, and all other arguments given unto us by Precept from His Majestie and your Lordships . . . the generality, save very few whose offers in the whole County came to about £70, refused to give otherwise than by Parliament, the ordenary and usuall way as they alledged'.[5] The invasion scare, then, was plainly inadequate as a means of inducing people to contribute. In default of this the Council was forced to rely on familiar techniques of persuasion and coercion; however, again its efforts were largely a failure.

Such methods required careful planning and attention to detail, which, during the crucial month of July, was something that the Council was unable to provide. It found that most of its time was taken up with preparations for defence, whilst the King, who might have imposed some direction on it, was preoccupied with diplomacy and the consequences of reorganizing his wife's household.[6] In addition to this, the scope of what the Council could actually do was severely limited by the way in which the levy had been framed. It was very difficult for it to equip the JPs with additional powers, and suggest coercive measures, when the benevolence was being presented as an opportunity for the loving

[4] *Proclamations*, ii. 97–101; *APC 1626*, pp. 55–61, 71–7, 87–90.

[5] The comment of some of John Rous's Suffolk neighbours was that this was 'a policy to draw monies': *Rous*, p. 8. 'The papers of Richard Taylor of Clapham', ed. G. D. Gilmore, *Bedfordshire Historical Record Society*, xxv (1947), pp. 106–8 (I am grateful to Gillian Ignjatijevic for this reference); PRO SP 16/36/34.

[6] *APC 1626*, pp. 50–154; Gardiner, *History*, vi. 134–8.

subject to show his affection for his monarch.[7] These limitations severely handicapped the service.

To start with it never received a proper launching and had no opportunity to develop a momentum of support. The Council tried to provide this by sending the judges to Westminster to put their case before local JPs and subsidymen; but this experiment ended in fiasco when the judges' speech was drowned out by cries of 'a Parliament, a Parliament' and only thirty, out of the 500 or so subsidymen present, agreed to contribute. The Council also tried to rally the goodwill which was supposed to exist amongst the peerage by sending out individual requests asking them to contribute, 'so as to encourage the people to follow your good example'; but most of these did not reach the counties until late August, by which time they were too late to have any affect.[8] The JPs, then, were left to rely almost entirely on the guidance provided by the Council instructions. However even here there were failings. The instructions included two crucial blunders. Firstly they suggested that the benevolence was in some sense an alternative to supply through Parliament and so increased fears for its future survival; secondly they allowed meetings with subsidymen to take place in large groups, thus reducing the opportunities for JPs to employ their personal influence. Both mistakes were rectified in a second set of letters sent out on 26 July, but by the time these reached the shires most of them had held their meetings and taken a decision to refuse.[9]

Perhaps the most serious shortcoming was the Council's failure to provide any adequate coercive support for JPs. This was necessary not only as a direct deterrent to refusers, but also to take some of the pressure off local governors. It was important, if they were to retain their local credibility, that at the same time as they were pushing their neighbours into making payment they were also seen to be defending them from even harsher impositions; and this could often be most readily accomplished where the Council was prepared to exert its own pressure from the centre. This it conspicuously failed to do. In theory it required JPs to certify refusers, but the instructions were so unspecific as to suggest that it was not entirely serious. No mention was made of punishment and there was no direct suggestion that it would

[7] See above, pp. 32–5.

[8] *CSP Ven 1625–6*, p. 495; *C. and T.* i. 130–1; *APC 1626*, pp. 154–5; HMC *Buccleuch*, i. 263, HMC *Cowper*, i. p. 280.

[9] PRO SP 16/31/31; *APC 1626*, pp. 133–4.

actually proceed against defaulters. As a result few JPs seem even to have bothered to send in names, and only six resisters were recorded as appearing before the board.[10] All this was typical of the Council's proceedings. It did little to launch the service properly and even less to persuade local governors that it was prepared to see it through to a successful conclusion. The result was a general unwillingness to co-operate.

This was unfortunate as there is evidence to suggest that where they wanted to, local governors could achieve a good deal, even with such a poorly conceived scheme as the benevolence. The Leicestershire JPs told the Council that they thought that their 'owne example and readines to give . . . often prevayleth more then eyther rules or reasons'; and William Lord Maynard demonstrated the truth of this within his home hundred of Dunmow in Essex. He informed the Duke that in spite of the fact that 'the townes adjoynings . . . doe all with one voice absolutely refuse' and 'my neighbours have incurred the scorne and I the envy of our Countrymen for our forwardnes in His Majestie's service . . . I have had the happines to prevaile soe farre with my neighbours . . . as the greatest part of them hath . . . ed [*illegible*] to give his Majesty to the proportion of two subsidies'. This was achieved largely through, what Maynard called, his 'creditt or power with them', and he begged Buckingham to help preserve this by releasing the subsidymen from payment if there was a general disinclination to give elsewhere.[11] The theme of 'creditt or power' was also elaborated by a Buckinghamshire JP—probably Sir Thomas Denton—who advised the Council of its significance in a local context. He urged that JPs be instructed to

> deale particularly with every man in their severall devisions . . . and to returne as well the names of the refractory as free givers, wherein His Majestie may bee assured that there is noe Justice of so little power in the place where hee dwelleth, or with his neighbours in the towns about him but, if hee will, hee may doe His Majestie a reall and good service herein. And by that meanes to disengadge and prevent the publique assemblies intended, where the one halfe of able persons will not appeare (as experience hath shewed) and yet the residue bee in hazard to bee drawne by example of a few negative voyces to joyne with them in a publique denyall, when by a more private and particular course His Majestie will bee better assured of supply, the ill affected discovered and their factious intentions either wholy prevented or in great measure suppressed.[12]

[10] *APC 1626*, pp. 230, 257–8; PRO SP 16/33/78.

[11] PRO SP 16/34/4; 524/100.

[12] PRO SP 16/34/69. The suggestion of Denton as author is based on internal

The Council appears to have heeded this advice in their second set of instructions, where they required JPs to deal with subsidymen individually 'by using such motives and perswations as you are best acquainted with'.[13] However by this time it was too late to alter the situation.

Most JPs were simply not prepared to put themselves out. The typical response was that of Denton's fellow Buckinghamshire Justices 'who did not assemble with the rest for effecting of the busines but so carry themselves as if they were not interested in the good success thereof'. Only twelve of the local governors attended the service here, and it was much the same story in Nottinghamshire and Hertfordshire, with ten each, and Cornwall, with only five.[14] In Essex Maynard's colleagues met at the quarter-sessions and conveyed to the Council the 'generall dutifull protestacon of the people's affections to supply His Majestie, but the generall desire that this should be done in a Parliamentary way and noe otherwise'. They then went on to ask that since the contribution was so small they be let off altogether.[15] And in the eastern division of Northamptonshire a memorandum by Sir Rowland St John described how

> The letters being reade it was said that wee the Justices did require theire answer and did hope and expecte that they would give freely unto His Majesty, whereupon they desired to goe together to consult thereof, after which they called us and tolde us as is expressed in our memoriall. They were alsoe asked whether they would not have the letters reade over againe unto them, that they might the more perfectly apprehende and understant them, whereunto a negative answer was made, for that they understande them very well already. They were asked whether they would not take some further tyme to consider of them, whereunto a negative answer was likewise given, that they neede not to take longer . . . Then wee sate still a good space of tyme to see if any would declare or expresse himselfe to be of contrary minde, but all men resting silent, we soe left them.[16]

With these replies we are apparently back with the obstructiveness and unwillingness to act which has been highlighted by local historians. However on closer examination there is rather more to it than this. As we have seen some JPs were in fact willing to act,

evidence and his signature on a letter which probably accompanied this: PRO SP 16/34/70.

[13] *APC 1626*, pp. 133–4.

[14] PRO SP 16/33/8; 34/69; 36/34; 37/50.

[15] PRO SP 16/34/62.

[16] Beds. RO St John MS 1296; NRO I. L. 2950, 3686.

for reasons which will be discussed later. There were also several ways in which their ability to act depended on the council. They needed support and backing which in this case was clearly not forthcoming. In the final analysis therefore what we are presented with is not a simple model of the working of localism, but something more complex, much closer to the interaction of local and national goverment depicted by Lake and Hirst.[17] This becomes even more apparent when we consider the loan.

III. THE FORCED LOAN

The loan was launched in circumstances which were a good deal more auspicious than those attending the benevolence. By September the campaigning season was drawing to a close and the Council was released from its responsibility to equip expeditions and prepare coastal defences. This left it ample time to deal with the task in hand. The King was also less preoccupied with the affairs of his wife, and the arrival of Bassompierre at the end of September promised a more harmonious period of Anglo-French relations.[1] Furthermore the failure of the benevolence and Charles's determination to do without a Parliament, released the Council from the constraints which had dogged its previous efforts. Since there was no longer an onus on avoiding coercion it was able to take positive steps to counter resistance. Finally, as we shall see, the character of the loan was such as to open up all sorts of possibilities for bargaining and negotiation, thus providing the Council with additional levers and inducements when it came to securing co-operation. These circumstances made for a levy which was altogether better prepared and supported than the benevolence.

Initially the Council learnt a good deal from the failure of the previous levy. It carefully vetted lists of commissioners and drew up a set of instructions which avoided the previous mistakes. Commissioners were ordered to deal with lenders individually, equipped with arguments to use against those standing on the principle of parliamentary taxation and given specific assurances that anyone who resisted would be punished.[2] It also made strenuous efforts to provide an adequate platform of support before launching the loan in the shires. The levy was agreed on by

[17] Lake, 'Ship money in Cheshire', 45–58; Hirst, 'Privy Council and enforcement', 46–66.

[1] Gardiner, *History*, vi. 141–7.

[2] PRO SP 16/36/43.

14 September, but the Council waited over three months before asking most of the taxpayers to actually contribute. In the mean time it was doing its best to persuade those over whom it had some influence to set an example.

This process began at the start of October with a series of meetings between Privy Councillors and local taxpayers in Westminster. This was chosen, rather than the City of London, because the City was still recovering from paying out a large loan on twenty ships furnished during the summer. Westminster was also smaller and more manageable, and had a large population of courtiers and royal officials who could be expected to co-operate.[3] The first meeting, in the wealthy parishes of St Margaret's and St Martin's, went well, with one of the residents, Sir Robert Cotton, commenting that 'he was glad to see yet the awe the people had of the lords of His Majesty's council and wished the council table could be carried into the country also, for then perhaps some good will be done'.[4] A few days later the process was repeated in the more densely populated area of St Clements, the Strand, the Duchy and Savoy, but there the Council encountered its first opposition. The subsidymen 'at the first when the subsidies were demanded cried out for a Parliament . . . most of them denying to paie, and stand ready for the press rather than yield a jot. Amongst them the Prophet Ball, the tailor, is the cheif man, who . . . in advising the lords to more lawfull councils . . . quoted scripture to them mightily'. The councillors, however, stood firm and set an example by immediately pressing Ball and twelve of the other ringleaders to serve the King abroad.[5]

This resolute approach was maintained as the Council carried its meetings into the five counties adjacent to London, between 19 and 26 October. It prepared extensively for these, sifting through lists of commissioners and drafting in local landowners who might be expected to provide support—including catholic courtiers such as Earl Rivers and Lord Wotton.[6] It also took steps to ensure that as many of its own members attended as possible, thereby

[3] V. Pearl, *London and the Outbreak of the Puritan Revolution* (Oxford, 1961), p. 76; M. J. Power, 'East and west in early-modern London', in E. W. Ives, R. J. Knecht, and J. J. Scarisbrick, eds., *Wealth and Power in Tudor England* (1978), pp. 167–85.

[4] *C. and T.* i. 154, 157.

[5] Ibid. 154; *CSP Ven. 1625–6*, p. 576; *APC 1626*, p. 313.

[6] BRL Coventry MS, commissions for the loan, nos. 12, 14; Quintrell, 'Gentry faction', 121; J. J. N. McGurk, 'Letter book relating to the lieutenancy of Kent, 1604–27', *Archaeologia Cantiana*, lxxxii (1967), 125–7.

presenting a united front to local commissioners and the newsletter writers. Councillors like Pembroke, Marlborough, Weston, and Coke—whose reservations about the levy were to surface later on—were much in evidence, signing warrants to summon refusers from these meetings; and Abbot was called out of semi-retirement and prevailed upon to host a dinner at Lambeth where Privy Councillors met the Surrey commissioners.[7] Such measures clearly helped to ease the early passage of the levy.

It is difficult to find out precisely what happened at these meetings, because the Council did not require reports; however such evidence as there is suggests that its main emphasis at this stage was on coercion. The only sign of bargaining is a hint that at the Kent meeting the county was promised first use of the loan to recoup its billeting charges.[8] Otherwise the Council chose to overawe opposition with a display of forcefulness. Buckingham and Dorset pointed the way at the Middlesex meeting, with tactics which were crude but apparently effective: 'when some denied to subscribe the loan, the Duke should say "Sirrah, take heed what you do. Did you not speak treason at such a time?"; and the Earl of Dorset asking a fellow who pleaded he was unable, what a trade he was of, and being answered a tailor "come, come" saith he "one snip will make amends for all" and other such like which they say was not wont to be in days of yore.' At the Essex meeting the Council squashed an attempt to organize opposition amongst the gentry by imprisoning two of the ringleaders; and elsewhere small groups of refusers were summoned before the Council.[9] In the short term these tactics appear to have worked well. The simple fact of the councillors' presence must have been enough to compel respect from most of the commissioners and subsidymen and, although the attendance was in some cases rather small, most of those who turned up accepted the levy. Within a month Surrey and Essex were making their first payments.[10] However, these successes did not allay all the misgivings. Newsletter reports generally harped on the early instances of opposition, and Pembroke's client Sir Benjamin Rudyerd, commented that 'what will be the success further from London and the awe of the council is much doubted'.[11]

[7] *APC 1626*, pp. 324–5, 328, 331; Rushworth, i. 444, 454–6.

[8] *C. and T.* i. 176; *APC 1626*, p. 372.

[9] *C. and T.* i. 162, 164; *Holles*, ii. 337–8; PRO SP 16/39/25; *APC 1626*, pp. 328, 331, 350.

[10] PRO E.401/2322, 'Collectoribus mutuum a communalitat'.

[11] *C. and T.* i. 159–67; PRO SP 16/39/25.

Such doubts could only have increased with the second stage of the levy. The object of this was not simply to get people to pay, but also to persuade prominent judges and peers to subscribe to the loan's legality. This would then provide a valuable justification when it came to launching it in the shires away from London. During October everything appeared to be going according to plan with most of the judges making their payment and agreeing to a meeting about subscription. However when this came, on 28 October, to the astonishment of most observers they refused to declare that it was legal; and within three weeks they had been joined by a group of fifteen peers.[12]

This combination of opponents constituted a very serious setback to the loan. Not only did it reopen discussion over the basic direction of policy, and undermine the arguments in favour of the legality of the levy, but it also threatened to make the service unenforceable in the shires. The peers who were either openly refusing to subscribe, or were hesitating to declare themselves 'uppon domesticall pretenses', included several of the country's leading territorial magnates, noblemen such as the Earl of Warwick, the leading peer in Essex, the Earl of Huntingdon, whose family had dominated Leicestershire politics for several generations, Lord Spencer, the richest landowner in Northamptonshire, the Earl of Essex, Lord Lieutenant of Staffordshire, and above all the Earl of Arundel who controlled the longstanding Howard influence in Sussex and Norfolk.[13] Without their co-

[12] PRO SP 16/36/43; 41/3; *C. and T.* i. 172; HMC *Buccleuch*, iii. 307–8.

[13] The precise identity of the fifteen or so peers mentioned as refusing subscription at this time is unclear. Some fifteen peers were removed from the Commission of the Peace during the following summer, most of them apparently because they had refused the loan; but reports in November suggest that others were involved as well and were probably waiting to see which way the wind was blowing before declaring themselves: SRO Phelips MS 219/35; *CSP Ven. 1626–8*, p. 55. The ringleaders of the refusal, mentioned in virtually all the records, were Warwick, Essex, Saye, Lincoln, and Clare: PRO SP 16/41/3; 54/821. In addition to these Bolingbroke, Bristol, Cromwell, Dacre, Deincourt, Gray of Wark, Kent, Lescalles, St John of Bletsoe, and Stanhope were removed from the Commission of the Peace in June 1627; PRO C. 231/4, fo. 227^{v}; BRL Coventry MS, Commissions of the Peace, nos. 69–81; whilst the peers also reported as refusing in November included Arundel, Buckerose, Darcy, Devonshire, Gray of Groby, Hertford, Huntingdon, Mordaunt, Northumberland, Oxford, Somerset, and Spencer: *Yonge*, p. 98; TCC MS 0.7.3., fo. 7^{v} (I am grateful to Maija Cole for this reference); PRO SP 16/54/821. Of these only Devonshire, Gray of Groby, Hertford, and Saye were recorded as having paid before the end of December; the remainder could therefore quite plausibly be seen as refusers: PRO E. 401/2322, 'Mutuum de magnatibus'.

operation it must have been seriously doubted whether any real progress could be made in dealing with local commissioners and taxpayers. For several weeks, then, the service hung in the balance whilst the King pressed for its enforcement and councillors like Coventry and Marlborough reminded him of the problems. Eventually, as we have seen, in the council debate on 27 November the King got his way; but this was only accomplished at a price.[14]

The moderates appear to have secured agreement to a marked shift of emphasis. Whereas at the early meetings for the loan the stress was very much on coercion, on overawing opposition by a display of forcefulness, the Council's new awareness of its difficulties seems to have prompted a much gentler approach. During the last week of November decisions were taken not to imprison the peers and not to press for subscription. More significantly the first of many orders was issued allowing counties to recoup their billeting and coat and conduct charges out of the loan.[15] This provided a clear pointer to the Council's intentions over the following months. It betokened a willingness to bargain and negotiate rather than coerce, a readiness to grant financial concessions in order to ease the passage of the service and above all a desire, whenever possible, to minimize the division and the resentment engendered by the levy.

The new approach was exemplified in the negotiations which took place—mainly during November and December 1626—between courtiers who supported the loan and a number of peers and leading local governors whose response was considered doubtful. These individuals found themselves alternately wooed with promises of preferment and intimidated with threats of disfavour. Such stick-and-carrot methods were, of course, a familiar part of the political scene—in the early-seventeenth century as in any other period—but their relevance to the successful implementation of council policy has perhaps not been sufficiently emphasized. Professor Hirst, for example, has alluded to their importance for conciliar enforcement, but has then gone on to discuss the loan in terms of more straightforward processes of coercion.[16] This is understandable in view of the difficulty of tracing such methods through the council registers; but it does, nevertheless, lead to a rather distorted picture of the operation of the council. It should be stressed that this was as much a political

[14] See above, pp. 54–6. [15] *APC 1626*, pp. 383–4, 388.

[16] Hirst, 'Privy Council and enforcement', 50, 52.

as an administrative process, involving the Court and the dispersal of patronage as well as the pursuivant and the council summons. One of the best ways of demonstrating this is to look more closely at the techniques employed at this time, and some of these can be illustrated from the experience of the Earl of Clare.

Clare had made it plain in a letter to his old friend Bishop Williams, on 13 November, that he was determined to oppose the loan. His refusal to subscribe two weeks later was therefore predictable.[17] However, as soon as it became known the Court set out to persuade him to change his mind. The first approach came from an old acquaintance, the Countess of Banbury, acting on behalf of the Duke. She put it to Clare that what was at stake in his action was not simply the prospect of favour from the Duke, but his whole reputation as a loyal servant to the King. This line of argument threw Clare off balance as he had treated the loan, up to this point, as entirely the doing of Buckingham. He admitted to his son that 'how to deale in it seeing the King is a partie perplexeth me not a little . . . yet would I be loathe in a free gift to refuse the King in a pressing necessitie, from what parent soever begotten'. He therefore returned the Countess an equivocal answer, being 'loathe to object or dispute where the King his service was a party', but uncertain

> how I might serve His Majesty by my purse without prostituting my reputation to a just condemnation, by eating up my word formerly given my lord treasurer, with which, though I might dispense for so much as concerneth my owne particular, yet His Majestie's service being in consequence, I am to be the more tender being by such an uncomly part justly to forfeit the good name I have in the world and all power with my friends by which hereafter I might serve His Majestie and be of use to your Ladyship.

This attempt to justify not subscribing in terms which made clear his continuing desire to serve the King gave the Countess just the opening she needed. She replied by suggesting that he could escape his dilemma either by offering a separate contribution—as a personal gift to the King—or else by allowing her to lay down the money on his behalf. She then announced, in mid-December, that to all intents he had paid.[18]

Clare, meanwhile, was trying to extricate himself by setting off home to Nottinghamshire. On the road north at Buntingford, however, he was overtaken by a letter from the Earl of Warwick,

[17] *Holles*, ii. 337–8; PRO SP 16/41/3.

[18] *Holles*, ii. 341–4.

warning him that the Court had used his reply to claim that he was about to lend his money and strike a tally. This tactic had probably been used a few weeks earlier to trick Lord Saye and Sale into appearing to subscribe—his name is recorded in the receipt rolls as having given £350 on 18 November in spite of the fact that a week later he was being described as an outright refuser—but Clare was alive to any such danger and wrote promptly to the Countess and the Duke, forbidding them to lay down any money for him and explaining his reasons for refusal. He also instructed his son to show an account of his actions to his friends in London so that if the Countess insisted he had paid they could repudiate her. He then lay low in Nottinghamshire for a couple of months and when he returned to London kept well clear of the Court.[19]

This episode illustrated not only the methods employed by the Court, and the lengths to which it was prepared to go, but also the crucial part played in the negotiations by Charles himself. From the start of the service he had shown a willingness to become personally involved which contrasted sharply with the behaviour of his predecessor Henry VIII, who—as contemporaries noted—in the similar circumstances of the 'Amicable Grant' had distanced himself and allowed Wolsey to carry the responsibility.[20] Such politic restraint seems to have been largely beyond Charles, and this had important consequences for those contemplating opposition. Perhaps his most significant intervention was the proclamation issued on 7 October containing what amounted to a royal promise that the loan would not be made a precedent.[21] This had originally been intended to allay fears for the future of Parliament; but in time—as opponents of the loan continued to harp on this theme—it helped to shift the central issue, from a debate about precedents and legality to the question of whether or not one trusted the King's word. For an individual like Clare—who had sought comfort in an assurance that the loan was all the work of the Duke—this could involve having to make a very uncomfortable choice and as we shall see, in the long term, this was to be deeply divisive.[22] In the short term, however, the King's approach provided valuable support to the efforts being made in Council and at Court.

[19] Ibid. 342–5; PRO E.401/2322, 'Mutuum de magnatibus'; SP 16/41/3. It was also claimed that Sir Edward Coke had paid his loan, although he later testified that he never did so: *CD 1628*, iv. 243.

[20] PRO C.115/N.4, 1 Oct. 1626; TCC MS 0.7.3, fo. 7^{v}.

[21] *Proclamations*, ii. 110–12.

[22] See below, pp. 170–85.

Alongside his more formal statements Charles had also let it be known that he regarded the loan as a crucial test of loyalty to his person. Those Lords who had refused to subscribe were reported to have escaped imprisonment only to be consigned to the 'black book' of royal disfavour. Buckingham warned the Earl of Northumberland that if he withheld his loan it would 'much prejudice you in the opinion of His Majestie'. And, as late as May 1627, Lord Clifford was reminding his brother-in-law, Sir Thomas Wentworth, that

> I cannot hope to see you receive the least favor that the great ones can abridge you if you still refuse; neither dare any move the King in the behalf of any gentleman refuser for his heart is so inflamed in this business as he vows a perpetual remembrance, as well as present punishment. And though the Duke will be gone shortly yet no man can expect to receive any ease by his absence since the King takes the punishment into his own direction.[23]

Not unnaturally such prospects had a sobering effect on many of those who were contemplating resistance. Wentworth himself thought long and hard before finally deciding not to pay. Nathaniel Tomkins remarked that 'most of the parlamentarie men likely to denie, that I know, are unwillingly determined to give all', and cited Sir Dudley Digges as an instance. And Clare noted that three of his acquaintances who might have been expected to resist—the Earl of Devonshire, Lord Russell, and Lord Mulgrave—had in fact all contributed, 'which', he observed caustically, 'shows the nature of man, cast only to the present, without care of future or consequence'. Indeed by the end of December some forty-one out of eighty-five peers had paid up, which constituted a considerable success given the difficulty of contacting many of them in their home counties.[24] The pressures being exerted in this direction seem to have worked at several levels, and something of their nature can be illustrated in the case of Sir Robert Phelips.

Phelips faced the loan at a crucial point in his political career. Like other leading parliamentarians in this period he had ambitions to serve the Crown and also needed backing at Court to secure his local offices. In 1624 he had been in high favour with the Duke after acting as one of his undertakers during the Parliament, but

[23] *C. and T.* i. 177; PRO SP 16/53/3; *Strafforde's Letters*, i. 38.

[24] *Strafforde's Letters*, i. 36–9; SRO Phelips MS 219/35; *Holles*, ii. 339; PRO E.401/2322, 'Mutuum de magnatibus'.

then in the following year—for reasons which are not entirely clear—he turned against him and led the Commons' attempt to uncover his abuses. As a result Phelips was first pricked as a Sheriff, to prevent him from sitting in the following Parliament, and then deprived of his local offices.[25] In order to regain these he had no alternative but to look to the Court, and so in November 1626 he entered into covert negotiations through his contact at the centre, Nathaniel Tomkins.

Tomkins approached various courtiers to discuss the prospects for Phelips being restored to favour and received the unanimous answer that it was 'hardly possible . . . but ex post facto'—in other words after he had paid the loan. The most helpful was the Earl of Holland who promised 'he would undertake upon your meriting of His Majestie in this busines . . . to sett you right at Court and putt you in as good a way as ever you were.' But the loan was clearly the crucial test. As far as Holland was concerned it put 'the King's honour . . . really at the stake, but the liberties of the subject but in opinion'; and partisan feeling was running so high that courtiers were vying to outdo each other in expressions of loyalty and heaping of abuse on those peers who delayed in committing themselves. On the strength of this Tomkins encouraged Phelips to support the loan, stressing 'the regard of a man's own particular, which to endanger without certen and apparent good to the publiq I doe not see manie wise men forward to doe in this age'. However as he recognised the mood the the Court was not the only consideration.[26]

Phelips also had to take account of opinion in Somerset, which on past experience could be very changeable. After his 'undertaking' in 1624 his popularity amongst the freeholders had declined sufficiently to encourage his local rival, John Poulett, to spread a rumour that he had 'forsaken the country and was turned courtier'; and his attack on Buckingham in 1625 together with his opposition to the benevolence of 1626, may have been intended to correct this impression.[27] He evidently had to tread carefully to avoid losing his one remaining political asset, and Tomkins's final advice reflected this: 'You who best knowe the constitution of your countrie can best advise your selfe which course to take . . . but I should not in this case judge the middle way a good way; if you

[25] Russell, *Parliaments and English Politics*, pp. 149–52, 170, 268.

[26] SRO Phelips MS 219/35.

[27] Russell, *Parliaments and English Politics*, pp. 19–20; Barnes, *Somerset*, pp. 163, 289.

deny faintly and are not a leader of those who shall refuse, you shall hardly be held a meritor among them; if you doe not avowedly declare yourself to advance the work, you shall have no thanks from the King.' In the event Phelips did choose the middle way and left his county for London just as the loan was being launched.[28] This in itself, however, was a significant demonstration of the pressure being exerted by the King and the Court.

If Tomkins's advice is a reflection of his friend's attitude, then, for Phelips calculations of political advantage and an awareness of the need to outmanœuvre his local rival seem to have been well to the fore in making the decision over the loan. For others this process was often influenced by more obviously principled considerations. This was perhaps particularly the case for members of the peerage, who had to take account of the widely accepted notion that the King was the fountainhead of all honour and virtue. The effect of this was to increase the pressure to conform. In its purest form it could be taken to imply that personal service to the monarch was the *raison d'être* of the peerage, and that denial of the opportunity for this service was the ultimate disgrace. Such considerations had obviously weighed heavily with Clare and caused him to reconsider before finally declaring himself; however they were not the only influence operating at this level. Alongside the ethos of service to the monarch there had also developed a sense of the obligations of godliness and service to 'the Country' which in circumstances like these could draw an individual in a different direction.[29] The consequence was that many peers faced an acutely difficult decision in which honour and principle were intimately bound up with considerations of self-interest and self-esteem. Whichever course they chose it was likely to lead to a good deal of discomfort and anguish.

These were clearly illustrated in a letter written by the Earl of Essex on learning that the King had deprived him of his Lord Lieutenancy for refusing the loan. Earlier in the 1620s Essex had fashioned a promising career for himself as a soldier/courtier in the mould of his father, and at the beginning of 1626 he seemed to be on the verge of preferment. He was chosen to act as a standard bearer at the King's coronation and received assurance from his courtly friend, the Earl of Holland, that after the Cadiz expedition the King had been heard to express the opinion that 'your currage

[28] SRO Phelips MS 219/35; PRO SP 16/53/88.

[29] M. E. James, *English Politics and the Concept of Honour, 1485–1642* (*P. and P.*, Supp. 3 1978), pp. 72–92.

and generositie would have done something more worthy of your countrie's honour'. However he was to be disappointed. His opposition, first of all to the Duke and later on to the loan, effectively blocked his advancement and caused him to retire to his estates in Staffordshire.[30] There in July 1627 he received news from the Earl of Monmouth that the King had removed him from office, and, moreoever, had done it in a particularly wounding manner:

> when the Kinge . . . tould me his plesur I thought of my dethe sooner then such a motion, but when I herd it I tould His Majestie . . . I hoped your Lordship had and would doe him good service there and humblie intreted him you myght continew in it still. His answer was no, you were a willfull younge man and desired more your owne glory then to doe him any acceptable service; and the Attorney standinge by, he caled him to him and commanded him to draw a commition redy for him to signe.

This must have reminded Essex of the treatment meted out to his father by Elizabeth, and not surprisingly he seems to have been completely flattened by the news. His letters from Holland suggest a constant anxiety about the King's interest in himself and his family, and to be told that Charles considered him a 'willfull younge man' must have been peculiarly hurtful. His reply to Monmouth indicated this:

> Be assured that I am infinitely sorry for that opinion His Majesty exprest to have of mee for I doe assure you I never framed to myself any other way of acquiring glorie or opinion then that by which I might with the most advantage do His Majesty the best service . . . And it is my hope that His Majesty wilbee pleased in his owne tyme and according to the mesure of his owne royal heart to remove this cloud which now hangs over mee and to receyve mee againe into his grace and favour which is the only glorie I doe and ever shall value in the world.[31]

Essex was not the only peer who felt the force of such a disgrace. During the 1628 Parliament Bristol, Arundel, Saye, Clare, Warwick, and Gray all spoke up, one after another, begging to be restored to favour, with Bristol describing 'the displesure of my Prince, being the debarre of all promotion or imployment in the state, to be fully equall to close imprisonment'.[32] Confronted with this sort of

[30] V. F. Snow, *Essex The Rebel* (Nebraska, 1970) pp. 162–7; BL Loan MS 23/1. fo. 170^{r}.

[31] BL Add. MS 46, 188, fos. 102, 107; Loan MS 23/1, fos. 170^{r}, 184^{v}, 205.

[32] *LP 1628*, pp. 468–9.

prospect it was perhaps hardly surprising that peers were tempted to adopt the craven approach castigated by Clare. However this was not necessarily an easy way out, and in some cases support for the loan led to a positive stand which was just as principled as that taken by the refusers. A good example was provided by Lord Montague, a leading Northamptonshire landowner, brother to the Lord President of the Council and one of the first non-courtier peers to make payment, on 20 November.

Several contemporaries supposed that over the loan Montague was simply responding to the dictates of the Duke, whom he had apparently served loyally in the previous Parliament. Closer examination suggests, however, that his motivation was far more complex. He was to claim early in 1628 that their relationship was relatively detached: 'I have been as true a friend to his Grace as any of my rank', but to add that 'there be not that familiarity between the Duke and me as may be hath been between the Lord Mordaunt and him'.[33] Montague was also very evidently aware of the possible implications of a levy like the loan. In 1622, after the premature dissolution of Parliament, he had written to his brother on his own initiative, warning of the apprehension amongst his neighbours 'lest some unusuall courses shall be taken for supply of present necessities, the people in general being in great necessity and want for money, and England not liking levies but by Parliament, as former ages shew'. If he needed any reminding of this dislike in November 1626 it was no doubt provided by 'a grave and godly Batchelour of Divinity'—possibly his own minister the renowned Robert Bolton—who visited Montague to put the case against the levy; and also by his own 'countrymen' who, as he remarked to his brother, thought him 'to be too forward in it because he had made such haste in paying, whereas divers good lords stand out who gain great applause'.[34] Montague, then, faced a difficult and complex choice and in the circumstances one might have expected him like so many other peers, to have simply kept his head down. Instead he seems to have gone out of the way to demonstrate his support for the loan, paying up promptly and then appearing on a platform alongside three of the Privy Councillors when they met with the Northamptonshire subsidymen the following January. Some indication of his reasons for doing this

[33] TCC MS 0.7.3., fos. 5^{r}, 7^{v}; HMC *Buccleuch*, i. 265; *Buccleuch*, iii. 321.
[34] HMC *Buccleuch*, iii. 225; NRO Montague MS 186 (unpaginated: I am grateful to Esther Cope for this reference); 3/205.

are provided by a statement issued at the time, to answer his detractors.[35]

In this he first of all rehearsed the main features of the King's case, restating his arguments for supply in fighting a just war; he then reiterated Charles's promise that the loan would not be used as a precedent; and finally, in response to suspicions about his relationship with Buckingham, he insisted that he had 'not been led by any by respects'. However the heart of the matter for him personally seems to have been the King's direct request to each member of the peerage. 'Upon this letter and the causes therein alleged', he wrote 'I could not with an upright heart and good conscience deny this desire of the King's. For if it be the duty of one Christian Brother being able to lend to another . . . how should I answer it before his tribunal seat if I should deny so amicable a desire of my sovereign Lord the King.' For Montague this sense of duty—undoubtedly enhanced by his elevation to the peerage in 1621—probably represented absolute bedrock. Throughout the 1620s his correspondence showed a deep concern with the obligations and responsibilities implied by his rank; and in 1642, at the age of eighty he was to respond in a very similar fashion when he again received what he felt to be a personal summons from his monarch.[36] There was however a price to pay for such open expressions of loyalty, and in Montague's case, as we shall see, it involved forfeiting the esteem and reputation he had enjoyed amongst his neighbours.[37] This was perhaps a measure of the pressure being applied through the Court and, more particularly, through the intervention of the King. It was a good deal subtler and much less visible than the straightforward coercion generally associated with the loan, but in many respects it was at least as effective, and at this stage played a crucial role in restoring a momentum of support.

The rallying of a substantial number of peers and local governors provided a base of support and some grounds for optimism when it came to the third stage of the levy, the meetings in counties away from London. However the prospects for these were a good deal

[35] PRO E.401/2322, 'Mutuum de magnatibus'; E., S. Cope, *The Life of a Public Man* (American Philosophical Soc., 142, 1981), pp. 119–22; HMC *Buccleuch*, i. 264–5.

[36] Cope, *Life of a Public Man*, pp. 95–6, 191–4; HMC *Buccleuch*, iii. 258.

[37] See below, pp. 224–5.

less bright at the end of November than they had been a month earlier. The refusals of the judges and the peers had been widely reported in the shires and served to undermine the early impression of a consensus in favour of the levy. In Hertfordshire many of the subsidymen, who had at first accepted the loan, changed their minds as a result of the judges' stand. Towards the end of November 600 of them were reported to have signed a letter to the Earl of Salisbury upbraiding him for 'inducing them to subscribe by making them believe the judges had subscribed' and refusing to pay until other counties had done so. From Northamptonshire Lord Montague lamented to his brother that 'if you be putt uppon it agayne, as it seemes you shall, your wellcom will be worse then it would have beene because men are deceyved of there hopes.' And when three of the council commissioners—Edmonds, Carleton, and Banbury—visited Reading early in December, their meeting was more or less boycotted by the Berkshire gentry. Only eleven of the thirty-three commissioners turned up, and the absentees included all but two of the senior JPs.[38] This sort of response must have confirmed councillors in their decision to adopt more conciliatory methods, and similar embarrassment was generally avoided.

The county meetings took place between December 1626 and March 1627 and as with other aspects of the loan were carefully prepared. The Exchequer provided councillors with full lists of subsidymen before they went down to the shires; the councillors themselves checked and altered lists of commissioners right up to the moment of departure; and messengers were sent around 'to inquire out all the persons of principall qualitie (which now remayne in or neere the city of London) to require them in His Majestie's name to make their ymediate repaire into there counties for the execucon of the service'. Even the King joined in the preparations and over Christmas was to be found stalking the corridors of his Whitehall palace, driving councillors out on their long winter journeys.[39]

The Council also took considerable pains over the visits of its own representatives to the counties. It drew up several lists of names for consideration, and then elevated three of the nominees —Savile, Exeter, and Suffolk—to the board, according to Clare, in

[38] *C. and T.* i. 176; *CSP Ven. 1626–8* pp. 62, 94; NRO Montague MS 3/205; PRO SP 16/40/39.

[39] PRO SP 16/47/44; 458/105 (miscalendared under 1640); HMC *Portland* iii. 22; *Buccleuch*, i. 264.

order 'to incurrage as in those days before a battell'.[40] The list of those chosen provides an interesting insight into the way in which councillors conceived of their relationship with the local governors. Where possible representatives were selected who combined loyalty to the regime with local influence. Thus Dorset was chosen to go into Sussex where his position as Lord Lieutenant and the territorial standing of his family could to some extent compensate for the absence of Arundel; and Buckingham's client Lord Savage, although not a privy councillor, was sent into Cheshire where his family had long been pre-eminent.[41] However, in some cases there was no such person available, and here the Council showed little hesitation in sending an outsider so long as he was either a councillor or someone who could be trusted by the Duke. Hence the representatives proposed for Leicestershire—where both Huntingdon and Lord Gray held back from co-operating—were Sir John Coke, Sir John Savile, and the Earl of Exeter, none of whom, except Coke, appear to have had a direct connection with the county; Holland was sent to accompany the Duke to Buckinghamshire, largely, it seems, because he was on particularly intimate terms with him at the time; and Lord Montague was proposed for service in Huntingdonshire, in spite of his insistence that 'being soe foreigne . . . I can effect little good'.[42]

In one sense this use of outsiders revealed a weakness of the Council. Because of the opposition of the peers it could no longer rely on the support of territorial magnates like Arundel, Warwick, and Essex, and their influence would normally have been considered crucial when it came to persuading the governors of their home counties to co-operate; however their omission from the service was also a comment on the Council's strength. The fact that it could contemplate launching the loan without them suggests that its representatives were thought to possess reserves of influence and prestige which went beyond mere territorial power. Just over 100 years before Wolsey's 'Amicable Grant' had been wrecked by the defection of local magnates;[43] but in the 1620s the Council apparently did not regard this as an insuperable problem. It seems to have believed that any lack of influence in this respect could be

[40] PRO SP 16/39/55; BL Add. MS 39, 238, fo. 74; *Holles*, ii. 339.

[41] Fletcher, *A County Community*, pp. 23–4, 195–6; VCH *Cheshire*, ii. 102–3.

[42] HMC *Cowper*, i. 119; SRO Phelips MS 219/35; NRO Montague MS 3/205.

[43] A. Fletcher, *Tudor Rebellions* (1968), pp. 17–20; M. E. James, 'Obedience and Dissent in Henrician England: The Lincolnshire Rebellion of 1536', *P. and P.* xlviii (1970), 52–3.

compensated by other means: through invoking the habits of loyalty and obedience deeply ingrained in local governors, and through proffering the benefits and concessions which, in an increasingly centralized state, lay at its disposal.

The journeys made by the Council's representatives were a quite extraordinary extension of its normal role. Perhaps the closest parallel would be some of the royal progresses of Elizabeth's reign, where there were similar opportunities for central governors to meet groups of gentry and freeholders, assess their mood and impress on them their prestige and power. The gatherings made it possible to detect disobedience and punish it immediately and publicly, without having to mobilize the cumbersome processes of a council summons. They also enabled local inhabitants to petition and bargain with councillors face-to-face, rather than struggling through the normal channels of access.[44] All of this was of considerable significance in providing a solid platform for the loan, as can be seen from the Norfolk meeting of January 1627.

Here the Council faced an initial problem in the Earl of Arundel's continuing exclusion from Court. Arundel was Lord Lieutenant and High Steward of Norwich, as well as being the leading territorial magnate in the shire, and in his absence the only councillor with extensive local connections was Sir John Suckling. Suckling was therefore sent down, accompanied by Lord Keeper Coventry—whose daughter had married a Norfolk landowner—and two complete outsiders, Sir Thomas Edmondes and Sir Humphrey May.[45] In the event this did not prove a particular handicap, and the councillors were able to make a success of the meeting through a combination of careful preparation and nimble footwork.

They were given their orders on 20 December, and by the 24th had written letters to the Sheriff requiring him to set up a meeting with the local subsidymen for 12 January. This unusually prompt action enabled the sheriff to write round to commissioners and high constables on 28 December, and allowed the Norwich corporation time to prepare a reception and banquet to enhance the dignity of the visit. It also gave the councillors an opportunity

[44] Clark, *English Provincial Society*, pp. 133–4; D. McCulloch, 'Catholic and Puritan in Elizabethan Suffolk', *Archiv fur Reformationsgeschichte* 72 (1981), 237–40.

[45] G. L. Owens, 'Norfolk 1620–41: Local Government and Central Authority in an East Anglican County' (University of Wisconsin Ph.D., 1970), pp. 45–7, 378.

to arrange for themselves some valuable patronage, in the form of licences for the Norfolk farmers to export grain.[46]

The precise sequence of events at Norwich is difficult to sort out because no report has survived; however the outline can be reconstructed from later letters and orders. There was probably a large crowd gathered on the 12th as the city was in the midst of preparation for the January quarter-sessions, and this meant that it was particularly important for the councillors to create the right impression.[47] They faced two main challenges to the service. The first was relatively direct and consisted of two of the leading commissioners—Sir John Heveningham and Sir John Corbett—openly refusing either to pay the loan or support it. The councillors responded promptly by binding them over to answer in London, and this appears to have deterred others from following their example.[48] The second challenge was more insidious and so more difficult to counter. It took the form of a petition from Yarmouth corporation, prepared by Corbett's brother, Miles, and begging the councillors to release the town from payment. The text of this particular petition has not survived, but if it was anything like the others which came from Yarmouth at this time, it would have emphasized the costs the town had to bear for coastal defence and its impoverishment as a result of trade losses.[49] Yarmouth had been harder hit than most towns by the war and there was therefore some justification for its plea; however for the Council to have accepted it would have been disastrous. It would doubtless have led to similar appeals from Norwich and the shire—who invariably insisted on like treatment in matters relating to taxation—and thus would have undermined the whole service. Equally, however, the councillors could not afford to dismiss it out of hand. The county looked to them for the protection of coasts and shipping, and expected sympathetic action in return for obedience and support.[50] The councillors therefore appear to have resolved upon a compromise by which Yarmouth withdrew its petition, and the local commissioners

[46] *State Papers relating to Musters, Beacons, Subsidies, Ship Money etc. in Norfolk*, ed. W. Rye (Norwich, 1907), pp. 45–7, 49–50; NNRO, Norwich Mayor's Court Bk. 1624–34, fos. 123, 124^{v}; *APC 1627* pp. 3–4; A. Hassell Smith, *County and Court* (Oxford, 1974), pp. 234–6.

[47] A. Hassell Smith, 'Justices at work in Elizabethan Norfolk', *NA* xxxiv (1967), 93–4.

[48] *APC 1627*, pp. 28, 40, 74.

[49] YRO 18/6, fo. 233^{v}; 19/5, fos. 7^{r}, 53^{v}; PRO SP 16/61/85i.

[50] Hassell Smith, 'Justices at work', 98–101.

promised to co-operate, in return for assurances that the coastline would be secured. Direct evidence for this has not survived, but something very similar was arranged a few days later when the councillors moved on to King's Lynn; and soon after their return to London a letter was dispatched to the Norfolk commissioners, informing them of the King's pleasure at their co-operation and his purpose 'toucheinge the garde of that coaste . . . to have an especiall care thereof'.[51] This was gratefully received and 'presently published' amongst the county's subsidymen, 'which gave them a great deale of comfort'. However the ships were rather slow in coming, and at the end of February it was necessary for the commissioners to remind the Council of its promise in a letter which strongly hinted at the implied terms of an earlier bargain: 'after soe great a measure of love and duty shewed in performeinge even beyond the strength and meanes of this poore countrey the late great loanes, the continuance of these insultes and infestations upon our coastes (to soe great losse of some and terror of all the rest) are very bitterly tasted by the generality of our countrey'. This helped to do the trick and within a few days the ships were on their way.[52]

Meanwhile at the meeting in Norwich the Councillors, having cleared away the main obstacles, had set in motion the collection of money. They took subscriptions and payments from several of the leading gentry and began to organize the allocation of commissioners to appropriate divisions. This was not as straightforward as it might have been because—even with seven additions to the normal bench—there were several divisions where no one was in residence who was prepared to serve.[53] The councillors therefore had to sit down with those commissioners in attendance and work out a way of distributing them so as to cover the gaps. This appears to have been managed with some success. The service got off to such a rapid start that already by the end of February some £3,456 had been paid into the Exchequer. It was also sufficiently well co-ordinated for council communications to reach the various divisions and commissioners to come together again in September to present a survey of their proceedings.[54]

[51] YRO 19/6, fos. 54^r, 55^r; PRO SP 16/61/81; *APC 1627*, p. 33.

[52] PRO SP 16/55/25; Owens, 'Norfolk 1620–41', pp. 165–70.

[53] Cust, 'A list of commissioners', 205; PRO SP 16/53/33; 76/24; 77/11.

[54] PRO E.401/2322, 'Collectoribus mutuum a communalitat'; *Musters, Beacons, Subsidies, Ship Money etc.*, pp. 50–2, 70, 83–4, 86–7; PRO SP 16/75/94.

The meeting at Norwich was in many respects typical. The mixture of coercion and gentler persuasion—whereby the council commissioners first of all punished a few refusers, as an example to others, and then sat down to some hard bargaining with the local governors—was common to most shires. However, circumstances varied, and the degree of force used and the precise nature of concessions tended to differ in each case. In the three counties which offered most resistance—Gloucestershire, Northamptonshire, and Lincolnshire—the emphasis at the start was on overawing opposition through a display of strength.

Here the initial meetings proved something of a mixed blessing, because, as well as giving councillors an opportunity to make their presence felt, they provided opponents with the chance to demonstrate their dissatisfaction publicly. At the Northamptonshire meeting on 12 January the council commissioners—Manchester, Coke, and Exeter—found a 'strong combination of two and twenty principle gentlemen which drew after them near halfe the shire and as they presumed would not only frustrate the service in the county, but infuse the confidence of contradiction into the next adjacent shires'. When the Earl of Rutland arrived in Lincoln towards the end of the month it was reported that the country 'did little better than rebel: for they would not hear the commission read and as is said went about to have untiled the house over the commissioners heads'. And at the Gloucestershire meeting on 16 February twelve of the twenty-four commissioners appearing refused point blank to support the loan, thereby jeopardising the service over the entire shire.[55] These setbacks would have been enough to destroy the service if left to the management of local governors; but the council commissioners, with their added prestige and resources, were to a large extent able to rescue the situation. In Gloucestershire the Earl of Northampton managed to contain the damage by impressing on commissioners that open resistance would be 'very ill taken by His Majestie and your Lordships'. In Northamptonshire the councillors improvised to

> break the opposition . . . partly by gentle and fair entreaty of those we found tractable and cheifly by improving the authority and power of our commission, first to divide the heads from the members by binding all the gentlemen to appear at the Council board, with demonstration of reproach and disgrace, and secondly to dishearten their followers by binding all the

[55] PRO SP 16/49/8; 54/28; *C. and T.* i. 190.

refractory persons to muster themselves in the Artillery yeard . . . for supply of the reviews to be sent for Denmark.[56]

And in Lincolnshire the Earl of Rutland, after being forced to withdraw, was able to reorganize in London and eventually launch the service in March. In the meantime he first of all had the opposition ringleader, the Earl of Lincoln, summoned and imprisoned in the Tower; then appointed thirty-four new commissioners to replace those who had failed to co-operate; and finally recruited Suffolk and May to accompany him on the return journey. The second set of meetings was carefully staggered to keep local commissioners and subsidymen apart and, although there was still some opposition, much of this was overcome by binding over fourteen of the refusers and threatening punishment or pressing to the remainder.[57]

In each of these cases the councillors had placed an emphasis on coercion; but it was not the only tactic they used. In Gloucestershire Northampton reasoned with the commissioners and apparently persuaded them of the disruption their example might cause within the local community; in Northamptonshire Manchester and his brother Lord Montague used 'gentle and fair entreaty', which consisted of stressing the King's commitment to carry on ruling with Parliament; and in Lincolnshire Rutland allowed 'bearers' to relieve the burden on the poorer subsidymen, 'which obtained the consent of a great many'.[58] Elsewhere this approach was more obviously to the fore, and a series of bargains were struck, providing the basis on which substantial numbers of local governors and subsidymen agreed to co-operate.

Sometimes the concessions involved took the form of pledges and reassurances about the political implications of the levy. For example in Nottinghamshire Viscount Mansfield, the Lord Lieutenant, and eleven of the local JPs were able to bring the subsidymen round by again emphasizing the King's promise:

The countrey at first not a little perplexed with the height of the demand and the manner of it, as not being moulded and concluded in Parliament, held off for some while. But being made more plainly to understand by us

[56] PRO SP 16/49/8; 54/28; 458/106.

[57] *CSP Ven. 1626–8*, p. 126, BRL Coventry MS, Commissions for the loan, no. 15; PRO C.193/12/2; SP 16/56/39; 71/50; *APC 1627*, pp. 142, 240–1, 253; HMC *MSS of the Duke of Rutland*, 3 vols. (1888–94), i. 481.

[58] PRO SP 16/54/28; 71/50; *C. and T.* i. 198; HMC *Buccleuch* i. 265; TCC MS 0.7.3., fo. 7^{v}. For 'bearers' see below, p. 258.

the pressing necessity at this instance for defence of God's true religion and the weale publique, and gracious promise of His Majesty to repaie the said moneys now lent so soone as he shall be enabled thereunto, and not to make use of this president in future, nor intermitt the summoning of Parliaments so often as the state occasions should require, but rather be invited to the frequency thereof by their cheerful conformity to the extraordinarie corse at this time desired for supply, they were persuaded generallie to submitt.[59]

In most cases, however, more direct material incentives were required.

In Buckinghamshire these turned what could have been a difficult meeting into a triumph for the Duke and the Earl of Holland. The majority of local JPs and freeholders had shown how they felt about unparliamentary levies in their unenthusiastic response to the benevolence; they were also aggrieved because central government had failed to reimburse over £1000 which they had expended on purveyance and coat and conduct money. The councillors therefore faced a hard task when they arrived in Aylesbury on 26 January, particularly as they were immediately confronted by John Hampden, refusing to pay or subscribe.[60] However, Hampden was quickly bound over to appear in London, and the Duke then went on to arrange a series of concessions which ensured the support of the other commissioners. These were outlined in a council letter, written a few days later on his return to Whitehall:

The King out of the full and faithfull relacion made . . . by our very good lorde the Duke of Buckingham takes speciall notice with what affeccion and cheerefulnesse you assisted his Grace and my Lorde of Hollande in that businesse about the loans, as also how readily and dutifullie the people of that countrie in generall appeared themselves to that which the commissioners required . . . which manner of proceeding both by you and them gave His Majestie much contentment, as hee esteems it above the value of the loane and hath commanded us to let you knowe so much . . . And that you may knowe the happinesse you had by the Duke's presence he hath with his report presented also to the King some desires from the countrie, to all which at his humble suite the Kinge hath condiscended: first that the composicion money which to the Greencloth shall appeare to be due to the countrie shalbe satisfied againe out of these loans; secondly the coat and conduct money arreare shalbe allowed and defaulked by you out of the said loanes; thirdly for those of the three

59 PRO SP 16/55/1.
60 PRO SP 16/34/69; 51/27; 76/21 i, ii.

hundreths of Alisbury the King will intrust it to your direccons what tyme to give unto the poorer sorte for paying their loanes . . .[61]

All this was a marked contrast to the rather heavy handed methods adopted by Buckingham at the initial Middlesex meeting, and the change of style typified the general shift of approach on the part of the Council. The concessions granted in Buckinghamshire were worth well over £1,000, but in return the Council secured substantial benefits.[62]

These were principally of two sorts. First of all the concessions undoubtedly helped to ensure prompt collection of the loan, with £1,590—out of an eventual total of £2,333—being paid in by the end of February. This was doubtless due in part to the provision whereby much of the money was to be kept by the county to reimburse ratepayers; however it also owed something to the local commissioners, who took the unusual step of nominating themselves as collectors.[63] Perhaps this was again a response to the assurances of Buckingham and the King. Not only did these provide a welcome pat on the head, but they also enhanced the prestige and popularity in being associated with the service.

In the second place the concessions also helped to strengthen general links between the Council and local governors. Here much depended on the Duke who, as Lord Lieutenant and a principal landowner in the shire, assumed a pivotal role. To be successful he needed to be seen by the county as someone able to represent its interests at the centre and deliver benefits in return for co-operation; however in this respect his record left a good deal to be desired. He had been Lord Lieutenant since 1616, and a local landowner since 1618, but because of his commitments at Court he had had little opportunity to get to know the local governors or understand their concerns. This was reflected in his lieutenancy book, which contained only the most cursory of instructions to his deputies; it was also revealed in his slowness over responding to the county's many appeals over coat and conduct money.[64] The visit in 1627, however, provided Buckingham with an opportunity to change all this and he seized it with both hands, not only securing concrete benefits and assurances of favours to come, but also clearly demonstrating that he had the county's best interests

[61] *APC 1627*, p. 45.

[62] PRO SP 16/76/21 i, ii.

[63] PRO E.401/2322–4, 'Collectoribus mutuum a communalitat'.

[64] Sainty, *Lieutenants of the Counties*, p. 12; Lockyer, *Buckingham*, pp. 26–7; BL Eg. MS 860, *passim*; *Letters and Papers of the Verney Family*, ed. J. Bruce (Camden Soc., 1st Ser. 56, 1852), pp. 121–2.

at heart. This promised to ease co-operation between central and local governors for the future, and the Council evidently felt that this sort of link was worth cultivating. On the same day as it confirmed the concessions to Buckinghamshire ten other counties were allowed to recoup their coat and conduct charges from the loan, and this grant was eventually extended to cover the whole country.[65]

The council commissioners in Cheshire faced an altogether lengthier struggle before persuading the local governors to co-operate. At the initial meeting, early in February, Lord Savage and the Earl of Derby met with a mixed reception. The City of Chester quickly agreed both to subscribe and pay, and had delivered in its money by the 10th. The county however held back and Savage had to report to the Duke that 'I find a Northampton and Warwicksheere infection in this Countye . . . to persuade and to bringe in there money must be a work of some tyme.'[66]

In doing this the basic method adopted by Savage was to demonstrate the benefits which followed from being helpful. To this end he wrote again to Buckingham on 6 February, urging the cause of some Chester merchants who had their goods impounded in a French ship at Beaumaris. He stressed that the request was from 'a body that will ever be ready to serve your Grace, itt being a cytty not rich but in all things most ready to . . . obeye His Majestie', and Buckingham duly responded. Savage also took up the city's case against a corrupt official, and eventually secured council backing for his dismissal.[67] These signs of approval were calculated to arouse the envy and sense of self-interest of the county, which had long been in competition for the Council's favour over a variety of matters ranging from local rates to broader questions of disputed jurisdiction. Savage recognized this and sought to push the process a little further by getting the Duke to secure a public recognition of the city's co-operation: 'if you would returne an answer to us how well His Majestie doth accept of it itt would do much good to the service in the adjacent shire'. A letter was duly sent containing fulsome assurances of the King's 'very gracious interpretation and acceptance of your forwardnes

[65] *APC 1627*, pp. 51, 98.

[66] PRO SP 16/53/18, 73. For the situation in Warwickshire: A. L. Hughes, 'Politics, Society and Civil War in Warwickshire 1620–50', (University of Liverpool Ph.D., 1980), pp. 163–9.

[67] PRO SP 16/53/28, 39; 57/12, 69; *APC 1627*, pp. 157–8, 165–6; *A Calendar of Chester City Council Minutes 1603–42*, ed. M. G. Groombridge (Lancs. and Cheshire Record Society, cvi, 1966), pp. 143–8.

and your good indeavors . . . and to lett you know that His Majestie will be mindfull of your dutifull and loving affecion in any occasion that shall be offered for the good of your said cittie'. This did the trick. By 10 March the county was co-operating, and most of the subsidymen had agreed to pay up.[68]

The Council's letter—assuming that its contents were widely known—seems to have worked on two levels. First of all it prompted the county governors to reconsider how the interests of the shire might best be served by touching on the long-standing rivalry with the city in which the Council was generally called on to act as final arbiter. It must have been clear to the Justices that such fulsome expressions of royal favour threatened to give the city a decisive advantage, and that ultimately the only way to prevent this was to respond with equal readiness. In the second place it may have worked at a personal level, particularly with the three leading signatories to the local commissioners' reply, Sir George Booth, Sir Richard Wilbraham, and Sir Richard Grosvenor. All three held markedly traditional views on the constitution, and they had probably refrained from supporting the loan initially because of fears about its consequences for the future of Parliament.[69] Alongside an exalted view of Parliament, however, they also fully accepted the supremacy of the monarch, and the need for obedience and loyalty, and this made it extremely difficult to hold back when the King's personal interest was demonstrated so clearly. The letter to Chester and another similar letter written to the shire—together with letters written in the King's name to most other counties—must have had much the same impact as the news of the King's involvement which was circulating at Court.[70] They confirmed that the loan was regarded as a crucial test of fidelity and therefore put added pressure on commissioners to make a choice one way or the other.

In Hampshire the main problem and priority for local inhabitants was the presence of soldiers, who had been billeted in the county since January 1626. By December there were about 650 of them dispersed in the larger towns throughout the shire and being supported on the local rates. The funds allocated to them by central government had run out in September, and the service was

[68] J. S. Morrill, *Cheshire 1630–1660* (Oxford, 1974), pp. 7–8; Lake, 'Ship Money in Cheshire', 45–52; PRO SP 16/53/18; 56/72; *APC 1627*, pp. 69–70.

[69] Morrill, *Cheshire*, pp. 58–9; Cust and Lake, 'Sir Richard Grosvenor', 40–53.

[70] *APC 1627* pp. 69–70, 158 and *passim*.

continued largely through the personal efforts of the Deputy Lieutenants.[71] This situation was not unusual late in 1626. All over the southern shires soldiers were being billeted and the central funds to pay for them were exhausted. The loan, however, presented a way out of this difficulty, as the Council seems to have recognized at an early stage. Prompted by a petition from Kent—and by that county's refusal to pay the loan 'till the regiment of soldiers there lodged shall be answered their pay'—they agreed that the money collected locally should be used to meet the needs of the soldiers; and this decision was confirmed on 29 November as part of the deliberately conciliatory approach adopted at this stage. In effect the Council was preparing to concede nearly £80,000 of loan money to the counties affected by billeting; but in return it stood to gain both administratively and politically.[72] Not only would this compensate for the shortage of funds available from the Exchequer and enable the billeting to continue in a relatively orderly fashion, it would also help to earn the council commissioners and local governors a considerable amount of goodwill. Thus when Lord Conway and Sir Richard Weston went down to the initial Hampshire meeting, at Winchester on 8 December, they were able to carry with them an extremely valuable concession.

The meeting was well attended, with some twenty-eight commissioners appearing. Eight of them immediately subscribed and paid in their money, but the remainder held back. This was the cue for Conway to start bargaining, and he later described how 'where wee found any doubtful and not coming in roundlie to the subscripcion and payment, wee dealt privatlie with them and by disabusing their owne apprehensions and shewing them the true reasons of this loane drew them to conformitie'. Precisely what apprehensions were disabused is not known, but they certainly included a concern over billeting payments, which Conway laid to rest with what Sir Thomas Jervoise, one of the commissioners and deputy lieutenants, described as 'your noble promise to the county that as they would be willinge to complye both to His Majestie's service and your lordship's desires you would be ever ready to assist them with your noble favour for that they may have a speedy satisfaction'. This seems to have convinced some of the commissioners, and twelve more of them immediately agreed to

[71] PRO E.179/272/10; BL Add MS 21, 922, fo. 79^{v}–85^{r}; HRO Jervoise MS 029.

[72] *C. and T.* i. 176; *APC 1626*, pp. 372, 388; PRO SP 16/85/77.

pay although not to subscribe to the loan's legality.[73] The effect of the promise, however, was even more apparent at the meetings with the subsidymen held in the following weeks. The commissioners for the New Forest division described how local taxpayers were eagerly awaiting council letters confirming Conway's undertaking 'which will cherish the good affeccones of the lenders and comfort the needie expectacon of a great many'; and Jervoise described how, in his Basingstoke division,

> the only labour at was to give them satisfaction that the soulders billetted upon them should be payd out of these monyes and also the conduct money . . . I after many disputes and promises . . . finding other partes of the contry to stand upon the same termes could find out no better way then to make sum reall performance of sum thinge to them, and thereupon I did issewe those monyes for the payment of Sir Sherfield Clapham's company, £6, and that did give so greate a satisfaction to the contry as after that difficulty was taken of we proseeded with much alacryty and I dare bouldly say it gained the Kinge a good sum of money.[74]

He was right. By February the Deputy Lieutenants were reporting that most of the county's three main divisions had subscribed and by 17 April £4,712 out of £7,514 had been paid over and then repaid to those who had incurred billeting charges.[75]

The financial benefit from these concessions was obvious, but this was not the only dividend. There were also less tangible political advantages which Jervoise alluded to when informing Conway of the county's reaction: 'it joyes my harte to see with what expressions of thankfulness to your lordship they both recieve and paie. I will not flatter, but do confidentlie beleeve there could not be a thinge done that doth do you more honour then the standing for your countrie's satisfaccon in which they see your power and desire to do them favour'.[76] Despite the disclaimer there undoubtedly was an element of flattery, or at least exaggeration, in this statement. The unease displayed by the commissioners over subscribing and the refusal to pay of several leading subsidymen—even after concessions had been granted—indicated that the broader constitutional implications of the levy

[73] HRO Jervoise MS 012/9, 10; 021/1, 34; 48/8 (N.B. Most of the documents in these boxes are unnumbered; the numbering is my own and roughly indicates the position in the box); Isle of Wight RO Oglander MS Box 17/105, 107.

[74] PRO SP 16/42/92; HRO Jervoise MS 48/8, 13, 14.

[75] HRO Jervoise MS 021/3, 33; 48/42, 53.

[76] PRO SP 16/54/77.

had not been entirely overlooked.[77] However Jervoise's statement does indicate the way in which the granting of concessions could offset some of the odium which those commissioners who co-operated in the service were likely to incur. Whatever the political doubts aroused by their actions, they could at least be seen to be acting as effective representatives of their county's interest, and this was a crucial element in their local reputation and standing. As Jervoise put it to Conway in another letter, through securing these concessions, 'you shall not only have power to commande, but assurance that what is commanded by you shalbe performed and thereby your ministers have more life and confidence to do acceptable servis, for where love and authority meetes together it ever provides of brave consequences'.[78]

The concession over billeting produced similar results elsewhere. The southern shires where it was granted were amongst the readiest loan-payers, and none witnessed the widespread opposition amongst ordinary subsidymen, apparent, for example, in Essex and Lincolnshire. In Sussex most of the money in the Lewes Rape was collected extremely rapidly, and payment in Pevensey was only delayed because of doubts about whether the Council would stick to its promises. In Berkshire the allowance was widely publicized, and was seen by Carleton and Banbury as largely responsible for the successful launching of the loan second time round.[79] And in Devon and Cornwall it relieved what was rapidly becoming a critical situation. The proximity of these two shires to Plymouth ensured that they had borne the brunt of billeting. Some 10,000 soldiers had been kept there since early in 1625 and the costs had been astronomical. Devon had been paid £11,000 out of the Exchequer and allocated a further £30,000 out of revenue from royal tin-mines, but this was not enough, and so much money had had to be found from local rates that by February 1627 inhabitants in Coulridge hundred—one of those worse affected—were in many cases owed the equivalent of ten, fifteen, or twenty times their subsidy assessment.[80] Concern over this transferred itself to the loan, so that in early February the south Devon commissioners were reporting that

the like sufferings of many hath laid a necessity upon them to make

[77] HRO Jervoise MS 012/9, 10, 15, 16; PRO SP 16/52/69; BL Add. MS 21, 922, fo. 86^{v}.

[78] HRO Jervoise MS 48/8.

[79] Fletcher, *A County Community*, pp. 195–6; PRO SP 16/49/34.

[80] *APC 1627*, p. 75; PRO E.351/288; 30/26/59.

> conditionary offers of lendinge, namely that if they might now be paid of the great charges which they have byn att in billettinge His Majestie's army . . . they would most willingly yeld to lend His Majestie by way of abatemente the somes proposed. . . . They are not ignorant that other counties have obtained the favour they desire to whom lesser somes have not byn so longe tyme due.

A similar plea went forward from Cornwall, and Sir George Chudleigh was dispatched to London to represent the two counties' case. It was supported in Council by Pembroke, the Lord Lieutenant of Cornwall, and by the end of the month the concession had been granted. This had the desired effect. Not only did it encourage payment and provide the Deputies with another source of revenue for billeting, it also helped to reinforce the sense of reciprocal trust and obligation on which effective links between centre and localities depended. As the Devon commissioners explained, in anticipating the concession from the Council, 'by this course your lordships shall infinitely establish His Majestie's honour and your owne justice in the hartes of the people to whom your lordships not long since vouchsafed the tytle of welldeservinge. . . Their trade almost overthrowne by the late imbargo will receave no little life by the stay of money amongst themselves . . . And they will be much encouraged in all future services'.[81]

This statement neatly encapsulated the benefits of the Council's approach when it came to dealing with the rather amorphous bodies of subsidymen and local governors in the shires. The most effective concession in such circumstances was the grant of a large repayment which put the loan money back in the pockets of the ordinary subsidymen and was sufficiently widely publicized to reflect credit on the local governors. When it came to dealing with the corporate towns, however, a slightly different emphasis often became appropriate. Here the most crucial consideration was winning the support of the local oligarchs, and this could often best be done by providing more narrowly for their financial and political interests.

To this end the Council was already furnished with several points of leverage. The economic decline suffered by many towns in the early seventeenth century had set several of these oligarchic groups at loggerheads with their own citizens, and in this situation they looked to the Council to bolster their position and maintain order. The warfare and trade depression of the 1620s

[81] PRO SP 16/53/96; *APC 1627*, pp. 75–6, 107–8; Devon RO Exeter Corpn. MS 60D. nos. 286, 295.

added to these pressures, making commercial interests dependent on the Council for protection against piracy and the disruption of trade, and local inhabitants reliant on it for help with fortifications and ordnance. In addition the demands for money and troops generated disputes over ratings and jurisdiction in which the Council played a key role as arbiter.[82] The effect of these circumstances can be demonstrated by looking at some of the towns of Norfolk and Suffolk.

For the ports of this area the most crucial consideration in 1627 was whether their fishing fleet would be able to make its annual journey to the North Sea and Iceland. The previous year this had been impossible because the Council had failed to provide an escort against the Dunkirkers, and the resulting loss of livelihood was claimed to have cost some £10,000 to £15,000, as well as the employment of several hundred local inhabitants.[83] The ports clearly recognized their dependence on the Council and, moreover seem to have understood that its readiness to help them was linked to their response to its demands for money. This had been apparent at the time of the benevolence, in August 1626, when the Suffolk JPs had informed their Lord Lieutenant that the 'said service was exceedinglye retarded . . . by lowde cries from the inhabitants neare the sea coasts, averringe that their shippes were taken and fired in their havens before their faces insomuch as they durst not look out of there portes, to the great impoverishinge of them in their trade of fishinge and other commerce by the sea'. The Lord Lieutenant, the Earl of Suffolk, had passed this on to the Duke, acting in his capacity as Lord Admiral, and at the same time had hinted at a possible bargain: 'if your Lordship hould it convenient to make unto me some such answere that may shew your particular care for reddres and the peoples ease . . . I shall not faile to make the best advantag I can. . .'. Buckingham, however, was more concerned with vindicating themself from any possible charge of negligence and he responded by simply reminding the local inhabitants that for the King to be able to help them they must make a contribution towards his needs.[84] On this occasion nothing concrete came out of the negotiations; however a few

[82] Hirst, *Representative of the People?*, pp. 44–50; J. T. Evans, *Seventeenth Century Norwich* (Oxford, 1979), pp. 62–4; B. E. Supple, *Commercial Crisis and Change in England 1600–42* (Cambridge, 1959), Chs. 3, 5; L. Boynton, *The Elizabethan Militia* (1967), pp. 37–40, 270.

[83] PRO SP 16/42/102.

[84] PRO SP 16/34/17; 17i; Minnesota University Library MS 435 (Suffolk lieutenancy book), fo. 27.

months later the process seems to have been repeated. In mid-December Suffolk came down to the county to launch the loan and doubtless put it to the taxpayers that they could only expect help if they first of all demonstrated their loyalty in this service. They duly co-operated, and a few days later Aldeburgh, Southwold, Dunwich, and Walberswick were petitioning the Council for ships. This time help was forthcoming. Buckingham's admiralty secretary, Nicholas, advised that 'for many important reasons' the petition was to be supported, and the Duke himself persuaded the King, sitting in Council, to grant it. The towns received an escort of four warships, and the £1,768 needed to pay for these was provided from the loan.[85]

This constituted a fairly straightforward quid pro quo, similar to the help given to Chester. Both sides would appear to have understood what was involved and the process of exchanging favours proceeded relatively smoothly. On other occasions, however, the process of negotiation was a good deal more roundabout, as can be illustrated by looking at the inland town of Norwich.

From the start of the service the Norwich aldermen had taken great pains to show their support. They had provided a £50 banquet for the council commissioners, and followed this up by appointing collectors as soon as the meeting was over and thereafter responding promptly to each new set of council instructions. There may well have been more in the appearance than in the substance of what they did, but, even so, their display of zeal was notable. As late as August 1627 167 subsidymen in Norwich had still failed to pay the loan, and there were indications that their resistance was making life difficult for the aldermen. Earlier, in February, one of the town preachers had been censured for having 'much upbrayded Mr. Maior and the Bretheren', and during September there was a particularly unruly shrieval election in which, against the aldermen's wishes, the freemen selected the obstreperous John Kettle.[86] In such circumstances, vigorous support for the loan was hardly calculated to calm things down. It becomes understandable only if we look at the incentives which the Council could offer for co-operation.

In the first place—as Professor Evans had demonstrated—it could make or break the aldermen in their struggles with the

[85] *Rous*, p. 8; BL Add. MS 39, 245, fo. 116–17; PRO SP 16/42/102; *APC 1627*, pp. 2–3; HMC *Various*, iv. 292, 305.

[86] NNRO Norwich MCB 1624–34, fos. 123, 124^{v}, 125^{v}, 127^{r}, 139^{r}; PRO SP 16/75/52, 94; Evans, *Norwich*, pp. 73–5.

freemen. These had arisen largely because the aldermen were trying to control elections by methods which were not sanctioned in their charter. During 1619 this had led to a dispute over the choice of mayor which was only resolved with the help of the Council and assize judges; and in 1627 the problem was blowing up again to culminate in the contest over the shrievalty. In these circumstances it was more than usually important for the aldermen to be able to defend their interpretation of the charter, and here they were in a very vulnerable position because, since 1625, it had been under review as part of a process of *quo warranto*.[87]

The *quo warranto* applied to a number of towns at the beginning of the new King's reign, and the outcome was of sufficient concern to cause Exeter to lay out £361 over three years and Gloucester to employ two aldermen for long periods in London.[88] Normally there was little doubt about privileges being renewed. James and Charles pursued a policy of supporting narrow oligarchies in order, as the Council explained to Norwich, that 'the orderly gouvernment of cittie and corporacions should be mayneteined, and that popular and factious humors that trouble the same should be suppreſt and punisht'.[89] However favourable treatment could not be guaranteed. Charles expected the Corporations to co-operate over the loan, and where they failed to do so they were liable to the sort of harassment that Londoners faced in mid-1627 when

> they are persuaded if the term could be conveniently removed from hence, His Majesty would willingly be brought to deprive them of the benefit thereof, and to have it transported and settled in some other part . . . And as they say he doth intend to keep his Court out of this place as long and as much as he can hereafter, purposing at this present . . . after he hath spent some time at Hampton, to where he is lately removed, to withdraw himself to Newmarket till Christmas.[90]

In the event Norwich was clearly thought to have done enough. The charter was eventually renewed on the old terms and in November 1627 the Council also upheld the Corporation's

[87] Evans, *Norwich*, pp. 66–76; NNRO Norwich Assembly Bk. 1613–42, fos. 216^r, 217^v, 225^r.

[88] W. T. MacCaffrey, *Exeter 1540–1640* (Harvard, 1958), p. 28; GRO Gloucester Borough Records, B8/13.

[89] *APC 1627–8*, pp. 140–1; Hirst, *Representative of the People?*, pp. 47–50.

[90] *C. and T.* i. 269.

proceedings against Kettle.[91] However this was not the only issue of immediate concern to the aldermen. They also faced a demand for ship money.

This had first arisen in July 1626 when the town was ordered to pay one-third of the costs of Yarmouth. The aldermen had protested, and as the risk of invasion passed the Council had allowed the demand to lapse. However it was revived in December 1626, just as the loan was being launched in the county. A good deal was at stake for Norwich. Not only was the town being asked to pay £900—which along with the £1,372 demanded for the loan would have stretched its taxpayers—but it also stood to lose from the precedent which would be created. This was particularly significant, because, as the aldermen pointed out, Norwich had previously paid only one-tenth or one-twelfth of the defence charges levied on Yarmouth. To accept one-third now would expose it to all sorts of additional demands in the future. At the end of January 1627, therefore, they pleaded for relief on the grounds of poverty, and hoped that this would be the end of the levy. Notwithstanding on 24 March the Council made a second demand and specifically ordered the town to contribute one-third. At this point the aldermen decided to change their tactics and, instead of simply begging, pointed out that the options open to it were limited. They reiterated the pleas of poverty and then asked that

> wee may be either freed from this taxacon or that some equalle apportionment of charges between them and us in this and other busynes may be sett downe accordinge to the presidents of former tymes . . . for the noyse of the taxacon hindreth the payment of the loane, and the earnest endeavour to procure payment of the loane will occasion the none payment of the entended assessment, unles yt may be sorted to so small a summe as may be warranted by former presidents.[92]

In essence the Council was being offered a deal. The aldermen were saying that they could go on collecting the loan money only if the ship money demand was reduced or dropped. However this was a deal which cut both ways. The Council may well have recognized the force of Norwich's arguments, but its response was to make no reply and keep its governors in suspense, whilst quietly allowing the demand to lapse.[93] This had the effect of

[91] Evans, *Norwich*, pp. 76, 81; *APC 1627–8*, pp. 140–1.

[92] *APC 1626*, pp. 150–1; *APC 1627*, pp. 160–1; PRO SP 16/35/1; 52/3; 61/83.

[93] See below, p. 133.

putting the ball back in Norwich's court. It had much to gain from relief from ship money, but in order for its pleas to carry conviction it had—on its own terms—to go on collecting the loan as vigorously as possible. If it failed to do this it would be defaulting on its side of the bargain, and would be giving the Council an opening for reimposing the demand. Hence the existence of this additional levy—with all it entailed in terms of ratings and precedents—served to provide an additional incentive for co-operation.

The response of the Norwich aldermen appears to have been fairly typical. Corporations were generally readier to support the loan than benches of county magistrates, in part, at least, because of their even more direct dependence on the Council. One of the clearest demonstrations of this was provided by the Lincolnshire port of Boston. This was an early centre of opposition to the loan, organized around the Mayor and a group of puritan aldermen and freemen, all of whom were connected with the charismatic local minister, John Cotton. However these men did not have things all their own way, and the levy opened up a split—which may already have been in existence—within the aldermanic bench. At least half of the aldermen were merchants and their main priority was to protect the town's financial and economic interests which, through a combination of circumstances, were almost completely at the mercy of the Council.[94] In the first place Boston was involved in a dispute with the county over the cost of repairs to sluice gates which were vital to prevent the port from silting up. After years of wrangling the aldermen had appealed to the Council for help and were still awaiting their verdict. Secondly the town was also facing a demand for ship money which it maintained would cost the equivalent of sixteen subsidies, over three times the amount demanded for the loan. And thirdly, like Norwich, Boston also faced a *quo warranto* on its charter which, as the aldermen said, 'occasioneth very chardgeable expence in the present and threatneth ruine and overthrowe to the corporacon if the same be prosecuted'. There was clearly a good deal to be

[94] See below, p. 172. Six of the twelve Aldermen—Thomas Askham, John Cannock, Leonard Cannock, John Wright, William Barnabye, and John Thorpe—were described as merchants: *The Port Books of Boston, 1601–60* ed. R. W. K. Hinton (Lincs.Rec. Soc. 50, 1956), pp. xxxiv–xxxviii, 64, 223. No connection has been traced between these men and Cotton and the Puritans; indeed the Cannocks were to the fore as accusers of the nonconformists in 1634: M. Spurrell, *The Puritan Town of Boston* (History of Boston Ser. 5, 1972), p. 17.

gained from co-operation with the Council, and this helps to explain why, on 7 March, the aldermen, presumably at the behest of the merchants, resolved that 'in case Mr. Maior at the meetinge at Lincoln . . . be asked and urged by the said commissioners in the behalf of the corporacon concerning the same loane, that then the said Mr. Maior shall yeald and assent to the same in the behalfe of the corporation'.[95] This decision was evidently not unanimous because two days later the Mayor and two of the aldermen went to the commissioners' meeting and refused to pay. However there was sufficient support on the remainder of the bench for collection to proceed, and by 14 June £400 had been paid into the Exchequer.[96]

From the Council's point of view the timing of the *quo warrantos* and ship money levy was peculiarly opportune. It is therefore worth considering whether it deliberately manipulated these demands to create more advantageous conditions for the loan. In the case of *quo warrantos* this seems to be unlikely, since most of the processes were begun long before the loan was launched.[97] With ship money however the situation was rather different and the circumstances surrounding it might lead one to suspect that the object was not simply to provide ships.

This levy was very widespread, and involved all the major ports, as well as inland trading centres and a number of counties. Some of these produced lists of precedents to show that they had been more favourably rated in 1597, and others complained that ship money would amount to several times the cost of the loan.[98] They therefore had everything to gain from seeing ship money dropped, even at the cost of collecting the loan; and in response to their petitions the Council gave a series of hints that this was about to happen. After reviving the initial demand in December 1626, it summoned representatives from the towns to attend a meeting in February 1627. There they were simply told that nothing had been decided and that they must continue 'to attend till by their

[95] C. Holmes, *Seventeenth Century Lincolnshire* (History of Lincs., 7, 1980) pp. 99–101; PRO SP 16/52/31; 61/18, 19; 524/119, 119i; Boston Guildhall, Boston Council Minute Book 2, 1608–1638, fo. 200r, 210, 216r.

[96] PRO SP 16/56/39; E.401/2323, 'Collectoribus mutuum a communalitat'.

[97] Evans is incorrect in asserting that the proceedings against Norwich were begun as a punishment for defaulting over ship money; here and elsewhere they started much earlier: Evans, *Norwich*, p. 81; NNRO Norwich A. B. 1613–42, fo. 216r, 217v, 225r; MacCaffrey, *Exeter*, p. 28; GRO Gloucester Borough Records, B8/13; Boston Guildhall, Boston C.M.B.2, fo. 218; J. W. F. Hill, *Tudor and Stuart Lincoln* (Cambridge, 1956), p. 120.

[98] Bodl. L. Firth MS c.4, p. 326; PRO SP 16/59/52, 55; 60/64; 61/17.

lordshipps they shalbe discharged'. Meanwhile the petitions continued to pour in, and in response to one of these, from Hull, the Council decided, 'for some reasons best known to themselves', to release the town from its charge. However three weeks later, on 24 March, this decision was reversed and Hull, along with the other towns and counties, was ordered to pay the charges as originally laid down. This produced a further batch of pleading and indignant letters, and in response to these the Council decided to form a committee to consider the future of the levy. This is the last one hears of it, but the towns were never told of any final decision, and as a result were left on tenterhooks, expecting a revival of the demand as soon as the fleet sailed for La Rochelle and left the coasts unguarded.[99]

All this was very helpful to the Council. Several towns responded as Norwich did and went on collecting the loan in the hope that this would free them from ship money. Exeter, for example appealed to the Council's sense of fair play, by pointing out that its taxpayers had 'submitted themselves in the hope of beinge freede from this and further disbursements'; whilst Yarmouth took a more forceful line, emphasizing to its High Steward, Marlborough, that 'yf these heavy burthens shalbe imposed upon the commons of our towne according as they are required . . . they would, by the conceite of impossibility of performance, rather breed a confusion and bee a great cause of difficulty to both then procure any conformity in either'.[100] The corollary of these pleas was, of course, that the towns be seen to be raising at least their fair share of the loan, and this doubtless encouraged the aldermen to stick at the service. How far the Council recognized all this, however, and calculated accordingly, is unclear. There is certainly something odd about this particular ship money levy. If the intention was really to create a second fleet then it was going about this task in what was—even by its own standards—a peculiarly haphazard fashion. The timing was also suspicious. It was pointless to ask for the ships in the middle of winter—when there was no emergency and they could be of no immediate use—unless the primary objective lay elsewhere. However to argue from this that the ship money levy was an ingenious manœuvre to bolster the loan would perhaps to be to impute too much subtlety to the Council. It seems more likely that the benefits were largely accidental, and that the meanderings

[99] *APC 1626*, pp. 447; *APC 1627*, pp. 48–9, 125, 159–61, 230.

[100] PRO SP 16/60/64; YRO 18/6, fo. 233^{v}.

over ship money were yet another example of the Council's inability to keep track of its decisions or to pursue a coherent policy during wartime.[101] Accepting this, however, the episode does also indicate that the Council possessed a basic political acumen. At least it could recognize that ship money was unlikely to succeed and that abandonment of it would be taken as helpful recognition of the towns' support elsewhere.

This principle of quid pro quo was central to the Council's success in securing co-operation over the loan. Its ability to proceed in this way—rather than through straightforward coercion—was a function of its position, in the absence of a Parliament, as the principal source of power at the centre of the political system.[102] As such it combined a variety of executive and judicial roles, being at the same time responsible both for raising supply and distributing the resources which this provided it with. These resources could take a variety of forms, ranging from material benefits—such as the money to repay billeting charges, or the ships and ordnance needed for coastal defence—to judicial decisons—whether in arbitrating factional disputes or clashes over ratings and jurisdiction—to political inducements—which included assurances of future favours and threats of the King's displeasure. Whatever their nature, all of these provided valuable points of purchase when it came to dealing with local governors. Local society, even in the most stable circumstances was far from monolithic, and in this period tended to divide more than ever as a result of ratings disputes and competition for resources. These divisions worked to the Council's advantage since they helped to transform local society into a series of interest groups, competing for conciliar favour on the understanding that this would be forthcoming only if they co-operated over its main priority, the collection of the loan. In this situation it was ideally placed to pursue a policy of divide and rule.[103]

This again illustrates the extent to which implementation of the Council's decisions was at bottom a political process. The dealings with local commissioners and aldermen were strongly reminiscent of the negotiations being conducted with various

[101] Hirst, 'Privy Council and enforcement', 54.

[102] Lake, 'Ship money in Cheshire', 51–5.

[103] D. Hirst, 'Court, country and politics before 1629', in *Faction and Parliament*, pp. 125–7. This situation is analogous to that existing during the Civil War when different groups at a local level were competing for favourable decisions in Parliament: A. L. Hughes, 'The King, the Parliament and the localities during the English Civil War', *JBS* xxiv (1985), 242–51, 260–3.

individuals around the Court. This whole process was unusually visible at the time of the loan, largely because of the gatherings held out in the shires which provided councillors and local governors with a rare opportunity to meet face to face and on something like equal terms. As both sides well knew the Council's desperate need for money impelled it to make substantial concessions and stick to them. In these circumstances, then, one sees what were basically the normal processes of contact between the centre and localities being thrown into relief and shown up in an exceptionally clear and straightforward fashion.

Perhaps the most difficult issue in all this is deciding how far the Council's actions were the result of deliberate calculation. It has been demonstrated that with the meeting on 27 November it took a conscious decision to try to raise the money by more conciliatory methods, and that these accorded with the political perceptions of moderate councillors. It has also been shown that the Council recognized the principle that one favour deserved another.[104] However beyond this it is difficult to offer any definite conclusion. The shifts over ship money were just as likely to have been a result of the Council's inadequacies as conscious planning; and for all its readiness to reward those who had co-operated the contrasting fortunes of Buckinghamshire and Devon demonstrated that much still depended on individual access to those with power. In these circumstances it is perhaps safest to conclude that its actions were as much accidental as calculated, the outcome of what Lake has described as 'the deep interdependence that bound the centre to the localities'.[105]

This emphasis on co-operation, however, begs important questions about the role of coercion in the collection of the loan. If so much depended on the recognition of mutual benefits why was there still considerable opposition; and if so much was the result of consent why did it earn the epithet 'forced'? Ultimately, questions like these need to be considered in the light of contemporary understanding of the Crown's intentions and the ideological framework within which the levy was perceived, and some attempt will be made to do this in the next chapter. However it is also relevant to look more closely at the place of coercion within the Council's scheme for raising the levy, and the consequences which followed from adopting forceful methods.

[104] See above, pp. 127–8. [105] Lake, 'Ship money in Cheshire', 54.

As we have seen, historians of the loan—notably Gardiner, Barnes, and Holmes—have tended to emphasize the part played by enforcement, and there is certainly no shortage of contemporary testimony to support their verdicts.[106] Those involved in collection frequently advocated a rigorous application of coercion, particularly where they were encountering extensive opposition. To cite just one instance, the Bishop of Worcester, in May 1627, was quick to remind councillors that requests from above, unsupported by actual punishments,

> moveth little or nothing froward minds. Wherefore I who sate for this service at least ten times, and observed the dispositions, shifts and evasion of men, doe intreate, that two purseventes . . . may be sent to the commissioners of Worcestershire with a letter to send up such refractory persons as wilfully deny their loane or refuse their appearance . . . The very shewe of the pursyvantes (as I am persuaded) will bring the King a thowsand poundes more then otherwise His Majestie is like to have.[107]

This sort of line tended to be argued most vehemently by those commissioners who felt least confident about their local standing and who were therefore particularly dependent on the Council. A good example was the plea from the two commissioners in the Holland division of Lincolnshire who urged the Council to consider that 'the not questioninge of the froward hath discouraged diverse that were forward, and they had soe infected one the other that, until very lately, these parts were in a great revolt . . . wee know assuredlye that upon the noyse of trouble to the most perverse, or a pursevant with a blanke (as the Lordes did threaten at Lincoln) all wilbe consummate on a suddaine'. Doubtless there was more to this than simply a concern with the collection of money. The experience of continually being defied and disobeyed must have been extremely uncomfortable and probably had an adverse effect on their local credit, particularly as these two were the only commissioners to participate in collection in this area.[108] In these circumstances it was crucial that the Council be seen to be upholding the actions of its servants, as the Earl of Northampton recognized in urging Conway to support the Gloucestershire commissioners: 'it may be very fit and expedient that the country might see that those that refused to lend, or absented themselves from attending the service might not pass so freely away. For it may embolden others to the like and make us suffer largely who

[106] See above, p. 93.
[107] PRO SP 16/64/53.
[108] PRO SP 16/71/50.

have been most industrious in His Majesties service and be laughed at for our pains . . . and every day subject to censure or contempt'.[109]

Statements like this undoubtedly struck a receptive chord with councillors. Conway responded to Northampton's letter by urging his fellow secretary, Coke, to take punitive measures against Gloucestershire:

> whereas there are 200 men to be leavied in Worcestershire . . . it being but a small countie, and a county which hath been much charged and hath ever willingly paid both in loans and otherwise . . . And Gloucestershire is a greater shire . . . And they having beene desperately averse to the last loane if they should now goe free and Worcestershire be burdened it would be a laughter for those of Gloucester and discouragement to those of Worcester . . . for equitie's sake and for the advantage of the King's service, I should thinke it more fitt that Gloucestershire should bear a larger part.[110]

Elsewhere Coke himself, in spite of his evident desire to minimise the divisions caused by the loan, explained the practical advantages of maintaining pressure on refusers: 'wee heare daily that the shires in al partes readily consent to the loanes: but the paiments come in slowly and I feare if some further course be not taken to call upon them they may gather confidence out of neglect. I could therefore wish that some commandment were sent from His Majestie to require the board to press for paiments in a more earnest manner'.[111] And other members of the Council would appear to have seen the sense in this advice, continuing the vigorous efforts made in the early stages of the loan into and beyond the summer of 1627. In this they were again supported by the King. He sat in Council during several discussions relating to the loan and issued specific instructions to cover contingencies such as the removal of prisoners into the counties. He also demanded regular reports of proceedings, personally examined several rolls of lenders, on his own initiative ordered a Proclamation for apprehending trouble-makers in Lincolnshire and even insisted on councillors forgoing their summer holidays to keep up the pressure for payment.[112] In response the Council displayed

[109] PRO SP 16/56/12.

[110] Melb. H Cowper MS Bdl. 28.

[111] PRO SP 16/56/1.

[112] *C. and T.* i. 261; *APC 1627*, pp. 140, 142, 422, 492; PRO SP 16/68/28; 71/25, 28, 44; 72/28; *Proclamations*, ii. 138–40; HMC *Buccleuch*, i. 266.

considerable persistence. Queries about eligibility to pay the loan were given detailed consideration and answered promptly to avoid delaying the service. Every month rolls of lenders were perused, and as a result the Council was sometimes able to send lists of defaulters to the local commissioners. And after the Duke's departure for Rhé in June, when councillors had more time for the service, they stepped up their efforts and proceeded 'at every sitting to call some before them (who have been certefied for refusers) and to committ them yf they continew soe, and doe dayly send out new warrants for fetching up of those whoe are certefied from severall counties'. Finally all this was complemented by reminders to the commissioners. On 22 June 1627 some forty-three JPs and Lords Lieutenant were removed from office to confirm the King's disapproval of those who had resisted, and then on 30 June and 20 August council circulars were sent round, calling on commissioners to re-summon defaulters and interrogate collectors.[113]

As Hirst has shown this level of application was unusual and contrasted very favourably with the Council's efforts over the militia;[114] however this alone is not enough to demonstrate the overriding significance of enforcement. The collection of money was never simply a matter of the Council issuing orders and then compelling obedience. It was a more complex process which required the co-operation of local governors and the balancing of different interests, and in these circumstances coercion was not always regarded as beneficial. Although, as we have seen, there were some local governors ready to stress its importance, there were others who regarded its effect as limited, and, in some situations, as positively disadvantageous. This can be better appreciated if we look in more detail at the task of collection in the shires, and the best documented in this respect is probably Norfolk.

Here, as in the majority of shires, most of the money was eventually collected; however the problems involved varied considerably from one area to another. In the western division of Freebridge Marshland, Freebridge Citra Lynn, and Clacklose, for example, there was little open opposition, but collection still demanded considerable persistence on the part of local commissioners. Led by the industrious Deputy Lieutenant, Sir John Hare, they made a rapid start to the service, and by 13 February had

[113] *APC 1627*, pp. 91–2, 113, 194–5, 243, 387, 395, 492–3; PRO SP 16/71/28; C.231/4. fo. 227, 259–62; BRL Coventry MS Commissions of the peace, 69–74.

[114] Hirst, 'Privy Council and enforcement', 52.

secured payment of £1,150 out of £1,369. Before July the deficit had been whittled down to £51. 3*s.* 4*d.*, most of which was owed by individuals who had died or whose estates had diminished since the previous subsidy. The five remaining defaulters were re-summoned during July and August, and three were persuaded to pay; but with the remaining two, little could be done because further action depended on the Council which, after being notified of the defaulters on at least two occasions, had simply failed to respond.[115]

This pattern of local initiative, supported with varying degrees of efficiency by the Council, was repeated elsewhere. In the southern division of Diss, Eresham, Henstead, and Deepwade the commissioners faced a mixture of delays and evasions which was overcome largely through their personal tact and persistence. By 5 February Owen Sheppard, another of the more active local governors, had returned a list of lenders to the Exchequer and had also made an enquiry about how to deal with the difficult cases of women lenders and those who were either absent from the county or who held most of their property in town. For once the Council responded promptly—mainly due to the efforts of Sir John Suckling whom Sheppard had contacted—and a comprehensive reply was dispatched which was then circulated amongst the commissioners. However it was still up to them to interpret this, and it was here that their common sense and experience counted for a good deal. Sheppard acted as generously as he could, granting exemptions on over one-seventh of the total payments due.[116] He was also careful to avoid giving offence to local gentlemen, such as Thomas Knyvett of Ashwellthorpe who from the start of the service had been looking for a way to evade payment, either by claiming his privilege as an official of the mint or offsetting the cost against his earlier privy seal loan. Knyvett's sympathies may well have been with the refusers since at the time he was in close contact with Sir John Heveningham and relatives of John Hampden; however technically he had done nothing wrong, and for Sheppard to treat him as a defaulter would have been to risk antagonizing an important local landowner. The commissioner therefore waited his opportunity and delayed until May before politely reminding Knyvett 'that some course may be taken for payment of your loan

115 *Musters, Beacon, Subsidies, Ship Money etc.*, pp. 84–9; PRO SP 16/75/94.

116 PRO SP 16/53/33; *APC 1627*, pp. 79–80; *Musters, Beacons, Subsidies, Ship Money etc.*, pp. 51–2.

money to the King for the collector cannot avoid to certify those that refuse any longer'.[117] This approach appears ultimately to have done the trick. Knyvett himself seems to have contributed—since he was not listed as a defaulter later in the summer—and in September, after appointing 'severall dayes of meeting for the partyes that were behinde', Sheppard and his fellow commissioners were able to persuade some thirty lenders, out of the fifty-nine still outstanding, to pay up.[118]

Similar persistence was also evident amongst the four commissioners in the northern division of North and South Erpingham, Holt, and Eynesford, this time after a nudge from the Council. They had been active for the early part of the service, but had then devolved responsibility to the collectors. This turned out to be a mistake as it was discovered in August that several collectors had been reducing assessments for certain subsidymen and then recovering the arrears from those who were poor or exempt. The Council demanded an inquiry and this not only exposed the full extent of the abuse, but also revealed that a good deal of money was still owing from absentees and individuals who had never been charged. The commissioners therefore gave the collectors a dressing down and strict instructions 'to perswade the refusers to lende and to give us tymely notice of the retorninge hom of the loane flyers'. This seems to have produced the desired effect. The collectors returned to those who had not paid and uncovered several blatant cases of evasion; commissioners and collectors then put renewed pressure on those still in default; and their combined efforts eventually brought in much of the money which was still owing: £50 out of £94 in the case of South Erpingham, £35 out of £38 for North Erpingham and £13 out of £24. 2*s*. for Holt.[119]

In all of the divisions considered hitherto the task of collection was supervised by resident commissioners. If none of these were active there were additional difficulties, as was the case in Tunstead, Taverham, and Happing where the main work was left entirely in the hands of the local collectors, Jonas and Lionel Pytt. The Pytts were industrious and conscientious enough, but with the leading local landowner, Sir John Corbett, opposing the service, they felt in need of additional support; so, on 23 February,

[117] BL Eg. MS 2715, fo. 322; NNRO Rye MS 72/2588, 2591; *The Knyvett Letters 1620–1644*, ed. B. Schofield (1949), pp. 72–4.

[118] PRO SP 16/75/94; 76/24.

[119] PRO E.179/153/604; SP 16/74/60, 60 i.

when they travelled up to London to pay in their receipts, Jonas 'attended the counsaile board . . . for some course from thence for the drawinge in the money from such as were slack or stubborne defaulters or recusants'.[120] The Council's response was clumsy and hesitant. The Pytts were told to inform the Clerk that they needed a messenger, but nothing was done until mid-April, when after securing the help of Sir Thomas Edmonds, an order was issued to send John Peniall into the shire. Peniall, however, must have been unavailable for on 30 April another messenger, Edward Wickens, was appointed. He finally reached Norfolk late in June.[121]

Wickens's presence proved to be something of a mixed blessing. He helped to uncover the abuses in North and South Erpingham, Holt, and Eynesford, and the threat of immediate delivery into his custody seems to have persuaded at least four defaulters to pay up at a meeting on 21 August. However he was of little help to the Pytts, largely because he had been so late in arriving. In February they had had arrears of £216. 3*s*. 4*d*. which through their own efforts had been reduced to £54. 5*s*. 8*d*. by 7 June; and this sum was still outstanding when Wickens left the shire in September.[122] Moreover his heavy-handed methods caused considerable disruption and embarrassment, especially in the case of the widow Spalding. She had refused to pay the 40*s*. assessed on her dead husband because his property had passed to her son who had moved away from home. The local collector, however, was reluctant to accept this and came to visit her one evening with Wickens in tow. At first the widow appeared not to be at home, but

> Wiggens swore he would find her. And at length finding her he tooke hold of her and told her that he came for money and money he would have before he went. Whereunto she answered that she had none. Whereupon he told her that she must then goe with him before the commissioners; and she being unwilling to goe out of her house at that tyme of the nyght . . . he dragged her along the ground out of her house and threatened to make her goe or he would tye her to his horse . . . But she crying out and making a great noyse they were at last content to lett her alone . . .

The messenger's actions constituted little short of assault and the aggrieved widow immediately began legal proceedings, which was

[120] PRO SP 16/59/48; 77/11 ii.
[121] PRO SP 16/79/70; *APC 1627*, pp. 78–9, 221–2, 255–6.
[122] PRO SP 16/74/59, 59i; 74/60; 77/11, 11ii.

the last thing either the local commissioners or the Council wanted. Up to this point the service had proceeded relatively smoothly in the shire, and public prosecution of a council messenger could not but be a considerable setback. They therefore combined to prevent the prosecution: the local commissioners, including Sheppard, interviewing the widow and mollifying her by laying the blame on Wickens and freeing her from payment; whilst the Council summoned her attorney and apparently persuaded him to drop the case.[123] A major check was therefore narrowly avoided and the process of collection could continue as before. However the whole episode provided a salutory reminder of the dangers of outsiders intervening and pressing enforcement too far. It also highlighted the importance of the men on the spot.

This was something which emerged again and again in the course of collecting the loan. However vigilant the Council might be, it obviously lacked the resources and manpower to supervise every aspect of the service; as in other areas of its work, it was therefore compelled to entrust a good deal of responsibility to local governors and local collectors. In the event this often turned out to be an advantage. These officials possessed the experience and knowledge needed to deal with local taxpayers, and were able to streamline and adapt the formal processes. In some cases their initiatives actually speeded up the process of collection: for example, in the Basingstoke division of Hampshire, where Sir Thomas Jervoise and his two fellow commissioners held a series of six meetings in five weeks, most of the money was brought in well inside the two months generally allowed by the Council. Their industry and attention to detail was also impressive. In Havering Liberty in Essex the collector spent much of December 1626 chasing up the sixty-five subsidymen who had either offered excuses or not been at home when he first called, and by the middle of the following January fifty-five of these had paid up. Similarly in the Devon division of Exminister and Wondeford East the two local commissioners interviewed over 400 subsidymen before presenting the collector with a roll of names sorted into those who had agreed to pay, those who could be excused as paupers, those who were absent and those who had refused.[124] This sort of activity and persistence was priceless to the Council and, of course, it was not something which could be secured

[123] PRO SP 16/44/15.

[124] HRO Jervoise MS 012/1; 021/11, 17, 20, 29; PRO SP 16/44/8; 52/64; 30/26/59.

simply by threats and coercion. As we have seen a crucial role was played by the subtler inducements offered through the initial meetings and the continuing contact with the centre; and just as these subtler inducements set the tone for contact between councillors and commissioners so they often predominated when it came to face to face dealings with the subsidymen.

There were good reasons for this which went beyond the simple consideration of how best to get the money in. For those commissioners who co-operated with the service the most difficult problem was often one of reconciling efficient performance with continued enjoyment of the esteem of their neighbours. The issues raised by the levy meant that it could rarely be treated as just another administrative task. The commissioners had constantly to take into consideration the political significance of what they were doing and the ways in which this would affect both their ability to perform the task and their own local reputations. In these circumstances they generally opted for the discreet methods of someone like Owen Sheppard, and, rather than leaping in heavy-handed, preferred to mobilize the 'powers, favours and creditts' which went with their position as landowners and local governors. Lord Maynard, for example, continued to demonstrate the effectiveness of these in his native Essex hundred of Dunmow. In spite of the opposition to the loan on the nearby estates of the Earl of Warwick and Sir Francis Barrington, he reported in July 1627, that he had obtained 'more money than any other part of the Country' and had delayed certifying refusers 'onely in hope to gett in the money by faire meanes'. In this situation punishment was something best kept in reserve, as was appreciated even by the hard-pressed Lincolnshire commissioners cited earlier, who explained that they had forborne requesting council help as long as possible 'in good expectacon to procure the people with gentlenes (for they be our neighbours)'.[125] Indeed, as we have seen in the case of Wickens, Council intervention could in itself create difficulties. This was the case in Yorkshire where the service was threatened with disruption when Sir Henry Savile, a West Riding commissioner, was ordered to summon his respected friend and neighbour Sir Thomas Wentworth. Savile was a conscientious local governor who tried hard to soften the impact of demands like the loan, and it seems likely that he had refrained from summoning Wentworth on previous occasions not

[125] PRO SP 16/71/50; 72/44.

only to avoid personal embarrassment, but also because this would have the effect of driving a powerful opponent out into the open. Faced with a direct command from the Council, however, he had little choice but to comply; and eventually the situation was rescued only because Wentworth chose to plead illness and then answer before the Council in London.[126]

These examples should suffice to demonstrate that coercion was not always thought appropriate and that when employed it required careful handling. This is not to say that it was not of considerable importance. Clearly taxpayers needed to be made to realize that if they did not pay up they were liable to be punished; and without the councillors taking a firm line the service in some shires would have failed to get off the ground. None the less, it is also evident that, like most policies relying on deterrence, coercion worked best until the Council had to carry out its threats. Whenever it did so it risked crossing the narrow divide between making an example and creating a martyr.

Unfortunately over the loan the latter often proved to be the outcome. Out of well over 100 refusers summoned before the Council only eight were recorded in the register as having submitted and agreed to pay. Others may have gone unrecorded, but there is little doubt that the majority of those interviewed remained obstinate. They were generally able to stand up to the ordeal and even, in some cases, to take advantage of it to publicize their cause more widely.[127] There were, of course exceptions, of which perhaps the most beneficial to the Council was Sir Nathaniel Barnardiston. He was one of the leading Suffolk commissioners, and was expected by his godly friends to make some sort of stand against the levy; however after being bound over to appear in London he, and the two Suffolk gentlemen with him, rather surprisingly made 'acknowledgement . . . of their error. . . and sett downe in writing under their hands to pay the money required from them by way of a loane as the Board should direct'. The Council hastened to make the most of this and immediately sent copies of the undertaking to the local commissioners, 'to give

[126] *APC 1627*, pp. 243–4; *Wentworth Papers*, p. 258; PRO SP 16/65/12, 12 ii. For a fuller discussion of Savile's attitudes as a local governor see below, pp. 243–4.

[127] *APC 1627*, pp. 84, 200, 232, 253, 413; *APC 1627–8*, pp. 83–4, 98, 103. Three of the Northamptonshire commissioners were also reported to have conformed within a few days of their meeting with the councillors; PRO SP 16/458/106. For the council summons as a platform for publicizing opposition, see below pp. 227–8, 232–4.

you notice hereof to the end that noe others be incourraged by theire example to goe on the lyke courses of backwardnes to his Majesty's service, and that you may appoynt the collectors to receive the moneys from them'. Barnardiston later withdrew his recantation and went to prison, but this came too late to destroy the advantage which the Council had gained.[128] Successes like this were, however, few and far between, and whenever the Council resorted to such methods it risked making matters worse through its chronic inconsistency and inefficiency. Perhaps the best illustration of this was its treatment of a group of refusers from Essex.

Essex was one of those counties recognized from an early stage as requiring particular attention. Heavy opposition had been reported since November 1626, and in February 1627 the Council decided to do something positive. It obviously lacked the facilities to summon all the refusers, so instead it instructed the Deputy Lieutenants to press fifty men from the hundreds of Chelmsford, Hinckford, Becontree, and Rochford, out of those who had 'promised to lend unto His Majestie and have not performed it'. The Deputies interpreted this as enabling them to levy outright refusers, and tried to implement the order on 12 March, during a meeting of the Chelmsford assizes. Seven promiment refusers from the town had appeared before them and declared the 'constant resolution . . . of themselves and the greatest parte of the residue for the absolute denyall thereof'. The Deputies therefore offered them press money which the refusers declined, whereupon a row broke out in which Christopher Harris, an attorney and client of the Earl of Warwick, informed Lord Maynard and Sir Thomas Fanshawe, two of the Deputies, that 'he was not willing to medle but it was against the law and Henry 8 durst not nor would not doe it'. This resistance was clearly an affront not only to the local governors, but also to the Council and the service as a whole, so the Deputies immediately sent Fanshawe off to London to seek further instructions.[129]

The Council faced a crucial decision over the Chelmsford refusers. After such a public display of opposition, the whole county was waiting to see what would happen, and reports were being spread far and wide by newsletter writers. The seven were

[128] *The Winthrop Papers*, 4 vols. (Massachusetts Hist. Soc., 1929–1943), i. 336; *APC 1626*, p. 427; PRO SP 16/55/10.

[129] *APC 1627*, p. 102; PRO SP 16/52/62; 57/1; 60/10; Bodl. L. Firth MS c.4, p. 301.

summoned to London and, as we have seen, on 16 March, the Council rejected the hard-liners' proposal that they should be hanged and decided instead to indict them in Star Chamber.[130] However, somewhere along the line either the resolve of councillors diminished or else the administrative machinery broke down. The hearing had been set for 30 March, but in early April the Attorney-General 'when asked if the Essex men came to the Star Chamber said he thought not'. By the 14th reports suggested that the Council was going back on its tracks and proposing that 'Sir Tho Fanshawe should offer that if they would retract their refusal of press money they should be set at liberty'. And three days later the refusers were told that 'if they will petition and acknowledge that the cause why they refuse press money was becaus they were not of abylyty to serve in war, and not out of disobedience, they shall have liberty'. Two of them apparently accepted this, but the rest remained obdurate, and in the meantime the Council had also issued instructions for the Deputies to abandon pressing of refusers.[131] All in all, then, this episode could be regarded as a humiliating defeat; however it was not the end of the Council's problems in Essex.

At the same time as the attempted press was taking place, the assize judges were being presented with a petition from 'some hundreds of poor people, to beseech them to move His Majesty for the release of their workmasters imprisoned, without which they must starve . . . whereof . . . the judges presently gave advertisement unto the state'. This referred to the Council's recent decision to counter resistance in the clothing town of Dedham by imprisoning three of the ringleaders, Thomas Wood, John Wilkinson, and Richard Barker, all of whom were wealthy clothiers. Dedham was one of the industrial centres of the Stour valley and was regarded by the Council as a likely centre of popular unrest, particularly during the recession of the 1620s. They therefore allowed the petition and released Wood and Wilkinson.[132] This however created new problems for the hard-pressed local commissioners. On 6 July they wrote to the Council informing them that opposition was continuing so strongly 'as

[130] *C. and T.* i. 207–8; *APC 1627*, pp. 130, 140. See above, pp. 57–8.

[131] PRO SP 16/60/10; *APC 1627*, pp. 143–4, 252–3.

[132] *C. and T.* i. 205; Supple, *Commercial Crisis and Change*, pp. 102–12; B. W. Quintrell, 'The Government of the County of Essex 1603–42' (University of London Ph.D., 1965), p. 328; *APC 1627*, p. 93, 363; *APC 1627–8*, pp. 49; PRO SP 16/76/13 ii.

wee have just cause to feare that itt exceedeth the habilitie of perswation to prevaile any further with many of them then wee have done alreadie'. They also asked for guidance 'that wee may understand what your Lordships pleasure was touchinge those of the Countie who appeared before your Lordships and are returned hom againe freed (as they alledge) from the loane by your Lordships, of whom wee can demande noethinge till wee can heare what your Lordships have done therein'. At this point the Council recognized its mistake and tried to repair the damage by recommitting the clothiers and sending a messenger with an open warrant to receive refusers. However the gesture came too late. Resistance in Dedham continued unabated, and the messenger was powerless even to bring refusers before the local commissioners.[133]

These proceedings stand as a demonstration of just how ill-equipped the Council was to take a firm line on enforcement, even where there appeared to be a pressing need to do so. In part this was a question of attitude. A majority of councillors still believed in an approach to governing which hinged on the ideas of consent and co-operation. They recognized that too firm a line could lead not only to practical problems—like unemployment in Dedham—but also to the raising of awkward and divisive constitutional issues. Attorney-General Heath, for example, was said to have remarked, in the context of dealing with the Chelmsford refusers, that 'it had been well if that man had bin dead that had opened that gapp'.[134] This made it very difficult to pursue a consistent direction since at one moment the King and hard-liners might be in the ascendant and at the next the moderates. Thus decisions over enforcement were at the mercy of the political struggles within Council.

There were also the practical limitations of its administrative machinery. These have already been described by Hirst and Dr Quintrell, but it needs to be stressed that they were just as apparent with regard to the loan as other services.[135] Time and time again the Council showed itself incapable of processing information or keeping track of its decisions. For example, after

133 Bodl. L. Firth MS c.4, p. 373; *APC 1627*, p. 426; *APC 1627–8*, p. 49; PRO SP 16/74/48; 76/13 ii.

134 PRO SP 16/60/10 (I am grateful to Christopher Thompson for this reference).

135 Hirst, 'Privy Council and enforcement', 52–63; B. W. Quintrell, 'Government in perspective: Lancashire and the Privy Council, 1570–1640', *Trans. of the Hist. Soc. of Lancs. and Ches.* cxxxi (1982), 40–7.

pressing refusers from Westminster in October 1626 it had neglected to arrange for anyone to receive them in Portsmouth. As a result they stayed in the town for a few days where they were treated like heroes by the local garrison—being roused every morning by 'drum and fife'—and then came home again 'with great reputation for standing out so stoutly'.[136] Letters went astray and orders were frequently delayed. Manchester complained to his brother that the circular letters of 30 June 'were ill conveyed for few tooke notice of them: therefore we sent new'; and the Earl of Northampton pointed out to the Council that these same letters were delivered 'soe late unto me that it was impossible for som countyes to receive them by the time limited for the returnes which I am desirous to signify unto your Lordships because it happen soe often times in busines which require expedition'.[137] Much depended on personal contacts with individual councillors. Sir James Bagg in Cornwall was able to get his requests—over the loan and other matters—executed promptly because he was hand-in-glove with the Duke and his secretary, Nicholas; but Sir George Chudleigh, in the neighbouring county of Devon, was kept waiting months for action against refusers because the Earl of Marlborough's secretary had lost his letter, and he eventually got something done only through the offices of his old acquaintance, Secretary Coke.[138]

The Council's attention to the loan also tended to ebb and flow according to its other commitments. The pressure for money and the involvement of the King ensured that it was given a high priority in the Council's order of business, but at times not even this was enough to guarantee proper attention. A good deal was done during February and March 1627—and the register is full of summons of defaulters and letters to commissioners—but during April and May the Council was overwhelmed with the preparations for Rhé, which may help to explain its haphazard proceedings with the Chelmsford men. It was only when the fleet had sailed in June that it was able to return to the loan once again and keep up pressure through the rest of the summer.[139]

This demonstration of the Council's shortcomings lends support to the verdict given by Hirst that 'a coercive policy could not be

[136] *C. and T.* i. 172, 178; HMC *Buccleuch*, iii. 314.

[137] HMC *Buccleuch*, i. 264–5; PRO SP 16/73/19.

[138] PRO SP 16/60/75; 68/16, 25; 70/79; 72/35, 35 i; 77/8; E.351/288; HMC *Cowper*, i. 257, 281, 283, 288, 302; *APC 1627* p. 248; *APC 1627–8*, p. 46.

[139] *APC 1627, passim.*

carried out by such a regime which was normally capable of little more than issuing a general order and then moving on'.[140] It also reinforces the stress laid earlier on the significance of conciliar bargaining and negotiation. In conclusion the collection of the loan can basically be seen as the outcome of a process of balancing interest groups and distributing favours, in which politics and administration were elaborately interlaced. Enforcement had a role to play in this process, but only alongside subtler methods of management and persuasion. It must be remembered that the task of collection fell largely on local officials and that their readiness to co-operate depended on more than simple coercion. This might deter those considering outright opposition, but it was still open to commissioners to simply absent themselves, as many did.[141] What were needed were more positive incentives, and these were largely provided by the personal favours and resources at the Council's disposal.

Collection of the loan was never simply a straightforward administrative process. Unlike a service such as the enforcement of militia obligations—where most were agreed on the necessity and the main problem was localist backsliding—the loan was politically sensitive and needed to be handled in a way which would avoid deepening the ideological divisions. Because of this there was invariably an element of risk attached to pressing coercion. Even if it avoided giving rise to fresh issues, punishment was always liable to publicize the stand being taken by resisters. This was something the Council appears to have recognized by the time of the ship money levy in the 1630s, and its methods of enforcement were fashioned accordingly.[142] However in 1626 and 1627 this lesson had not been sufficiently absorbed and—driven on by the hard-liners and the desperate need for money—the Council sometimes added to its problems with an ill-judged lack of restraint.

[140] Hirst, 'Privy Council and enforcement', 54.

[141] R. P. Cust, 'The Forced Loan and English Politics, 1626–1628' (University of London Ph.D., 1983), app. iii.

[142] Lake, 'Ship money in Cheshire', 55; N. P. Bard, 'The ship money case of William Fiennes, Viscount Say and Sele', *BIHR* l (1977), 177–84.

3

Political Opinion and the Loan

I. INTRODUCTION

In financial and administrative terms the loan was a considerable success. It provided the Crown with much needed finance at a crucial stage in the war and did so, moreover, in a way which minimized disruption to the links between centre and localities. The levy was burdensome and the demands made on local governors were heavy, but these were often compensated by benefits and concessions which the localities were allowed when they co-operated. However financial and administrative considerations were not the only ones which affected the levy. As we have seen, in looking at the Privy Council, the loan also had political implications which made its repetition undesirable and, in the eyes of some, well nigh impossible. These will become clearer if we look at the ways in which it was perceived and understood within the framework of contemporary ideas.

In many respects this is the most problematic aspect of the loan. For a variety of reasons—some of which have already been touched on—contemporaries were reluctant to talk openly about the levy. So whilst one can occasionally find private denunciations—along the lines of the anonymous diarist who claimed that 'if it be yielded to it wilbe the greatest conquest that ever was since William the Conquerer'—it is unusual to encounter this sort of statement amongst the answers given to commissioners or the correspondence of local governors.[1] The reasons why individual taxpayers co-operated or resisted were revealed only rarely, and because of this there has been considerable disagreement about how to interpret their response. Whig historians have stressed that they perceived the levy as a threat to the traditional order and resisted as a matter of principle, whilst local historians and so-called 'revisionists' have argued that they were relatively unconcerned about principle and responded to the immediate local effects of any particular policy.[2] Given the shortcomings of the evidence this debate is not easy to

[1] TCC MS o.7.3., fo. 7^{v}; see above, pp. 9–12.

[2] See above, pp. 5–6.

resolve; however it is possible to offer some suggestions, and initially these can be based on a broader view of the extent to which contemporaries were concerned with national politics.

One of the clearest conclusions to come out of recent research has been that the amount of political news disseminated to the localities was increasing very rapidly during the early seventeenth century.[3] The Council maintained strict controls over what was printed, but it could not prevent material circulating in manuscript, either as newsletters or as the transcripts of proceedings of Parliament, state trials, diplomatic negotiations, etc., known as 'separates'. These formed the basis for a network of news which faithfully reproduced what was being reported and discussed in St Paul's Walk and the Exchange in London, and which was transmitted not only to the literate county gentry, but also—by means of local gossip—to the 'middling sort' and the lower orders. The political effects were considerable. During the 1620s, for almost the first time, local people had access to detailed and continuous coverage of many aspects of national politics. Politicians were exposed to much greater public scrutiny than previously, whilst at the same time being provided with increased opportunities to influence public opinion. And the tendency of the news to concentrate on dramatic events affected the way in which the political process was represented. It often came to be treated in terms of a series of conflicts, between two sides which were sometimes described as 'Court' and 'Country'. This helped to break down the emphasis on consensus, which pervaded much contemporary rhetoric, and further highlighted divisions of principle. Hence the news helped to develop a framework within which local taxpayers could recognise and understand the broader implications of what was happening within their shire; and some of the consequences of this were revealed in the opposition to the loan.

II. IDEOLOGY AND THE OPPOSITION TO THE LOAN

To understand the roots of the hostility aroused by the loan it is necessary to go back at least as far as the early part of James's

[3] F. J. Levy, 'How information spread among the gentry, 1550–1640', *JBS* xxi (1982), pp. 20–4; Hirst, *Representative of the People?*, pp. 132–88; A. Fletcher, *The Outbreak of the English Civil War* (1981), pp. xxv–xxx. The conclusions in this paragraph are based on Cust, 'News and politics', 60–90.

reign. One of the more striking features of debates in Parliament during this period was the frequency with which fears were expressed for its future survival. The precise origin of these is unclear, but they were in evidence as early as 1604, in the oft-quoted statement from the Commons' Apology: 'The prerogatives of princes may easily and do daily grow; the privileges of the subject are for the most part at an everlasting stand'.[1] By 1610 this was coming to appear prophetic. The King's recent use of proclamations, his proposals for the Great Contract and, above all, his continuing resort to impositions, gave rise to considerable anxiety, as expressed most eloquently by James Whitelocke:

> the ancient frame of the commonwealth is much altered in points wherein it differs in fortune and blessedness from many other commonwealths. One is that we are masters of our owne and can have nothing taken from us without our consents; another that laws cannot be made without our consents, and the edict of the prince is not a law; the third is that the Parliament is the storehouse of our liberties. All these are in danger to be lost by this power . . . we know not how far this may stretch.[2]

Such fears intensified in 1614. Impositions were again a subject of heated debate; the Crown's efforts at 'undertaking' were seen as an attempt to control membership of the house; and the premature dissolution of the Parliament was described by the normally restrained Sir Thomas Roe as 'a dissolution not of this, but of all Parliaments'.[3] There followed a seven year interval before the next meeting, and during the Parliaments of the 1620s

[1] J. R. Tanner, *Constitutional Documents of the Reign of James I, 1603–1625* (Cambridge, 1930), p. 222; Hirst, *The Representative of the People?*, pp. 66–9. Some of these fears may have been a legacy of the 1590s when, in order to meet the shortfall in supply from Parliament, Elizabeth's Council was drawn into extending the scope of the prerogative. This generated considerable unease in counties such as Norfolk, and in the Parliaments of 1601 and 1604: Hassell Smith, *County and Court*, chs. 12–15; J. E. Neale, *Elizabeth I and her Parliaments, 1584–1601* (1957), pp. 369–432; R. Munden, 'James I and "the growth of mutual distrust": King, Commons and Reform, 1603–1604' in Sharpe, ed., *Faction and Parliament*, pp. 43–72. There are also indications of such concern back in the 1560s and 1570s: Hirst, 'Revisionism revised: the place of principle', 85–6.

[2] *Proceedings in Parliament, 1610*, ed. E. R. Foster, 2 vols. (New Haven, 1966), ii. 109; J. S. Levy 'Why was it feared Parliament might be in danger of extinction between 1610 and 1614' (unpublished paper), pp. 5–8 (I am grateful to Jacqueline Levy for allowing me to make use of this); A. G. R. Smith 'Crown, Parliament and Finance: The Great Contract of 1610', in Clark, Smith, and Tyacke, eds., *The English Commonwealth*, p. 124.

[3] Russell, 'Parliamentary history in perspective', 9; Hirst, *Representative of the People?*, pp. 9–11.

MPs were constantly reminded of their precarious future by speakers such as Sir Benjamin Rudyerd and Sir Robert Phelips. The effect of all this was to greatly increase sensitivity over their powers and privileges. Issues such as the imprisonment by the Privy Council or interference in elections came to be vigorously contested where before they had been allowed to pass; and MPs reacted particularly strongly whenever they perceived a threat to the principle of parliamentary taxation.[4] These fears within Parliament provided the basis for a similar concern outside.

It first became widely apparent in 1614, with James's unfortunate decision to revive the benevolence. This form of taxation had been abandoned by the Crown since 1546, largely, it seems, because it was politically contentious. On previous occasions it had sometimes been raised successfully, but had also aroused considerable opposition, resulting in a series of statutes which outlined the threat to principles of parliamentary consent. It was to avoid infringing these that Mary, Elizabeth, and James himself, up to 1614, had employed the more acceptable method of raising personal loans by Privy Seals.[5] Thus when the benevolence was reintroduced, in the wake of parliamentary protests about impositions, its appearance was all the more sinister. The Council did its best to allay suspicion, by stressing the emergency and the voluntary nature of the levy. It also kept the use of coercion to a minimum, refraining from punishing defaulters in all but a few cases.[6] But these efforts were largely futile, and the doubters mounted a considerable opposition.

Initially this came from the JPs of Devon, Somerset, and Warwickshire, all of whom shared the same basic objection, that 'a generall scruple of exceeding prejudyce . . . may come to posterity by such a president'.[7] The fullest reply was that from Somerset, which has survived in the hand of Sir Robert Phelips and may well have been drafted by him. He was more aware than most of the precarious nature of Parliament's existence, describing benevolences in 1623 as 'a way of dangerous

[4] Russell, *Parliaments and English Politics*, pp. 55–8, 146, 149; Hirst, *Representative of the People?*, pp. 9–11, 65–70; Levy, 'Why was it feared Parliament might be in danger of extinction', p. 12: John Eliot, *Negotium Posterorum, or an Apology for Socrates*, ed. A. B. Grosart, 2 vols. (1881), i. 46–50.

[5] See above, pp. 35–6; Dietz, *English Public Finance*, i. p. 211–12; ii. 17, 62–3, 94, 115, 149.

[6] *APC 1614*, pp. 492–3, 557–9.

[7] Ibid., pp. 566, 629, 650. The words come from Devon's reply.

consequences, and that for a twofold aspect: the first that levies of this kind will seem by use and practice to create and invest a right of property in the King in the goods of his subjects, at his owne pleasure and by any pretence to be exercised; that it will procure an utter destruction of Parliaments when one of the principal works of a Parliament may be done another way'.[8] The 1614 reply of the Somerset JPs was scarcely more guarded and indicated a similar attitude. After consulting the local subsidymen—since they 'thought ytt fytt to tast the ynclination of the countrymen to that which was propounded'—they declared that

> when we call to mynd how that o^ur predecessors have at all tymes byne accustomed to relieve the wants and necessityes of theyr Kyngs only by Parliament, as being a course of less daunger unto themselves and more honour unto theyre Majesty, and howbeyt the contrary hath byn attempted to be effected yet hath ytt always mett a strong and prevaylying oppositten in so much as at length itt gave occasion of constituting that law whereby all such courses are directly and playnely prohibited, . . . we are constrayned to refuse to render unto His Majesty such satisfaction as in our harts wee desyer. . . .

The Council quickly summoned the JPs and gave them a lengthy lecture on the legality of benevolences; but this appears to have had little effect. Once back in their county they exhibited no enthusiasm for the levy; and even Sir Edward Rodney, normally a loyal crown servant, was to confess, several years later, that he had never been able to see the justification for either this or the benevolence of 1622.[9]

Elsewhere there was similar hostility which produced some well-publicized confrontations. In West Kent an initial meeting had shown that some JPs were ready to press the service by specifying the amount each should give, whilst others maintained 'that they woulde neither perswade nor diswade, but woulde leave it to every man's disposition to doe as him listed'. Some of this latter group—described as 'men of greate place'—were also thought to have backed a declaration made at a second meeting by Josias Nicolls, a deprived nonconformist minister. This called on the JPs 'to become petitioners unto the honorable Lords of His Majesty's Counsell that there maye be a Parlyamt by which wee maye be taxed, for the wysemen of the realme can better judge what wyll serve to supplye His Majesty's wants then wee are able

[8] SRO Phelips MS 223/113; Russell, *Parliaments and English Politics*, pp. 55–6, 149.

[9] *APC 1614*, p. 630; Add. MS 34, 239, fo. 45[v].

to doe . . .'. It also expressed a specific concern for the survival of Parliament:

> for which purpose I reade in the French cronacle a notable commendacon of the state of Englande, for he calleth the Kyngs of Englande happye because that if att anye tyme they lacke monye they maye call a Parliament and the subjects of England are very readye to geve hym whatsoever shalbe thought necessarye, & needfull for hym . . . further wee cannot tell whether this maye become a president in tyme to come for that which is well used in one tyme maye in ages followinge be used in worser manner.

Nicolls was reported to the Council and eventually imprisoned; but not before his arguments against the benevolence had been copied and thoroughly aired.[10]

A similar clash in Wiltshire produced similar results. A Marlborough gentleman, Oliver St John, decided to refuse the benevolence and make clear his reasons in a detailed reply to the local JPs. This argued that the benevolence was against 'law, reason and religion': law in that it was contrary to Magna Carta and to various statutes; reason in that it questioned the 1614 Parliament's decision not to provide supply; and religion in that it encouraged the King to violate his coronation oath. St John was again reported to the Council and committed for trial in Star Chamber;[11] however the notoriety which his case attracted led to his views being spread far and wide. His letter and accounts of the trial were circulated as 'separates', and as late as 1625 it was still possible for the Norfolk antiquary Sir Henry Spelman to obtain copies in London.[12] More significantly, his case appears to have prompted Sir Walter Raleigh to compose an influential treatise on 'the Prerogative of Parliaments'.[13]

In essence this was a historical examination of Parliament's place in the political order; however it also contained discussion

[10] BL Add. MS 34, 218, fos. 146–8; Staffs. RO D/593/S/4/60/1; 65/4, 5; P. Clark, 'Josias Nicolls and religious radicalism, 1583–1639', *JEH* xxviii (1977), 133–50.

[11] *The Works of Francis Bacon*, ed. J. J. Spedding, R. L. Ellis and D. D. Heath, 14 vols. (1857–74), v. 132–4, 140.

[12] BL Add. MS 34, 599, fos. 94–5 (I am grateful to Christopher Thompson for this reference). For copies of this letter: BL Add. MS 40, 838, fo. 19^{v}; Add. MS 44, 848, fo. 96; Harg. MS 226, fo. 28; Sloane MS 1856, fo. 1.

[13] Sir Walter Raleigh, 'The Prerogative of Parliaments Proved in a Dialogue between a Counsellor of State and a Justice of the Peace', in *Harleian Miscellany*, 10 vols. (1808–13) v. 194–225 (a copy of the 1640 edition). This takes as its starting-point a discussion of the St John case.

of a number of threats to the future of Parliament, amongst which were benevolences. Raleigh was careful to distance himself from the abrasive tone of St John's statement, but nevertheless argued firmly against this type of levy. He posed the question 'Why should not our Kings raise money as the Kings of France do, by their letters and edicts only?', and answered it by pointing to the fundamental differences between the two nations. In the first place France 'was never free in effect from civil wars' which often arose out of unparliamentary taxation, whilst England had avoided this, at least in the recent past. Secondly, whereas France's strength consisted in its great lords, that of England lay in its people and 'the content of them should not be neglected . . .'. Thus Raleigh insisted that 'The motive of all dangers that ever this monarchy hath undergone should be carefully heeded, for this maxim hath no postern: potestas humana radicatur in voluntatibus hominum.'; and advised James to accept the 'common answer of all the sherrifs in England when the benvolence was commanded . . . that his loving subjects in general are willing to supply him if it please him to call a Parliament'.[14] The Council did its best to suppress Raleigh's treatise, refusing to allow publication in spite of a fulsome dedication to the King; but their efforts could not prevent it from circulating widely. It was published with a Middleburg imprint in 1628 and quickly ran into five editions; and before this had been copied as a 'separate' which—as Sir John Eliot explained in May 1626—'passeth from hand to hand'. Those who read it during the 1620s included Sir Thomas Wentworth, the Earl of Clare, Bishop Williams, and Bishop Laud, and they—along with Eliot himself, who annotated his copy and drew on it as a source for precedents and analogies—evidently acknowledged it as something approaching a definitive discussion of the position of Parliament.[15]

Resistance to the 1614 benevolence had important implications for the discussion of extra-parliamentary taxation since Raleigh and the other opponents were effectively providing a framework within which its effects could be perceived and understood. Raleigh and Nicolls gave a historical perspective and drew attention to the contrasts, and possible future parallels, with the situation in France; whilst St John and the Somerset JPs had outlined the legal aspects and the way in which the levy infringed

[14] Ibid., pp. 194, 202, 207, 224.

[15] PRO SP 16/27/18; 96/31; *Wentworth Papers*, p. 266; Sharpe, *Sir Robert* Cotton, p. 243 n.

personal liberties. All this was to be extremely influential, not only in helping to provide a common stock of ideas to which later commentators would return again and again, but also in publicizing such views to a wide local audience, including ordinary subsidymen and freeholders.

The concerns displayed in 1614 resurfaced in 1622, when the King tried to levy a benevolence to support his daughter in the Palatinate. Opposition on this occasion was more muted, largely because of the widespread sympathy for Frederick and Elizabeth; nevertheless, there were still expressions of disquiet.[16] At Oxford a young divinity student named John Knight preached a sermon—based on the writings of the Calvinist resistance theorist, Paraeus—arguing that unruly or tyrannical rulers could be corrected by their subjects. This may not have been directly related to the benevolence, but its relevance in the context was evidently recognized as the Bishop of London replied with a sermon defending the levy and affirming that 'what we have is not our owne, and what we gave was but rendering and restoring'.[17] These were the sorts of themes that were to recur with Sibthorpe and Manwaring in 1627. Alongside this there were more orthodox objections. The Somerset JPs, although deprived of the leadership of Phelips, remained reluctant to contribute, providing as their reason that 'the countrie seemed to be troubled att this manner of giveinge, apprehendinge the president to be dangerous'; Lord Montague was moved to write to his brother reminding him of England's 'notliking levies but by Parliament as former ages shew'; and Lord Saye was imprisoned for refusing to give, in spite of it being well known, according to Walter Yonge, a Devon diarist, 'that he affected the good of the Palatine as much as any man, and would give in a legall course by Parliament, if it were half his estate'. Saye's qualms were based on his concern that 'he might enjoy with favour that freedom and liberty which he conceaved himself and every subject in the land that had freehold was borne unto, that is that he might not be pressed for his owne parte nor urdged to presse any other to parte with money which was their proper goods in any other course than by theire owne full and free consent in Parliament . . . if any subject was pressed

[16] This benevolence raised £116,000, compared with only £66,000 from the 1614 levy; Dietz, *English Public Finance*, ii. 116; Gardiner, *History of England*, ii. 265.

[17] Judson, *Crisis of the Constitution*, pp. 312–13; Sommerville, *Politics and Ideology*, pp. 72, 75, 80; *APC 1621–3*, p. 237; *Chamberlain*, ii. 434, 439, 443.

to parte with his money without his free consent his liberty touched'.[18] Saye was stressing the extent to which coercion invalidated the levy more than the opponents of 1614—largely because he was answering before the Privy Council—but in essence his views were the same as theirs; he firmly believed that the best safeguard for liberty and property was the need for the King to consult Parliament. Doubtless many agreed, even though in 1622 they did not see this principle being infringed. It was therefore perhaps predictable that the 1626 benevolence should meet with widespread resistance.

This 1626 levy again highlighted concern over the future of Parliament. Like the 1614 benevolence it was requested within a month of a parliamentary dissolution, after a stormy session in which government policy had been challenged and criticized. It was also based on a rather dubious invasion scare, which MPs and newsmongers had been quick to dismiss as conciliar invention, manufactured 'as a spur to obtain money'.[19] Furthermore it was linked to two new problems, thrown up by the Parliament: firstly the issue of how to finance the war against France and Spain, and whether this was to be done through the traditional means of parliamentary supply; secondly the question of how to deal with the Duke. The resolution of both of these was tightly bound up with the fate of the benevolence and there are indications that contemporaries recognized this.

With regard to Buckingham it is understandably hard to find much evidence of local opinion; but what there is suggests that ordinary subsidymen shared the concerns expressed by MPs. The widespread circulation of 'separates' relating to proceedings against the Duke, the content of contemporary satirical verses and the views picked up amongst local inhabitants by the Suffolk diarist, John Rous, all point to this.[20] So too does an intriguing account of the response to the benevolence in Nottinghamshire.

[18] PRO SP 14/130/81: HMC *Buccleuch*, iii. 225; *Yonge*, p. 61; M. L. Schwarz, 'Lord Saye and Sele's objections to the Palatinate benevolence of 1622', *Albion*, v (1971), 12–22.

[19] HMC *Skrine*, p. 72; *CSP Ven. 1625–6*, pp. 447–8; *C. and T.* i. 116, 125.

[20] J. S. Morrill, 'William Davenport and the 'silent majority' of Stuart England', *Journal of the Chester Archaeological Society*, lviii (1975), pp. 118–22; *Poems and Songs Relating to George Villiers, Duke of Buckingham*, ed. F. W. Fairholt (Percy Soc., xxix, 1850), *passim*; *Rous*, pp. 1–22. This material is discussed more fully in Cust, 'News and politics', 65–9, 80–5.

Writing to Conway in August 1626, the Lord Lieutenant, Viscount Mansfield, complained that his neighbours were not responding well to the request for money, but were being 'governed by ill presidents, and I finde factions the dregges of the late Parliament. God sende them see clearer and nott to be governed by their intelligencer, fame that never speakes trewth'.[21] Whether Mansfield intended 'factions' to refer to particular individuals—perhaps Clare and his son, or Sir Thomas Hutchinson, all of whom had been involved in the Parliament—or simply to a mood prevailing in the shire, is not really clear. But what seems inescapable is his conviction that events in the shire were connected with the views expressed in the previous Parliament, perhaps through a recognition that the levy's success would delay the Duke's removal.

Evidence of concern about the threat which the benevolence posed to Parliament is rather more plentiful, although again comment was guarded. Subsidymen seem to have recognized that if they were too specific about reasons for not giving they were liable to face the sort of treatment meted out to Nicolls and St John, and JPs had no wish to antagonize the Council by dwelling on their refusal. As a result the answers sent in from county meetings were almost uniformly bland, with at least eleven shires sending replies which closely matched that from Hertfordshire: 'all . . . are . . . most willinge to contribute for the defence of the Kingdome & for the supply of His Majestie's wantes in that behalfe, by waye of subsidie in a parliamentarie manner, even beyond their habilities. But as touchinge any contribucon in this kynd wee finde them altogether unwillinge thereunto'.[22] Sometimes these were accompanied by pleas of poverty or lists of excuses which may indicate that some subsidymen were unable or unwilling to contribute in any case;[23] however the widespread readiness to restate commonly held beliefs relating to parliamentary supply also suggests that there was a good deal more to this non-payment than simple 'localist' obstructionism. Subsidymen were evidently aware that there were broader principles at stake and that these could be invoked to legitimate their stance.

Sometimes it is possible to see these principles being given quite a wide airing. In this respect the King's letter read out at the

[21] PRO SP 16/33/126.

[22] PRO SP 16/33/8. The other replies are: SP 16/33/41, 57, 59, 84; 34/4, 30, 62; 35/46; 36/34, 39; 37/50.

[23] PRO SP 16/33/57; *Fairfax Correspondence*, i. 73–4; Fletcher, *A County Community*, pp. 211–12.

initial meetings was of considerable significance.[24] In the first place it pointed out the connection between the benevolence and parliamentary subsidies—by requesting the equivalent of the four subsidies agreed on, but not granted, in 1626—and thereby drew attention to the way in which the one might come to replace the other. Secondly it provided what must have been a disturbing insight into the King's intentions with regard to the war effort. If the subsidymen failed to contribute, it declared, 'noe ordinary rules can prescribe a law to necessity and the common defence and safetye, and even the very subsistence of the whole might warrant us if out of our Royall Prerogative and power we should take a course any way more extraordinarye or less indifferent'. Given these warnings it was hardly surprising that there should have been extended discussion amongst the subsidymen, in some cases leading to the sorts of views expressed by earlier opponents. In Pembrokeshire—normally regarded as a political backwater, isolated from considerations of national politics—they asked for a week to talk about the levy and then presented an answer similar to other shires. In Surrey the JPs, after encountering opposition at their initial meeting decided to drop all mention of the term 'subsidye . . . because we heare that so much distasted in other countryes . . .'. And in Norfolk the subsidymen's deliberations touched on ship money and the lieutenancy, as well as the benevolence, and bred 'strong conceyts . . . putt into the heades of the generalitye of the people'.[25] Precisely what these 'conceyts' were was not explained, but it seems likely that they included the misgivings revealed in the two counties where opposition was most fully described, Somerset and Bedfordshire.

Somerset maintained its former stance on benevolences with a response which harked back to 1614 and 1622. County governors such as Phelips were less open in providing a lead than before; nevertheless there was considerable opposition, and Sir Edward Rodney found that, as he went his rounds trying to raise the money, he was bombarded with queries from his neighbours. Some wanted to know whether there was a real danger of invasion; others what had happened to the money given in 1622; but the most frequent complaint was the 'scruples in the mindes

[24] PRO SP 16/31/30.

[25] H. A. Lloyd, *The Gentry of South-West Wales 1540–1640* (Cardiff, 1968), pp. 120, 211; PRO SP 16/33/57; BL Harl. MS 387, fo. 71^r (I am grateful to Christopher Thompson for this reference); *Musters, Beacons, Subsidies, Ship Money, etc.*, p. 33.

of many who persuade themselves that by law all benevolences are forbiden . . . Why', they asked, 'should we give since the Parliament did not think fitt? Shall wee bee wiser then the Parliament?'[26]

Similar views surfaced in Bedfordshire, where for once the subsidymen were pressed to give a detailed explanation for their refusal.[27] Their meeting took place at Bedford on 17 August in front of five of the local JPs. The King's letters were read out and then Richard Taylor, the JP chosen to sponsor the service, gave 'a narration of the state of the busines', dwelling on 'the state of christendom as it stands this day . . . shadowed and cast over with clouds of darknes, with the alarms of war and battling of arms'. As was the case elsewhere, this made little impression, and after discussing the matter for some two hours the local constables returned 'the opinion and vote of every hundred to be, not to give to His Majesty in this way, but in a parliamentary way. Notwithstanding the hardness of the tymes and the generall poverty of the county they woold strayn themselves to give that that then should be agreed'. This was a common enough answer and would normally have sufficed, but in this case the JPs had also received the second set of council letters dispatched on 26 July; so, following instructions, they moved to interview the subsidymen individually. This revealed that only two men were actually prepared to contribute, the rest remained 'resolutely in the same opinion as the high constables did report'. The JPs therefore turned back to the constables and tried to exert pressure on them 'willing them to consider better of it and to be persuaded by the reasons alleged by us and to conforme themselves thereunto or els to render reasons to us of their willfullness'. This led to a further conference between constables and subsidymen, and at length they produced a more detailed account of their reasons for refusing a contribution:

> they made some question whether this course now holden were not agaynst law, and they conceived it was not grounded upon good presedent and they feared future danger by such a presedent. They much insisted that the parliamentary way of raysing money was most equall and most indifferent . . . And moreover they alleged that as the parliamentary way of giving was most equall so it did produce good effects, making good lawe, redresse of grievances if anything were amisse, pardons etc. And they did

[26] PRO SP 16/36/46; 37/5; BL Add. MS 34, 239. fos. 45v, 50.
[27] 'Papers of Richard Taylor', pp. 106–8.

declare that the generall opinion was that in a parliamentary way every man would be willing to contribute to his abylity.

This is one of the few occasions on which it is possible to hear ordinary taxpayers speaking for themselves and it clearly indicates that their objections to the benevolence were based on much more than simple obstructionism. They were able to make distinctions between different forms of taxation and at the same time recognize that parliamentary subsidies were a necessary part of the political process. All this was evidently founded on a wider view of the functions of Parliament and its place in the common weal which accorded closely with the notions of MPs themselves.[28] Moreover they were also aware of the dubious legal status of benevolences and, although not actually able to cite the statutes condemning them, were at least sufficiently knowledgeable to recognize that they had been challenged in the past.

If this sort of argument was being put forward by the lesser gentry and subsidymen one would also expect it to have been familiar to leading gentry and local governors; however in their case it is even more difficult to find opinions being openly expressed. We have occasional hints from observers such as John Poulett that 'ill spiritts' were attempting to disrupt the service; but the fact that, even in Somerset, he found it hard to provide substantive allegations suggests that opponents were keeping a very low profile.[29] Again this is understandable. Local governors were even more exposed than subsidymen when it came to the risk of a council summons; and besides they must have recognized, on tactical grounds, that open opposition was unnecessary to defeat the service. It was so flimsily based that anything less than wholehearted support would probably condemn it to failure, and this could easily be withheld whilst still going through the motions of obeying council orders. Hence it is quite common to find later opponents of the loan—like Barrington and Masham in Essex—turning up to their meetings, reading the Council's letters and then doing little more than accept the subsidymen's refusal.[30] Such a response should not be taken to indicate that local governors were unconcerned at the broader issues: rather it reflected a realistic compromise, made to fit the circumstances.

This was the case in Buckinghamshire where lack of positive enthusiasm and disagreement over the way to proceed appeared to

[28] Russell, 'Parliamentary history in perspective', 6–7.

[29] PRO SP 16/37/5.

[30] PRO SP 16/34/62.

mask more fundamental concerns. The JPs had launched the service at Aylesbury on 3 August with decisions to hold separate meetings for the shire's two divisions and invite Sir Francis Goodwin to make the keynote address, 'as the most popular man . . . being a Deputie Lieutenant, knight of the Parliament and held to bee a potent man to swaye a greate parte of the sheere in the Upland Chilterne where hee usually inhabited'. Goodwin duly appeared at the first meeting, but, instead of throwing his weight behind the service, handled the proceedings in a way which a hostile observer, probably Sir Thomas Denton, interpreted as blatant obstructionism:

> making a short speech to the people, expressing the tenor of the King's letters but not reading them, he did withall tell the people that the justices did not expect an answere from them at that tyme bycause it was harvest and a busie tyme. And therefore he thought good to give them day till satterday before Michaelmas to give their answere . . . to which many people (though privately) answered they had rather have given their answers then and soe not bee troubled any more. *The Kings letters and instructions requiring expedicon not delaies.*[31]

On the following day, at the second meeting, Goodwin failed to appear and was replaced by Denton, who revelled in the responsibility and 'verie worthily declared the King's pleasure to the people . . . effectually inciting them to due consideracon thereof'. The subsidymen in response maintained a long silence, eventually broken when a Mr Skepwash of Hambledon proposed 'that this was a businesse of great weight, and required a longer tyme of consideracon, which hee desired to bee graunted'. Denton and some other justices, recognizing this as an attempt to push the meeting into the previous day's dead end, resisted the proposal as 'needlesse'; however they were undermined when the senior justice present, Sir William Borlase, 'asked the people what they said to Mr Skepwash his motion to which . . . Mr. Chace of Gt. Marlowe said it was a good motion and after him not above sixe or seaven urged unto the same, the residue standing all mute'. As a result it was decided to delay the answer, and after further discussion—in which Denton argued for the earliest date and Borlase for the latest—this was postponed for six weeks.

Neither meeting, then, saw any real discussion of the substantive issues raised by the benevolence; but in the context this was

31 SP 16/34/69, 70. The use of the adjective 'popular' in this context—a report to the Council—was probably intended by the writer to be double-edged.

hardly surprising. With hostile observers present Goodwin and Borlase would have risked severe punishment from the Council if they had opposed the levy openly; and the ideas expressed in Denton's report to the Council would certainly have been unpalatable to local subsidymen. Both sides kept their opinions largely to themselves; however this did not mean that the broader implications of the levy were ignored. The disagreement over whether or not to postpone the answer appears to have reflected more general conflicts of political allegiance. Much of Goodwin's eminence in the shire depended on his popularity amongst the freeholders, and this probably influenced his response, which the Council interpreted as a deliberate attempt to obstruct. Denton, on the other hand, enjoyed close contacts with the Court—via his two friends, Sir Edmund Verney and Sir Thomas Tirringham, who were both Gentlemen of the Privy Chamber—and this must, in part, explain his display of zeal.[32] Neither side, then, was able to divorce its actions from the wider implications of the service. Indeed what seems to have happened was that broad issues, rather than being excluded, were disguised and presented as a disagreement over postponing the answer. In other words principle became identified with a narrow practicality and conflict proceeded along the lines which this laid down. Given the pressures on spokesmen in these meetings such a situation was probably not uncommon—it can be seen, for example, in some of the conflicts over ship money ratings in the 1630s[33]—and this should be allowed for when it comes to assessing reactions to the loan.

The issues initially raised by the loan were similar to those presented by the benevolence. The Duke's future still appeared to hang in the balance and anxiety over the King's direction of the war effort was increased by his failure to summon an expected Parliament in September 1626. Moreover, in spite of the Council's careful attempt to distinguish the two levies and thereby avoid falling foul of the statutes relating to benevolences, opponents generally seem to have perceived them as offering the same sort of threat to the traditional constitution. Awareness of this was sharpened by two fresh considerations which made the loan

[32] L. L. Peck, 'Goodwin v. Fortescue: the local context of parliamentary controversy', *Parliamentary History*, iii (1984), 33–56; *Verney Papers* pp. 103–5, 120–4, 128

[33] Holmes, 'County community in Stuart historiography', 65–6; Barnes, *Somerset*, pp. 213–22.

perhaps the most difficult test of loyalties that most Englishmen faced during the 1620s.

In the first place early measures taken by the Council tended to weaken its own case for regarding the levy as legal. The instructions to commissioners, the pressing of the refusers and the attempt to force the judges to subscribe all undermined the main argument used in support of benevolences, that they avoided coercion and could therefore be regarded as 'free gifts' which were not covered by statute. And this tendency was reinforced by the newsletter reports of these proceedings which drew attention to the precedents being established and brought out parallels with earlier examples of royal oppression, such as 'the Amicable Grant'.[34]

Even more significant was Charles's personal involvement with the service. As we have seen, he put pressure on individuals to subscribe and issued a public assurance that the levy would not be repeated, all of which had the effect of compelling lenders to decide whether or not they trusted his word.[35] This was potentially very divisive. For those who were not dissuaded from resisting it became much more difficult to justify their actions on the grounds of legal scruples or opposition to the Duke; in theory, at least, they had to face the fact that they were opposing the King himself. The practical consequences of this were, of course, limited because most still sought refuge in a belief that the King had been led astray by his advisers; but at least the issue had been raised, and once out of the box, as we shall see, it could lead to some dramatic shifts in attitude.

In immediate terms the effect of the King's intervention was to inhibit open discussion of the loan even more than had been the case with the benevolence. When it came to considering something as delicate as the trust and faith reposed in the monarch, most contemporaries were extremely wary, preferring to skirt round the matter and assume that his intentions were always of the best.[36] As a result one finds that even those who were prepared to face a council summons and imprisonment remained tight-lipped when it came to discussing their refusal in public. The general absence of comment in the council registers suggests that most, on being summoned and asked to explain themselves, maintained a

34 *Works of Bacon*, v. 138–9; *Rous*, pp. 7–8; *Yonge*, p. 97; HMC *Buccleuch*, iii. 314; PRO SP 16/41/3; C. 115/N.4/1 Oct. 1626.

35 See above, pp. 55, 105–6.

36 Hill, 'Parliament and people in seventeenth century England', 110–11.

dignified silence, or at most mumbled a few words of excuse. Even Richard Knightley leader of the widespread opposition in Northamptonshire, chose to register his disapproval not by openly arguing the issues of principle but by refusing to kneel, 'lest, as they interpret it here, he should seem to acknowledge a fault and crave mercy where not guilty'.[37] However there were exceptions, and one of the most striking—and a response which was obviously treated as out of the ordinary by both the Council and newsletter writers—was the interview of George Catesby of Northamptonshire, along with William Coryton, perhaps the most stubbornly awkward of all refusers. When summoned, he at first refused to explain his opposition, declaring that 'the Council was no fit place to contest . . . he came not to contend but to suffer'; however the councillors continued to press him and he eventually replied that he thought 'the King's proclamacion declaring His Majesty's intention in this way of the loane was no warrant to the subject to trust to for though the King in one place say it shall not be made a president, yet often in the same proclamacion he saieth it shall not be annuall and usuall so as he may use it every second or seventh yeare . . .' Moreover he pointed out that at the initial meeting in his county he had heard the Earl of Manchester 'affirm . . . that the setting a-foot or practising of this loan was, ipso facto, a precedent; and every precedent a flower of preogative'. Clearly this was not what the Council wanted to hear. Instead of crediting him with uncovering a legal loophole, they delivered 'a sharpe reproofe' and 'censured him for this cause to be commited to the Marshallsea, there to remayne till the King's further pleasure be known'.[38] In these circumstances it was perhaps unsurprising that most refusers declined the opportunity to explain themselves.

In addition to this, however, there were other considerations which inhibited them when it came to speaking out, particularly at the meetings within their own shires. Most Englishmen accepted that the King's position at the head of the social and political hierarchy was unchallangeable and that the principle of obedience to his commands was one of the linchpins holding this together.[39] His promises and insistence on involving himself

[37] *APC 1626, 1627, passim; C. and T.* i. 189–91.

[38] *APC 1627*, p. 62; *C. and T.* i. 198. For some other examples of the Council responding vigorously to defiance on the part of refusers: *APC 1627*, pp. 2, 42.

[39] Judson, *Crisis of the Constitution*, ch. 1; D. Hirst, 'Court, country and politics before 1629' in K. Sharpe, ed., *Faction and Parliament*, p. 131.

personally in the service therefore put them in a considerable dilemma. They had no guarantee that the King would not be misled into breaking his word as Catesby had implied; but on the other hand to appear to challenge him would be to set an example which could easily rebound against them. In short they had to try to refuse without being seen too obviously to defy a higher authority. The majority resolved this difficulty by presenting themselves as submissively as possible, expecially in front of their own subsidymen. Sir Nathaniel Barnardiston, for example, deliberately arrived late at the West Suffolk meeting, apparently to avoid the unedifying spectable of a public wrangle with the Privy Councillors; Barrington and Masham allowed themselves to be led away from the Romford meeting with barely more than a refusal to answer on oath; and four Dorset refusers, including Sir Walter Erle, were reduced to silence when told that they risked 'incurring the King's high displeasure'.[40] Perhaps the most revealing episode concerned the twelve commissioners who refused at the Gloucestershire meeting on 16 February. Since these included two of the Deputy Lieutenants and five of the most active JPs, the Council's representative, Northampton, put it to them 'that their denial might be a great hindrance to the service in respect of their neighbours'. This was evidently something they wished to avoid, in appearance at least. As individuals they felt bound in conscience to refuse, but when it came to their fellow subsidymen 'they answered that they would by no means hinder it either by perswasions or other ways . . . refused in the fewest words and arguments that could be imagined . . . and when they were moved to enter into bond they did it as willingly and did submit themselves as dutefully to His Majestie's and your Lordships' pleasures as can be expressed'.[41] This sort of attitude ensured that open contestation of the loan was comparatively rare, but it did not silence it altogether. In some instances particularly determined and committed individuals went ahead and publicly expressed their reasons for opposition.

The arguments they used were for the most part unoriginal, being based on the earlier objections to benevolences; nevertheless they served at least two important functions. In voicing opinions which might otherwise have gone unheard they promoted discussion of the levy, sometimes in public; and in placing opposition within sets of familiar and broadly acceptable assumptions they

[40] *Winthrop Papers*, i. 336; *C. and T.* i. 161–3; PRO SP 16/49/11i–iii, 35.
[41] PRO SP 16/10/5; 35/43; 54/28, 28i.

helped to rescue it from the smears of 'popularity' and 'resistance' being spread by royalist propagandists.

This was apparent in the first public demonstration against the loan which took place at the Northamptonshire meeting on 12 January.[42] Led by Knightley, twenty-two gentlemen and 205 freeholders were reported to have appeared and presented a petition to the council commissioners in which payment was 'generally excused except by Parliament, and they besought the commissioners to be humble suitors to His Majesty'. This was mild enough; perhaps too mild since it seems to have been taken as a sign of weakness by the commissioners, who hastened to reject the petition and press for conformity. Nevertheless it did bring about a public discussion of some of the issues relating to the loan, leading the Earl of Manchester into his damaging admission about its status as a precedent. It also presented the Northamptonshire public with an alternative to the views which Robert Sibthorpe was to preach at the following assizes, in his sermon *Apostolike Obedience*.

This petition, however, was probably less influential than the protests of the Cornish refusers, Sir John Eliot and William Coryton, which were widely circulated as 'separates'. Eliot's 'Petition from the Gatehouse' has survived in at least twenty manuscript copies, and soon after its production, at the height of interest in the Five Knights Case, it was to be found 'wandering amongst the subjects in Cornwall'.[43] Coryton's earlier treatise, 'A Relation of Soe Much as Passed Between the Lordes of the Counsell and Mr. Corinton at the Counsell Table', was less widely dispersed, but a cursory search of the British Library has still revealed three copies.[44] Thus it appears that the two treatises were part of a co-ordinated campaign to publicize the moderate case for opposition.

Both were similar in content and form and focused principally on the threat to law and tradition. Eliot's 'Petition' consisted largely of an exposition of the main statutes against benevolences —25 and 33 Ed. I, 25 Ed. III and 1 R.III—culminating in an appeal to the subjects' freedom from aribitrary imprisonment enshrined in Magna Carta. Its basic argument was obviously in

[42] *C. and T.* i. 184, 198; PRO SP 16/49/8; Sibthorpe, *Apostolike Obedience*, dedication.

[43] J. Forster, *Sir John Eliot*, 2 vols. (1864), ii. 87–93; H. Hulme, *Sir John Eliot 1592–1632* (1957), pp. 165–72.

[44] BL Harl. MS 39, fos. 452–7; 737, fos. 159–65; Add. MS 30, 926, fos. 1–8.

opposition to the Crown, but this was tempered by the author's acknowledgement of his trust in the King's 'pious disposition to preserve the subject's liberties' and his declaration that he had refused the loan only out of 'fear that succeeding ages might thereby take occasion to strike at the property of the subject, contrary to the intention and piety of your Majesty so graciously exprest'.

Coryton's 'Relation' was less elaborately rhetorical, but presented what, in many respects, was a more formidable case. The author set out to demonstrate that if one accepted contemporary commonplaces on the nature of law and its position within the constitution then it was virtually impossible to justify the loan. He began by emphasizing that his refusal to pay was based on the letter of the law and nothing else, and then went on to provide a long description of the statutes against benevolences. There followed a discussion of the various obligations imposed by law in which he stressed that one of its principal functions was to uphold the prerogative and provide a guide whereby 'wee ought to obeye our Kinge'. And the 'Relation' then shifted into a dialogue, in which Coryton responded to various challenges which Privy Councillors had made to his basic defence. First of all they suggested that his appeal to statute was irrelevant because the statutes cited were 'noe lawes but charters and graunts from the Kinge to the people'. This he countered by pointing out that they had been 'made with a full consent of all sides, selfe sworne and confirmed with a curse . . . and weare in the open printed, Statute Bookes which every subject might take notice of'. Then they argued that, like a privy seal loan, 'this loane was asked freelye, men weare not compelled to paye it, and whie might not the King soe demand'; at which he simply 'marvayled whie any weare restrayned for not paying it'. And finally they put forward perhaps the most difficult argument to counter, that based on the text used by Sibthorpe: 'whether the Kinge weare not to command me, whether tribute weare not due to him'. To this Coryton replied carefully, accepting 'the Kinge to be the greate power ordayned of God to command me', and allowing that tribute was 'to be payde to him', but then inserting a crucial qualification: 'if this weare tribute, they woulde shewe by what lawe it was due otherwise it was not the power ordayned of God that requyred it of me, neither was it due, soe there weare not lawe for it neyther was I bound to obaye it'. This, according to the account, eventually silenced the councillors, who 'replyed not, but after a little stoppe moved their hands to me and gave me leave to depart'.[45]

The defences of Coryton and Eliot, then, were scrupulously legal and grounded in commonplaces which even the Privy Councillors appeared unable—or possibly in some cases unwilling—to dispute. This was perhaps their greatest polemical strength. They presented a series of arguments against the loan which must have appeared virtually watertight; they drew on statutes concerning the property rights of the subject which were familiar and, in the case of Magna Carta, virtually sacrosanct; and they showed respect and moderation when it came to discussing the power and prerogatives of the King. In the circumstances, this was probably the most effective response that could have been made to the propaganda of the Crown.

Neither of the two protests which remain to be considered could be said to have displayed either moderation or any particular respect for the monarch, and both differed fundamentally from the statements made by Eliot and Coryton. Instead of couching their appeals in terms of the law and a return to tradition, they were essentially summons to action, calling on the individual taxpayer to rise up and openly oppose the Crown's actions. Moreover the arguments they used and the language and style in which these were presented, all differed markedly from the attacks on previous levies and, as I hope to demonstrate, mark an important shift from earlier forms in the rhetoric of opposition. These two protests therefore deserve to be considered in some detail.

The first took the form of an anonymous manuscript pamphlet, dated 24 January 1627 and directed 'To all English Freeholders from a Well-Wisher of Theirs'. The probable author of this—and certainly the moving force behind its distribution—was Theophilus Clinton, Earl of Lincoln.[46] Although only twenty-seven and

[45] Assuming that this is a reasonably accurate account of Coryton's interview then this probably took place on 28 May 1627. The heading to the 'separate' implies that the interview was in April, but this would hardly have been possible because Coryton and Eliot were not summoned from Cornwall until the 27th of that month. If Coryton did indeed make this address on 28 May then he would probably have faced a particularly 'hard-line' audience, including Dorset, Laud, Neile, and the Duke himself, all of whom were in attendance: *APC 1627*, pp. 248, 297–8; BL Harl. MS 39 fos. 452–7.

[46] The only copy of this document which has been found is, PRO SP 16/54/82i. It is clear, however, from the various descriptions of its content that this was similar to the document circulated by Lincoln's servants before the meeting of the Nottinghamshire loan commissioners and on other occasions: BL Add MS 12,946, fo. 125; Add. MS 48,057, fo. 35^{v}: Harg. MS 321, fo. 137;

lacking in political experience, he inspired and directed one of the most effective protests against Crown policy in the entire pre-Civil War period. It wrecked at least one of the meetings held by council commissioners in the country, mobilized over seventy subsidymen to make a combined protest against the loan and successfully disrupted collection of the levy over much of southern Lincolnshire.[47] The Earl's part in all this was crucial. Along with peers such as Warwick, Saye, and Clare he had refused subscription in November 1626; but in the early months of 1627, whilst others were running for cover, he was still championing the cause of opposition. One newsletter writer identified his intervention as the main cause of the debacle at Lincoln in January: the Earl 'being askte whether he would give, answered he had made his answer already to the Lords . . . prest to give a better answer sayd he would neither give, subscribe, nor execute the commission and so went away, whereupon the whole assembly made a noys and departed'. As a result of this Lincoln was summoned before the Privy Council and, after refusing to answer on oath in Star Chamber, was incarcerated in the Tower, having 'showed himself an enemy to the King's proceedings and done harm to others both by his example and speeches'.[48] However this did not prevent him from continuing to influence the opposition. His estate steward, Thomas Dudlye, remained in the county to organize resistance and obstruct the local commissioners; and whilst the Earl was travelling up to London in early February, four of his household servants were distributing the anonymous pamphlet. This probably circulated through much of southern Lincolnshire and eventually reached as far afield as Kings Lynn—where a copy was found and sent to the Privy Council on 23 February—and Nottingham—where copies were 'scattered in the Kings waye when the King's commissioners sate for the loane'.[49] As we shall see it was to have a considerable effect on the service.

Lincoln's militancy and determination in opposing the loan was remarkable, and quite exceptional amongst the peerage. This may have had something to do with the fact that he had spent much of

PRO SP 16/527/53; *C. and T.* i. 202. It is not possible to identify the author on the evidence currently available, but Lincoln himself seems the most likely candidate, as argued by a Star Chamber reporter: BL Add. MS 48,057, fo. 35^{v}.

[47] *C. and T.* i. 190; PRO SP 16/56/39; 71/50.

[48] PRO SP 16/41/3; C. 115/N.4/2 Feb. 1626–7; *C. and T.* i. 207.

[49] A. Johnson and D. Malone, ed., *Dictionary of American Biography* (New York, 1930), Dudlye, Thomas; *APC 1627*, pp. 73–4; PRO SP 16/54/82, 82i; 72/36; BL Add. MS 12,946, fo. 125.

the previous three years away from the restraining influence of the Court, commanding one of Mansfeldt's regiments in Germany or involving himself in local government within his shire; however more than anything it appears to have been the consequence of a fervent godly zeal. For Lincoln stood at the head of a group of Puritan sympathizers centred on the charismatic figure of John Cotton, the minister at Boston where he was High Steward. This included leading county governors—such as Sir William Armyne and Sir Anthony Irby—several godly ministers—such as Samuel Skelton, Anthony Tuckney, and Samuel Whiteinge—and a group of Boston townsmen who like Lincoln were involved in colonizing ventures in Massachusetts—Isaac Johnson, his brother-in-law, Richard Bellingham, Recorder of Boston, and Thomas Leverett and Atherton Hough, both common councilmen.[50] This group provided the bedrock of opposition in the area and stood behind the Earl as he maintained his commitment to resisting the levy. The views which inspired this were outlined in the address 'To all English Freeholders'.

This began conventionally enough, if rather bluntly, by setting out the usual arguments against the loan:

> Beware and consider what you doe conserning theise subsidies and loanes which are now demanded of you least you give away not only your money but your liberty and propriety in your owne goodes. For, howsoever you may be promised that it shalbe no presedent against you, yet it is most certaine that it wilbe a thing of most dangerous consequents and that is more aymed at then the money, the gaining of a presedent to raise moneyes without law, which was the overthrow of Parliament and of the freedom that now we injoy in France. And if it goes forward we make ourselves and our posterityes subject to perpetuall slavery without recovery and to be taxed at pleasure without any limitts . . . This course have ever beene disprooved of in Parliament and there are many lawes made against it of Rich 3: 2 chap, 34 of Edw 1: 2 chap.

However the pamphlet then proceeded to draw out the implications

[50] GEC vii. 696–7; *Lincs. Archives Office*, Lindsey Quarter Sessions Rolls 1625–30, A.I./169; H. Hajzyk, 'The Church in Lincolnshire c. 1595–1640' (Univ. of Cambridge, Ph.D. thesis, 1980), pp. 330–3, 344–8, 457, 463–6; PRO SP 16/85/99; P. Thompson, *History of Boston* (1856), pp. 428–31; M. Spurrell, *The Puritan Town of Boston* (History of Boston series, v, 1972), pp. 9–17; M. F. Keeler, *The Long Parliament* (American Philosophical Soc. xxxvi, 1954), pp. 230–1. For the very close links between Lincoln, Cotton, Johnson, Bellingham, Dudlye, and Lord Saye and Sele see Johnson's will made in April 1627: *Winthrop Papers*, ii. 49–56. For the response of some of these individuals to the loan see below, pp. 298–9.

of the levy in a manner which most refusers shrank from. First of all it declared unambiguously that this was a levy devised to rescue the Duke. 'Be sure whatsoever is given out of Parlament wilbe cast away and not dispersed for the good or safetie of the commonwealth . . . but for private uses and the satisfieing of the ambitious desires of favourityes at the Court who are afraid of Parlament and therefore devise theise courses'. Then it proceeded to cast doubt on the King's promises and assurances, strongly implying that Charles was bent on rule without Parliament: 'It maybe you wilbe told the kindome is in present danger and they cannot have time to call a Parlament but that is but a pretence . . . That which is laboured at is to suppresse Parlament that so great offenders might not be called in question, and so they might imposse what burthens they please uppon the people and never be called to account'. And finally, instead of trying to contain the damage caused by the levy and restore harmony with an appeal to tradition, it deliberately set out to stir up opposition. In terms which echoed exhortations to the godly to stand up and be counted, it called on all 'honest men and wise men' to 'shew themselves either now or never': 'shall we to avoyd a little present feare or danger of being impressoned or the like plunge ourselves into an unrecoverable mischiefe. Now let us unite ourselves to stand for our owne liberties whatsoever comes of it. Refuse the oath and refuse to be bound to appear before the Lordes of the Counsaile and the commissioners may threaten you, but they cannot hurt you, for they have no law on their side'. This was directed to the freeholders, but it was not intended to encourage autonomous action on their part. They were to look for leadership from the ruling class, or at least from those amongst it who had shown themselves 'best affected for the good of the commonwealth'. This included the judges 'who have all refused to subscribe to it', those peers who 'have refused to give' and those gentry 'that hold out and are most esteemed in every man's harts . . . gentlemen you chuse to stand for you . . . if there should be a Parlament'. With this coalition the pamphlet confidently asserted that the levy, and the evil intentions behind it, could be defeated:

> if you couradgeously and boldly withstand this course you may be sure it wilbe the only way to have a Parlament whereby the bloodsuckers of the commonwealth shall receave dew punishment for their faulte . . . but this is most certaine, that it is generally conseaved by the most wise and best men that stand for the good of the commonwealth, that if this course be not withstood, but take effect, we shalbe ourselves the instruments of our

owne slavery and of the losse of the priviledge which we have hitherto enjoyed, that our goods cannot be taken from us without consent of Parlament.

As has been observed this pamphlet was a marked contrast to the appeals to sense and moderation made by other opponents of the loan. In both style and content it anticipated many of the views being put forward by parliamentary spokesmen between 1640 and 1642.[51] It treated a situation in which opinion was polarized and the nation divided, and, instead of advocating peace and neutrality, it summoned the 'well affected' to action in language which, in spite of its secular tone, was strongly reminiscent of a godly minister seeking to separate good from evil. All this was extremely significant and its implications will be discussed in due course. In the meantime, however, it is important to recognize that the views expressed in the pamphlet, although radical and militant, were evidently not beyond the pale of respectable political discourse. The pamphlet was emphatically not a call to social revolution; neither was its principal target the monarch himself, but rather the favourite who had led him astray. And whilst it certainly advocated 'resistance' to the Crown, it envisaged this as being led by the ruling class and directed towards securing a Parliament. Thus it reflected some of the more radical oppositionist ideas put forward within Parliament itself; and, although these surfaced only occasionally outside, they appear to have been acceptable to a wide range of subsidymen.[52]

The strongest evidence for this comes from the meetings held in Lincolnshire early in March, when large numbers of subsidymen 'refused to lend or enter bond'. This was an unusually strong line for refusers to take and perhaps reflects the advice given in the anonymous pamphlet. As we have seen it circulated widely in February 1627, and this was accompanied by considerable debate. Tirringham Norwood of Spalding, who complained to the 1628 Parliament about prerogative taxes, was 'suspected to have diswaded the country' from the loan; and remarks by Bishop Williams implied that some Puritan clergy were resisting it. There was also considerable activity amongst supporters of the levy. Peter Titley, former chaplain of Bishop Neale—and responsible for railing off the communion table in Grantham church—was said to

[51] Judson, *Crisis of the Constitution*, ch. 9; M. J. Mendle, 'Politics and political thought 1640–1642', in Russell, ed., *Origins of the English Civil War*, pp. 219–45.

[52] Gardiner, *History of England*, vi. 59–121, 230–337.

have preached that 'they were all damned that refused the loan'; and the nonconformist minister of Stamford, John Vicars, 'read the Kinge and Councill's letters and sayd that tribute must be given to Caesar and . . . perswaded the people to a liberall contribucon for His Majestie's necessity'.[53] The effects of this discussion were apparent when the council commissioners returned to Lincoln on the 7–10 March. At the first days' meeting seven of the local commissioners refused to lend or be bound, including Sir Thomas Darnell who 'beinge tolde that such as refuse doe incurre the King's high displeasure . . . answered he hoped he should have the libertie of a subject to dispose his money and estate at his pleasure'. Two days later it was the turn of the subsidymen, and sixty-four of them delivered a similar refusal, many having travelled forty or fifty miles from the isolated villages of the fens. The answers of some of these—from the area of Lincoln's estates around Tattershall and Sempringham—indicated that the issues relating to the loan had once again been discussed well below the level of the county governors. One Christopher Harte of Tattershall, a lesser subsidyman, assessed at £2, refused 'bycause he saw so many emynent men refuse'; John Diconson of Billingborow, also assessed at £2, refused saying 'that in a way of Parliament he will give anything'; and William Savell of Newton, assessed at £8, echoed the address to freeholders in declaring that 'he may scarcely . . . [two words illegible] a goode mann in givinge against his conscience'. How far these individuals agreed with everything that was said in the pamphlet is impossible to determine; but what does seem clear, from these meetings, is the strength of support for Lincoln and his opposition. Each of these refusers faced the risk of the press or imprisonment and yet they persisted in their action.[54]

This response provides the strongest indication we have of widespread sympathy for a more radical opposition to the loan; however it is not the only protest of its kind to have survived. We also have an incomplete treatise written by the Canterbury Puritan, Thomas Scott—not to be confused with Thomas Scott,

[53] PRO SP 16/56/39; 85/99; *CD 1628*, iii. 336, 351; *Commons Debates for 1629*, ed. W. Notestein and F. H. Relf (Minneapolis, 1921), p. 133; Holmes, *Seventeenth Century Lincolnshire* pp. 114–15; *Cases in the Courts of Star Chamber and High Commission* ed. S. R. Gardiner (Camden Soc. New Ser. xxxix, 1886), pp. 209–10.

[54] PRO SP 16/56/39. The council commissioners pressed one man and had a further two refusers summoned before the Council. In spite of this only six of the seventy-seven original refusers agreed to pay up: *APC 1627*, p. 139.

author of *Vox Populi*—which suggests that amongst some of the godly opinion was moving towards even more extreme conclusions.

Scott's treatise consisted of a reply to the sermon preached by Isaac Bargrave, Dean of Canterbury, in March 1627. To judge from its form it was intended for circulation, and may well have been a contribution to the struggle between Bargrave and the godly within Canterbury; however Scott ranged far more widely than this might imply, and produced a remarkably radical and far-reaching indictment of the King's policies over the previous two years.[55] In this exchange were encapsulated many of the ideological differences which surfaced at the time of the loan. Both Bargrave and Scott ended up with extreme formulations of a particular viewpoint; but these were developed out of the wide range of conflicting commonplaces which made up contemporary political thought. As we have seen Bargrave—in common with Sibthorpe and Manwaring—drew out the implications of the King's divinely ordained authority, and delivered what was basically a homily on obedience.[56] Scott, on the other hand, began by emphasizing the mixed and limited nature of English monarchy.

His starting point was what he described as Bargrave's attempt to apply the 'doctrine of absolute obedience unto God, unto that obedience which hee saith is . . . due unto Kings and make all Rebellion of subjects against theire King's will parallell to that of the King against God's will'. He therefore commenced by carefully drawing out the distinctions between God and a temporal ruler: 'He may command against the lawe of armes to which Kings are subject . . . and against the law of nature, justice and religion, beyond which noe obedience is due unto Kings'. Part of this comparison involved stressing the contractual basis of monarchy: 'for we must knowe that wee have not made or created God to be our Kinge for our good and service as . . . we have made and created Kings and other Magistrates, but that hee hath made and created

[55] KAO Knatchbull MS U.951/Z.10; P. Clark, 'Thomas Scott and the growth of urban opposition to the early-Stuart regime', *HJ* xxi (1978), 1–26. This treatise is addressed 'To the Reader' and survives in a neat manuscript copy. It also refers to a series of earlier comments on Bargrave's sermon which Scott presumes his audience to have read. Most of Scott's writings survive in the form of a diary providing a commentary on political events in the 1620s and 1630s from a godly viewpoint. There is a fair copy of much of this in the Knatchbull MSS, the papers of his wife's family. There are also several copies of miscellaneous items by Scott surviving in different collections. These sources are described in Clark, 'Thomas Scott and the growth of urban opposition', 2 n.

[56] See above, pp. 62–7.

us'. Moreover, whilst not actually denying the divinely ordained nature of monarchy, he tended to avoid reference to it and instead reminded the reader that 'the Parliament, State and subordinate Princes and Magistrates are noe lesse God's ordinance then the Sovereign Magistrate'. Hence his ideal was the balanced monarchy represented in the Bible by Moses and Aaron, who 'tooke not upon them absolute rule, but that limited authority onely which the State and the law gave them for the service of the Church and Commonwealth . . . Kings are lifted up by the Congregacon of the Lorde, for the wealth & service of the Congregation'.[57]

After this careful exposition of the bounds of royal authority, Scott devoted most of the remainder of the treatise to a discussion of the subject's duty to resist a tyrannical ruler. He introduced this by outlining the obligations of what he called 'the Conscientious Puritan'. This readiness to use the term 'Puritan' to describe his own viewpoint is one of the more striking features of the treatise and already suggests the extent to which Scott viewed the broader political perspective in terms of division and polarization. Most contemporaries, after all, would have dissociated themselves from the term—even those like John Pym to whom it might readily be applied—because of its connotations of separation, nonconformity and reluctance to accept the established order. Scott, on the contrary, seems positively to have revelled in it and—in much the same way as a godly author such as William Bradshaw—employed it to distinguish those who were most devoted to the preservation of Protestantism.[58]

Scott's discussion of the obligations of a Puritan was initially framed as a response to Bargrave's claim that they were those 'whose purity consists in parity, whose conscience in disobedience'. He carefully deflected the first charge by pointing out that 'the Puritans indeede teach a paritie between Bishopps and other Inferiour persons, some of them rightly, some of them over rigidlie; but none of them denie subordination in the commonwealth, much lesse with the Anabaptists that there ought to be noe Magestrates. This is not Puritan paritie, but Anabaptisticall paritie'. The second, however, he allowed to stand and, instead of

[57] KAO U.951/Z.10, pp. 1, 4, 6–7, 14 (my pagination). I have retained Scott's use of capitals where this might be significant.

[58] P. Collinson, *English Puritanism* (Historical Association General Ser., cvi, 1983), pp. 7–11; Russell, 'John Pym', pp. 151–2, 160; P. G. Lake, *Moderate Puritans and the Elizabethan Church* (Cambridge, 1982), pp. 268–78 (I am grateful to Conrad Russell for alerting me to the significance in Scott's self-application of the term).

trying to qualify or excuse this attitude, maintained that it was a principal attribute of the Puritan:

It is true the puritan's Conscience consists (in some cases) in disobedience; they dare not but disobaye Pharaoh or Herod yf they command to massacre the infants; their conscience bindes them to disobaye Nebuchadnezzar yf hee commaund them to worshipp his goulden image; their Geneva puritan Bible saith that the three puritans despised the King's Commaundment and that the twoe midwives theire disobedience was lawfull. Naye (theire puritan meaning is) it was their duety. Their Conscience in this matter consisted in Disobedience; and in generall all Juditious puritans houlde that it is against conscience to yeald obedience to Tyrannicall and lawlesse commaunds as of duety.

For Scott the supreme example of 'the Conscientious Puritan' was Samuel and he used the same Old Testament text as Bargrave—1 Sam. 15: 1–31 (the story of Saul and the Amalekites)—to show how a Puritan should proceed in dealing with a tyrant. In this case Samuel had acted in response to God's wishes by disobeying his ruler and slaying the evil Agag, thereby lifting from the Israelites the curse they had suffered for ignoring divine ordinance; however Scott was at pains to stress that he had done this not as a prophet, with 'an extraordinary commission'—as Bargrave and others seeking to defend royal authority tended to argue—but as a lesser magistrate: 'Samuel indeed was a prophett; but he did not all things as a prophett. He needed not any such extraordinary authorities to doe this extraordinary justice, with the consent of the State and he being himself a publique Magistrate'. This argument was to all intents and purposes an espousal of resistance theory. Scott was to stop short when it came to discussing the problem of who was to depose the King—and like most Englishmen of the day seemed to envisage this as being done only by God—but in most other respects—particularly in his view of the capacity of the lesser magistrate and the extent to which royal authority derived from below—he appears to have been in broad agreement with mid-sixteenth century authorities, such as the editors of the Geneva Bible whom he cited approvingly.[59] This was unusual enough for someone writing in the 1620s; but Scott went even further.

When it came to considering such a sensitive subject as tyranny

[59] KAO U.951/Z.10, pp. 7–8, 10, 14; R. Tuck, 'Power and authority in seventeenth century England', *HJ* xvii (1974), 45–51; Sommerville, *Politics and Ideology*, pp. 69–77; Tyacke, 'Puritanism, Arminianism and counter-revolution', pp. 140–1.

most early-seventeenth century writers, at least in print, confined themselves to discussing hypothetical or historical situations, leaving their audience to apply the conclusions.[60] Scott, however, did not. He was quite definite in pointing out that what he had to say bore direct relevance to the political situation of his own day. At first he argued this in general terms: 'wee ought, if wee bee as Samuel was in place and authoritie and have fitt opportunitie as hee hadd, to reproove our Kinge, in all loyall & duetifull manner nevertheless freely and plainely, saying, as that conscientious puritan, wherefore hast thou not obeyed the voice of the Lord'. Then he became more specific, castigating those who out of 'pittie', or 'rather than a worse mischiefe should follow', hesitated to face up to their responsibilities: 'this it is that makes soe many men now loute [i.e. submit] to those loutes our lawlesse deputie lieutenants and Captaines, and theire usurpinge and Tyrannizing Lords, and to lend and give away their moneyes and to suffer themselves to be pressed over the Seas and oppressed very strangly; not that they ought to doe this (for they doe better that will die rather than obay in such a case) but because they dare noe other'. Finally he brought home the full relevance of his argument and the immediate parallels with the story in the Old Testament:

> Subjects may disobey and refuse an unworthie Kinge his command or request if it be more then of duety wee ough unto him. Yea gracious subjects ought of duety in theire places to discountenance & disharten gracelesse Tyrants, that will not kill Agag, but in his defence fall out with the Parliament and with loanes & impositions & exacted services, contrarie to right and libertie, oppresse & exhaust the people and the wealthe & strength of the Kingedome.[61]

With this remarkable denunciation of the King, Scott encapsulated the central argument of his treatise and indicated its relevance to the loan. What was most striking was the readiness with which he specifically identified Charles as a tyrant and therefore argued that the subject had not only a right, but a positive duty, to disobey him. This was an extraordinary step to take, even for a godly zealot like Scott, and it requires some further consideration.

More than anything it seems to have been a response to the Duke. It is possible, through Scott's writings, to see the direction in which his ideas were developing, and these indicate that he had come to regard Buckingham as the main obstacle to harmony and

[60] Judson, *Crisis of the Constitution*, ch. 8.
[61] KAO U.951/Z.10, pp. 8, 9, 12.

good government in England. Indeed this would be something of an understatement. It appears that Scott hated the Duke with an intensity which was almost obsessional, endowing him with all the attributes of a popish demon. In a lengthy treatise on medieval history he compared him to the eleventh century Mercian ealdorman, Eadric Streona, who had betrayed his country in wartime and been responsible for the slaughter of some 40,000 Kentish folk. He also reiterated the charge that the Duke had been responsible for murdering King James, an act which invited comparison with the gunpowder plotters or the Jesuit regicide, Ravaillac. And finally, and perhaps unsurprisingly he was able to detect in him the mark of the beast, and argue that his ascendancy was the precursor to the millennium.[62] Of course once Buckingham had been identified as such a monstrous creature it was a relatively short step to regarding the King, who had defended him as a tyrant. The parallels with the story of Saul and Agag were inescapable, as Scott had indicated; so too were the oft-quoted examples of Gaveston and Sejanus. Charles's protection of the Duke was enough to seal his own fate. There was perhaps a touch of the irrational, even the hysterical, in the processes by which Scott reached this conclusion; but there was no lack of reason about the way in which he discussed and presented the basic features of his argument. It was framed in accord with conventions and commonplaces of contemporary political discourse, and would have been recognized as such by his readers. Two features in particular would have been reassuringly familiar.

The first of these was the idea that Parliament had a duty to advise and direct the King. Scott explained this by equating its position to that of Samuel, the divinely ordained subordinate magistrate, acting with the consent of the people:

> To denye this authority and power and more unto the State, people, commonwealth or Parliament in some cases, is against all grounds of government and state wisdom and to putt a sword into a madd man's hand, to cutt all our throates none daring to resist him because forsooth all the authoritie is in him. If Saul will not doe Justice and hereby bring a curse uppon him and the whole land what remedie, if the people or parliament may not, to expiat this sinne . . . hew Agag to pieces . . . if the King abused by his Streona or Gaveston will exhauste the people's wealth, the Kingdome's strength, in sending forth our marriners and souldiers and shippes unto certaine and probable destruction because untill justice be

[62] Clark, 'Thomas Scott and the growth of urban opposition', 7–8, 17–19; KAO U.951/Z.10, p. 13; U.951/Z.17/1.

done on King James his murtherers . . . we are accursed and cannot prosper & because the manageinge of these businesses is committed to him that is more likely to betraye us all then to deliver us out of our enemies hands; what remedie if the people or Parliament may not in this case rescue the state and the King himself, whom the traitor soe much abuseth to the ruine of himselfe & the whole realme?

To argue this was of course to claim an extremely exalted position for Parliament, and Scott seems to have gone even further in maintaining that the 1626 assembly 'which is not yett legally dissolved . . . may in such a case summon themselves'; but at least he was proceeding along lines which were familiar. The idea that Parliament, as 'the representative of the people', had a responsibility to advise the King was widely accepted, and many others apart from Scott regarded this as a crucial guarantee of an ordered and balanced polity.[63] Scott's views on Parliament, then, served to locate him, at least partially, within the pale of respectable political discourse. Much the same could be said of his discussion of the King's two bodies.

He introduced this in addressing the problem of what was to be done where the king was

soe bewitched or otherwise nose ledd or desperately resolved, as to sett his citties on fire, or his navie, or to sett open his ports to invadours, or lend or give awaye our shippes, ordinance, powder and marriners to our enemies . . . or massacre his most loyall & true hearted peeres & other patriottes. Must he be suffred to doe all this? If hee cannot otherwise be entreated and perswaded may hee not bee resisted? Are they not Traitors . . . even against himself whoe doe not resist him?

Unfortunately the treatise is incomplete and breaks off soon after this point; however it seems clear from what survives that in this situation—which bore obvious resemblances to the England of his day—Scott again believed the subject had a right to intervene, because the King's person was in a sense public property: 'Is it not lawfull in such a case to rescue King Saul (when hee would have killed himself and the Kingdom) from Saul the Kinge . . . To obay his Prince (or rather the man that was his Prince) in this case was it not to betray his Countrye and Prince'. This alluded to a distinction, developed and popularized in the sixteenth century, between the King's personal, natural body and the body politic,

[63] KAO U.951/Z.10, pp. 17–18, 19; Lake, 'Constitutional consensus and puritan opposition', 815–18; Cust and Lake, 'Sir Richard Grosvenor', 44–8.

residing within the person of the King but enjoying an independent existence. Scott was using an updated version of this idea, similar to that outlined by his namesake, the author of *Vox Populi*, who had argued for distinguishing between the King as 'publique person' and 'private man'. According to this when he acted in the public capacity, abiding by law, both human and divine, then his actions were unchallangeable; however 'when he doeth any acte of Justice without a law then he layes by the prerogative and dignity of a publique person and acts the parte of a private man. Because the law is the instrument and sword of a publique magistrate without which to strike is to tyrannize and without which to converse in any publique busines is to become private'.[64] 'Canterbury' Scott was utilizing precisely the same distinction, but unlike his namesake was prepared to employ it in a sense which was openly derogatory to his monarch.

This was perhaps the most remarkable aspect of his writings. Much of what he said basically consisted of taking the implications inherent in a series of political commonplaces and drawing them out to their logical conclusion. Obviously in doing this Scott went further than most, particularly in his espousal of resistance theory; nevertheless what would probably have struck contemporaries most forcibly was his readiness to apply these directly and unambiguously to the political situation of the day. This was the sort of thing which must sometimes have happened in private discussion; but it was extremely rare in a pamphlet intended for circulation, albeit to a restricted readership. Scott's arguments, if they had fallen into the wrong hands, would almost certainly have led to a council summons and severe punishment.[65]

This makes it particularly difficult to assess how far his views accorded with a broader body of contemporary opinion. Two possible conclusions suggest themselves: either Scott can be regarded as completely out on his own, putting forward arguments and expressing opinions which would have been completely unacceptable to most contemporaries; or he can be seen as representing a particular response to the loan, a response which because of its peculiarly perilous implications remained largely submerged. It would be unrealistic to expect to know, with any

[64] KAO U.951/Z.10, pp. 20–2; M. Axton, *The Queen's Two Bodies* (Royal Historical Soc. Studies in History, v. 1977), ch. 2; Lake, 'Constitutional consensus and puritan opposition', 814.

[65] See, for example, the fate of Hugh Pyne who was tried for treason for similar denunciations of the Duke and the King: below, p. 193.

degree of certainty, which of these is nearer the mark; but it is possible to offer some suggestions.

Much of the evidence—or rather lack of it—points to the first conclusion. There is nothing that I am aware of relating to the loan which approaches Scott's treatise. The Lincolnshire pamphlet was a call to opposition, but opposition on far more limited and specific terms and containing little of the rhetoric of resistance employed by Scott. Similarly the views on the loan and the Duke presented in contemporary newsletters and diaries never really matched the sustained invective of Scott. Perhaps the nearest equivalent would be some of the political ballads recited in alehouses; but their tone was altogether less serious.[66] The obvious deduction would be that his views were those of an isolated extremist who had perhaps become unhinged by his obsession with the Duke and his concern at the impending millennium. Yet such an explanation does not appear entirely satisfactory. It is important to remember that Scott's treatise was produced for an audience. We do not know of whom, precisely, this would have consisted, but it seems likely that it included friends and acquaintances amongst the godly of Canterbury, and there is no doubt that in such circles Scott enjoyed a considerable reputation. He had been called on to represent their interests in all but one of the previous Parliaments of the 1620s and was to be entrusted with their support again in 1628. He was also closely associated with influential figures at a national level, including Sir Dudley Digges, Knight of the Shire for Kent, Sir Randall Crewe the former Lord Chief Justice, and Sir Robert Cotton, the antiquarian.[67] It seems, then, that Scott was not completely out of touch with the realities of contemporary politics. Moreover extreme as his views on the Duke were, they accorded at least partially with the perceptions of others. One of his main charges, that Buckingham was responsible for the murder of King James, had been alluded to by the House of Commons in the articles of impeachment in 1626, and on the strength of Dr Egglesheim's scurrilous allegations seems to have been widely discussed.[68] It is therefore not possible simply to dismiss Scott as someone out on his own. Others may not have

[66] Cust, 'News and politics', 66–9.

[67] Clark, 'Thomas Scott and the growth of urban opposition', 4–23; *Proceedings in Parliament 1628*, vol. 6: Appendixes and Index, ed. M. F. Keeler, M. J. Cole, W. B. Bidwell (New Haven 1983), pp. 228, 230–1, 235, 239–40.

[68] Gardiner, *History of England*, vi. 101; *Rous*, p. 20; *C. and T.* i. 98–9.

wanted to go as far or as fast as he did, but it seems that some at least would have felt they were moving in the same direction.

In this context it is important to recognize—as Dr Somerville and Dr Tyacke have pointed out—that resistance theory was not entirely alien to early-seventeenth-century Englishmen. Indeed its main tenets were publicly rehearsed at Cambridge during 1627, in a famous series of history lectures given by Isaac Dorislaus.[69] It was also clearly visible in the advice given by Jeremiah Burroughs, chaplain to the Earl of Warwick, in 1638. In a series of statements which closely parallelled those of Scott, he argued—in the context of the Scottish Covenant—that the people 'did originallie choose their Kinges, and prescribe them conditions and limited their power by lawes' and that 'if the Supreme magistrate refuse or neglect that which he ought to doe and is necessarie to be done, maye not the people give power to some other to supplie his neglect and defect?' Not surprisingly Burroughs was hounded by the authorities and eventually driven into exile for expressing such opinions—and this helps to explain why they so rarely came out into the open—but this does not mean that they were entirely unacceptable.[70] On the basis of this case, and Scott's treatise, it seems plausible to suggest that in certain godly circles ideas of resistance represented part of a continuing tradition, and were liable to come to the surface when events made it appropriate, as in 1627.[71]

Their emergence at this time was extremely significant. For it should be evident that the writings of Scott, and to a lesser extent the Lincolnshire pamphleteer, reflected a situation which was rapidly progressing towards breakdown. The extent of this can be appreciated if we compare some of their basic assumptions which those revealed in more conventional criticisms of the loan. It was implicit in the statements of Eliot, Coryton and other critics that, however corrupted those around the King might be, Charles himself remained pure and virtuous. Whether they actually believed this was another matter. In public, at least, they committed themselves to the view that the King was not personally responsible for the measures taken over the loan; and

[69] Sommerville, *Politics and Ideology*, pp. 69–77; Tyacke, 'Puritanism, Arminianism and counter-revolution', pp. 140–1.

[70] K. W. Shipps, 'Lay Patronage of East Anglian Puritan Clerics in pre Revolutionary England' (Yale University, Ph.D. thesis, 1971), pp. 179–83, app. xiv.

[71] I am grateful to Gerry Bowler for suggesting this.

this meant that all that was needed to nudge him back towards traditional policies was a limited display of dissent and the advice of Parliament. With Scott and the Lincolnshire pamphleteer a completely different scenario presented itself. Both of them had come to face up to the evidence of the King's personal involvement in the loan, his oft-publicized objections to the re-summoning of Parliament and the fact that moderate councillors had been unable to persuade him to change his mind. Both had also accepted that he was playing a principal role in protecting the Duke. Taken together these revelations led to a strikingly different conclusion. Their arguments quite clearly implied that consensus could no longer be restored through a display of understanding and goodwill, or even through the more drastic, but still traditional, remedy of afforcing the Council. What was needed to deter the King from his tyrannical intentions was nothing less than an aggressive demonstration of opposition. With such assumptions we are within measurable distance of the Civil War.

All this is not to suggest that Civil War was about to break out in 1627. Rather it is an indication of the shift in attitudes which had taken place since the beginning of 1626. This, of course, was not due simply and solely to the loan. The agitation over the Duke and the sense of shock when the King put his preservation before the re-summoning of Parliament made an enormous impact; so, to a lesser extent, did the rise of Arminianism at Court.[72] The loan came on top of these two developments as another alarming sign of the breakdown in unity and drift towards prerogative rule. Its greatest significance perhaps lay in the fact that it provided an issue on which the individual could stand and fight. There was little a local politician could do about Buckingham's ascendancy at Court; and, as Russell has demonstrated, most were at this time ignorant of the implications of Arminianism.[73] But the loan was quite different. It raised issues which had been widely publicized and discussed since at least 1614; its implications for the future of Parliament appear to have been common knowledge right down to the lowlier subsidymen; it was something on which each taxpayer was called to make a personal decision; and it involved the issue of trust and faith in the King himself. For many, therefore, it provided perhaps the clearest test of basic political loyalties to be found anywhere before 1640.

[72] Russell, 'John Pym', pp. 159–65.

[73] Russell, *Parliaments and English Politics*, pp. 29–32.

4

Local Governors and the Loan

I. INTRODUCTION

REACTIONS to the loan have so far been discussed largely in ideological terms; however it should be obvious that this was not the only consideration influencing an individual's response. As with most political actions, this was as much a result of personality and circumstance: individual nerve, external pressure, and perceptions of immediate or long term advantage were all extremely important, and help to explain why those with similar views could often act in ways which were diametrically opposed. This is not to say that ideas can be discounted. As we have seen, the implications of the levy were so familiar and so widely discussed that few of those involved could have been entirely ignorant of them; and the way in which both the Crown and the local subsidymen approached it was shaped by their ideological preconceptions which therefore helped to influence the pressures each exerted. Rather it is to suggest that the effects of ideas can only be understood with regard to their particular context.

To say all this is perhaps to state the obvious; but it does seem necessary because there is a danger of assuming that the response to taxation was a literal indication of an individual's viewpoint, and thence to argue that the absence of open opposition demonstrated a lack of concern over the broader implications of levies such as the loan.[1] S. R. Gardiner pointed to the fallacy of this when he observed that the fact that most people paid the loan should not

> afford matter for surprise. The immediate risk was great. The refuser might be cast into prison or sent to be knocked on the head in some chance skirmish in the German wars. Except for the most resolute and self-sacrificing the temptation to escape the danger by the payment of a few shillings or a few pounds was too strong to be resisted. Yet small as the number of refusers was, the Government could not afford to pass lightly over their denial. It represented a vast amount of suppressed discontent . . .[2]

[1] This is implied for example in Morrill, *Revolt of the Provinces* pp. 20–9, although here the author was basing his conclusions on a study of ship money.

[2] Gardiner, *History of England*, vi. 154–5.

If the responses recorded in the previous chapter are anything to go by then Gardiner's analysis was largely correct. There is no doubt that in many cases individuals with reservations were pressed into making payment; and these even included Thomas Scott of Canterbury who paid his £8, as he said later, not 'willingly or in hope to have it again out of the subsidies, but, as I told the mayor and aldermen, to escape imprisonment and death'.[3] The threat of coercion was a powerful incentive and often the most obvious element in an individual's decision; however it was by no means the only one. Ordinary subsidymen were also influenced by the prospect of concessions, the effectiveness of enforcement and the example of leading gentry; whilst these gentry were themselves conscious of the state of local opinion, the balance of power within the shire and their standing in relation to the Court. Immediate circumstances impinged at every point in the process. Before attempting to explain individual responses, then, we should investigate some of the recent developments in local politics.

II. COUNTY POLITICS AND THE COURT

Something of the character of county politics after the 1626 Parliament was revealed in mid-July, in an incident at the West-Riding Quarter Sessions. Sir Thomas Wentworth, who was presiding over the court as *custos-rotulorum*, was suddenly delivered a note informing him that he was dismissed from his post. Wentworth's speech on this occasion has survived, and it shows that even in these embarrassing circumstances his customary eloquence did not desert him. He protested his loyalty to the King, his love of justice and his desire to serve his country. He also expressed his wish to pass out of office with 'the opinion of an honest man'. Finally he delivered a sidelong thrust at the two men responsible for taking away his place:

> I would wish they who succeed me had forborn this time, this service, a place in sooth ill chosen, a stage ill prepared for venting such poor, vain, insulting humours . . . Therefore shame be from henceforth to them that deserve it. For I am well assured now to enjoy within myself a lightsome quiet as formerly. The world may well think I knew the way which would have kept my place. I confess indeed it had been too dear a purchase and so

[3] *P. in P. 1628*, pp. 222–3.

I leave it, not conscious of any fault in myself, nor yet guilty of the vertue of my successor that should occasion this removal.

This successor was Sir John Savile, of whom Wentworth had said some years earlier, 'if Sir John Should supply the room in my place it would justly be taken as the greatest disgrace that could be done unto me'.[1] The loss of the custosship was a shattering blow. Not only did it subject Wentworth to public humiliation, it also forced him out of his main local office and deprived him of much of his influence in Yorkshire politics. It was perhaps not surprising, then, that this episode marked a watershed in his early career; however it was also significant for another reason, as an illustration of the interference from the Court which was becoming a feature of county politics subsequent to the dissolution of the 1626 Parliament. For the man ultimately responsible for Wentworth's removal, and Savile's promotion, was the Duke of Buckingham.

The dismissal was part of a purge of office-holders by which Buckingham punished his enemies and rewarded his friends. This was an unusual operation in the early seventeenth century and its impact was therefore all the greater. A little pruning had taken place late in 1625, when Lord Keeper Coventry had removed those who were inactive as JPs or otherwise unsuitable;[2] however the removals of 1626 were quite a different exercise, including five *custodes-rotulorum* and several other leading justices.[3] The purge took place in several stages. An initial list of seventeen names appeared in a letter from the Lord Keeper on 8 July; this was followed by piecemeal exclusions during August and September; and then a final batch of eleven names on 28 October. The causes of removal were not the same in every case, but the majority can be traced back to the Duke. There is little doubt that he was profoundly alarmed by proceedings in the 1626 Parliament and, as soon as he was released from the threat of impeachment, he

[1] *Strafforde's Letters*, i 36; J. J. Cartwright, *Chapters in Yorkshire History* (Wakefield, 1872)., p. 190.

[2] These removals went largely unrecorded in the Crown Office Docquet Books, but they have been picked up in local studies: PRO C.231/4; Fletcher, *A County Community*, pp. 129–30; A. L. Hughes, 'Politics, Society and Civil War in Warwickshire, 1620–1650' (University of Liverpool, Ph.D., 1980), pp. 102–3.

[3] For a list of the removals: Cust 'The Forced Loan and English Politics', app. 2. Gardiner has suggested that the removals were primarily intended to further the collection of the benevolence, but this seems unlikely given that two of those excluded—Digges and Earle—were chosen as privy seal collectors in August 1626: Gardiner, *History of England*, vi. 125–6; *APC 1626*, p. 168.

decided to take revenge on those responsible. The 8 July removals included six of the MPs who had offended him in 1625—Wentworth, Edward Alford, Sir Robert Mansell, Sir Guy Palmes, Sir Robert Phelips, and Sir Francis Seymour—together with a further ten involved with the impeachment proceedings of 1626—William Coryton, Sir John Eliot, Sir Dudley Digges, Sir Walter Erle, Sir Thomas Hoby, Edward Kirton, Walter Long, Sir John Strangeways, Sir William Walter, and Christopher Wandesford. A newsletter writer commented that 'most if not all of the parliament men that were justices and against the duke were put out of the commission'.[4] This first batch of expulsions accounted for many of the Duke's most obvious enemies, but there were others who had defied his friends and were now vulnerable as targets for persecution. John Poulett secured the removal of three men who had opposed him in Somerset—Hugh Pyne, John Symes, and Thomas Lyte—and two East Riding Justices—Sir William Constable and Sir John Hotham—were probably put out at the instigation of Viscount Dunbar.[5] Other dismissals seem to have come as a result of individuals being involved in the 1626 Parliament's committee for investigating papists in local government. This had been used to harass the Duke's most powerful Catholic friends and at one point had seemed to threaten Buckingham himself. A further four of those dismissed were closely involved in its work—Sir Francis Barrington, Sir Gilbert Gerrard, Sir Thomas Grantham, and Sir Richard Grosvenor.[6] The remaining removals consisted of another MP who had attacked the Duke in 1626—Sir William Armine—a local justice who had spoken out against the benevolence—Sir Francis Goodwin—and several gentry whose offence is unknown; however, Buckingham's vindictiveness did not end there. On 1 July he launched the processes by which Sir John Eliot was hounded out of his admiralty office in Devon, and a few days later he initiated a purge of the Essex lieutenancy by removing the Earl of Warwick from his office of Lord Lieutenant.[7]

[4] *C. and T.* i. 136.

[5] Barnes, *Somerset*, p. 163; see below, pp. 195–6.

[6] *CJ* i. 726, 823, 828, 863: HMC *Portland*, i. 477, Forster, *Sir John Eliot*, i. 491.

[7] PRO SP 16/31/2; *C. and T.* i. 124 (Warwick was not finally removed until 11 Sept. 1626: Sainty, *Lieutenants of the Counties*, p. 20. Buckingham may also have had a hand in the investigation of Sir Robert Mansell's glass patent begun immediately after the Parliament and resulting in a *Quo Warranto* in November 1626: Berks RO Trumbull MSS, misc., xviii, 19; *C. and T.* i. 165. Lockyer has sought to minimize the seriousness of these proceedings by arguing that 'there was no general purge . . . the punishment of ingratitude was

At the same time as punishing those who had crossed him the Duke also reduced the range of his own patronage. As we have seen, those who came to be promoted to the Privy Council and the Lord Lieutenancies were almost all men of proven loyalty, and even the granting of peerages was restricted to those whom he felt to be reliable.[8] All this had a decisive effect on the shape of politics, both at Court and in the counties. Probably the most damaging consequence was to reduce the opportunity for expressing dissent and securing change through normal channels. The advantages of a Court which was open to different opinions and different factions have been stressed by Russell and Professor Elton. Above all it helped to ensure that political conflict was 'earthed' to the Court, and to a large extent contained within it, under the supervision of the monarch. This had been the situation for much of the sixteenth century and continued even under Buckingham; but the changes after the 1626 Parliament began to alter the pattern, dividing a part of the political nation into 'ins' and 'outs' and forcing opposition to move beyond the confines of the Court and into the country.[9] The beginnings of the process can be seen if we turn back to Sir Thomas Wentworth.

The origins of Buckingham's distrust of Wentworth are something of a mystery. Hostility towards him amongst the Duke's clients in the Commons was evident during the first parliamentary session

simply the negative aspect of patronage, and an offender could usually work his way back into favour if he so wished: *Buckingham*, pp. 331–2. This considerably underestimates the significance of what was taking place. Although Buckingham chose his victims carefully—and avoided his most powerful enemy, Pembroke, who still had the King's favour—the relatively small number of obvious opponents who escaped shows that the purge was not far short of being general. It is also clear that its effects were to make a future working relationship with the victims far more difficult. One or two, such as Wentworth, were eventually reconciled, but the vindictiveness displayed by the Duke—for example in his pursuit of Digges (see below, p. 207)—drove many into uncompromising hostility. Buckingham generally seems to have seen loyalty in personal rather than ideological terms. This helped to maintain a broad range of outlook within his patronage network—and ensured that moderates such as Coke and Coventry still had a say in his counsels—however it also meant that once he felt his trust had been abused it was very hard to regain.

[8] See above, pp. 24–6.

[9] Russell, *Parliaments and English Politics*, pp. 9–12; G. R. Elton, 'Tudor government: the points of contact: iii. The Court', *TRHS* 5th Ser. xxvi (1976), 211–28; Hirst, 'Court, country and politics', pp. 133–5. The immediate extent of this division should not be exaggerated. Even in November 1626 it was still possible for Phelips to gain access to the Court and secure promises of future favour: see p. 107.

of 1625, which may have been due to Sir Thomas's defence of his former patron, Middlesex, in 1624. However it seems that the most damaging suspicions can be traced to the Oxford session of 1625 when, as Wentworth was informed by his court contact, Sir Arthur Ingram, the Duke 'was and is possessed that there were four in the higher House, that upon any complaint that should come up of him to them, that they with all their strength would set it forwards there. He is likewise possessed that there were divers combined against him in the lower House . . . many who had their conferences with these four Lords and others that were depending upon them, among which, you are not altogether free.' In fact Sir Thomas's main intervention—a speech which advocated withholding additional supply on 10 August—appears to have been innocent of any anti-Buckinghamite intent; and one of the 'four lords', his old friend, Lord Keeper Williams, specifically vouched for him to the King. However, given Buckingham's paranoia at the time, this was unlikely to have been sufficient. Williams's statement suggested that he was already suspect and the very mention of an association between the two men was probably enough to ensure his condemnation. Thus when a group of the Duke's enemies were pricked as sheriffs in November 1625 it was no surprise that Sir Thomas's name was amongst them.[10] This represented a considerable set-back, not only in preventing his sitting in the following Parliament, but also in indicating that he was *persona non grata* at Court; however Wentworth was nothing if not an opportunist, and whilst the Duke was casting around for allies to help him survive impeachment he seized the chance to manœuvre himself into favour. Under the auspices of his friend, Sir Richard Weston, he met with Buckingham, accepted his explanation that he had not been responsible for his pricking as sheriff and negotiated 'a contract of friendship, all former mistakes laid asleep'. Unfortunately the contract barely outlasted the Parliament. Wentworth's close links with Christopher Wandesford and the Earl of Clare, two of Buckingham's principal parliamentary critics, continued to render him suspect, and according to Abbot he was still thought to be collaborating with opponents in the Lords.[11] It was therefore predictable that as soon

[10] Eliot, *Negotium Posterorum*, i. 93–105. Russell, *Parliaments and English Politics*, pp. 168–200; *Strafforde's Letters*, i. 28; *Wentworth Papers*, pp. 236–9; J. Hacket, *Scrinia Reserata: a Memorial Offered to the Great Deservings of John Williams, D.D.* (1692), pt. ii, 17; Gardiner, *History of England*, vi. 33–4.

[11] *Strafforde's Letters*, i. 34–5; Rushworth, i. 450–1.

as the Duke felt more confident of his position, the order should go out for his dismissal. The initial impulse for this may well have come from his old rival Savile; but it is clear that by this time Buckingham distrusted him sufficiently not to stand in the way. The punishment had a considerable effect.

Wentworth had probably felt frustrated by Buckingham for some time; but whilst access to the Court remained comparatively open he had kept his feelings in check and tried to work through the favourite. In April 1625 he had written to his friend Wandesford of his 'pretences and hopes at Court . . . How to sett my cards uppon this new shuffle of the packe'. In August he was careful to dissociate himself from the first stirrings of opposition at the Oxford Parliament, and indeed responded encouragingly to an approach from the Duke. And even after the disappointment of being pricked as sheriff he had declined to join in a scheme to defy the Court by having himself returned as burgess in another county. Instead, as he explained to Wandesford, he was determined to

> fold myself up in a cold silent forbearance, apply myself chearfully to the duties of my place . . . For my rule which I will not transgress is never to contend with the Prerogative out of Parliament; nor yet to contest with a King but when I am constrained thereunto, or else make shipwreck of my integrity and peace of conscience . . . expecting that happy night that the King shall cause his chronicles to be read wherein he shall find the faithfulness of Mardochus, the treason of his Eunuchs, and then let Haman look to himself.[12]

He maintained this passive posture during the early months of 1626 and avoided any public expressions of support for the proceedings of Wandesford and the other leaders of the Commons; but his dismissal in July was the last straw. Presented with clear evidence of the influence of Savile and the duplicity of the Duke, he publicly denounced his enemies at the Quarter Sessions and later came to defy the Court openly by refusing to pay the loan.[13]

A similar progression can be seen in Somerset, again as a result of Buckingham's purge. In this case the individual concerned was a short-tempered and tactless lawyer named Hugh Pyne. He had already used his position as chairman of Quarter-Sessions to urge the grand jury to present militia ratings as a grievance in April 1626; however this was mild in comparison with his conduct after

[12] *Wentworth Papers*, p. 229; *Strafforde's Letters*, i. 33–5.
[13] Hirst, 'Court, country and politics', p. 133.

his dismissal in July. Poulett described him as raging round the county like 'a madde dogge' and striving 'to keepe backe the justices from the sessions and ... disorder businesses'. He was also alleged to have said that the King was 'noe fitter to be a King then Hicke Wright, which Hicke Wright is Mr. Pine's shepherd and ane naturall foole.'; and to have encouraged his son in the opinion that 'there would be a comotion in this kingdome and that wee should shortly bee at one ane others throtes by reasone that the Kinge was soe governed as he was ... that itt would never be otherwise untill the Duke's head was sett farther from his shoulders ...'. Predictably he was summoned before the Council and eventually tried for treason; but this only happened after his neighbours in Somerset had been treated to a spectacular display of defiance, towards both the favourite and the King.[14] This could do nothing but harm to the stability of the political order. Opposition was being channelled away from the centre and directed instead towards stirring up anti-Court feeling amongst local gentry and freeholders. As the events which followed were to show this was dangerous and divisive.

A second consequence of Buckingham's actions was to upset the balance of power and aggravate factionalism in a number of counties. This balance is often an elusive quantity, easy enough to recognize but hard to explain. It seems to have rested partly on the personalities and friendships of local governors, partly on their sense of the obligations of office and the expectations of their county, and above all, perhaps, on their maintaining continued and open access to support at Court. The central government had the final say in a whole variety of local matters which could curb even the most ruthless county politician and help to preserve the status quo. However for it to function effectively in this role of arbiter, it was necessary that all parties should be able to secure a hearing. If this was prevented, and one side gained exclusive access, then the balance would rapidly be undermined. The consequences were illustrated in the struggle between Wentworth and Savile in the West Riding of Yorkshire.

This started when Sir John Savile had voluntarily surrendered his custosship to Wentworth in 1615. Two years later he decided that he wanted it back and appealed to the new favourite

[14] PRO SP 16/36/46; 438/37: Bodl. L. Clarendon MSS nos. 251, 256 (I am grateful to Conrad Russell for these references); Barnes, *Somerset* p. 34; *C. and T.* i. 295; *Yonge*, p. 114.

Buckingham; however Wentworth was able to prevent this with a series of vigorous protests which the Duke was unable to ignore. Three years later the struggle flared up again with a disputed county election. Savile lost, but appealed to the House of Commons and had Wentworth reprimanded for threatening reprisals against those who failed to vote for him. In 1624 it was Wentworth's turn to protest, and he was able to prevent Savile obtaining a charter for Leeds on behalf of a group of wealthy clothiers. Finally in 1625 Savile was again defeated at the county election, but secured a fresh contest through winning the support of 'the major part of the courtiers' in the House of Commons.[15] There was little love lost in these disputes. Each side was out to destroy the other and was generally prevented from doing so only by the exercise of influence at the centre; however, in the absence of a Parliament, this could only operate whilst both had some purchase on the Court. Once this was denied to Wentworth there was no holding his rival.

Savile had become firmly attached to the Duke in the course of the 1626 Parliament, and it was this which tilted the balance of power. The first fruits of their relationship emerged in May 1626 when, with Buckingham's backing, he obtained substantial reductions in Yorkshire's privy seal loan. This was intended to offset some of the dislike he had incurred for his actions in Parliament and 'to make him popular in the country'; however it also enabled him to transfer the collectorships to his own friends and use the assessments to penalize Wentworth's allies. Further benefits followed when the Parliament ended: on 7 July Savile had Wentworth removed from the custosship; on the 18th he finally secured the incorporation of Leeds and was able to nominate himself and his friends as the first aldermen; on the 19th he was granted a commission to compound for all lands held by knight's fees in the West Riding; and by the end of the month he had been appointed Vice-President of the Council of the North, giving him virtual control in place of the discredited Lord President, Lord Scrope.[16] These grants ensured Savile's political dominance within

[15] Cliffe, *The Yorkshire Gentry*, pp. 282–6; A. Gooder, *The Parliamentary Representation of the County of York*, 2 vols. (Yorks Archaeological and Record Soc. xci and xcvi. 1935–8), ii. 168–71; H. Heaton *A History of the Yorkshire Woollen and Worsted Industry* (1920), pp. 220–4; Eliot, *Negotium Posterorum*, i. 93–105.

[16] *Wentworth Papers*, pp. 249–54; PRO SP 16/33/30; M. Beresford, 'Leeds in 1628', *NH* xi (1975), 140; Heaton, *Yorkshire Woollen and Worsted Industry*, pp. 220–4; Rymer, xviii. 739; R. Reid, *The King's Council in the North* (1921), p. 398.

the West Riding, but it was a dominance which depended largely on backing from outside. He had long been unpopular amongst the leading gentry—something which was demonstrated during the shire elections—and even his new found influence did little to change this. Sir Arthur Ingram came over to his side briefly, and regained a place on the Council on the North; but Ingram was a court operator with limited roots in the shire, and apart from him Savile could count on only two of the West Riding JPs—his son, Sir Thomas, and John Kay—together with some gentry and clothiers from the area around Leeds.[17] This weakness, however, was compensated by the backing he received elsewhere. Sir John Lowther, a Cumberland landowner who had also served the Duke in Parliament, was appointed to the Council of the North and the Yorkshire bench during July;[18] and Savile could also draw support from Buckingham's clients in the East Riding who had been secured in office through the dissolution of the Parliament.

These comprised a group of JPs with pronounced Catholic sympathies. The leader was Viscount Dunbar, a wealthy courtier who protected the Duke's interests in the north-east; and he was supported by Sir William Alford, who was alleged to keep 'company much with Papists, particularly Lord Dunbar', Sir Thomas Metham, who was a JP in spite of the complaints against his notoriously popish daughter, and Nicholas Girlington, a suspected church papist. During the period when Lord Scrope was President of the Council of the North these men had prospered. Dunbar, Alford, and Metham had all acted as Deputy Lieutenants, and Scrope's own catholic sympathies allowed them to follow their religious inclinations in neglecting duties such as the disarming of recusants.[19] With the summoning of the 1626 Parliament, however, this position came under threat. There had been an upsurge of anti-Catholic feeling, particularly in the East Riding, which encouraged the staunchly protestant local MPs, Sir Thomas Hoby and Sir William Constable, to move against Scrope, Dunbar, and the others. Their names had been presented to the Commons committee on Papists and then forwarded in the petition to the King. Informed sources believed that Scrope was almost certain to lose his place, and this would doubtless have

[17] Cliffe, *The Yorkshire Gentry*, pp. 282–3; Reid, *Council in the North* pp. 399–400; Rymer, xviii. 729; *APC 1627*, pp. 312–13; *Wentworth Papers*, pp. 250–1; *Fairfax Correspondence*, i. 30–1.

[18] *Lowther Family Estate Book*, p. 229; PRO C.231/4, fos. 203^{r}, 206, 207^{r}.

[19] PRO SP 16/67/105; 84/16; Cliffe, *The Yorkshire Gentry*, 289–90; *CJ* i. 825; Rushworth, i. 391; Reid, *Council in the North*, p. 391.

accounted for the East Riding group as well. However the petition was eventually rejected and Scrope reprieved after apparently receiving a personal assurance of Charles's protection. With this Dunbar and his friends were also secure, and their hold was further strengthened when Hoby and Constable were removed from the bench and Alford was appointed *custos rotulorum*.[20]

These changes ensured that the East and West Ridings became dominated by groups with strong court backing and relatively few ties amongst local gentry or freeholders. The balance of power in the North Riding is more difficult to assess, but the influence of Scrope and other allies of Buckingham, such as the Cliffords, meant that it was unlikely to stand in Savile's way.[21] The situation was tailor-made for him. His allies held most of the positions of power and there was no risk of his being brought to account by the Privy Council. He proceeded to exploit this to the full. Wentworth's friends were hounded for their privy seal loans and reported to the Council when they refused to accept Savile's assessments. The incorporation of Leeds was used to establish a narrow, self-recruiting oligarchy by which Savile and his allies forced local guilds and cloth-workers 'to bee a companye and submitt themselve to such rules and constitutions as they shall please to make, to bee fined, and imprisoned and called from their labour at their wills'. Savile also sponsored a series of drainage projects in Hatfield Chase, under the supervision of Cornelius Vermuyden, which led to complaints and riots by local smallholders. And most blatantly of all he abused the powers granted under a special commission of June 1627. This allowed him to equip a fleet of six ships for protection of the northern coasts, the money being provided by compounding with recusants and levying 6*d*. a chauldron on coal shipments. Local recusants seem to have received some benefit from the generous composition rates, but virtually everyone else suffered. The gentry resented his high-handed exercise of authority; Scrope and Ingram quarrelled with him as they were increasingly ignored; and Savile's idea of protection consisted of stationing a ship at the mouth of each port and threatening to press anyone who tried to leave without paying the levy. According to Christopher Wandesford, by September

[20] S. P. Salt, 'Sir Thomas Wentworth and the parliamentary representation of Yorkshire, 1614–1628', *NH* xvi (1980), pp. 143–4; *CJ* i. 823, 828; Rushworth, i. 391–3; *Fairfax Correspondence*, i. 27; HMC *Report on the MSS of the Duke of Rutland*, 3 vols. (1888–94) i. 477; BL Harl. MS 286, fol. 297.

[21] Cliffe, *The Yorkshire Gentry*, pp. 3, 165, 297.

1627 'Sir John hath lost many by his harsh carradge of things'; however neither he nor his friend Wentworth were in any position to take advantage. At the time of writing this, Wandesford was removed from the Commission of the Peace, Wentworth was confined in Kent and both were isolated from influence at Court. The only hope of bringing Savile to account was a Parliament, and Wandesford acknowledged as much by going on to explain that he and Ingram were already making their preparations.[22]

The events in Yorkshire were exceptional, but by no means unique. This much is apparent if we look at some of the other shires affected by Buckingham's intervention. In Nottinghamshire, for example, the Duke's backing settled a long standing struggle for pre-eminence and installed another of his clients in a position of authority, although with less disruptive consequences. This was William Viscount Mansfield, later Earl of Newcastle, who had been striving to make his mark since the death in 1616 of his former patron, the Earl of Shrewsbury. Much of Shrewsbury's land had passed into Mansfield's hands, and this provided him with a strong claim to succeed to the Earl's political dominance within the shire; however he was resisted by a group of long established county grandees which included the Earl of Clare, Lord Stanhope, and Sir Robert Pierrepont. It seemed unlikely that the struggle would be resolved until someone was appointed to fill the Lord Lieutenancy, kept vacant since the 1590s because of hostility to Shrewsbury, and in this respect Buckingham's favour proved the deciding factor. Whilst Stanhope and Pierrepont had been largely uninvolved during the 1626 Parliament, and Clare had figured prominently in the opposition, Mansfield remained loyal and gave the Duke his proxy vote. His reward was not long in coming: on 6 July he was appointed Lord Lieutenant.[23]

Mansfield's position was not dissimilar to that of Savile; but he was a man of very different personality, far more attuned to heeding the interests of his neighbours and so better equipped to combine the roles of court servant and county magnate. He was an assiduous and hard-working local governor who commanded the

[22] *Wentworth Papers*, pp. 251–2, 264–5, 271–2; Cartwright, *Chapters in Yorkshire History*, pp. 234–8; Heaton, *The Yorkshire Woollen and Worsted Industry*, pp. 225–6; L. E. Harris, *Vermuyden and the Fens* (1955) pp. 41–53; Reid, *Council in the North*, pp. 402–3.

[23] J. R. Dias, 'Politics and Administration in Nottinghamshire and Derbyshire, 1590–1640 (Oxford University, D.Phil. 1973), pp. 282–97, 309–18; Russell, *Parliaments and English Politics*, pp. 281 n., 314; HLRO Lords Proxy Book, 1626; Sainty, *Lieutenants of the Counties*, p. 29.

loyalty of most of the bench when it came to executing a service such as the loan; his 'great estate, liberal hospitality and constant residence in the county' earned him the praise of the otherwise hostile Lucy Hutchinson; and he was particularly adept at public relations, as was shown during the re-equipping of the county militia in 1626–7. After raising some £500 from the local taxpayers Mansfield had voluntarily 'ordered . . . that the same amount should be recorded amongst the sessions rolls, and be published in open sessions to the end that the county might take notice how their monies were disposed of: for which act of justice my Lord was highly commended'.[24] This example is a reminder that it was still possible to be a client of Buckingham and build a favourable reputation in one's shire; however Mansfield was the exception rather than the rule. Elsewhere the Duke's men attracted considerable, often deserved, opprobrium.

In Essex this need not have been the case as his principal allies, Earl Rivers and Lord Maynard, possessed much of the tact evident in Mansfield; however, the divisions in the county ran very deep and, as we shall see, could not easily be papered over. These were caused initially by the dismissal of the Earl of Warwick, who stood head and shoulders above other local landowners as the pre-eminent magnate in the shire. He had inherited a vast estate in 1619, consisting of over fifty manors within Essex alone, and in addition held the right of presentment to twenty-two advowsons and exerted sufficient influence to ensure that his clients were returned in forty-one out of the shire's sixty-four parliamentary elections between 1603 and 1640. This position was strengthened still further when he was appointed joint Lord Lieutenant in September 1625 and given the job of organizing the shire's defence against the invasion threat to Harwich. He performed this difficult task so capably that later in the year he felt able to ask for Buckingham's co-operation in securing the removal of his co-Lieutenant, the idle and inefficient Earl of Sussex.[25] This, however, proved to be the height of his local fortunes in this

[24] PRO SP 16/31/101; 55/1 i, ii; 73/32; Lucy Hutchinson, *Memoirs of the Life of Colonel Hutchinson*, ed. J. Sutherland (1973), p. 61 *The Life of William Cavendish Earl of Newcastle*, ed. C. H. Firth (1907), p. 5.

[25] Shipps, 'Lay Patronage of East Anglian Puritan Clerics', pp. 167–8; B. W. Quintrell, 'The Government of the County of Essex, 1603–1642' (University of London, Ph.D., 1965), p. 33; B. W. Quintrell, 'Towards a 'perfect militia'; Warwick, Buckingham and the Essex alarum of 1625', *Essex Archaeology and History*, xv (1983), 96–105; Bodl. L. Firth MS c.4, pp. 175, 179.

period. During the early months of 1626 he fell out with the Duke, first of all at the York House Conference and then during the Parliament, where his clients in the Commons played a leading part in the attempted impeachment. After the dissolution it was clear that Buckingham no longer trusted him. By 7 July it was being reported that he would be dismissed from the lieutenancy because the Duke 'would not have him joy too much in his service of overseeing the work at Harwich . . .'; and, although this was delayed for several months, the knowledge that it was about to happen proved disastrous since it gave the irresolute Sussex the encouragement he needed to cling to his post and submit himself to Buckingham's guidance and protection. In September 1626 he drew up a list of the names of his proposed Deputy Lieutenants for the Duke's approval. Notably absent was Warwick's client Sir Francis Barrington, who had served as leading deputy since 1603; and once the list had been presented another of Warwick's allies, the recently appointed Sir Harbottle Grimstone, was also struck off.[26] This purge marked the start of a period in which the Earl and four of his leading supporters—Sir Francis and Sir Thomas Barrington, Sir Harbottle Grimstone, and Sir William Masham—were all excluded from the government of the shire. Warwick was formally removed from his Lieutenancy in September and at the same time was deprived of his governorship of the fort at Landguard Point; the two Barringtons were removed from the Commission of the Peace in the same month; and Grimstone and Masham were struck off during the following June. The county was thus deprived of the services of five of its most active local governors; their attendance at Quarter Sessions ceased abruptly after September 1626 and did not resume until June 1628. In the meantime Warwick devoted most of his energies to a series of privateering ventures; Sir Francis Barrington, Masham, and Grimstone were imprisoned for refusing the loan; and Sir Thomas appears to have kept out of the way. This did not completely destroy the Earl's local influence—two of his clients, Sir Thomas Cheeke and Sir Arthur Harris, remained active on the bench—but it reduced it enormously; and, as a result, the shire came to be governed by a group of men who looked towards the Court and towards Buckingham.[27]

[26] C. Thompson, 'The origins of the parliamentary middle group, 1625–1629', *TRHS*, 5th Ser. xxii (1972), pp. 76–81; *C. and T.* i. 124, 149–50; PRO SP 16/35/24.

[27] PRO SP 16/36/22; 38/57; 41/55; E.163/18/12; BRL Coventry MSS,

In the frequent absences of the Earl of Sussex the all-important lieutenancy was dominated by William Lord Maynard. Maynard was not a courtier, preferring the life of a country gentleman, but was nevertheless firmly attached to the Duke's following. He later claimed a friendship with Laud which may have existed at this time; he wrote personally to Buckingham over the benevolence in the terms usually employed by a client; and he was sufficiently trusted to be given an English peerage in 1628 when the Duke was trying to increase his following in the Lords.[28] Maynard was the most important of the local governors in this period, but scarcely less influential, although enjoying little in the way of formal authority, was Thomas Earl Rivers. Rivers's pricipal connection with Buckingham was provided by his son-in-law, Thomas Lord Savage, who had long been a close adherent and had helped procure Rivers's titles. The Earl was a recusant and after being complained of by Sir Francis Barrington in the 1624 Parliament had been removed from the Commission of the Peace; however he remained useful to the Duke, acting as his intermediary in election negotiations with Colchester and providing another proxy vote in the 1626 Parliament. He also continued to wield considerable power within Essex. In September 1626 he was appointed along with Maynard and Sir Henry Cary to investigate Warwick's conduct as governor of the Landguard fort; the following month he was chosen as one of the shire's principal loan commissioners; and he seems to have been allowed some say in the choice of Deputy Lieutenants, probably being responsible for the selection of his close friend, William Smyth of Cressing Temple, who was not yet a JP.[29] Between them, then, Rivers and Maynard had temporarily supplanted Warwick as the dominant force in Essex politics.

They were supported by a group of men who were largely unaccustomed to playing the leading role and were similarly dependent on Court favour. The Deputy Lieutenants had all been

Commissions of the Peace, no. 74; ERO Q/SR, 249/61; Morant MS, D/DY/2/4, pp. 55, 63, 83; Quintrell, 'Government of Essex', pp. 44–5; *C. and T.* i. 215; *APC 1626*, p. 328; *APC 1627*, p. 262; Shipps, 'Lay patronage of East Anglian Puritan Clerics', p. 168 n.

[28] Quintrell, 'Government of Essex', pp. 121–5; PRO PCC Wills 24 Eveleyn (I am grateful to Nicholas Tyacke for this reference); SP 16/524/100; *Dep. Keepers Rept.*, xlvii, app., p. 114.

[29] *Chamberlain*, ii. 387; *CSPD 1625–6*, p. 468; *LJ* iii. 394; PRO E. 163/18/12; SP 16/37/64; PCC Wills 30 St John; ERO Morant MS D/DY/2/4 p. 59; HLRO Lords Proxy Book, 1626; Quintrell, 'Government of Essex', p. 138.

specifically approved by the Duke, including Sir Thomas Fanshawe whose promotion had previously been blocked by Warwick. One of the leading local JPs, Sir Thomas Wiseman, had been complained of for recusancy in 1624 and presumably owed his continuance in office to support at the centre. And the group as a whole lacked the personal and territorial influence enjoyed by Warwick's clients, something which was reflected in the fact that none of them gained a local parliamentary seat during the 1620s.[30] In more normal circumstances this need not have been a handicap. Much depended on the attitudes and personalities of the leading figures, and Maynard and Rivers were in many ways the ideal men to hold the situation together. Maynard was an industrious and conscientious local governor with a sure grasp of the best way to deal with taxpayers; Rivers was careful and responsive when it came to protecting the interests of his neighbours; and both were extremely respectful in their dealings with Warwick. They gave him a clean bill of health after the investigation into his governorship at Landguard; whilst Maynard, at least, refrained from involving himself in the ill-judged attempt to pre-empt the Earl's election plans in 1628.[31] This helped to reduce the tensions created by the purge of his supporters and prevented gentry politics from degenerating into overt factionalism; however, as we shall see, it was not enough to avoid considerable conflict and division.

In Cornwall the upheavals of this period also started with the displacement of a local magnate, in this case the Earl of Pembroke who was Lord Lieutenant and Lord Warden of the Stannaries. Pembroke did not actually lose his offices, but he seems to have been forced to surrender most of the local influence which he and his Vice-Warden, William Coryton, had used to build a following in the 1626 Parliament. By October he had removed Coryton from the vice-wardenship in favour of the Duke's nominee, John Mohun; he also dismissed Coryton, Sir Richard Buller and Charles Trevanion from their Deputy Lieutenancies; and during the 1628 election appeared to be doing his best to co-operate with Buckingham's supporters.[32] This left his own clients unprotected

[30] PRO SP 16/9/63; 35/24; *CJ* i. 395; Quintrell, 'Government of Essex', pp. 44–5, 139; *Returns of the Names of Every Member Returned to Serve in Each Parliament*, 2 vols. (1878), i. 450–79.

[31] Quintrell, 'Government of Essex', pp. 44–5, 121–5, 139–40; PRO SP 16/37/64; Quintrell, 'Gentry politics and the Witham affray', 122–4.

[32] Rowe, 'The influence of the Earls of Pembroke', 246–51; PRO SP 16/12/78; 36/37; 37/91; 68/25; 74/34; Russell, *Parliaments and English Politics*, p. 14 n.

and allowed the initiative to pass into the hands of the Duke's principal local adherent, Sir James Bagg.

Bagg is one of the more striking characters of the 1620s. He was spectacularly obsequious, even allowing for the patron-creature conventions of the day, and habitually subscribed his letters to Buckingham 'your excellencie's humble servant and slave'. He had a remarkable reputation for corruption, allegedly making a fortune out of supplying rotten victuals to the navy and earning the nickname of the 'bottomless Bagg'. And he seems to have shared to the full his patron's paranoia about plots and conspiracies. Hardly a letter passed between them without some mention of 'that pattern of ingratitude' Eliot, 'malicious' Coryton, or 'those who love not my Lord Duke'; and his unmasking of Buckingham's enemies during the 1626 Parliament was a masterpiece of poisonous invective, concluding 'knowe the instruments your enemye, and judge whether the principalls be your friends'. To contemporaries Bagg represented the worst type of corrupt, court-backed local tyrant, much in the mould of Sir Giles Mompesson; however this did not prevent him from exerting a dominating influence within Cornwall.[33]

His position was due almost entirely to the backing of the Duke. Bagg had first come to Buckingham's notice as Vice-Admiral for Cornwall in the early 20s. In 1625 he was given responsibility for victualling the fleet and after its failure sought his protection against charges of maladministration. He seems to have become one of the Duke's inner circle soon after this, and fully demonstrated his worth by uncovering the machinations of opponents during the 1626 Parliament. In the course of 1626 he was given the additional office of Captain of Plymouth and Collector of Customs in the southern ports; he was also entrusted with the task of hounding Eliot out of his admiralty offices, and came to be treated by Buckingham as an exclusive source of information on all matters relating to Cornwall. Bagg worked this connection for all it was worth, plying the Duke and his Secretary, Edward Nicholas, with a constant stream of malicious, and often false, gossip which served to discredit not only Eliot and Coryton, but also less obvious enemies such as Sir Richard Buller, Ambrose Mannington, and Nicholas Trefusis. All of these men were removed from office in the course of 1626 and 1627 and in

[33] S. R. Gardiner, 'Notes by Sir James Bagg on the Parliament of 1626', *Notes and Queries*, 4th Ser. x (1872), 325–6; Forster, *Sir John Eliot*, i. 204–5; ii. 142; *Yonge*, p. 89.

their place Bagg was able to secure power for a group of his own friends led by Sir Reginald Mohun and his son, John, Sir Bernard Grenville, Sir Richard Edgecumbe, and Sir William Wray.[34]

These six men enjoyed a position similar to that of Savile in Yorkshire. They controlled the lieutenancy and the vital service of billeting soldiers in the county; their enemies had been stripped of office and in some cases imprisoned in London; and there was little or no prospect of their being brought to account before the Privy Council. In these circumstances they were able to do more or less what they wished and this led to charges of tyranny and corruption. The Deputy Lieutenants were accused by Coryton of levying an illegal rate for the repair of Pendennis Castle; Walter Yonge, the Devon diarist, recorded allegations of neglect and profiteering in the supply of soldiers at Plymouth; and evidence presented to the 1628 Parliament suggested that John Mohun had been running a protection racket in the Stannaries. He was accused of selling tin-miners' privileges—to allow individuals who were not normally eligible to escape the jurisdiction of the Common Law—and imprisoning those who challenged him or requiring them to yield to warrants in which he simply declared 'To this submit or you will provoke me.' He was also supposed to have been preparing to sell similar exemptions to the whole governing body of the Stannaries, with the proceeds being used 'to defend them if in Parliament they be questioned'.[35] This was understandable since a Parliament was now virtually the only thing which could threaten him and his friends. In October 1626 it had seemed to be on the cards and an ally of Bagg's wrote apprehensively that 'thos friends of my Lord's such as Elyott was, geveth outt that the day is appoynted which is the second of the next moneth; and they have laboured for places allredie, and are sure of it, and geve great wordes what wilbe donne; and nottes taken whatt speaches have been geven, and notte bookes be fyled, and many other words given outt which wilbe to long to writt.' However this was not to be, and the reckoning had to wait until 1628 when, through Eliot's efforts, Mohun and his allies were summoned to answer before the Commons. In the meantime, although Eliot and Coryton might snipe at the lieutenancy and

[34] PRO SP 16/12/22; 60/75; 68/16; 74/78, 78i; C.66/2389, 2393; Hulme, *Life of Eliot*, pp. 153–7; *APC 1627*, p. 248.

[35] PRO SP 16/34/35; 74/34; 84/2; 85/8; *Yonge*, pp. 89, 97, 110, 112; Forster, *Sir John Eliot*, ii. 284–301; *CD 1628*, iii. 625–6.

encourage subsidy men to resist taxation there was little they could do to shift the balance of power.[36]

The pattern of events in Somerset closely resembled that in Cornwall. Again Pembroke's abdication of influence in the shire enabled an ally of the Duke to take control and purge his enemies. In this case the man was John Poulett. He had first become linked with the Court when the King stayed at his house in September 1625, and thereafter maintained contact by acting as host to the exiled Huguenot leader, Baron de Soubise. Poulett cultivated this connection assiduously, sending a stream of letters to Buckingham and Conway which combined a desperate concern for social propriety with a more than ordinary officiousness. In one letter he would be moaning about his gout and begging Conway to excuse his attendance on the King; in the next he would send up a local JP to complain of some words 'spoken in derogation of His Majesty's honor and virtues'.[37] His main concern in all this was to secure himself against his long-standing local rival, Sir Robert Phelips. The two men had been at loggerheads ever since the disputed Somerset election of 1614. Whilst both retained local office and support at the centre they were evenly matched and it was difficult for either to gain the upper hand; however Phelips's position began to crumble late in 1625 when he was removed from the lieutenancy, presumably at the behest of the Lord Lieutenant, Pembroke. The Earl's motives in this are not easy to discern, but it seems likely that he wished to avoid any association with the Duke's enemies of the previous Parliament and was therefore ready to dismiss someone described by his client, Sir Benjamin Rudyerd, as a 'rank weed' given to 'undutiful and seditious speeches'. Phelips's misfortunes continued after the 1626 Parliament, when as part of the July purge, he was removed from the Commission of the Peace, to be joined soon after by his allies John Symes and Thomas Lyte.[38] This deprived him of his official role in the running of county business and what little influence he had left depended largely on his popularity amongst the freeholders; however this was more or less useless, until a Parliament was

[36] PRO SP 16/37/52; *Yonge*, p. 115.

[37] Barnes, *Somerset*, p. 37; PRO SP 16/7/57; 36/7; 82/53; 83/21.

[38] Barnes, *Somerset*, pp. 163 n., 285; Russell, *Parliaments and English Politics*, pp. 20, 266–7. It is difficult to tell precisely when Phelips lost his deputyship, but it was probably between August 1625—when he received a circular from Pembroke to the Deputies—and November—when his signature was absent from a report of the musters: SRO Phelips MS 222/6; PRO SP 16/10/48.

summoned. As we have seen, in the autumn of 1626 this seemed distinctly possible and the prospects for Phelips and his allies immediately began to look brighter. Poulett reported that

> uppon the rumor of the overthrow given to the Kynge of Denmark all this county was filled with the news of a Parlament which should be verie shortly, and uppon that faith I heare some popular men doe allready seeke after places, and from there I conceave these men take upon them to make there conjectures . . . that Sir Robert Phelippes, Hugh Pyne, the lawyer, and John Syme shall be restored agayne to their offices of Justice before Easter, doe all men what they can.[39]

Their hopes, however, were unfulfilled and in the meantime Poulett was left in control of the shire. Pembroke's lack of involvement in the lieutenancy meant that he more or less ran this institution, supported by three of his clients, Sir Edward Rodney, Sir John Stawell, and William Walrond, and one of the few neutrals amongst the local governors, Sir Ralph Hopton. He was also able to use his influence at Court to have George Poulett and Sir Francis Rogers appointed to the bench and to secure the trial and imprisonment of another of his enemies, Hugh Pyne. For the period between 1626 and 1628 he and his allies enjoyed almost complete freedom of action. Phelips used what little influence remained to him to press a charge of corruption against Stawell at Quarter Sessions; but this was blocked when Stawell appealed to the Council. Similar complaints were also made by Walter Yonge, including an allegation that Stawell had billeted soldiers on Taunton freeholders who refused to support him in the 1628 election. However nothing could be done to remedy these abuses until the 1628 Parliament; and then Phelips launched a blistering attack on the lieutenancy, which resulted in Stawell and Walrond being summoned to answer charges.[40]

These examples should suffice to demonstrate the imbalances that could occur in county politics as a result of Buckingham's purge and the narrowing of the Court. The basic pattern of an assault on his enemies followed by the exercise of more or less untrammelled power by his friends was repeated in Somerset, Cornwall, and Yorkshire and to a lesser extent in Essex and Nottinghamshire. However it is important not to overstate the

[39] PRO SP 16/37/5.

[40] Barnes, *Somerset*, pp. 34, 42–3, 102–4, 249–58, 297; *C. and T.* i. 292, 295; PRO SP 16/86/37; *APC 1627*, pp. 453–4; *Yonge*, pp. 96, 114–15; *CD 1628*, ii. 254–5, 570; iii. 419–26.

effects of this. Beyond these shires the balance of power appears to have remained largely as before.[41] A good deal depended on particular personalities and the nature of relationships between the members of a county élite. Where there was a history of stability, or the leading individuals had avoided the purge, there was little apparent alteration. Hampshire, for example, survived largely unscathed, with co-operation amongst the county leaders remaining notably close during the following two years, in spite of the fact that two of the Deputy Lieutenants, Sir Benjamin Tichborne and his son, Sir Richard, had been reported to the Commons committee on recusants.[42] In Sussex the removal of Edward Alford from the bench, and the absence of Arundel from the lieutenancy, made little discernible impact since Alford remained a Deputy Lieutenant and Arundel's duties were assumed by Dorset, with whom he had previously been acting in harness anyway.[43] Similarly in Cheshire the dismissal of Sir Richard Grosvenor and Peter Daniell had no obvious effect. Their allies, Sir George Booth and Sir Richard Wilbraham continued to exercise an overriding influence in local government and the only client of the Duke's prominent in local affairs was Lord Savage, a long established and much respected member of the county élite.[44] In some cases changes at the centre may even have brought a positive improvement in the local situation. The drawing in of Buckingham's clientage network was probably one of the factors encouraging Lord Montague and the Earl of Westmorland to patch up their differences in the Eastern Division of Northamptonshire.[45] The experiences of these areas were probably just as representative, if not more so, than the counties examined earlier, and this should be allowed for before it is assumed that the problems of the period stemmed simply from an intensification of factionalism. This was not a rerun of English history in the 1450s.[46] There were novel factors at work, most notably the conflicts arising out of religious division and the

[41] There are, however, hints from Buckinghamshire and Kent that the Duke's following was becoming more aggressive and that this was again leading to conflict: *Verney Papers*, pp. 103–28; Clark, *English Provincial Society*, pp. 337–8.

[42] Rushworth, i. 396; BL Add. MS 21, 922, fos. 1–154; HRO Daly MS 5.M.50/1954; Jervoise MS 44.M.69/ 37–40, 45, 48, 012, 029.

[43] Fletcher, *A County Community*, pp. 176–7; 'Minute book of the Sussex Deputy Lieutenantship', *Sussex Archaeological Collections*, xl (1896), 1–37.

[44] C. P. Higgins, 'The government of early Stuart Cheshire', *NH* xii (1976), 50–1; VCH *Cheshire*, ii. 101–2.

[45] Cope, *Life of a Public Man*, pp. 111–12.

[46] R. L. Storey, *The End of The House of Lancaster* (1966).

ideological uncertainties engendered by the benevolence and the loan. Having made these qualifications, however, it is still possible to detect a certain change in atmosphere—not always immediately obvious, but probably recognizable enough to those involved in local government—which can be traced back to developments at the centre.

One of the clearest manifestations of this was the more prominent role assumed by leading papists. The Commons proceedings in 1624, 1625 and 1626, the increased numbers of presentments at Quarter Sessions and the disarming of prominent recusants must all have been considerable blows to the morale of those with catholic connections; but this was more than offset by Buckingham's willingness to welcome them at Court and the King's efforts to treat them as loyal subjects, in spite of the war.[47] Thus, many of the leading Catholics in this period actually appear to have been gaining in confidence, something which was reflected in their activity as local governors. As we shall see, several were particularly prominent at the time of the loan; and even before this, individuals such as Scrope, Dunbar, Savage, Rivers, Brudenell, and the Tichbornes were exercising their authority quite openly, in spite of the Commons attempts to curb them.[48]

Another sign of the times, not unrelated to the confidence enjoyed by the papists, was the much clearer stress on loyalty to the established regime. Several individuals found that, try as they might, there was no escaping this fact. One was Sir Dudley Digges who during the 1626 Parliament had been a leading opponent of the Duke, but afterwards made a determined effort to regain favour. The only obvious means to do this was through performance of the one local office which remained to him, that of privy seal loan collector in Kent; so, during the summer months of 1626, he threw all his energy into this thankless task. Before long, however, somebody must have told Buckingham what Digges was doing; he received a sharp letter from the Council ordering him to 'surcease from proceeding anie further or medling anie more with collecting anie such monies', and thereafter he was persistently harried by the Duke and his adherents.[49] As we have seen, others suffered in

[47] *CJ* i. 776, 828, 853; *Commons Debates for 1625*, pp. 18–27; T. S. Smith, 'The persecution of Staffordshire Roman Catholic recusants, 1625–60', *JEH* cxxx (1979), 330–1; Quintrell, 'The practice and problems of recusant disarming 1585–1642' *Recusant History*, xvii (1985), 214–20.

[48] See below, pp. 248–50; Quintrell, 'Recusant disarming', 218–19.

[49] *APC 1626*, p. 168, 257; *APC 1627*, p. 2; Phelips MS 219/35; Rushworth, i.

this atmosphere of suspicion and intolerance. The scheme for privy seal loans itself became a means of punishing those who had crossed the favourite; the malicious reports supplied by Bagg and Poulett achieved their effect largely because loyalty and subservience were at a premium; and Sir Francis Goodwin, the Buckinghamshire JP, was summoned before Council and removed from the bench after what were really no more than hints that he was obstructing the benevolence.[50] The threat of a summons now hung over local governors to an extent which they had not experienced before. In part this was due to the pressures of running a war, which tended to make the Council's responses cruder and more reflexive;[51] but it was also a result of the tenseness which pervaded the Court, increasingly drawn in on itself and inclined to imagine plots in every corner.

Perhaps the clearest reflection of the new atmosphere was the growing wariness which contemporaries displayed when it came to discussing national politics, particularly anything relating to Buckingham. Newsletter writers such as Clare or the Cambridge theologian, Joseph Mead, enquired anxiously whether their correspondence had gone astray; an Ipswich minister found himself under investigation for a sermon in which he intimated the Duke's responsibility for the dissolution of Parliament; and John Preston made preparations to flee to Basle after the discovery of a letter advising his friends that Buckingham could no longer be trusted.[52] Given the existence of informers like Bagg and Poulett these mishaps were always likely and demonstrated the need for those involved in local government to tread carefully. It was no longer enough for them simply to carry on as usual, performing their traditional role of reconciling the interests of their neighbours with the demands of the centre. They had constantly to be looking over their shoulders and asking themselves how the Court would view their actions and whether they would be seen as a threat to the Duke. Issues on which they had previously been agreed became fraught with tension and required careful handling; and as a consequence much of the neutral ground in local politics was swept away.

450–1; PRO SP 16/42/65; 475/49 (I am grateful to Conrad Russell for this reference).

[50] See above, pp. 163–4.

[51] Hirst, 'Privy Council and enforcement', pp. 50–1, 54–5, 60–2.

[52] NUL Ne.C. 15,405, p. 123; BL Harl. MS 390, fos. 181–2; PRO SP 16/33/60; Morgan, *Prince Charles' Puritan Chaplain*, p. 165.

These changes were linked to a third development which can be traced back to the Duke: the espousal, by some amongst the local gentry, of the anti-parliamentary ideas which were being mooted in some circles at Court. The roots of this development were present much earlier, and can probably be traced back to the broadly 'royalist' strain in much of the political thinking of the early seventeenth century; however it was the peculiar conditions of 1626–8 which brought it out into the open and provide evidence for its reception at a local level.[53] Perhaps the best way of tracing this is by looking in detail at the views of those gentry who gained control in Cornwall and Somerset. Not only has sufficient evidence survived to reconstruct some of their attitudes, but they can also be regarded as a reasonably coherent entity. Both groups of local governors were linked to Buckingham and the Court; they had experience of working together, with Poulett and Bagg combining to get Pyne removed from the Somerset bench; and they were regarded by an outsider, such as Walter Yonge, as belonging to the same genus of Court-backed local despot.[54]

The assumptions which they shared were based on a number of widely accepted political commonplaces. They supported the notion of a balanced political system in which royal authority acted as the keystone of order and hierarchy; without it, they believed society would be plunged into chaos and their own position undermined. They also subscribed to the idea that a Parliament should bring unity and consensus. All this was largely unexceptionable. Where they differed from the majority was in their idea of where the point of balance lay and how this unity was to be achieved. For, while most contemporaries ascribed a fundamental role to Parliament and the law, these local governors placed an almost exclusive emphasis on royal authority and the royal prerogative. This emerges from one of the most consistent themes of their discussions, the dangers of 'popularity'.

The idea that the lower orders were 'a many-headed monster' posing an ever present threat of social anarchy was again a commonplace of seventeenth century political thought; however it is significant that when Sir James Bagg referred to this threat, it was seen as emanating from a much higher social group than was normal. Usually the 'many-headed monster' was taken to refer to the shifting population of day labourers and vagrants who were

[53] Sommerville, *Politics and Ideology*, pp. 9–56; Judson, *Crisis of the Constitution*, pp. 107–217.

[54] PRO SP 16/36/46; *Yonge*, pp. 114–15.

thought to be responsible for a good deal of crime and disorder; and this group was distinguished from the respectable lower orders, consisting of yeomen and tenant farmers who attended church, filled parish offices, paid subsidies and voted in county elections.[55] In Bagg's view, however, the latter were just as potent a threat. This emerged from his discussion of Cornwall's response to Sir John Eliot's 'Petition From the Gatehouse', circulated in 1627. Bagg accused Eliot in this of 'an aim to popular glory although to his sovereign's unprosperity', and declared that 'I held it dangerous to roam up and downe among the many headed people, in these times made discontented by him and his accomplices.' Now, since the Petition was an attack on the forced loan, Bagg's reference to the 'many headed people' can be presumed to refer to the subsidymen who were being asked to pay and were likely to have an interest in Eliot's arguments.[56] In effect, then, Bagg was identifying the 'popular multitude' of contemporary rhetoric with a relatively elevated social group; and by doing so was able to obliterate some of the distinctions which were customarily drawn between different levels of the lower orders. Once this had been done it was open to him to regard almost any form of political activity amongst those below the gentry as potentially subversive.

John Poulett reflected a similar view in drawing Buckingham's attention to his actions in raising the benevolence. Again the 'popular' element consisted of local subsidymen and Poulett described how he and his friends 'for theire labour have not escaped without envye, reproaches, and the racking of ill tonges . . . yet that did not discurrage them nor me, who reverence the Majesty of Kyngs and their government to doe His Majestie all dubtifull service'.[57] Here Poulett was writing to vindicate the trust placed in him and his friends and the views he expressed can be taken to indicate what he thought the Duke wanted to hear. Thus it is particularly suggestive that he framed his account in such a way that unpopularity amongst the subsidymen was taken as additional proof of loyalty and fitness to serve the King. It reflected the awareness of a tension between the expectations of 'popularity' and the royal service which was fundamental to the outlook of these gentry.

[55] C. Hill, 'The many-headed monster' in *Change and Continuity in Seventeenth Century England* (1974), pp. 181–204; Cust and Lake, 'Sir Richard Grosvenor', 45–51.

[56] PRO SP 16/87/11.

[57] PRO SP 16/37/5.

This emerged perhaps most clearly from an appeal to the King by Bagg's Cornish allies after the shire election of 1628. The summoning of a Parliament directly threatened this group through the opportunity it gave their enemies for launching an enquiry in the Commons. The Deputy Lieutenants therefore responded by mobilizing their influence against Eliot and Coryton and sending out letters to landowners and office-holders to dissuade them from giving support. In the event they failed, and one of Coryton's first actions on being elected to the Parliament was to demand an investigation, which resulted in Sir William Wray, John and Edward Trelawney, and Walter Langdon being summoned and imprisoned. They responded by producing two petitions to explain their actions, one apparently addressed to the Commons and the other to the King.[58] These differed markedly, both in their rhetoric and the nature of their arguments. They therefore provide an interesting insight into the Cornishmen's perceptions of what each audience wanted to hear. The petition to the Commons was directed mainly towards demonstrating that their actions had been governed all along by precedent and local practice, and that their intention had not been to impede a free election, but 'to avoid faction amongst the gentlemen and a great expense to the freeholders'. That to the King took an altogether more aggressive and self-confident line. It began by requesting him 'to take these proceedings against us into your provident consideration and to foresee how dangerous the precedent of our suffering herein may prove for the discouragement of your best affected subjects'. The basic reason for their actions, they said, was that 'Our gracious King in his declaration of the dissolution of the last parliament, f. 19, has a passage that the House was then abused by the violent passions of some few members thereof. Therefore out of our duties to His Majesty we thought good to advise our country gentlemen to beware of giving their voices for our shire knights unto men of unquiet spirits.' The sort of continuing disruption that could be expected from such men had been amply demonstrated during the election campaign when Coryton had 'laboured . . . the whole county, by means of himself and his friends, divulging amongst the vulgar the . . . pretence that he had suffered for his country'. This the Cornish deputies conceived to be 'an unworthy way, tending to the alienation of

[58] *CD 1628*, ii. 33; iii. 7; PRO SP 16/106/14, 14i; 471/69 (I am grateful to Conrad Russell for this reference. This does not have a heading, but the petition is addressed 'To the House', presumably the Commons).

people's hearts from our gracious sovereign'. They had therefore opposed the election, 'lest' as they explained elsewhere, 'His Majesty suspect our fidelity'.

Perhaps the most interesting aspect of this statement was the way in which it demonstrated that these local governors were coming to be influenced by the 'new counsels' mooted at Court. The reference to the King's *Declaration*, the concern with the threat of 'unquiet spirits' and the recognition that the demands of 'popularity' were incompatible with the demands of the Crown were just what one might have expected from the Duke's entourage. The fact that such views were being espoused by local governors out in the shires was potentially extremely significant. For like Bagg and Poulett, these Cornish local governors seem to have taken 'popularity' to mean respecting the interests of subsidymen and freeholders; and once this happened many of the traditional assumptions pertaining to the role of MPs or local governors came into question and a good deal of the political middle ground was in danger of being swept away.

Much the same point can be made by looking at the ways in which these same local governors regarded Parliament and the law. For most seventeenth-century Englishmen Parliament was the linchpin of the political system. It provided an opportunity for King and subject to come together; it marked the point at which the individual freeholder was most fully involved in the process of government; and it constituted the moment in which power was transferred upwards, from the subject to the sovereign. A meeting of Parliament was therefore something to be sought after and celebrated. Not so, however, for Bagg and his allies. They had come to view it as a threat precisely because of that feature which others revered and valued, the opportunity which it gave for broad participation in the political process. Hence Bagg, in September 1626, decried Parliament as that 'which your Lordship fynds the vulgers cry for, thinkinge that to be the waye unto their ends and their libertie, which I grieve is soe muche'. In the same vein Poulett noted that in Somerset it was regarded as a means by which the 'popular men' would recover their places and attain their ends.[59] And, most strikingly, John Mohun, envisaged some sort of permanent alternative, arguing that whilst Parliament continued

no state could ever be well ordered, because in Parliament every man

[59] PRO SP 16/37/5, 91.

would have his own fancy and so nothing would be brought into any certainty of settlement by that course. For his own part he would prefer to commit, under authority from the Privy Council, the direction of business in the severall counties to a certain number of men selected in each for the purpose, whereby he was convinced public affairs would be better ordered and disposed.[60]

This was an obvious echo of the advice being given by some of Buckingham's clients at the time of the launching of the loan. Beyond this, however, it was also a reflection of the very limited view of the functions of a Parliament which the Cornish members of this group, in particular, seem to have entertained.

Bagg was perhaps the most forthright. He described Parliament's position as analogous to 'a garden of His Majestie's delights . . . so as in it the roses of his prerogative be preserved'. Accordingly it should play an entirely passive and submissive role, its scope for advising the King being severely restricted, because counsel ought to be 'as secret as night' unconstrained by 'the barbarous people's misconceit of their prince's actions, which lights first upon his nearest and dearest councillors as most obvious to the vulgar eye'. This in turn led him to offer a vision of 'that Union betwixt His Majestie and his people . . . that he love them for their obedience and they render him service and love for his protection and power, which God still increaseth'.[61] This was obviously an extreme viewpoint but it was one not totally divorced from notions held by other contemporaries. There were parallels in the view of Parliament put forward by royalist divines like Manwaring; and it is perhaps significant that Bagg employed the term 'recusant subjects' to describe the loan refusers, a usage probably coined by Manwaring.[62] There were also distinct echoes of Bagg's ideas in one of the letters sent out by the Cornish Deputy Lieutenants during the 1628 election. In this they urged Coryton to desist from his candidature since

we are to prefer a petition that His Majesty would lend us ships and to have some salt etc., and to be paid conduct money and to gratify our county, and to exempt us from billets and to obtain a magazine all which are to be presented to the knights. Now how gracious you and Sir John Eliot are, you know, and how many ways His Majesty hath expressed his displeasure against you. And His Majesty will conceive your election to be

[60] This is a summary of Mohun's views, given by Sir William Courtenay to Sir John Eliot in July 1628 and cited in Forster, *Sir John Eliot*, ii. 112–13.

[61] PRO SP 16/87/11; 101/56.

[62] PRO SP 16/87/11; Manwaring, *Religion and Obedience*, pp. 31–2.

an affront to his service and so we shall draw the displeasure of the King upon us.[63]

On the face of it, this request seemed reasonable enough; however it did imply a rather unusual view of the way Parliament should proceed. Whereas it was normally regarded as an opportunity for the people's representatives to offer advice on their needs and grievances, and secure benefits through an exchange of gifts, these Cornish deputies envisaged gaining concessions simply through submitting themselves to the generosity of the monarch; and this in turn suggested a view of Parliament as largely bereft of independent power and entirely subordinated to the sovereign's will.

The same high prerogative line was apparent in their view of the law. Bagg and his allies justified this, at least initially, by invoking the doctrine of necessity, that in a just war the King had an obligation to take the measures necessary for the country's defence. Sir Edward Rodney expounded it in an address to the Somerset subsidymen, delivered during collection of the 1626 benevolence. He began by declaring that he had not thought any previous benevolences to be justified and had therefore resisted them; on this occasion, however, the King was 'ingaged in a just warr which must be supported with money . . . and shall not the King bee rewarded, shall not hee bee suplyed and suported with our bodyes, with our purses, with any thinge we have in doeing our busines, the busines of the commonwealth'.[64] This was a common enough argument and would have been acceptable to most Englishmen; however it needed only a slight shift in emphasis and tone to be seen as posing an alarming threat to fundamental liberties. This was demonstrated in Sir James Bagg's reply to Eliot's 'Petition', which argued very much the same case, but pointed to some distinctly worrying possibilities:

> Must the land be tied to the positions of peace in war? Or, in violent weather, must the traveller be tied to a Spanish pace? Or shall martial law be regulated by common law? . . . wars are necessitious; honour and safety are both at stake. Shall not the head then use all his counsels, ways, acts and policies of state to keep off foreign and suppress homebred dangers . . . Yes! and that with both praise and glory! For necessity hath no law.[65]

Much depended on the spirit in which the doctrine of necessity was interpreted and the precise extent to which it was seen as

[63] *CD 1628*, ii. 33. [64] BL Add. MS 34, 239, fos. 45, 49.
[65] PRO SP 16/87/11.

being bounded and limited by the law. This was where disagreements over its application originated, and where both Rodney and Bagg were out of step with a good deal of contemporary opinion.

Rodney's views seem to have been shaped largely by his experiences as a Deputy Lieutenant during the war years. As he explained to the 1628 Parliament, in attempting to justify himself against charges of issuing illegal warrants for billeting,

> The reason that guided us to do as we did is the example of other countries that have given way to the execution of those commands. Let us not then be blamed alone. We were also induced because we heard of the King's absolute power in Westminster and we know the great power of Kings in arms, all which transcends the law. Also we had an inevitable necessity which was apparent and visible. The soldiers came to us as soon as the letters: they came with weapons by their sides and merit in their hands from the King's service in France, and with necessity and hunger in their bellies.

This was a good deal more extreme than most of the Commons were prepared to stomach and Rodney's argument were immediately denounced by a succession of speakers: however at least they could be interpreted as a temporary response to the needs of the war.[66] Bagg's views on the subject contained no such saving condition, implying a much broader perspective and an even more limited role for the law. He appears to have accepted that there was something called law, which was binding on both King and subject; but its scope was so restricted that it could offer no effective limitation to the monarch's powers. This emerged from his clause by clause analysis of Eliot's objections to the loan.[67] To start with Eliot had cited conscience, which obliged one to obey the law, as ground for his opposition, something which Bagg dismissed by pointing out that conscience, 'which is the centre of virtue', could never 'deny tribute to Caesar'. He had then argued that payment was illegal on the basis of the statutes relating to benevolences. In response to this Bagg had taken each statute in turn and shown that they were either granted 'by the grace of a prince' and therefore 'must not be urged as a duty' or that they had been obtained under duress from monarchs anxious for their 'own quiet and subject's safeguard'. Finally Eliot had cited Magna Carta, and this drew from Bagg his most extreme pronouncement. He described this traditional bulwark of Englishmen's liberties as

[66] *CD 1628*, ii. 254–5.

[67] PRO SP 16/87/11.

not originally freely and regally granted nor . . . voluntarily confirmed. The beginning was in Henry the first's time who was but a usurper and to establish himself in that usurpation did by it curry favour with the nobles and smooth the people . . . And for the confirmation of his Magna Charta, King John having as crackt a title as Henry the First had used the same policy in selling his regality . . . Not yet was Magna Charta thus extorted, a law till the 52nd year of Henry the Third. Neither was it then so freely enacted by the royal assent (which is the form and life of a law) as wrung out by the long, bloody and civil wars of those never to be honoured barons. Yet sithence hath many pious princes suffered them to enjoy an equal liberty under it, preserving to every man his own vine. But it never was, as now . . . made a chain to bind the King from doing anything and a key to admit the vassel to everything.

The last sentence epitomized Bagg's outlook. He saw the law, like Parliament, as completely subservient to the royal will, bounded by the King's grace and useful only in so far as it allowed for the unfettered exercise of the royal prerogative.

This was obviously an extreme viewpoint, put by somebody who had imbibed the royalist ideas circulating at Court;[68] but as with 'Canterbury' Scott it would be unwise to dismiss Bagg as completely out of touch with other contemporaries. As we have seen, several of his allies from Cornwall and Somerset subscribed to similar ideas: Poulett shared his abhorrence of 'popularity', Mohun his distrust of Parliaments and Rodney his views on the implications of necessity. Perhaps none of these was prepared to go as far as Bagg, or was capable of presenting such a rounded view of the king's overriding authority; but clearly they were moving in the same direction and were ready to accept many of his basic assumptions.

This response appears to have been shaped by two particular influences which applied more widely than just these two shires: first of all the tone and content of discussion at Court, especially within the entourage of the Duke; secondly the experiences of local governors within their local context. The impact of the first of these can be seen, for example, in Sir John Lowther's anxieties at the pressure from the 'Multitude' or the determination of the Lincolnshire JP, Sir Nicholas Sanderson, that in spite of the misgivings of his neighbours, 'we must obey necessity'. Both men were basically local governors, active and hardworking within their shires, but also enjoying experience in Parliament and

[68] For similar comments on Magna Carta made by Laud, probably in 1628: PRO SP 16/96/31.

contacts with the Court.[69] As such they were typical of the means by which 'new counsels' were conveyed outwards; however the acceptance of ideas depended to a large extent on individual experience, and here the pressures and problems encountered during the war years played a significant part.

Most local governors faced increasing opposition and hostility as they were required to enforce burdensome and often unpopular measures on their neighbours. The majority, of course, did not react in the manner of the Deputy Lieutenants in Somerset and Cornwall; but there is evidence that quite a significant minority were being drawn in this direction. As we have seen one of the Buckinghamshire JPs, probably Sir Thomas Denton, was prepared to recommend extensive conciliar interference over the benevolence, that 'the ill affected' might be discovered 'and their factious intentions either wholy prevented or in great measure suppressed'. A similar recommendation came from the Gloucestershire commissioners at the time of the loan, when they went in fear of 'being laugh'd at for our paines'. And another Lincolnshire JP, Sir Edward Heron, after being reduced to exasperation by his neighbours' obstructiveness turned informer against them with the comment that 'I had rather offend in too much officiousnesse than negligence, especially to the King's service.'[70] This was the sort of response that led logically to the proposals put forward by Mohun, or to Rodney's speech in the 1628 Parliament.

As has been observed, all this helped to produce a markedly different atmosphere in local politics after the 1626 Parliament. Purges of local officials and informing against neighbours were rapidly becoming the order of the day, and with the narrowing of the Court and no immediate prospect of a Parliament, the opportunities to obtain a hearing at the centre became much more limited. In these circumstances responses became cruder and

[69] *Lowther Family Estate Book*, p. 229; Holmes, *Seventeenth Century Lincolnshire*, p. 107; PRO SP 16/78/11; *The Works of Robert Sanderson*, ed. W. Jacobson, 6 vols. (Oxford, 1854), ii. 1–2; iii. 1–2; vi. 288, 296.

[70] Hirst, 'Privy Council and enforcement', 49–50; Russell, *Parliaments and English Politics*, pp. 70–84, 324–34; PRO SP 16/34/69; 56/12; 72/36; Holmes, *Seventeenth Century Lincolnshire*, p. 107. For evidence of Heron's excessive zeal in summoning Lincolnshire men before the Council: *APC 1627–8*, pp. 161, 175, 206. He was also a notably aggressive landlord whose efforts to exploit his manorial rights in Surfleet had led to lengthy litigation with his neighbours. This helps to explain his political attitude: C. Holmes, 'Fenland disturbances in seventeenth century Lincolnshire' in A. Fletcher and J. Stevenson, eds., *Order and Disorder in Early Modern England* (Cambridge, 1985), pp. 182–6.

divisions inevitably deepened. Perhaps the most disturbing development was the spread of 'new counsels' out into the shires; for arguments about doing away with Parliament, casting aside the constraints of the law and teaching the subject a lesson in obedience represented a virtual mirror image of the views being put forward by more extreme opponents of the regime. In common with these they tended to assume that consensus had broken down, the middle ground largely swept away and that nothing less than a display of force would restore the rightful balance. This was the sort of view calculated to exacerbate differences still further.

III. RESPONSES TO THE LOAN

It is appropriate to begin this analysis of local governors' reponses to the loan by looking at those who refused, since it was their actions which did most to influence the later course of events. A precise estimate of numbers is almost impossible because the sources tend to be uneven and unless someone was actually summoned before the Council there is often no record of their refusal. Some seventy-six leading refusers were released at the time of the Councils' amnesty in January 1628, but allowing for those released earlier or never recorded the total was probably well over a hundred.[1] These were concentrated in the four shires where resistance was heaviest: Essex, Gloucestershire, Lincolnshire, and Northamptonshire. Elsewhere opposition was spread relatively thinly and there were rarely more than two or three leading refusers per shire.[2] The first task then must be to try to understand the motives of these individuals. Why were they prepared to stand up and be counted when their fellow local governors—who in many cases demonstrably shared their views—kept their heads down?

Obviously, to some extent, the reasons were personal. The state of a person's health or finances must have been an important factor, particularly as the more prominent refusers knew that they

[1] *APC 1627–8*, pp. 217–18. The rolls of lenders prepared for the Exchequer sometimes indicate additional defaulters; however the survival of these is extremely patchy. For a prominent refuser who appears to have escaped the attention of the Council see the case of Christopher Wandesford: *Wentworth Papers*, p. 267.

[2] This is based on a detailed analysis of the responses of loan commissioners in twelve shires contained in my thesis: Cust, 'The Forced Loan and English Politics', app. 3.

were liable to a spell of imprisonment; so too must individual determination and conviction. There was undoubtedly a sense amongst some refusers that they were involved in a crucial struggle for Englishmen's liberties, and the significance of this sort of idealism should not be underrated. It often seems to have supplied the resolution needed to face up to what was, after all, a very unpleasant ordeal. Several of the loan refusers died, either during their period of imprisonment or soon after, and virtually all of them were subject to worries and pressures from anxious relatives.[3] In these circumstances it helped to have a sense of personal purpose. This was clearly revealed in the prison letters of George Radcliffe, a Gray's Inn attorney from Yorkshire who was also a close friend of Sir Thomas Wentworth.

Radcliffe had been in London since the early days of the loan and had been able to observe at first hand the mounting excitement as the judges refused to subscribe and then large numbers of gentlemen resisters began to arrive from the shires. It took him until almost the end of April 1627 to decide to join them, but once his mind was made up be became fully involved in the excitement of the struggle. In an early letter to his wife—responding to reminders about his earlier doubts—he observed

> It is very true my resolution always was rather to yield by compulsion than to stand out to prejudice of my estate or course in profession. I always tould you so, neither is my minde altered from it, if nothinge else had come betweene; but now when it shall be thought I shall prejudice the public cause, beginning to conforme, which none hath yet done (of all that have been committed), except two poor men (a butcher and another) and they hooted at like owles amongste their neighbours.

Elsewhere he recalled that, although 'God hath blessed us at Overthorpe with many comforths, and I hope in his mercy he will continue them . . . they would scarce be comfortable if they should be hurt either with an unquiet minde or with public infamy and shame, which every honest man will and must respect, and take care to avoid; yea and every wise man too, that hath such a profession as I have.' And he frequently hinted at the elation, and sense of moral release, which accompanied imprisonment in these

[3] The loan refusers who died included Sir John Pickering and Sir Edmund Hampden of Northamptonshire and Sir John Corbet of Norfolk: PRO PCC Wills, 19 and 53 Barrington; *C. and T.* i. 318. Their sufferings were to be recalled in the Grand Remonstrance of 1641: S. R. Gardiner (ed.), *The Constitutional Documents of the Puritan Revolution 1625–1660* (3rd edn., 1936), p. 209.

circumstances: 'although restraint of libertye be a thing which naturally all avoid, yet in this restraint I thank God, I enjoy as much contentment as ever I did in my life, nether more comforth of, my friends, nay never . . . more joy then at this time . . .'; 'I have done hitherto what I thought fitt to be done; and I never begunne nor continued any action in my life with more courage and constancye.'[4]

Radcliffe's letters provide an unusually vivid insight into the thoughts and sensations experienced by one particular loan refuser; but his sense of being part of a worthy and ennobling cause was not unique. Others recognized this, and sometimes showed signs of wanting to get in on the act. The Cornish refuser, Sir Bevil Grenville, for example, wrote to his imprisoned friends, Eliot and Coryton, with a sense of regret that he had been left at home whilst others were summoned to answer:

> I cannot but out of the fulnesse of my griefe be verie passionate at your long suffering, from which there hath not wanted the prayers of many good men to redeeme; but whence it growes that I am thus long left at home, when now of late also more of the honest knot are fetched, drives me into wonder and amazement. No man hath with more bouldness declared his resolution in this perticular then myselfe, which noe torture can divert me from, while in my owne heart I am satisfied that it belongs unto the duty of an honest Englishman so to do.[5]

This sense of facing a moment of decision and a test of one's mettle was particularly marked amongst Puritans. They sometimes appear to have seen the act of resisting the loan as an extension of their religious experience, as in the case of the Essex refuser, Sir Francis Barrington. When he took his stand in November 1626 he was already sixty-five and sufficiently conscious of his fragile health to draw up a will as soon as the Council ordered him into confinement. Within a few months he was reported to be 'in so deep a consumption (having sucked a woman's breast these five weeks) that he is not likely to live long' and, although he survived this illness, he was to die soon after his release in July 1628.[6] The whole episode must have been peculiarly harrowing, for both himself and his family; but Barrington did not falter. Until ill

[4] *Radcliffe Correspondence*, pp. 133–7, 139, 148, 150, 153.

[5] R. Granville, *History of the Granville Family* (1895), pp. 163–4.

[6] G. A. Lowndes, 'The history of the Barrington family', *TEAS* New Ser. ii (1884), 23; *APC 1626, p. 328;* Russell, *Parliaments and English Politics*, p. 30; *Barrington Family Letters 1628–1632*, ed. A. Searle (Camden Soc., 4th Ser. xxviii (1983)), pp. 8–9.

health overcame him he maintained his stance as public spokesman and 'father' of the gentleman refusers; and much of the support and inspiration which sustained him in this was provided by a group of godly ministers. They visited regularly and preached to him whilst in prison, combining personal encouragement with efforts to persuade him of the wider religious significance of his sufferings. This was illustrated in a letter from James Harrison, the lecturer in his home parish of Hatfield Broadoak:

> there is a holy and unerring providence that ordaineth all things and will, I verily beleeve, so dispose all these occurrences in this good tyme as . . . shalbe both with glory to his owne name and increase of comfort to ourselves . . . It is noe small mercy to be able to deny ourselves and willingly to take up our crosse and follow the lord in sincerity of heart . . . it is noe other then of which it hath pleased God to teach your worship not the theory only but the practicke also. Such a work cannot but have a good windeing up; the patient abideing of the godly shall not be forgotten, for he that hath a good pilot may . . . sayle in a rough sea. What though this frayle barke of our flesh be a little weatherbeaten so longe as the passenger is safe and sure to land well.[7]

The psychological support that this sort of encouragement could provide can be readily appreciated, and it is surely no accident that many of those who most obviously emulated Barrington's courageous stand were individuals with a reputation for godliness, such as Richard Knightley or the Earl of Lincoln. Personal and religious factors, then, often played an important part in the decision to refuse; alongside these, however, there were motives of a more obviously political nature.

The variety of these is perhaps most apparent in the letter from Nathaniel Tomkins to Sir Robert Phelips, quoted at length above.[8] It demonstrated the interplay of a whole range of influences, from Phelips's ambitions for preferment at Court and concern for the liberties of the subject, to calculations of the effects for his reputation with local freeholders and worries about his standing in relation to John Poulett. All had to be weighed and balanced before he came to a decision. In this respect he was obviously not alone and we can see similar considerations impinging on the decisions of other local governors, of whom the best documented is Sir Thomas Wentworth.

Wentworth, like Phelips, harboured ambitions for preferment at

[7] PRO SP 16/60/10: *C. and T.* i. 188; BL Eg. MS 2644, fos. 250–1; ERO D/Ba/F 43.

[8] See above, pp. 107–8.

Court and was involved in an increasingly bitter contest with his local enemy, Sir John Savile. Both were important influences as he came to make what was undoubtedly one of the most crucial decisions of his early career. The loan had been launched in Yorkshire during February 1627, whilst Wentworth was at home looking after his wife and newly born son. He had been nominated as a commissioner, but had avoided the initial meeting and kept out of the way, perhaps hoping for a change in the Council's policy towards refusers once the Duke had departed for Rhé. However during May a decision was forced upon him by a council letter ordering that unless the Yorkshire refusers 'shall speedily paye' the local commissioners were to take bonds of them 'to appear to answer that contempt before this body'. According to Wentworth's friends at Court this letter had been procured by his old enemy, Savile, who was hoping thereby to 'bring you on this stage . . . to see you act your own notable harm'.[9]

In these circumstances they advised him to pay up as speedily as possible. His brother-in-law, Lord Clifford, sent him a warning about the King's enduring displeasure and told him that 'every man that loves you wishes you may not run so much hazard of your life and fortune'. The former Secretary of State, George Calvert, reminded him that 'the conquering way is sometimes yeelding . . . it may be yet interpreted obedience to your soveraigne and zeal to his service'. And even the Earl of Clare, who was his father-in-law, urged on him the problems of being 'separated from his young wyfe and young sonne and having an infirme boddy, agreeing better with ease and comfort then with payne'. Wentworth must have considered this advice carefully, but at the same time he was also being counselled in other directions. Radcliffe, with whom he was in regular contact, was presumably urging on him the peace of mind and reputation to be gained from resisting; and Clare's son, Lord Haughton, reminded him of the implications of his actions in a local context: 'your antagonist brags he hath you in a toil or dilemma; if you refuse you shall run the fortune of the other delinquents; if you come in at the last hour into the vineyard, he hopes it will lessen you in the Country'.[10] These shrewd reflections must have struck a receptive chord with Wentworth. As he was well aware, the Yorkshire electorate was

[9] *Holles*, ii. 350, *Radcliffe Correspondence*, pp. 142–4; *APC 1627* pp. 243–5; *Wentworth Papers*, p. 258; *Strafforde's Letters*, i. 37.

[10] *Strafforde's Letters*, i. 38–9; *Holles*, ii. 350; *Radcliffe Correspondence*, pp. 136–58.

sensitive to the behaviour of its local governors and liable to regard his response to the loan as a crucial test of his fitness to serve the shire.[11] He was also aware that Savile's ascendancy at Court meant he had little hope of regaining the initiative simply by keeping his nose clean. The most obvious way to retrieve some of his local power, was to make a nuisance of himself, secure his credit with the freeholders and hope for an early summons of Parliament; and this was precisely what he proceeded to do. Within a few days of receiving the letter from Haughton, he told the Yorkshire commissioners that he would be travelling down to London to deliver his refusal before the Council.[12]

The concerns reflected in the correspondence of Wentworth and Phelips were probably typical of many leading loan refusers. The majority would have been less ambitious for preferment than these two, but they were certainly just as conscious that their decision had implications for local politics and their local reputation. As we have seen, this was largely due to the recognition that the loan threatened the liberties of the subject. Contemporaries were often able to locate it within an analysis which saw politics as increasingly polarized between the 'Court' and the 'Country'. The 'Court' was perceived as representing everything which was impure, popish, and disruptive whilst the 'Country' stood for a virtuous Protestant commonweal and a whole range of traditional liberties.[13] Of course, as Russell and

[11] S. P. Salt has argued that 'Even in 1628, after the forced loan, there is little sign that the electorate looked at candidates in terms of their attitude to high politics': *NH* xvi (1980), pp. 145–7. However there is ample evidence in Wentworth's papers to contradict this view. In the 1620 shire contest electors were obviously responsive to Savile's claims against Secretary Calvert, of his 'Non residence and being the King's servant and out of these reasons by law cannot and in good discretion ought not to be chosen . . . whereas himself is their martyr having suffered for them.' In 1626 Savile himself seems to have forfeited much of his local credit because he became too closely identified with the Duke. In 1628 Wentworth's stand over the loan, although in itself not enough to ensure electoral success, was thought to have considerably helped his cause. And later in the same year his reconciliation with the Duke led to him losing much of this popularity, 'the common opinion', according to his friend Wandesford, 'passing you now under Sir John Savile's character and that there is a Thomas as well as a John for the King.': *Strafforde's Letters*, i. 11, 13, 34 (misdated; relates to 1628); *Wentworth Papers*, pp. 259–60, 262–3, 301; J. H. Hexter, 'Power struggle, parliament and liberty in early Stuart England', *JMH* 1 (1978), 27–8; P. Zagorin, 'Did Strafford change sides?', *EHR* ci (1986), 149–63.

[12] *Wentworth Papers*, p. 259.

[13] Zagorin, *Court and Country*, pp. 33–9; L. Stone, *The Causes of the English Revolution 1529–1642* (1972), pp. 105–8; Lake, 'Constitutional

Hirst have demonstrated, the 'real' situation was much more complex than this; individual politicians found it difficult to operate unless they had links with both.[14] However at the level of ideas and rhetoric this analysis was increasingly accepted, and within it the loan was seen as providing a crucial test of allegiance to the 'Country'. The effects of this were apparent in the reaction against Lord Montague in Northamptonshire.

During the 1600s and 1610s Montague had enjoyed a considerable reputation in the shire, principally because of his readiness to stand by the godly ministers deprived in 1604. This was said to have 'won and wedded to him such honor and high esteem that what he said ordinarily went for currant and that he was alwayes chosen by the better sort to be one of the knights of Parliament'.[15] By the 1620s, however, there were signs that this reputation was slipping. As he became more closely associated with the Court—through his elevation to the peerage and the preferment of his brother, the Earl of Manchester—so he seems to have been less readily perceived as sharing an identity of interest with his neighbours. A libel was published against him locally accusing him of being 'the grand promoter or informer of this country'; he lost most of the influence he had previously wielded in shire elections, largely because the freeholders no longer seem to have trusted him; and during the 1626 Parliament he was seen locally as standing for the interests of the Duke.[16] The really decisive decline in his reputation, however, came with the loan. As we have seen, he thought long and hard about this and gave as the main reason for paying his personal loyalty to the King; however this seems to have cut little ice with his neighbours.[17] He was compared unfavourably with the 'good lordes' who 'stand out . . . and gayne great applause'; he was put under pressure to refuse the levy by 'a learned counsellor and a grave and godly Batchelur of Divinity', who argued against the levy at Montague's own house; and it was even suggested that the only reason he was paying was

consensus and puritan opposition', 805–25. These views are developed more fully in, Cust, 'News and politics', 75–90.

[14] Russell, *Parliaments and English Politics*, pp. 5–26; Hirst, 'Court country and politics', pp. 33–7.

[15] NRO Montague MSS, vol. 186, unpaginated (I am grateful to Esther Cope for this reference); HMC *Buccleuch*, iii. 91; *Beaulieu*, 45–6.

[16] HMC *Buccleuch*, iii. 264 (misdated); PRO Sta. C. 8/217/17; J. K. Gruenfelder, 'The parliamentary election in Northampton, 1626', *Northants P. and P.* iv (1968–9), 159–65; TCC MS 0.7.3., fo. 5^{r}.

[17] See above, pp. 110–11.

because he had been 'led by . . . respects', presumably towards the Duke. All this was extremely harmful. A diarist with local connections recorded that 'his credit lay at the stake for it', and he was still not forgiven several months later, in spite of the fact that he did his best to secure concessions out of the loan to benefit the shire. In the long term it caused permanent damage, his biographer—the local minister, Joseph Bentham—recording in the 1640s that 'his paying the loan lost him the love of the countrye untill which tyme they would have lyved and dyed with him'.[18]

Montague was perhaps unfortunate in the conjunction of circumstances which led to such a permanent loss of esteem; but the hostility he encountered was by no means unique. Those JPs who had identified themselves too closely with raising the benevolence had risked 'envy, reproaches and racking of ill tongues'. By the time of the loan reactions were if anything even harsher. Montague's fellow Northamptonshire commissioner, Robert Sibthorpe—whose sermon *Apostolike Obedience* was preached at the county assizes in February 1627 and was said to have caused 'much distaste' amongst his neighbours—was reported to have had his house burnt down in what was evidently seen as a judgement of God. Sir John Scudamore, active in Herefordshire, was approached by a neighbouring minister, and treated to 'some seditious rhetoric and inducements' against paying. Lord Maynard in Essex fell victim to a series of threatening letters dispersed around the shire. And Henry Gent, another Essex commissioner, was denounced publicly by a local cleric, who told him that 'he was very harsh, and harsh against his brother, and tyme would come when he might answer it'.[19] On the other side of the coin this hostility was matched by a considerable enthusiasm for those who stood out against the levy. The use of the term 'honest' to describe loan refusers hinted at this; Tomkins clearly envisaged something of the sort in his letter to Phelips; and Wentworth and his friends seem to have been counting on it as a response to his stand in Yorkshire. It manifested itself most clearly in the enduring public reputation that some of the refusers enjoyed amongst their neighbours and contemporaries. Lucy Hutchinson was to describe her father-in-law, Sir Thomas, and others who had

[18] NRO Montague MS vol. 2/205; vol. 10/16; vol. 186; HMC *Buccleuch*, i. 265–6; *Buccleuch*, iii. 326; TCC MS o.7.3., fo.7^{v}; Cope, *Life of a Public Man*, p. 121.

[19] PRO SP 16/37/5; 76/22i; Rushworth, i. 436–8; *C. and T.* i. 207, 212, 292.

suffered imprisonment over the loan as 'worthy patriots . . . those gentlemen that had been most faithful defenders of their countrie's interests'. Sir Francis Barrington was still 'renouned' forty years after his death for what many seem to have regarded as a virtual martyrdom. A Boston refuser, Sir Anthony Irby, was remembered in his home town during the 1640s for 'his carriage against the loan money and other projects tending to public detriment'. And during the 1650s Sir Nathaniel Barnardiston was being hailed by his biographer—the local divine, Samuel Fairclough—as 'Pater Patriae, a true father of his country', a title he merited above all for 'standing up for his country and the defence of the just rights and liberties thereof . . . witness his suffering under the imposition of ship money, coat and conduct money and the loan, for refusing whereof he was a long time imprisoned in the gatehouse'.[20] The use of such emotive language and the existence of such enduring sentiments indicate the importance which was attached to the loan as a test of loyalty to the 'Country'. It was also—as the Lincolnshire pamphleteer had recognized—an obvious way of assessing someone's fitness to serve as Knight of the Shire. This was doubtless something which county politicians were aware of, and it perhaps explains why a relatively high proportion of those who refused—over a quarter in a sample of counties—were men with aspirations or experience as shire MPs.[21]

In the case of Phelips and Wentworth a concern with status and reputation was also linked with calculations relating to their factional enemies and struggles for local power. Again this was not unique. In Cornwall, for example, supporters and opponents of the loan were seen as being divided along factional lines. Bagg stressed repeatedly that he and his friends were the most active of the commissioners, whilst those opposing the service largely consisted of 'Elliott, Corrinton Arrondall and their associates and faction'. In fact the claims were slightly exaggerated: several of Elliot's allies did indeed refuse—such as Sir Bevil Grenville, Nicholas Trefusis, and Ambrose Nicolls—but others—such as Charles Trevanion—felt able to support the service, probably

[20] SRO Phelips MS 219/35; *Wentworth Papers*, pp. 259–60, 262–3; Hutchinson, *Life of Colonel Hutchinson*, p. 23; *Barrington Family Letters*, p. 9; Keeler, *Long Parliament*, p. 230 n.; S. Clarke, *Lives of Sundry Eminent Persons* (1683), p. 109. For the significance of the term 'honest' in a different context: D. Underdown, 'Honest' radicals in the Counties 1642–9' in D. Pennington and K. Thomas, eds., *Puritans and Revolutionaries* (Oxford, 1978), pp. 187–9.

[21] See above, p. 173; Cust, 'The Forced Loan and English Politics, app. 3.

because the money paid was not actually leaving the shire.[22] Nevertheless the general point being made was sound enough. Refusal in Cornwall was in a sense a continuation of the struggle between those who had been excluded from power after the Duke's purge and those who had benefited from it. Opposition was a way for those excluded to obstruct those in power, and damage their credibility as crown servants, whilst at the same time securing their reputations as the 'honest knot' in the eyes of their neighbours.

Much the same also seems to have been the case in the East Riding of Yorkshire, where resistance was led by those whom the Earl of Dunbar described as 'in all things . . . opposed to the Duke'. Two of the leading members of this group—Sir William Constable and Sir John Hotham—refused point blank, whilst a third—Sir Matthew Boynton—avoided co-operating with it. These were joined by Hotham's brother-in-law, Marmaduke Langdale—who had strong catholic connections—and Boynton's friend, Henry Alured, both of whom refused, and Sir William Hildyard, who paid his money in London and acted as a messenger for his friend Constable. Meanwhile the task of collection was carried out almost entirely by Dunbar and his three henchmen, Alford, Metham, and Girlington.[23]

These examples show something of the complexity in the pattern of pressures, opportunities, and circumstances which generally shaped a decision to refuse. It was rarely just a straightforward response to the issues raised by the levy. It was a decision which affected the balance of power and influence within the shires as well as having personal repercussions and implications for one's local credit.

Similar observations can be made as we move on to looking at the behaviour of refusers after they had taken their initial decision; here, however, the calculations were often as much about national as local politics. To appreciate this we need to be aware of the effects of political news. As has been suggested much of this was London news. Reports from the provinces did reach London, and were then recirculated to give an impression of events over the country as a whole; however the really detailed day-to-day

[22] PRO SP 16/60/75; 72/57; 73/103; 75/43i; 106/14i; Hulme, *Life of Eliot*, p. 174.

[23] PRO SP 16/37/28; 60/52; 68/51i; Cliffe, *The Yorkshire Gentry* pp. 290, 293, 346; *Fairfax Correspondence*, i. 68–9.

reporting was largely concentrated on events in the capital itself. This tended to mean that once refusers were brought up to London, to answer before the Council, their actions were scrutinized much more closely than before. Someone like Wentworth, who had been able to maintain a relatively low profile whilst in Yorkshire, now found himself thrust, willy-nilly, on to what Calvert called 'this stage'. The result was that he, and others in his position, were given considerable opportunity to shape national politics. Like MPs they could bring issues to the public's attention, influence the formation of public opinion and affect the deliberations of the Council.[24] In these circumstances, then, it was perhaps not surprising that differences of approach and divisions of opinion began to emerge amongst the refusers.

A majority were content to follow the line taken by the Gloucestershire gentry and present their refusals in as submissive a fashion as possible.[25] This meant maintaining a discreet silence when they were summoned before the Council and accepting whatever punishment was meted out to them. However there was also a sizeable minority who were determined to be as obstructive as possible and to publicize their grievances at every opportunity. To understand how this approach developed it is necessary to go back and examine the intentions of those peers who had refused subscription in November 1626.

For the most part evidence of these is hard to come by. The only peer for whom a continuous run of correspondence survives is the Earl of Clare and he was not always in the mainstream of events. Nevertheless his letters still suggest the approach of this group as a whole. He had been making gloomy predictions about the future—with the growth of 'Prerogative Government, where Book Law submits unto Lex Loquens' and the 'secret will of power not to be approached'—since the latter part of 1625, when his close friend Williams had been removed from the Lord Keepership and his son-in-law Wentworth pricked as sheriff. His opposition to the Duke in the 1626 Parliament was an attempt to stem the tide, but with the dissolution, followed by the various schemes for prerogative finance, he became even more pessimistic. By September 1626 he was confiding to his acquaintance, Lord Saye and Sele, his view that 'we gallop all to the overthrow of Parlament and consequently to that of the state . . . I speake to a

[24] Cust, 'News and politics', 69–73; Russell, *Parliaments and English Politics*, pp. 19–22, 388–9; Hirst, *Representative of the People?*, pp. 178–81.

[25] See above, p. 167.

good patriot and therefore more freely; the way by privy seales and benevolences is so easy and that of Parlaments so conditionall and uncertayn, as nothing is more in thought than their abrogation, a diminution of monarcall power'. His action in refusing subscription was therefore in keeping with his principles, and he rather caustically dismissed those other peers who apparently shared his views, but were ready to temporize, 'without care of future or consequence'.[26]

On the face of it Clare was making a limited protest against the Duke and the prerogative policies with which he was associated. He evidently saw Buckingham as the architect of the loan and was taken aback at evidence of the King's involvement. He was also a good deal more restrained and moderate than some of the later refusers and beat a retreat into Nottinghamshire at the first sign of trouble.[27] And yet if one looks more closely there are hints of collaboration with a wider scheme of resistance. As we have seen, he was in touch with Saye and Sele during September; he also received advice from Warwick about the use that might be made of his appearing to subscribe; and throughout these early months of the loan he looked to Lady Hatton, mother-in-law to Warwick and a close friend of the Earl of Essex, as a source of refuge and support.[28] This linked him in with the three individuals most often mentioned as the ringleaders of the peers' refusal and suggests that, in some respects at least, this was being coordinated.[29]

For further evidence of this we have to turn to the activities of the Earl of Warwick. These are not easy to follow, but from occasional glimpses he appears to have been forging a moderate strategy designed to unite opposition and reinforce those councillors who were trying to persuade the King against the levy. This first emerged at the Romford meeting, on 24 October, when two of his leading clients, Barrington and Masham openly resisted payment of the loan and refused to take an oath to answer the Council's questions. Accounts of what happened are very sparse,

26 *Strafforde's Letters*, i. 31; *Holles*, i. lviii–lix; ii. 334–5, 338–9.

27 *Holles*, ii. 342–3.

28 *Holles*, ii. 342–6; L. Norsworthy, *The Lady of Bleeding Heart Yard* (1935), pp. 24, 74, 130, 244.

29 Mead picked up a report suggesting that Pembroke's client, Dr Turner, was riding round the countryside organizing opposition on the basis that the loan 'was the Duke's; if it failed he was assured of a Parliament': *C. and T.*, i. 171. This may be true, but it is extremely unlikely that Pembroke himself would have been involved.

but one of them—provided by Clare—suggested that the actions of Barrington and Masham had been conceived as part of a wider effort, which involved the Earl himself: 'Sir Francis Barrington and his son-in-law, Sir William Massam ar committed for refusing to take the oath that they and others consulted not to deny; it being discovered that the gentlemen of Essex had had conference together, among whom Sir Nathaniel Riche lefte him with the rest in the plaine field; they ar still in the Marshallsea.'[30] This is slightly obscure, but it seems to indicate that there had been some sort of 'conference' amongst the Essex gentry before the meeting, and that Warwick's cousin and man of affairs, Sir Nathaniel Rich, had been involved. Possibly the preparations for this had been made at the time of the Essex Quarter Sessions, some two to three weeks earlier, when Warwick had been in attendance and the newly arrived loan commission had almost certainly been discussed.[31] Whatever the origins, the opposition seems to have collapsed when the Council got wind of what was happening and persuaded the other local governors to abandon Barrington and Masham; and in this respect the scheme was obviously a failure. However it had at least notified the Council of the existence of opposition, and this may well have been Warwick's principal objective.

His other interventions were apparently made with this very much in mind. Not only was he busy rallying peers like Clare, he was also mobilizing his contacts with Puritan ministers. We know that he requested Hugh Peter to preach a controversial sermon in London on 30 November, in which he prayed openly that God would commune with the King's heart 'and reveale unto him those things which were necessary for the government of his Kingdome'. He may also have influenced a sermon delivered at this time at Court by his friend John Preston, in which he lamented the loss of unity at home and the abandonment of Protestantism abroad.[32] Both aroused considerable controversy and coming as they did at the height of the Council's discussions about the future of the loan were surely intended to provide further hints of the depth of division and the resilience of opposition. Warwick must have been well aware that some of the

[30] *Holles*, ii. 337–8.

[31] ERO Q/SR/255/130; *C. and T.* i. 161–2.

[32] R. P. Stearns, *The Strenuous Puritan* (Illinois, 1954), pp. 29–30, 41; C. Hill, *Puritanism and Revolution* (1965), pp. 251–7; Morgan, *Prince Charles' Puritan Chaplain*, pp. 27–31.

moderates in the Council—possibly including his own brother Holland—favoured a return to more traditional methods of government; he also presumably knew that the future of the levy was still uncertain. It therefore seems likely that he was trying to strengthen the hand of the moderates by demonstrating that in political terms the levy would be counterproductive. He was not actually prepared to go to the King and ask him to abandon it—as he was to do in 1637 with ship money—but he must have hoped that others would do this for him.[33]

This was a strategy which demanded a good deal of co-ordination. As many peers as possible had to be persuaded to hold out and refuse subscription, or at least avoid making a payment; hence the significance of the warning given to Clare in December. Equally it was important to avoid any extremes of action which might provide a justification for the sort of draconian measures being advocated in Council by Dorset. For a while this moderate approach was relatively successful. As we have seen, those peers who withheld payment included not only the fifteen or so refusing to subscribe, but also a good many who had simply failed to make a contribution; and it was the reticence of this wider group—which included territorial magnates of the status of Arundel, Hertford, Huntingdon, and Spencer—which lent substance to the Council's doubts over whether the loan could be collected.[34] The strategy of this group, however, hinged around the Council moderates, and once they had been over-ruled, and a decision taken to persevere with the loan, it largely fell apart.

By the end of 1626 there was little option for the 'recusant' peers but to accept that the levy would go ahead and do their best to minimize the damage to their personal fortunes. Most of them had too much to lose—in terms of office and opportunities to serve the King—to feel comfortable in continuing with open opposition. Accordingly they turned for cover. Peers such as Somerset and Spencer after lying low, eventually consented to pay up; others returned to their shires or, like Lord Saye and Sele pleaded illness; and Warwick concentrated on his privateering ventures for which, amongst other things, he needed a commission from the King and the approval of the Council.[35] There were to be indications that he

33 See above, p. 54; V. Rowe, 'Robert, second Earl of Warwick and the payment of ship money in Essex', *TEAS*, 3rd Ser. i (1962), 162.

34 See above, pp. 102–3.

35 PRO E.401/2322, 'Mutuum de magnatibus'; SP 16/57/49; TCC MS 0.7.3., fo. 8v; *Holles*, ii. 345–6; *APC 1627*, pp. 204–5.

at least was still active behind the scenes. His brother petitioned the Council on behalf of Sir Francis Barrington and he himself met with Eliot and Coryton when his ships docked at Plymouth. But, like the other peers he avoided standing out against the loan in public.[36]

The one exception to this pattern of withdrawal was the Earl of Lincoln. During November he had been associated with Warwick, Saye and Sele, and Essex, and seems to have been content to follow their line of moderate opposition. As we have seen, however, by the following January he was changing tack and showing a determination to stand and fight on his own. On the 24th the pamphlet addressed 'To all English freeholders' was drawn up under his sponsorship; a few days later he appeared at the first Lincolnshire meeting and openly defied the Council's representative; and on being summoned to answer in London he refused to testify on oath and was incarcerated in the Tower.[37] In part Lincoln's actions can be explained by his relative distance from the Court; he had fewer contacts than the other leaders of the opposition, and therefore less to lose. However they also represented an obvious response to the changed situation facing refusers. Now that the opportunity of working through the Council had been closed off, the logical alternative was to appeal to opinion outside, amongst the wider public; and since there was no longer a premium on the contacts at the centre enjoyed by politicians such as Warwick, the initiative passed to those who were prepared to protest openly.

The first to come to the fore in this respect was Warwick's protégé, Sir Francis Barrington, and this again suggests the Earl's continuing involvement. As the earliest of the refusers, Barrington naturally attracted a good deal of public attention and he used this to set himself up as a focus for opposition. His prison became a regular resort for visitors to London and every Sunday he had two sermons preached before him, the tone of which was probably reflected in the text taken by John Dod: 'Fear none of these things which thou shalt suffer. Behold the devil shall cast some of you into prison, that ye may be tried and shall have tribulation ten days.' He also received news about resistance from friends such as John Winthrop in Suffolk, and provided a rallying-point for the other prisoners who were said to describe themselves as 'brothers'

[36] PRO SP 16/60/10, 75.

[37] PRO SP 16/54/82i; C.115/N.3, 2 Feb. 1626–7; *C. and T.* i. 207.

and Barrington as 'their father'.[38] Sir Francis's performance in this role, however, depended on his fragile health and by June 1627 he could no longer stand the strain. He had to be moved away to the comparative comfort of Surrey and with his departure public attention shifted to a group of Northamptonshire refusers led by Richard Knightley.[39]

Knightley's involvement pointed to the existence of another clearly defined network amongst refusers: those who were allies of Knightley himself and his two close friends, Lord Saye and Sele, and John Preston. This included virtually all the leading refusers in the western division of Northamptonshire and northern Oxfordshire: Sir Erasmus Dryden, Sir Edmund Hampden, and Christopher Sherland, recorder of Northampton, all of whom were friends of Knightley; Sir John Pickering, close to Dryden and Hampden and an acquaintance of Preston; Thomas Ball, rector of All Saints, Northampton, who was Preston's pupil and biographer; and Sir William Cope of Hanwell and Thomas Hallhead of Banbury, both allies of Lord Saye and Sele. It also included two prominent refusers from further afield: Knightley's friend and Sir Edmund Hampden's nephew, John Hampden, in Buckinghamshire, and Saye and Sele's adherent, Sir Walter Earle, in Dorset.[40] Throughout the service these refusers maintained an impressively united front. In January 1627 they organized a petition and protest to accompany the Privy Councillors' visit to Northamptonshire; in February Dryden, Pickering, and the two Hampdens petitioned together from the Gatehouse; and in the following November Earle and Sir Edmund Hampden were amongst those involved in the Five Knights Case.[41]

Their initial strategy was to seek public attention through provoking incidents which would be widely reported in newsletters. Knightley showed the way by refusing to kneel when summoned before the Council and later on standing 'unmoveable as a rock'

[38] *C. and T.* i. 188; *Winthrop Papers*, i. 336–7; PRO SP 16/60/10.

[39] Lowndes, 'History of the Barrington Family', 23; *APC 1627*, pp. 346–7; *APC 1627–8*, p. 217.

[40] Morgan, *Prince Charles' Puritan Chaplain*, pp. 31, 63, 203; PRO PCC Wills, 19 Barrington, 186 Harvey; NRO I.L. 3434–5, 3665–6, 3686; Russell, 'John Pym', pp. 148–9 n.; VCH *Oxfordshire* II vols. (1939–83), ix, 119–20; D. E. M. Fiennes and J. S. W. Gibson, 'Providence and Henry Halhed, Mayor of Banbury 1630–1', *Cake and Cockhorse*, vii (1978), 199–208; Gardiner, 'Notes by Sir James Bagg', 325–6.

[41] *C. and T.* i. 184; PRO SP 16/526/18; *APC 1627*, pp. 39, 46; Gardiner, *History of England*, vi. 213.

when 'threatened by their Lordships with seven years imprisonment if he would not yield to pay the loan . . .'. He was followed by other Northamptonshire refusers, notably George Catesby who, as we have seen, infuriated the Council by voicing his concern about the loan becoming a precedent.[42] By April, however, they were concentrating on efforts to get their imprisonment tested in the courts. It was reported that William Noy, acting as their Attorney, had secured a promise from the Exchequer Barons of 'oyer of the commission for the loan and of the condition of the recognisance'. This was to come to nothing, as the Council sidestepped the challenge; but it did indicate that the refusers were going on the offensive, in much the same way as Saye and Sele was to do over ship money in 1637.[43] They must have hoped that if a trial was held they would have a good chance of a favourable verdict, since the judges had already indicated their doubts over the loan's legality; but even if this was not forthcoming they would still have secured a public show-piece in which the Crown's actions would have been tested and discussed.

By this time the divisions between the militant refusers and their more moderate counterparts were starting to emerge quite clearly. This was largely because of the Council's decision to order refusers out of London and into the Home Counties. The more militant regarded this as a political manœuvre, designed to deny them a platform, and refused to go; the moderates, however, were willing to do as they were told.[44] In part this was because of a habitual reluctance to defy commands from above. The Council was ordering them to go and they did not wish to argue. However the implications of their actions went a good deal further, and, in some cases at least, reflected a continuing concern to build bridges with the moderate elements in the Council. They wished to show that loan refusers were not necessarily irresponsible or bent on undermining co-operation between King and subject, but sought to create the conditions for a future reconciliation. Again this is illustrated by Wentworth.

From the time of his first summons to London in May, Sir Thomas's behaviour towards the Council was a model of sub-

[42] *C. and T.* i. 190–1, 193–4, 198, 249; *APC 1627*, pp. 42, 62. Knightley's refusal to kneel was sufficiently widely noted to be recalled by Digges when, in 1628, he discussed with Thomas Scott how he should comport himself when appearing before the Privy Council: *P. in P. 1628*, p. 230.

[43] PRO SP 16/60/10; Bard, 'The ship money case of William Fiennes', 177–84.

[44] *C. and T.* i. 241; *Holles*, ii. 359–61; PRO SP 16/72/28.

missiveness. His discretion and restraint at his first interview in June earned widespread approval amongst his acquaintances at Court; and he was still clearly anxious to please in July when he told Sir Humphrey May that 'I am none of those which will refuse confinement. I will not dispute but obay . . . I was ever of that minde from the first as one naturally more delighting, more comforted to serve my soveraigne his owne way then my owne: and when I doe otherwise seemingly I shall allways judge it my misfortune, nay my greatest misfortune.' This readiness to go along with the Council gained him credit in some unexpected quarters. When he needed to leave his confinement in Kent to attend to business in Yorkshire during November, Weston and the Earl of Dorset petitioned on his behalf and the King himself 'was pleased to give way to itt and named the tym'.[45] He had apparently gained the status amongst the refusers of a figure of moderation and compromise, someone with whom the Privy Councillors could do business; and this perhaps helps to explain his rapid advancement after the 1628 Parliament.

All this was, of course, immensely useful from the point of view of Wentworth's ambitions since it did something to restore his credit at Court, without in any way damaging his standing in his county. However there was more to this than crude self-interest. Wentworth's actions reflected his continuing belief that the way to heal political division was to restore unity. As he had hinted in his letter to May, he was looking for a way to reconcile the different pressures produced by the loan and repair the damage; and the ramifications of this were worked out in a lengthy correspondence with his friend Christopher Wandesford. Unfortunately only Wandesford's letters have survived, but the past record of co-operation between the two men, and the tone of the exchanges, suggests that on most issues they were in agreement. To start with both seem to have accepted that the country faced a crisis and that in these circumstances the King could justifiably expect some form of extra-parliamentary aid. Wandesford confessed, in November 1627, that 'For my part . . . when the privy seals cum, I think itt will be the proportion only that shall trouble me, for the King's wants must be supplyed and since he declines the ordinarye way what can be more warrantable for the subject than this?'. If privy seal loans were acceptable, however, the forced loan and the judgement in the Five Knights Case were not. Wandesford was

[45] *Wentworth Papers*, pp. 259–61, 273, 279.

extremely worried by the implications of both of these, as he indicated in chastizing the apathy of his Yorkshire neighbours: 'so little doe we esteeme our libertyes and so lowe a valewe do we sett uppon thos that are borne to defend them; there being no man I mete with more sensible of the ryght we have then my neybor was when he only inquired for the quota pars of Richmondshyre'. However he did not wish to go to the other extreme and advocate wholesale resistance to the levy. The essence of redressing the situation was to restore a sense of proportion and balance:

> truly if I were to give direction for after adges howe people should carry themselves to there King, they should be animated and manadged to maintayne that hereditary and naturall interest which God and nature hath given them in there libertye (because princes should be mayde sensible how equallye the daingers respect them and there people) . . . And unless there be such a fatalitye upon us that the goodly tree which hath borne the blessed fruit of tranquillitye and peace in this kingdome some hundreds of yeares . . . shall nowe be cutt downe and the roote thereof bounde about with iron that itt may never growe agayne. Why should there be this litigation, this darknesse proceding betwixt the heade and the member; the weaker must be drawen up to the stronger or else they will never be joyned and confirmed together.

What was needed, therefore, was moderation and restraint to bring together the divided parties: 'All we can doe that are lookers on is to implore the almighty to direct his Majesty's heart and hands aright in these great and important necessityes. For my part if the howse doe mete I pray God send them a mixture of patience and curradge to apply the proper cure to these bleeding wounds. The fewer Corritonns and Katesbyes the better: itt is no tyme nowe to play at sharpe with the crowne.'[46] This was, of course, precisely the approach Wentworth was trying to put into practice; but as Wandesford's last comment indicated it was not always that of their fellow refusers.

For Coryton, Catesby and others the divisions were now running too deep to be healed over by concessions and goodwill. William Anderson, one of the Lincolnshire refusers and son of an Elizabethan judge, was consulting with Eliot and his friends about his father's notes on the Council imprisoning without showing cause; and at the end of June it was reported that he, along with Sir Thomas Darnell and Lincoln's friend, Sir William Armine,

> have a resolution not to accept of a confinement in that manner as it is

[46] Ibid., pp. 7–8, 259–60, 267–8, 276, 278, 285–6.

now tendered, that is to say not except the warrant do leave them as prisoners with the sherrifs, lest by that means they should bar themselves of the benefit of a Habeas Corpus which it is said cannot be denied them the next term, or might have been the last term if it had been demanded; by that means they look to have a judicial trial in Kings Bench, whether they have committed any offence or no.

The following month this refusal was reinforced by an even more defiant response from Coryton and Catesby, who declared to the Council that 'wee are no way provided to remove from this prison unless it might be to our oune houses . . . And wee were confident theyr Lops would have beene pleased to lett us know our offences and so have either punishment or freedom from this place.'[47] Both replies were in effect challenges to the Council to allow them to stand trial, and this became the basic aim of the thirty-five refusers who resisted any attempt to remove them from London during the summer. The Council responded for the most part by trying to cool the situation down, placing those whom they regarded as ringleaders—Coryton, Catesby and Earle—under close confinement, but otherwise refusing to rise to the bait. It was only when the King intervened in October that the refusers secured the trial they had been seeking.[48]

In the event this was not to be a test of the loan's legality; however it still aroused enough interest to serve their ends. The courtroom was packed throughout the hearing and the defence pleas were greeted 'with wonderful applause even of shouting and clapping of hands which is unusual in that place'. Accounts of the case circulated widely in newsletters and 'separates' and commentators were quick to recognize the disturbing powers that it gave to the Crown. Walter Yonge underlined passages in his copy drawing attention to the way in which the King was infringing past judgements and statutes; and Clare, writing to Wentworth on his release, expressed fears which were widely shared:

I cannot term you nor myself a freeman when law hath no protection for us: this diseased body our councillors have left us and the disease still strengtheneth upon us. Neither do the lawyers, the physicians for this

[47] *CD 1628*, ii. 229, *Fairfax Correspondence*, i. 68–9; *Holles*, ii. 356–7; PRO SP 16/72/28.

[48] *APC 1627–8*, pp. 58–9; *C. and T.* i. 280. The thirty-five most defiant refusers also included Eliot, Corbet, Heveningham, Darnell, Armine, and five of the Chelmsford refusers. Knightley, Dryden and Bernardiston were amongst those still in London on 20 July and may also have been causing difficulties: *APC 1627*, pp. 395–6, 430.

subject, heal us any whit, for meum and tuum between commen persons they croe in every corner, but when the question transcends between the hed and the boddi, they are crestfallen and have nothing to say and if accidentally something of them be heard and show themself in the lawne they only beray the place and leave the matter wurrs than they found it; witness the late Habeas Corpus.[49]

Thus the refusers had succeeded in their aim of stirring up discussion and public concern; however in doing so they had prompted a decision which actually seemed to strengthen the prerogative and led Charles to tamper with the controlment roll in order to establish a precedent.[50] This pointed to the dangers which their approach carried, and which so alarmed more moderate refusers. Whereas the likes of Wentworth and Wandesford believed the situation could still be redressed by restraint and compromise, the militants appeared to think that the only way to make progress was through confrontation. Their actions were in many respects the logical counterpart to the rhetoric of 'Canterbury' Scott and the Lincolnshire pamphleteer. They had come to accept that the nation was divided and that the time for compromise and moderation was past; they therefore wished to raise the stakes and oppose the King openly and directly. Of course this view was still held by only a small minority and, as we have seen, even amongst the refusers, most were still in favour of patching up the differences; however the fact that even a small minority were prepared to go this far was another indication of the way politics had become polarized by the loan.

Moving across the spectrum of responses those closest to the refusers were the local governors who paid up, but abstained from involving themselves in the service. Again, because of the nature of the sources, it is difficult to obtain precise estimates of their numbers; however from a survey of sixteen counties, or portions of counties, where responses can be reconstructed it is clear that they were often in a majority. Only five of these—Bedfordshire, Derbyshire, Norfolk, Nottinghamshire, and the North Riding of Yorkshire—show anything like a full complement of commissioners executing the service. In the remaining eleven the numbers involved were well under half: for example two out of seven in the Holland division of Lincolnshire, five out of twenty-two in

[49] *C. and T.* i. 292; BL Add. MS 35,331, fos. 4–8; *Wentworth Papers* pp. 287–8.

[50] Guy, 'Origins of the Petition of Right', 291–6.

the East Riding and thirteen out of forty in the Western division of Northamptonshire. In the case of Gloucestershire and Western Northamptonshire a good many of these absentees were outright refusers.[51] Elsewhere factors like illness and habitual non-attendance have to be taken into account.[52] However even when these are allowed for there remained, in each of these shires, a hard core of local governors, who were normally active, but who quite deliberately distanced themselves from the service of the loan. What were their reasons?

For some, abstention offered the easiest way out of a difficult choice. A favourite tactic of those who found themselves faced with this was to leave their county altogether and go up to London where they could pay their money directly into the Exchequer and avoid the embarrassment of being seen to support the loan in front of their own freeholders. The best documented instance of this was Sir Robert Phelips who, as we have seen, faced problems whether he paid or refused. His friend Tomkins had advised him to act decisively, one way or the other, but in the end he adopted a middle way and 'tooke his journey to London as the businesse beganne to be handled'.[53] He was followed by others. The Yorkshire knight of the shire and enemy of the Duke, Sir Thomas Hoby, abandoned his county once the levy was being made. The godly lord of the manor in Earls Colne, Essex, Richard Harlakenden, took himself off to London for the duration. The Warwickshire Deputy Lieutenant and MP, Sir Thomas Lucy, opted out of directly refusing—as had been expected at one time—and chose instead to leave his shire and pay in London. And Sir Roger Townsend, the Knight of the Shire for Norfolk, did likewise rather than emulate the resistance of his close friend, Sir John Corbet.[54]

[51] Cust, 'The Forced Loan and English Politics', app. 3. Other areas with low turnouts were Essex, Alton and Basingstoke in Hampshire, Herefordshire, Kesteven in Lincolnshire, Surrey, and Warwickshire (for Warwickshire: Hughes, 'Politics, Society and Civil War in Warwickshire', pp. 163–70).

[52] In Essex, for example, three of the absent commissioners seem to have been suffering genuine illnesses: Richard Franke and Anthony Luther, both of whom died during the year, and Sir William Maxey, who took up his duties once recovered: PRO PCC Wills, 87 and 106 Skinner; SP 16/39/31, 76/13. A further seven were not normally active as JPs: Lord Denny, Sir Paul Bayning, Sir Robert Quarles, Richard Hales, William Fanshawe, William Towse, and Thomas Winiffe, DD: ERO Q/SR/249–262.

[53] SRO Phelips MS 219/35; PRO SP 16/53/88.

[54] PRO E.179/214/389; SP 16/39/31; E.401/2323; Hughes, 'Politics Society and Civil War in Warwickshire', p. 166; W. Prest, 'An Australian holding of Norfolk manuscripts: the Bacon-Townsend papers at the University of Adelaide', *NA* xxxvii (1979), 121–2; *Knyvett Letters*, pp. 72–4.

All these were individuals who were likely to come under considerable pressure, both from sections of local opinion hostile to the loan and from the Court. Their response was a way of reconciling otherwise irreconcilable forces, and in this sense it was akin to the neutralist stance adopted by large numbers of gentry in the summer of 1642. However this was not all that it represented. Just as neutralism had a more positive edge so too did non-co-operation. It could imply not simply opting out, but also making a positive protest in a relatively secure and inoffensive fashion. Certainly this seems to have been the intention of John Pym.

At the time of the loan Pym was living in Hampshire where he had been nominated as a commissioner. He kept out of the way during the initial meeting at Winchester, but his brother-in-law, Henry Hooke, laid down £10 on his behalf and allowed him to be listed as a lender. When Pym found out he was furious and immediately wrote off to the local commissioner, Sir Thomas Jervoise, demanding that the money be recorded as paid by Mr Hooke and offering to return his acquittance. His concern in this was not simply with correct accounting. Pym was in close contact with Warwick at the time and was presumably aware that the Council was using any evidence of payment as propaganda for the loan. He therefore wished to make it quite clear that whilst he was not actually refusing—and felt a strong sense of 'Duty and Humble Affection whereby I am ernestly disposed to His Majestie's supply'—he was nevertheless not prepared to be recorded as having lent.[55] Given the lengths to which he was prepared to go he clearly felt that this was a distinction which mattered a good deal.

Pym may well have been slightly unusual in the contortions he was required to perform, but the basic line he was following was not. The desire to steer a course which, whilst not involving open opposition at the same time avoided indicating any positive approval for the levy, appears to have been quite widespread. The twenty-two Berkshire commissioners who failed to turn up to the meeting at Reading, in December 1626, appear to have been manœuvring in just such a fashion; so too do the twenty Hampshire commissioners who appeared and paid at Winchester, but nevertheless refused to subscribe to the loan's legality.[56] These were significant gestures, as the Council recognized in its early

[55] PRO C.193/12/2; HRO Jervoise MS, 012/15, 16; Hunts RO dd.M. 73, bdle. 3 (I am grateful to Christopher Thompson for this reference).

[56] PRO SP 16/40/39; HRO Jervoise MS 021/1,34.

efforts to secure subscription; for the levy's success depended not just on avoiding opposition, but also persuading commissioners to provide positive support.

Those who abstained from making these efforts were often undermining the loan as surely as those who opposed it. There are several instances of this. In the Norfolk hundred of the Gallow the absence of Sir Roger Townsend, the senior local commissioner seems to have ensured that only £12. 6*s.* 8*d.* was received from the subsidymen.[57] In the Northamptonshire division of Spelhoe, Newbottle, and Wymersley, the non-involvement of Lord Spencer and his eldest son, Sir William, both friends of Richard Knightley, left only one active commissioner and considerably hampered collection.[58] Whilst in the Hampshire division of Basingstoke the example of Sir Henry Wallop again did much to disrupt the service. This case is particularly instructive. Lord Conway recognized the influence wielded by Wallop as the leading local landowner and a regular Knight of the Shire, and wrote before the Winchester meeting specifically requesting his attendance since 'it is feared there may be some opposition in his division. If it is so and he is not present it would be laid to his absence.' Wallop duly appeared, but instead of displaying the commitment Conway had hoped for he refused to subscribe and withheld his payment to a later date. He was also conspicuously absent when it came to performing the duties of a commissioner, in spite of carrying on as a JP. It was therefore surely no coincidence that his area was reported as one of the centres of heaviest resistance within the shire.[59]

As this example indicates, non-co-operation implied more than simple quiescence. It was often an extremely effective form of passive resistance, a half-way house towards refusal, calculated to achieve much the same ends; and if enough commissioners had followed Wallop's line the loan would surely have had to be abandoned in the same way as the benevolence or the ship money levy of 1628. The gap between those who refused and those who

[57] PRO E. 401/2322–4; SP 16/75/94.

[58] PRO SP 16/49/8; 458/106; PCC Wills, 186 Harvey; E.401/2322–4; HMC *Buccleuch*, iii. 256. Sir William Spencer's non-involvement probably reflected a distaste for the service. At a meeting of Northamptonshire Deputy Lieutenants to discuss privy seal loans, early in 1626, he was alleged to have said that 'the King wanted noe monie and that if he did he might call on Parliament': BL Spencer of Althorpe MSS A 2.

[59] Keeler, *Long Parliament*, pp. 376–8; HMC *Portland*, iii. 22; HRO Jervoise MS 012/17; 021/1; PRO SP 16/52/69.

would not actively co-operate was often very narrow. Some commissioners, such as Sir Harbottle Gimstone in Essex—who first of all excused himself and then decided to openly refuse—shifted from one course of action to the other; others evidently recognized that collection of this particular levy differed significantly from their other duties as local governors and therefore distanced themselves from it.[60] Thus it is apparent that hostility to the loan, and some awareness of its damaging implications, went much further than just those local governors who stood out openly. It embraced a broad section of moderate county opinion.

Perhaps the most difficult part of this analysis is identifying the motives of those local governors who actively supported the loan. They were often in a small minority, facing criticism from local freeholders and their colleagues on the bench, and yet they were prepared to undertake one of the most time-consuming and tedious tasks of the period. What prompted this?

Habit, ambition, altruism and ideological conviction all played a part and were often so closely intertwined that they defy separation; however it is still feasible to make a broad distinction between two approaches to the task of collection and examine some of the influences at work in each. The first involved going about it in such a way as to minimise the disruption and inconvenience caused to local inhabitants. This tended to be adopted by those most firmly rooted in local society and therefore most conscious of their neighbours' interests. The second stressed the need to squeeze out as much money as possible by whatever means came to hand; and this tended to be the line taken by those who felt a strong pull towards the Court. Of course the real situation was more complex than this. The same local governor could often adopt more than one approach. Nevertheless for the purpose of investigating attitudes the distinction provides a useful starting-point.

The first approach was the more widely adopted. In most shires there was a group of hard-working justices who, in spite of all the hazards, were prepared to support the levy. In doing this they were probably moved for the most part by the sorts of consideration which persuaded them to take up their normal duties. In some cases it was a desire to demonstrate their fitness and readiness to serve. Hence one finds Sir Francis Goodwin throwing himself into

[60] PRO SP 16/39/31; 54/47; A. L. Hughes, 'Warwickshire on the eve of the Civil War: a "county community"?', *Midland History*, vii (1982), 55–9.

the service in Buckinghamshire having been chastened by his removal from the bench after the benevolence. In others it was an awareness that the exercise of any office carried with it power and status. Sir Henry Savile, the Yorkshire commissioner, had been reminded of this when earlier in 1626, he had been removed from the collectorship for privy seals which not only gave his enemies the opportunity to raise his assessment, but also carried with it 'shew of indignity as though wee weare nott worthie to be still trusted with the king's money as well as such as are farre our inferiors'. In other cases still it was the effects of deeply ingrained habits of obedience and a sense that, in order to keep the wheels of local society turning, it was necessary to obey commands from above. Thus when it became clear that the King was directly concerned in the service the three Cheshire commissioners, Sir George Booth, Sir Richard Grosvenor, and Sir Richard Wilbraham, overcame their earlier misgivings and responded positively.[61] These attitudes were part and parcel of the make-up of most local governors and doubtless applied in some measure to all who supported the service. What tended to set the first approach apart was the emphasis on doing this in such a way as to balance the interests of Crown and neighbours.

This principle was to the fore in most of the activities of local governors whether they were JPs attending to the distribution of grain supplies, ship money sheriffs examining ratings or Deputy Lieutenants supervising billeting and levies of conscripts.[62] In the case of the loan, however, there were particular reasons for observing it, both ideological and practical. The former can be illustrated in a series of remarks made by Sir Henry Savile in May 1626. These were included in a letter to Sir Richard Weston, Chancellor of the Exchequer, in which he sought to justify his performance as a collector of privy seal loans after this had been slighted by Sir John Savile. Whilst making his case Sir Henry revealed some of the assumptions underpinning his role as a local governor, assumptions which he seems to have expected Weston to share and which also, presumably, applied to his work as a loan commissioner. He explained that he felt pulled in different directions by his 'zeale to doe His Majestie service' and the 'love of my neighbours'. He accepted that the King's case for demanding

[61] PRO SP 16/76/24i; *APC 1626*, p. 230; *Wentworth Papers*, pp. 250–5; see above, p. 122.

[62] Hassell Smith, 'Justices at work in Elizabethan Norfolk', 98–101; Lake, 'Ship money in Cheshire', 44–71.

supply was a strong one, since the money was 'for the greater advantage of His Majestie's affairs, the necessitie whereof was the cause I thought my countrymen were justly bounde att this tyme to stretche their purse strings'. At the same time, however, he was concerned that his neighbours should be able to pay 'without sinking under the burthen' since 'I may nott too muche agravate any thinge against the country where I and my posteritye intende to live'. This encapsulated the classic dilemma of the local governor—how to mediate between the interests of the Crown and the interests of his locality—and Sir Henry's solution was typical, echoing the statements of umpteen MPs discussing parliamentary supply and anticipating Cotton's remarks on the moderate councillor, as represented by Burghley. This was to emphasize that, above all, the levy must be assessed with a sense of justice and balance. If this was achieved, not only would it be accepted by his neighbours, but ultimately it would work to the advantage of the Crown, 'the rather because His Majestie is never truly served by his subordinate instruments when pressures are imposed to extinguishe love of subjects'.[63] The last comment illustrated the way in which the pursuit of balance accorded with contemporary ideals of limited monarchy. The notion of the subject meeting the King's needs, whilst he in turn took account of their abilities and grievances, was widely regarded as essential to nurturing a spirit of co-operation between Crown and people. Thus the process envisaged by Sir Henry was a model for the sort of exchange which underpinned the existing political order; and this in turn helps to explain why he was prepared to justify it to the face of a Privy Councillor. However his comments also reveal something further: how he could reconcile his actions as a loan commissioner with the defence of the existing order. For if one accepted the King's arguments about necessity and believed that the levy would not be repeated, it became possible to regard the loan not as a threat, but rather a temporary expedient, helping the King to meet his immediate needs and encouraging him to work with Parliament in the future. This would not perhaps have persuaded a hostile subsidyman; but for those who felt under pressure to respond positively to the loan it offered a means of presenting themselves as exponents of unity and co-operation and thereby retaining the esteem of most of their neighbours.

This was the point at which practical considerations also came

[63] *Wentworth Papers*, pp. 253–5.

to apply; for, in order to avoid falling from grace, local governors had not only to present a good case for their actions, but also to demonstrate that their dealings were impartial and materially beneficial. In the case of the loan this could be done in a variety of ways, some of which have already been discussed: for example through the care which Owen Shepphard took in assessing cases of poverty, through the concern which Maynard displayed for avoiding coercion, or through Jervoise's efforts to protect his county's concessions on billeting.[64] However one particular aspect of this approach requires further explanation, that is the readiness of some commissioners to oppose, simultaneously, other demands being made by the Crown.

On the face of it this is one of the most puzzling features of their behaviour. One finds that at the same time as they were collecting the loan many commissioners were also resisting ship money. Sir Henry Savile, for example, was one of the leading signatories to a refusal to collect ship money by the Yorkshire JPs which stressed that 'though wee were never soe willing to rayse money for any service, yett haveing noe legall power to levie the same upon the subject wee dare not presume to doe itt and that upon consideracon taken of the present estate and povertie of the Country, wee conceive it is not possible to rayse these moneyes'. Precisely these arguments could have been used against the loan, and yet in the week they met to draft this letter the same local governors were busy summoning refusers and collecting payments.[65] In similar fashion Lord Maynard, whilst making every effort to persuade his neighbours to pay the loan, was doing his best to obstruct the new levy. As the leading Deputy Lieutenant he was heavily implicated in a manœuvre which involved first of all presenting the demand to the Essex Grand Jury and then conveying their refusal to the Privy Council in an unusually forthright letter: 'we takeing into consideracon by what power we maye taxe the Cuntrye for the setting forthe of this shippe canot finde that there have beene any levies of this nature made by any other power, but either by continued presidents or by the power derived unto us by a generall and unanimous consent of the whole countye'. This produced a stinging rebuke, but undeterred the local Justices sent their representatives up to the Council and 'made it appeare unto them by shewinge unto them the former

[64] See above, pp. 123–5, 139, 143.

[65] Yorkshire Archaeological Soc. Fairfax MS 38 fos. 94–5; *Wentworth Papers*, pp. 257–8.

Book of President, that they had proceeded in this business noe otherwise in effect then had beene done upon the like occation in the yeare 1594. Whereupon their Lopps were pleased to forebeare any further proceedings therein'.[66]

What Savile, Maynard and others were hoping to achieve by these actions is hard to tell precisely, and even harder to document; however it is possible to discern what may have been some of the intended consequences. The key to understanding these lies in the relatively low priority accorded to ship money by the Council. As we have seen, its resources were so stretched that to secure the success of the loan it had to direct most of its energy away from other projects.[67] The more experienced local governors undoubtedly recognized this and it gave them a good deal of room for manœuvre. They could trade off continuing co-operation over the loan for the assurance that they would not be penalized for resistance elsewhere, as was at least tacitly implied in the Yorkshire JPs letter about ship money. The loan commissioners were thereby provided with a means of repairing their local credit which was all the more effective for the fact that ship money—with its revised ratings and the precedents these would create—could be depicted as even more menacing than the loan.[68] Thus the commissioners could present themselves as the champions of local liberties who, by acceding to one set of demands, were in fact protecting their counties from other, and greater, burdens. In short they could be seen as fulfilling a mediating and balancing role to perfection; and in part, at least, this was surely what was intended.

Overall, then, this approach made it possible for local governors who shared the attitudes of their neighbours, and who valued their esteem, to co-operate with the levy. The emphasis on moderation and balance enabled them to accommodate their stance within the middle-ground of contemporary opinion; whilst the stress on preserving and defending their neighbours' interests meant they could emerge with their credit intact. Of course this was not always how it worked out. Much depended on the strength of feeling within a particular shire. In those counties when concessions were substantial and opposition was limited commissioners could often emerge relatively unscathed. Hence Sir Thomas Jervoise seems to have suffered no adverse effects from promoting the service in Hampshire. However where local opposition was

[66] PRO SP 16/59/52i; *APC 1627*, pp. 222–3; Bodl. L. Firth MS c.4, p. 326.
[67] See above, pp. 147–8. [68] See above, pp. 130–3.

heavy and feeling was running high, it was that much more difficult to escape damage. Thus Lord Montague's reputation in Northamptonshire was permanently tarnished, in spite of his public declaration and his efforts to secure concessions for those who had recently paid privy seals.[69]

From all this it should be apparent that, in terms of attitudes and assumptions, the difference between those who supported the loan, those who avoided involvement and those who refused, was often minimal. The ideological stance of Sir Richard Grosvenor was very close to that of Sir Thomas Wentworth. If anything Grosvenor's views, with their greater emphasis on the threat from popery, were more likely to lead to opposition; and yet he supported the loan whilst Wentworth resisted.[70] This again indicates the broad spectrum of responses which were still compatible with holding moderate opinions.

It is only with the final category of local governors—those who felt the pull of the Court and who tended to push their neighbours' interests into the background—that we are obviously dealing with individuals who departed from the moderate consensus; however even within this category there were many to whom this did not apply. For some commissioners a hard line with their neighbours was simply a way of preserving respect for their authority. They probably felt uncomfortable in adopting such a course, but the alternative would have been humiliation at the hands of social inferiors. This was apparently what was behind the readiness of Sir Edward Heron or the Gloucestershire commissioners to invite the Council to take stern measures on their behalf.[71] The result, however, was that they often came to be seen as opposed to the liberties of the subject. Their actions might be no different from those of a normal Deputy Lieutenant, but with feelings running high and so many commissioners opting out, any invitation to the Council was liable to be interpreted at best as unneighbourly and at worst as an indication that such commissioners were aligning themselves with 'the Court' and all it stood for. This might only be temporary, and once the animosities had subsided, the old pattern of relationships might well be re-established; but as we have seen it was still significant.

[69] See above, pp. 224–5.

[70] Cust and Lake, 'Sir Richard Grosvenor', 40–53; *Wentworth Papers*, pp. 7–8, 152–7.

[71] See above, pp. 136–7.

The common perception of a division between 'Court' and 'Country' might well obscure the complex motivation of individual local governors; but it nevertheless remained true that those most conspicuous in adopting a hard-line approach were those with connections at Court. In large part this was because of the extreme pressure exerted from the centre. Both the King and Buckingham threw all their weight behind the levy and insisted that loyalty could only be demonstrated by really committed support. As we have seen, for most local governors this created considerable problems; in a few cases, however, it was the ideal opportunity to demonstrate their adherence and their fitness to serve, and they seized it with both hands.[72]

There were four groups particularly prominent in this respect. All to some extent overlapped and all were already closely identified with the more narrowly based Court created since early 1626. First there were the Duke's own clients and supporters in the shires. These included Mansfield, who carefully supervised the service in Nottinghamshire; Maynard, Rivers, and their friends Wiseman and Smythe, who were conspicuously active in Essex; Lord Clifford who busied himself in various parts of Yorkshire; and Sir John Savile who travelled up to the West Riding specifically to preside over the collection.[73] Secondly there were recusant and crypto-catholic peers who had come to enjoy an enlarged role both at Court and in their counties: for example Rivers and Lord Petre in Essex; Scrope, Dunbar, and Lord Eure in Yorkshire; Lord Paulett and Lord St John in Hampshire; Lord Tufton in Kent; and Lord Savage in Cheshire.[74] Thirdly, there were the divines anxious to gain the favour of high church Bishops; men such as Bargrave, Sibthorpe, and Titley, all of whom preached prominently in support of the levy, and Sibthorpe's main clerical ally in Northamptonshire, Dr Samuel Clarke, who was active as a commissioner.[75] Fourthly there were those local governors who looked to the Court for support in factional struggles. These included Bagg and Poulett and their friends who took the lead in

[72] See above, pp. 105–10.

[73] PRO SP 16/39/3; 55/1; 59/35; 72/44; E.179/204/437; 209/383; 218/200; Hull RO Corporation Minute Book, no. 5, 1609–50, pp. 157–160.

[74] PRO SP 16/39/3; 42/65; 51/35; 52/30,67; 53/18; 55/11; 60/52; 67/49; 68/51; E.179/218/200; *APC 1627*, p. 2; HRO Jervoise MS 012/1, 021/11, 17, 29.

[75] *C. and T.* i. 195, 214–15; *Commons Debates for 1629*, p. 133; Sibthorpe, *Apostolike Obedience*, dedication; W. J. Sheils, *The Puritans in the Diocese of Peterborough, 1558–1610* (Northants Rec. Soc. xxx, 1979), p. 146.

Cornwall and Somerset, and Dunbar and his associates, similarly involved in the East riding.[76]

Where it is possible to gain an insight into the attitudes of these men, they usually exhibited a strong sense of recognition that their service was bound up with personal loyalty to the King or the Duke. For example, Lord St John coupled his efforts in the Hampshire divisions of Basingstoke and Kingsclere with his earlier attempt to show that, in spite of his recusancy, he was as faithful as any other peer. In April 1627 he wrote to Conway reminding him that he and his father had previously spent £2,000 at the King's Coronation by which 'I presume we both expressed our readiness to serve the King; neither do we desire longer to live then to continue the same uppon all occasions, and I hope your Lordship can witnes how ready I was to further the King's service here in Hampshire.'[77] Lord Clifford displayed a similar sense of personal obligation when writing to Conway about the privy seals of 1625, and presumably he felt the same way about the loan. He had begged the Secretary

> to sett him aright in His Majesty's opinions . . . for since the first day I entered into the government under His Majestie of blessed memorie I have applyed myselfe with more diligence and care to the discharge of the dutie of that place then to anie particular of my owne estate . . . if I should be guilty of soe silly and unmannerly an action as the deferring an answering of soe speciall direccons from His Majestie at any tyme . . . I shall not onely be soe ashamed to goe aboute to make an appologie, but blush to looke His Majestie againe in the face.[78]

And Sir John Savile displayed a characteristic recognition that not only self-esteem, but also self-interest were tied up with the levy. Writing to the Duke about the vacant Controllership of the Household he included a trenchant declaration of his fitness for office hinging on his service over the loan:

> in troth my lord I must ever reckon my self amongst the number of your truest servantes. Whilst I am consious to myself that I beare as unfeigned, constant and reall a hart unto your Grace against all the world as anie man in it, which I assure myself will now plead for me to your Grace . . . without anie further outward protestations at which I never was cunning. And the rather in regard my absence is now occasioned by His Majestie's most espetiall service; for having procurred all this countrie to subscribe I was desirous . . . to see the monie paid allso.[79]

[76] PRO SP 16/60/52, 75; 68/51, 51i; 72/57; 73/103; 75/43i; E.179/204/431, 433, 436; 218/200.

[77] PRO SP 16/59/9.

[78] PRO SP 16/18/101.

[79] PRO SP 16/59/35.

Given such attitudes it was hardly surprising that those connected with the Court were ready to put the demands of the monarch before those of their neighbours. There were exceptions —such as Maynard and Mansfield—who succeeded in balancing the two interests; but most were so intent on demonstrating loyalty that their neighbours got short shrift. This showed itself in the way in which they were prepared to resort to the powers of the prerogative at the slightest sign of opposition. Lord St John invited stern measures against defaulters by frequently describing them as 'obstinate' or 'contemptuous'. Sir Thomas Tyrringham, a Gentleman of the Privy Chamber, requested a messenger with blanks to deal with a relatively harmless group of refusers in Buckinghamshire. And from Northamptonshire it was reported that 'the sedulity of . . . Dr. Clarke . . . was so great in this business that he bound one woman thither . . . He sent one man up for twopence . . . and if a constable had not holden his honour, he would have beaten the refusers'.[80] It was also evident in the manner in which some commissioners denigrated their neighbours so that their own service would stand out more clearly. This was often done for blatantly factional ends, but it nevertheless still reflected the way in which the loan was regarded as a crucial test of loyalty. Bagg's efforts in Cornwall typified the approach adopted by others.[81] In Kent, for instance, Lord Tufton was able to make Sir Dudley Digges's promise of payment in London look like a refusal and thereby had him summoned before the Council and ultimately imprisoned.[82] In the East Riding Dunbar embarrassed his enemies by sending constables after them with warrants of summons and then reporting their consequent evasions to the Council, in the most damning terms available.[83] And from the North Riding Lord Eure delivered a lengthy epistle to the King, contrasting his own service in moving 'the Country . . . the most part [of which] had yielded by my earnest mediacon with them', with the obstructiveness of his neighbour, Sir John Jackson and 'those men that have Parliament men to their maisters'.[84]

Such episodes indicated the divisive consequences stemming from the loan's status as a shibboleth in the eyes of certain

[80] PRO SP 16/52/67; 58/16; *C. and T.* i. 195.

[81] PRO SP 16/60/75; 68/16; 74/78, 78i.

[82] PRO SP 16/42/65; 475/49 (I am grateful to Conrad Russell for this reference); *APC 1627*, p. 2.

[83] PRO SP 16/60/52.

[84] PRO SP 16/51/35.

sections of the Court, and these were not just confined to the hard-line attitude displayed by certain commissioners. An even more damaging development was the way in which this helped to extend support for the idea of avoiding a Parliament. In part this was directly attributable to the harsh methods being employed by some of the commissioners. Where they found themselves being threatened with investigation or having to answer before a future assembly it was not unnatural that they should look to the Council and the prerogative to defend their interests and avoid this possibility. However, beyond this, it was also a consequence of assumptions inherent in the notion that the loan was a test of loyalty. For where there was loyalty, there must also be disloyalty, and according to the version of events being presented in a good deal of official rhetoric this disloyalty could be identified with 'popular' elements such as the 'Parliament men' alluded to by Lord Eure. This, of course, did not necessarily lead all those who were conscious of such distinctions towards wanting to avoid Parliament. Individuals such as Lord Montague and the moderates within the Council clearly remained wedded to traditional policies. But it certainly contributed to the acceptance of 'new counsels' amongst those who, by dint of circumstance or inclination, favoured the use of the prerogative.

From all this it should be apparent that the loan was bringing to the surface distinctions which normally remained hidden. The peculiar pressures created by the levy, and the unusual clarity with which it presented basic issues was leading to a situation where, as Barnes has observed for Somerset, 'the individual justice faced for the first time the terrible choice of either serving the King or respecting the interests of his countrymen and the law'.[85] Of course, in many cases local governors fudged the issue and did all they could to avoid making a choice. Thus one finds a majority—from refusers across to supporters—who continued to cling to notions of unity and balance in much the same way as they were to do in 1642. However, as on that occasion, there had also emerged two significant groupings who were regarded by many contemporaries as clearly polarized and standing at opposite ends of the spectrum. One of these accepted the King's word and felt impelled to respond to his request as vigorously as possible; the other, either implicitly or explicitly, rejected his assurances and was prepared to go to considerable lengths in order to oppose

[85] Barnes, *Somerset*, p. 168.

him. These groups included individuals who on other matters of local government had been seen to work in close accord: men such as Richard Knightley and Lord Montague in Northamptonshire, Sir Francis Barrington and Lord Maynard in Essex, Sir Thomas Hutchinson and Viscount Mansfield in Nottinghamshire, and Sir Thomas Wentworth and his brother-in-law, Lord Clifford, in Yorkshire.[86] The fact that they could now be regarded as diametrically opposed again indicates that between 1626 and 1628 things had gone very badly wrong.

[86] HMC *Buccleuch*, iii. 257–8; Quintrell, 'Government of Essex', pp. 119–39; Dias, 'Politics and Administration in Notts and Derbys.', pp. 309–18; *Wentworth Papers*, pp. 119, 169–71.

5

Subsidymen and the Loan

I. INTRODUCTION

IF we turn from looking at the response of commissioners and county governors to that of subsidymen we are presented with a rather different set of problems. Foremost amongst these is simply the lack of detailed evidence about their views. With local governors we are sometimes provided with statements of attitudes and intentions, either in private correspondence or communications elicited by the Privy Council. In the case of the ordinary subsidymen such statements were rarely sought and, of course, little has survived in the way of letters or diaries. There is therefore a chronic shortage of rounded expressions of opinion. It is perhaps this, more than anything else, which has led some historians to suggest that these subsidymen were largely unconcerned by the broader issues raised by levies like the loan.[1] As I have already attempted to demonstrate, such a view would be misleading. Even if we set aside the statements of Scott or the Lincolnshire pamphleteer, the evidence we have of subsidymen discussing the loan as a threat to traditional liberties or treating it as a gauge of loyalty to 'the Country' indicates that it was not regarded simply as another demand for money. Far from being unconcerned some were sufficiently aroused to organize a concerted opposition against it, in spite of the unpleasant consequences which might follow. It therefore becomes important to try to account for their response.

This task can perhaps best be approached by looking at the patterns of co-operation and resistance revealed in lists of loan payments; however such an examination presents obvious problems. The most immediate of these is the difficulty of assessing the significance of a particular response. If one wants to use payment and default as indications of political attitudes it is particularly important to establish context. This has already been emphasized with regard to the local governors, but it is even more

[1] Morrill, *Revolt of the Provinces*, pp. 22–31; Russell, *Parliaments and English Politics*, pp. 333–4.

apparent when we look at the subsidymen. One cannot simply treat the response as an undiluted test of support or opposition.

Non-payment, for example, could stem from a whole variety of causes. It might indicate concerns of the sort evident amongst those who followed the Earl of Lincoln; but equally it might indicate a breakdown in the machinery for collecting and enforcing the levy, or simply a response to poverty or unemployment. Fortunately the task of identifying the latter is made easier by the fact that the Council's instructions established a system for reviewing and relieving those who were suffering genuine hardship. It was open to these individuals to plead their case before the local commissioners, thereby securing release from payment; and the numbers freed in this way were relatively high—around 10 per cent in a sample from three areas—which suggests that most commissioners applied the instructions in quite a generous fashion.[2] Thus it seems likely that most of those who ended up as actual refusers—having neglected the opportunity to plead poverty or having had their pleas rejected—represented a hard core who were able, but unwilling.

Within this hard core, however, there were still distinctions which need to be allowed for. Some evidently felt themselves to taking a stand on principle; but others must have been primarily concerned simply to evade payment. Ultimately, of course, it is very hard to tell these apart, and indeed both sorts of motive must often have been inextricably mixed in the mind of the individual refuser. Nevertheless it should be feasible, given a sense of context and attention to the tone of an individual's reply, to gain some insight into how far a particular response was seen as appropriate or legitimate within a particular group of subsidymen; and from this one can perhaps draw useful pointers to the nature of political causality at this level of society.

In connection with this it also has to be remembered that in many areas the service was run relatively efficiently, with hard-working groups of commissioners often backed by valuable concessions. It was these two factors which contributed more than anything else to ensuring that most of the money was collected, since, whatever their misgivings about the loan's

[2] These were Gloucester City, with 7 per cent being released (19 out of 266), Havering Liberty in Essex with 10 per cent (11 out of 114) and Coulridge Hundred in Devon with 11 per cent (76 out of 748): PRO E.179/116/531; 112/616B; SP 16/44/8; 52/64; 30/26/59. See also the amounts excused in various Norfolk hundreds: PRO SP 16/75/94.

legality, subsidymen who faced the prospect of a council summons or pressing for service overseas, were liable to think twice before refusing—especially as in many cases the money would be paid straight back into their own pockets. It is therefore necessary to beware of reading too much significance into the act of payment. The fact that Thomas Scott or Lord Montague's neighbours in the eastern part of Northamptonshire ultimately contributed—in spite of their complaints and evident hostility—indicates that this was not always a sign of approval for the levy.[3]

With these reservations in mind I have decided to concentrate on looking in depth at the shire which has perhaps the best records for this purpose, Essex. This is not to suggest that its experience was typical, or that the conclusions drawn can automatically be applied to other areas. Clearly in the extent of opposition and the level of political interest aroused during the levy Essex was untypical, and perhaps comparable only with other regions which showed intense resistance—the western division of Northamptonshire, the Holland division of Lincolnshire and the Cirencester, Whitstone, and Bisley division of Gloucestershire.[4] However the keynote of the response within Essex was its variety. Whilst some hundreds resisted long and hard, others paid up with a readiness and a degree of conformity which compared favourably with any part of the country. This means that it is possible not only to investigate the reasons for resistance, but also some of the preconditions and influences which helped to secure co-operation. Indeed in many respects the experiences of subsidymen in Essex can be taken as representing a heightened and intensified version of the experience facing subsidymen as a whole. This was because they were being presented with a comparatively open and unrestricted choice. Whereas in most shires the efficiency of enforcement or the level of concessions was such as to close down the range of options, in Essex this was emphatically not the case. Subsidymen within the shire had refused, and in many cases got away with it, often in a blaze of publicity; and the stand taken by Barrington, Masham and the Chelmsford refusers had ensured that there was a widespread awareness of the implications and legal status of the levy.[5] When the individual subsidyman came to make his decision in Essex, then, he must often have been conscious of a whole variety of considerations, going far beyond

[3] See above, p. 187; NRO Montague MS 2/205; *APC 1627*, p. 51.
[4] *APC 1627*, p. 51; PRO SP 16/56/39; 58/110; 71/50.
[5] See above, pp. 145–7, 229–30.

the simple experience of being asked to pay and threatened with punishment if he defaulted. Because of this it should be possible, through examining the various responses, to secure a handle on the otherwise largely unmanageable task of exploring political motivation below the level of the gentry. Before commencing, however, it is necessary to look more closely at another problem, that of identifying subsidymen.

The term has been used up to this point to indicate those groups immediately below the county governors and substantial gentry who were responsible for paying national taxes. In social terms it has been taken to encompass a range stretching from the lesser gentry down through the yeomen, husbandmen, and urban artisans. This rather vague application has perhaps sufficed hitherto whilst the subsidymen have been treated largely as a collective entity; however now that we are coming to deal with them as individuals it is necessary to identify them more precisely.

This is no easy task since by the 1620s subsidy assessments had ceased to bear any obvious relationship to wealth. When first introduced in Henry VIII's reign the subsidy had provided a relatively reliable register of the propertied classes; however since then assessments had fallen, and the overall number of taxpayers had been sharply reduced. Responsibility for this has generally been laid at the door of local governors who treated the system as a form of local patronage, reducing assessments on their friends or releasing them from payment altogether.[6] What has often been overlooked, however, is that at the same time as conniving at the abuses these same local governors occasionally made provision—unofficially and quite outside the bounds of the statute—for redressing some of the anomalies created by the system. This had the effect of further complicating the identification of subsidymen, and we therefore need to know how it operated.

The chief anomaly which concerned subsidy assessors was the fact that by the early seventeenth century only a small proportion of those coming within the tax threshold were actually liable for payment. In each parish there appears to have been a large pool of able individuals who were rarely, if ever, called on. Their existence was quite clearly revealed in the much fuller listings for paying local rates and the ship money levy. In the Essex village of

[6] Dietz, *English Public Finance*, ii. 380–97; Fletcher, *A County Community*, pp. 202–5; Quintrell, 'The Government of Essex', pp. 313–18.

Earls Colne, for example, only seven of the twenty-six most highly rated ship money contributors in 1636—those assessed at over 5*s*.—can be identified in the surviving subsidy rolls of the 1620s; and those assessed to pay subsidies at this time included a further three from the thirty-four less substantial ship money contributors —assessed at between 6*d*. and 4*s*. 6*d*.[7] Some of the absentees in the first group may be accounted for by non-residence in the village, or death or migration before 1636; but this surely cannot be the explanation for all of them. It seems instead that, by dint of local custom or favouritism on the part of the assessors, certain individuals got stuck in the subsidy roll whilst others escaped, regardless of their wealth. This view is supported by evidence from the neighbouring villages of Kelvedon and Terling where again only a small proportion of the wealthier villagers actually appeared in the rolls. Substantial, well established, yeoman farmers—men like John Savell and John Clench in Kelvedon, and Robert Greene and Richard Tabor in Terling—regularly escaped without making any subsidy payment.[8] This was the situation local commissioners sometimes tried to redress.

One way of doing this was to allow for a rough and ready rota system whereby different individuals out of the pool of taxable persons were included each time a subsidy was requested. This appears to have been operating in parts of Sussex where the rate of replacement amongst the lowest group of subsidymen was too rapid to be accounted for by death or migration. It may also have been practised in some Essex towns where a similar situation is apparent.[9] However it was clearly not universal, and seems to have depended a good deal on local initiative and local tradition. Elsewhere in Essex—in Earls Colne for example, where the same four £1 subsidymen appeared on each surviving roll in the 1620s—there is no indication of any such rota.[10] From our point of view this is perhaps just as well since if the system had been employed extensively it would greatly complicate the task of identifying those liable to lend.[11]

[7] PRO E. 179/112/588, 607, 638; SP 16/358, p. 109.

[8] PRO E.179/112/638; J. Sharpe, 'Crime and delinquency in an Essex parish 1600–1640' in J. S. Cockburn, ed., *Crime in England 1500–1800* (1977), pp. 94–5; K. Wrightson and D. Levine, *Poverty and Piety in an English Village: Terling, 1525–1700* (1979) pp. 74, 178.

[9] Fletcher, *A County Community*, p. 204; Quintrell, 'The Government of Essex', pp. 313–18.

[10] PRO E.179/112/588, 607, 638.

[11] This is because for many areas the subsidy assessments which have

As an alternative to the rota system some areas adopted a system known as providing 'bearers' which again, if it had been widely practised, would make the task of identifying subsidymen far more difficult. This was a system whereby local assessors chose certain individuals from the potential taxpayers to bear a part of the burden of those returned in the subsidy-roll. Henry Best explained the practice within his own East Riding village of Elmeswell where three bearers were usually linked to the two men officially named to pay the subsidy. A similar system appears to have operated in parts of Lincolnshire, and there 'bearers' were employed to distribute the heavy burdens on the poorer subsidymen at the time of the loan. Beyond these two shires however I have been unable to find any evidence for this system; and indeed the comments made on loan lists from Essex make it quite clear that the whole burden was expected to fall on the person whose name appeared in the roll.[12]

Apart from helping us to recognize and allow for some of these vagaries, an exmination of the subsidymen also enables us to draw two useful conclusions about their social status. First of all it is apparent that the social spectrum covered by the subsidymen was often very broad. As one might expect most were either gentlemen or yeoman farmers who comprised the top layers of village society; however it is also clear that some were drawn from considerably lower down the village hierarchy. In Earls Colne, for example, of the eight subsidymen in 1628 who can be identified with reasonable certainty in wills one was an esquire, one was a gentleman, one was a wealthy linen draper and four were yeoman farmers; however, the eighth subsidyman was probably an illiterate tanner with a small cottage and tenement.[13] A similar picture emerges from the Cambridgeshire village of Chippenham, where five of the 1628 subsidymen can be identified in a manorial

survived are those for 1628. Given a normal turnover of names—and allowing a margin for error of around 10 per cent—these can be used to indicate most of those who would have been liable to lend according to the 1625–6 assessment; however with widespread operation of a rota system this would obviously become impossible.

[12] *Rural Economy in Yorkshire in 1641, Being the Farming and Account Books of Henry Best of Elmeswell in the East Riding*, ed. C. B. Robinson (Surtees Soc. xxxiii, 1857), pp. 85–92 (I am grateful to Nicholas Tyacke for this reference); PRO SP 16/39/3i; 54/47, 47i; 58/110; 71/50.

[13] PRO E.179/112/638; A. MacFarlane, S. Harrison, C. Jardine, T. King, and J. King, *Records of an English Village: Earls Colne 1400–1750*, 3 vols. (Cambridge, 1980), i; Church court records, probate.

survey of 1636. Four of these were substantial gentry and yeoman with holdings of ninety acres or more, but the fifth was a relatively humble smallholder with only six acres.[14] Doubtless a similar pattern could be detected elsewhere where the right sort of data exist. This serves, then as a useful reminder that subsidymen were not confined to the village élites. The inequities of the assessment system ensured that those further down were often lumbered with burdens which should have been borne by their wealthier neighbours.

In the second place it is also apparent that the assessments returned, although bearing no obvious relation to an individual's property, nevertheless reflected, in a very crude way, the hierarchy of wealth in local society. Checking these assessments against biographical data and local ratings reveals a rough order of ranking. The top category comprised those who were assessed at £10 or over, for the most part landowners and office-holders who held property and enjoyed an influence beyond the bounds of their native parish. The lords of the manor in both Earls Colne and Terling—Richard Harlakenden and Robert Mildmay—came into this category, serving the county as either JP or sheriff and holding substantial amounts of land. The second category comprised those rated at between £3 and £10 in lands, and over £4 in goods. These were generally the lesser gentry and substantial yeomen, individuals whose influence was usually limited to their own village, but who were often dominant within this, acting either alone or in tandem. In Kelvedon the resident gentleman—William Sammes—and two substantial esquires—John Wakering and John Cudmore—were assessed at this level; and the integrity of this group was emphasized in the ship money ratings, where virtually all of them were rated for at least £1. The third category was the broadest and most diffuse, comprising those assessed at £1–2 on lands and £2–4 on goods. They covered a very wide social spectrum indeed ranging from minor gentry and substantial yeomen who had managed to keep their contributions down—such as Edward Cressner and Henry Abbott in Earls Colne—to small husbandmen and artisans—such as Thomas Smith. This range was reflected in the ship money rate where some were as high as 15*s.* whilst others were as low as 1*s.* 4*d.* or 2*s.*[15] Given this

[14] PRO E.179/83/392; M. Spufford, *Contrasting Communities* (1974), p. 69.

[15] A. MacFarlane, *The Family Life of Ralph Josselin* (Cambridge, 1970), pp. 63, 78; Wrightson and Levine, *Terling*, pp. 35, 137–9; Sharpe, 'Crime and delinquency in an Essex parish', pp. 95–5; PRO SP 16/358, pp. 99–102.

variety it would be unwise to try to read too much into an individual assessment;[16] none the less in the majority of cases the general categories appear to hold good and can therefore be used to provide a rough rule of thumb when it comes to identifying the relative status of those involved in opposition. This is very useful as we turn to looking in detail at Essex.

II. ESSEX AND THE LOAN

The reaction of subsidymen within Essex varied considerably from one part of the county to another. Only about half the shire is adequately covered by the sources, but within this responses ranged from stubborn resistance to almost complete conformity. The best way to approach it therefore is hundred by hundred, starting in the north-eastern corner and working towards the divisions nearest London. The first area to take is that covered by the hundred of Tendring and the half-hundreds of Winstree and Thurstable.

Of all the county taxpayers the inhabitants of this area showed perhaps the greatest readiness to pay up. At their initial meeting, held at the end of October 1626, the local commissioners found 'the people in those parts that appeared before us for the most part very willing and forward to lend to His Majestie . . . and albeit some of them at the first made delatorye aunswer, yet in the end they assented and sett to ther hands save only a few persons'. This was in spite of the fact that between 1625 and 1627 they suffered heavier charges than any other part of Essex. Tendring contained within its boundaries the port of Harwich and its inhabitants were therefore put to 'more charges then any' during the invasion scare of September 1625 and the mutiny of April 1627. In consequence by August 1627, when they were asked to make yet another contribution, Earl Rivers had to report to the Council that 'the inhabitants are soe weak in estate that they are not able to undergoe this burthen . . . I heare they take it very ill and I feare this commande wilbe obayed not without great difficulty'. None of this, however, appears to have affected the loan. As he also explained, 'they were the first that gave and fewer defalts then in any other hundred'. By December 1626 they had already collected

[16] For example Thomas Guyon of Coggeshall was assessed at only £2 in goods, in spite of being one of the wealthiest clothiers in England, reputedly worth £100,000 at his death: P. Morant, *History of Essex*, 2 vols. (1768), i. 165.

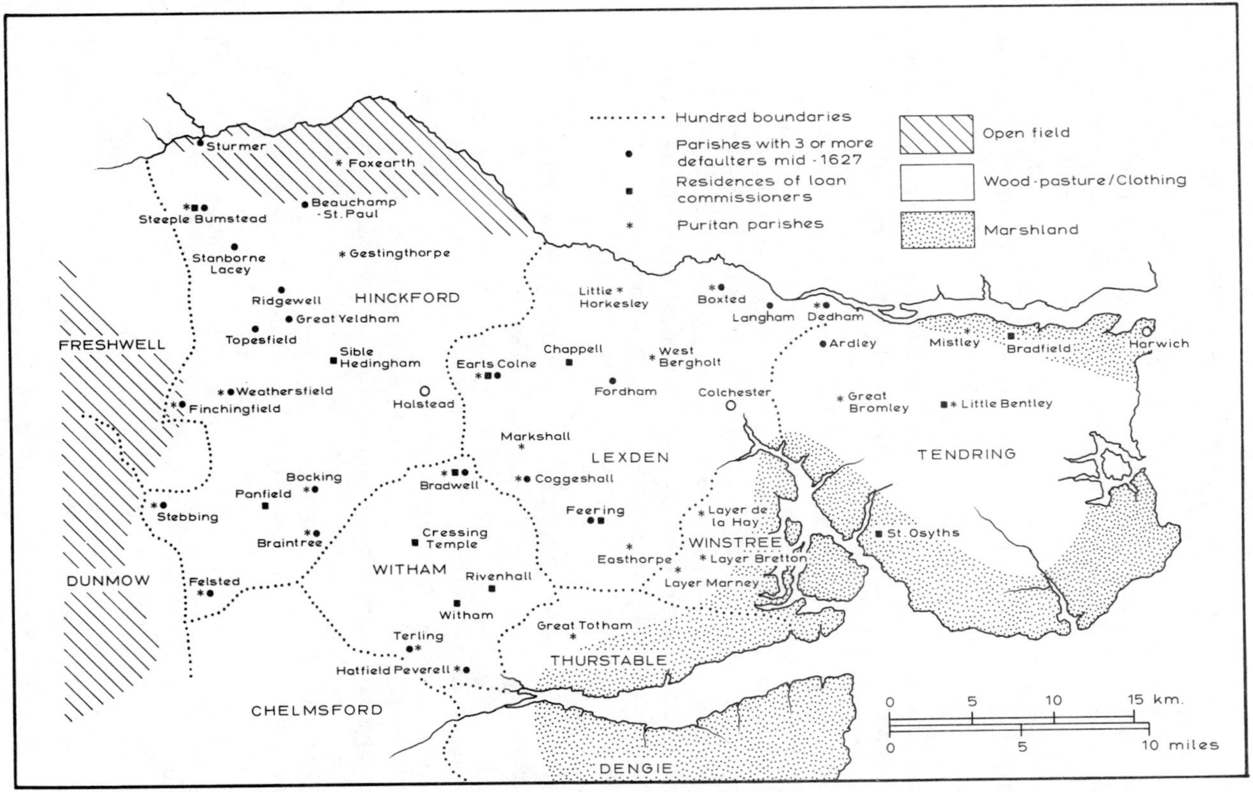

MAP 1: North-eastern Essex and the Loan

and paid into the Exchequer some £533. 3*s*. 4*d*. out of £632. 16*s*. 8*d*., and the final arrears totalled only £38, of which £25 was due from Sir Harbottle Grimstone.[1]

The basic reason for this conformity is not hard to find. This was a sparsely populated, largely rural area, in which there was little to restrict the influence of the leading landowners;[2] and chief amongst these, by a very substantial margin, was the Duke's loyal servant, Earl Rivers. His family had been settled there since the mid-sixteenth century and owned a string of sixteen manors stretching from Little Oakley, just south of Harwich, down and round the coast as far as Tolleshunt Darcy; and Rivers himself, in spite of being tainted with suspicions of popery wielded considerable clout in local politics. He regularly claimed a right to intervene in the disposal of freeholders' votes in nearby Colchester and—as his letter to the Council indicated—he tended to represent the interests of local inhabitants when it came to dealing with the central government. Within Essex he was probably the nearest thing to an old-fashioned territorial magnate, enjoying a relationship with his tenants and freeholders in this relatively underdeveloped area which must have been akin to the traditional notions of 'good lordship'.[3] The local subsidymen, then, naturally looked towards Rivers to provide leadership, and there is no doubt that over the loan he set a very positive example. He presided over the early meeting in October and thereafter helped to chase up defaulters and provide support for the collectors.[4] None of the other local landowners could match him in terms of power and prestige. The largest of these was Sir Paul Bayning, who held several manors in the northern part of Tendring; but he was too preoccupied with his business affairs in London to give much thought to his country estates and did not even attend the service. There was also Sir Harbottle Grimstone, a hard-working and conscientious JP, but without the territorial weight of Rivers. After initially subscribing, he decided to resist

[1] Quintrell, 'Towards a 'Perfect Militia', 96–105; PRO SP 16/39/3,31; 71/29; 76/13, 13i, 13ii; E.401/2322–4, 2444. These volumes are unpaginated, but the sections covering loan payments from the shires are headed 'Collectoribus mutuum a communalitat'.

[2] F. Hull, 'Agriculture and Rural Society in Essex, 1560–1640', (University of London, Ph.D., 1950), pp. 5–15, 72–83; J. Thirsk, ed., *The Agrarian History of England and Wales, iv, 1500–1640* (Cambridge, 1967), pp. 53–5.

[3] Morant, *Essex*, i. 455–90; ERO D/DY2/4. pp. 55, 59, 63; M. E. James, *A Tudor Magnate and the Tudor State* (Borthwick Papers, xxx, 1966), pp. 5–9.

[4] PRO SP 16/39/3; 76/13.

the loan, but few followed his example, even within his own parish of Bradfield. The only substantial defaulting was in the small township of Ardley, and there it was probably encouraged by proximity to Dedham, one of the principal centres of resistance.[5] It seems evident therefore that a principal factor in securing conformity in this part of Essex was the territorial influence and example of Rivers.

In the neighbouring hundred of Witham the pattern was much less uniform. Most of the parishes of this area—including the clothing centre of Witham itself—were eventually willing to pay, and by August 1627 all but £25 of the money due from the hundred had been collected. However along the way there had been signs of resistance, particularly in the two townships of Terling and Hatfield Peverell.

The conformity of much of the hundred can again probably be accounted for by the influence of local landowners. As Dr Quintrell has pointed out, Witham hundred contained a concentration of local governors who were ready to do the bidding of the Court. Foremost amongst these was Sir Thomas Wiseman of Rivenhall, a senior JP—inspite of having a recusant son—and a constant ally of Maynard and Rivers. He was perhaps the most active loan commissioner in the entire county, involving himself not only in his native hundred but also in the neighbouring areas of Hinckford, Lexden, Tendring, Winstree, and Thurstable. Immediately adjacent to Wiseman lived his colleague, and Rivers's close friend, William Smythe of Cressing Temple, who was also consistently active as a commissioner; and directly to the north, at Bradwell, was the seat of Sir William Maxey, another commissioner, who once he had recovered from illness, worked hand in glove with Wiseman and Smyth.[6] It was the presence of these three men—possibly supported by some of the catholic and crypto-catholic landowners living in the vicinity of the town of Witham—which seems to have ensured the compliance of the northern part of this hundred. Writing at a later date Wiseman was able to refer to the fact that 'the Townesmen of Wytham had been most conformable in paying the loane monies . . .'; and the only

[5] Morant, *Essex*, i. 447, 462, 464, 468, 480; Ashton, *The Crown and the Money Market*, pp. 18, 73–4, 99; PRO SP 16/39/3i; 54/47; 73/13i.

[6] Quintrell, 'Gentry faction', 121–3; Quintrell, 'Government of Essex', pp. 44–5; PRO SP 16/39/3, 3i; 76/13,22; PCC Wills, 30 St John.

sign of an absolute refusal in this area was, somewhat surprisingly, in Maxey's own parish of Bradwell.[7]

To the south, however, in Terling and Hatfield Peverell it was a different story. Four of the fourteen Terling subsidymen were in default in February 1627 and a further three out of sixteen from Hatfield. Although these numbers were by no means large they were exceptional within the hundred as a whole. In part this can again be explained in terms of the influence of local landlords. Both Robert Mildmay of Terling and Edward Alleyn of Hatfield failed to pay up and refused a council summons early in 1627, which must have encouraged a similar response on the part of their tenants.[8] However this was far from being the whole story. Both townships also showed clear evidence of puritan sympathies and these may have played some part in shaping their response. Hatfield had a strong tradition of supporting godly ministers, extending back into Elizabeth's reign; and Alleyn worked closely with at least one of these. In Terling support for godliness became evident rather later, but during the 1620s the local minister was the fiery Thomas Weld, who regularly flouted authority and, in concert with the village leaders, did his best to work a godly reformation.[9] It seems likely that someone of Weld's forceful personality would have had some part in deliberations relating to the loan and may even have encouraged opposition. Certainly his presence suggests a link which will become even more obvious elsewhere, between puritanism and resistance.[10]

The next neighbouring hundred of Lexden illustrates this more clearly. In contrast to those already considered it did not contain any particularly influential landowners. Sir Paul Bayning held more property than anyone else in the area, but, as has been noted, he was mainly an absentee. Instead the hundred was dominated by the clothing interest, concentrated in the towns of the new draperies at Dedham, Langham, Boxted, and Horkesley in the

[7] Quintrell, 'Gentry faction', 121–3 n.; BL Add. MS 34, 679, fo. 61 (I am grateful to Brian Quintrell for this reference); PRO SP 16/54/47, 47i; 76/13i.

[8] Wrighton and Levine, *Terling*, pp. 139, 154; Morant, *Essex*, ii. 131–2, 134.

[9] H. Smith, *The Ecclesiastical History of Essex* (Colchester, 1932?), p. 15; W. Hunt, *The Puritan Moment* (Harvard, 1983), pp. 100, 147; Morant, *Essex*, ii. 131–2, 134; Wrightson and Levine, *Terling*, pp. 158–62.

[10] In identifying puritan parishes I have looked first of all for evidence of puritan sympathies amongst the local parishioners and gentry and then for indications of nonconformity on the part of the minister—as provided in Shipps, 'Lay patronage of East Anglian Puritan Clerics', apps. ix, x, xv.

north and Coggeshall in the south. These were the main centres of population and employment in the hundred and exerted a profound influence on its social and economic life.[11] It is therefore important to consider the condition of their economy.

By 1626 and 1627 the cloth industry in this area was enjoying a period of relative recovery after the disastrous recession earlier in the 1620s, when unsold cloths had been piling up in London warehouses and there had been widespread unemployment. The effects of this were still being felt in 1625, with emergency poor relief schemes continuing in nearby Braintree; however the area avoided most the mortality and disruption caused by the plague of that year and the worst effects of a fall in trade during the war were not to become apparent until 1628 and 1629. The industry in general was still in a state of chronic stagnation, but overall these towns were probably better placed to sustain a high level of taxation than at any other time in the 1620s.[12] This is of some significance when it comes to assessing the motives of defaulters.

Besides dominating the local economy, however, these towns also tended to set the tone for religious life. There was a long tradition of support for nonconformity within clothing areas and this doubtless helped to account for the concentration of puritan parishes within the hundred in the early seventeenth century. The livings at Boxted, Coggeshall, Easthorpe, Little Horkesley, Markshall, Earls Colne, and West Bergholt were all filled by nonconformists and in addition there were two renowned godly lecturers in the area, Thomas Shepherd at Earls Colne and John Rogers at Dedham. These ministers were also supported by an enthusiastic laity: gentry, such as Richard Harlakenden of Earls Colne and Robert Honeywood of Markshall, left them generous bequests; and the ordinary parishioners reputedly flocked from miles around to hear Rogers preach.[13] This connection was again to be significant for the loan.

From the start of the service Lexden had shown a good deal

[11] Morant, *Essex*, ii. 238–40; J. E. Pilgrim, 'The rise of the "New Draperies" in Essex', *Birmingham Historial Journal*, vii (1959–60), 45–51.

[12] Supple, *Commercial Crisis and Change*, pp. 8–13, 102–8; *Early Essex Town Meetings*, ed. F. G. Emmison (1970), pp. x–xi; E. A. Wrigley and R. S. Schofield, *The Population History of England* (1981), pp. 314–15, 328, 497, 638–43, 676.

[13] P. Collinson, *The Elizabethan Puritan Movement* (1967), pp. 222–32; Shipps, 'Lay Patronage', pp. 119–22, apps. ix, x, xv; R. Newcourt, *Repertorium Ecclesiasticum Parochiale Londinense*, 2 vols. (1708–10), ii. 56, 160, 186, 239, 408; PRO PCC Wills, 109 St John and 67 Skynner,

more intransigence than its neighbours. At the initial meeting, in October 1626, eleven of its subsidymen had appeared before the commissioners and refused to pay and a further twenty-five had simply failed to appear. Even more significantly none of the three local commissioners were prepared to co-operate, in spite of normally being active as JPs: Richard Harlakenden was absent in London, Robert Sandford of Chappell refused to pay and Dr Aylett of Feering simply failed to appear.[14] This was surely in part a reflection of the strength of local feeling. In the absence of these three men the service passed into the hands of the Tendring and Witham commissioners—Rivers, Wiseman, Smythe, and Maxey—and their position as outsiders created additional problems. Lacking local influence they depended on support from the Council which was not to be forthcoming. As early as November 1626 Rivers and the other commissioners had notified the board about refusers and urged prompt action, since 'the willinger sort seeme much discontented if those that stand out goe free'. In return however they simply received a letter of congratulation and more books of instructions on how to proceed. By February 1627 a second summons of lenders revealed resistance on a much heavier scale, particularly in the clothing towns.[15] Table 1 indicates its extent and distribution. On being notified this time the Council responded more positively and summoned six refusers to appear before it. One of these immediately submitted; but, as we have seen, when it came to the crucial test of dealing with the Dedham clothiers, the Council backed down and the consequences were

TABLE 1. Lexden defaulters, October 1626–August 1627

Townships with 3 or more defaulters	1628 subsidymen	Non-appearers and non-payers	Outright refusers	% of resisters
Boxted	16	4	—	25
Coggeshall	40	11	2	33
Dedham	45	38	2	89
Earls Colne	14	4	—	29
Fordham	9	3	1	44
Feering	10	3	—	30
Langham	16	4	5	56

Source: PRO E.179/112/638; SP 16/39/3i; 54/47, 47i; 76/13i, 13ii.

[14] PRO SP 16/39/3i; 54/47; ERO Q/SR/253–63.
[15] PRO SP 16/39/3; 54/47, 47i; *APC 1626*, p. 352.

disastrous.[16] By July the situation was so out of hand, that the county commissioners were complaining—presumably with Lexden very much in mind—that

> we cannot finde any one man from whom the money of the loan hath not beene more than once demaunded, in soe much as wee have just cause to feare that it exceedeth the abilitie of perswation or other power which we have to prevail more with many of them then wee have done alreadie. For as there are many which refuse to paie accordinge to their former consent soe in some partes of the countrie wee meete with divers who never would appeare or send us any resolution . . .

In August collection virtually ground to a halt, with some fifty-five of the sixty-four earlier Lexden refusers still holding out and one of the collectors, William Glasscock, 'obstinately refusing to warne to appeare before us the defaulters . . . or to shew us tallies for the satisfieing of what moneys he has paid into the Exchequer'. Prompted by this information the Council's machinery finally creaked into action. Glasscock was summoned before it and submitted to pay; and the Dedham clothiers were resummoned and committed. However all this had happened far too late. The last payment from the hundred was made in June 1627, and out of a total of £648. 3*s.* 4*d.*, £129. 6*s.* 8*d.* remained uncollected.[17] The pattern of this resistance suggests three principal causes.

First of all there was obviously the failure of the Council's attempts at coercion. Its treatment of the Dedham refusers was particularly ham-fisted and helped ensure that this town served as a centre of opposition and an example to the whole surrounding area. However this alone could not account for everything since strong resistance had been clearly evident as early as the initial meeting.

Another significant factor was undoubtedly the lead given by local landowners and employers. As we have seen two of the three resident JPs very obviously distanced themselves from the service and they were supported by a number of leading local gentry: the Cottons of Fordham and West Bergholt—one of whom was a minister—refused to subscribe; the Maidstones who were the leading landowners and employers in Boxted failed to appear at the first meeting; and William Glasscock, the obstructive collector, was lord of the manor in Aldham. Their actions were also supported by prominent clothiers, including the three Dedham employers, John

[16] See above, pp. 146–7.

[17] Bodl. L. Firth MS c.4, p. 373; PRO SP 16/76/13, 13i; E.401/2322–4, 2444.

Wilkinson, Richard Barker and Thomas Woode, and the wealthy Coggeshall manufacturer, Thomas Guyon who openly refused at the first meeting.[18] None of these individuals was as influential as a Rivers or a Wiseman, but in the absence of a dominant magnate within the division, they formed a substantial segment of the leading property-owners, and their example must have been a considerable encouragement to those below.

A similar lead also appears to have been given by the godly. This is most clearly indicated in the substantial overlap between townships involved in resistance and those which were obvious centres of puritanism. Six out of twelve of those containing defaulters were served by puritan ministers—Dedham, Boxted, Coggeshall, Little Horkesley, West Bergholt, and Earls Colne; and only two townships with non-conformists were not involved in resistance—Markshall and Easthorpe. In addition to this the main focus for opposition—around Dedham and along the Stour valley—was precisely the area where lay puritanism was most firmly entrenched. Occasionally the links between godliness and opposition became visible. In Dedham, for example, the charismatic John Rogers set his congregation a firm example by failing to appear at the initial meeting; whilst in Coggeshall one of the leading defaulters was John Sparhawke, a friend of the local minister and an unlicensed preacher in his own right who during the 1630s publicly denounced the Crown's prerogative levies.[19] More often, however, the precise nature of the connection remains obscure. Whether the initiative in resistance came from ministers or laity, and why the godly should apparently have felt so strongly about the loan, are questions which are better answered at a later stage. For now we should simply note the correspondence.

This is again evident in the next hundred of Hinckford. Like Lexden it contained a strong clothing interest and considerable support for puritanism. The towns of Bocking, Braintree, and Halstead were major centres of the new draperies and at least nine godly parishes can be identified within the area: Braintree and Bocking were noted for the zeal of their parishioners; Gestingthorpe supported a nonconformist lecturer; and Felstead, Finchingfield, Foxearth, Stebbing, Steeple Bumstead, and Wethersfield all had

[18] Morant, *Essex*, ii. 165, 198; *The Visitations of Essex*, ed. W. C. Metcalfe (Harleian Soc. xiii and xiv, 1878–9), p. 384; PRO E.179/112/638.

[19] PRO SP 16/39/31; 54/47; 76/131; Shipps, 'Lay Patronage', p. 203 n.

nonconformist ministers.[20] Unlike Lexden, however, the hundred contained two substantial landowners: Horace Lord Vere who held a string of five manors in the north western part, around Tilbury; and Robert Earl of Warwick whose property stretched down from Braintree and Felstead almost to Chelmsford. Vere's local influence was insignificant since he was absent serving abroad for most of the 1620s; but Warwick was clearly the dominant figure in the area. He spent much of his time in residence at Lees Priory, just south of Felstead, and as we have seen, was fully involved in the day-to-day running of the shire until his removal from the Lieutenancy in 1626. He also worked closely with several local ministers such as his former chaplain, James Gardiner, at Bocking, Samuel Wharton at Felstead, and Stephen Marshall at Finchingfield. And he evidently regarded Braintree as a local power base since in 1620 he made it the new venue for county elections, presumably so that he could exert his influence more easily.[21] He himself was, of course, absent from the county for much of the period of the loan; but his indirect impact on proceedings appears to have been considerable.

Although we have no account of the early stages of collection the evidence of payments into the Exchequer suggests that this was an uphill struggle. By the end of February 1627 the collectors had paid in only £233 out of £1290. 12*s*. 4*d*.; and their difficulties were confirmed in a report from the commissioners made in September in which they explained how they had called defaulters before them during the two previous months 'and used all the best meanes wee could to draw them to conformitie in that behalfe, and some of them that appeared were perswaded by us and paid their money, but some others were soe obstinately affected and combined together as they did not only refuse to lend and gave dilatory answers, but also gave peremptory and unreverend speeches unto us . . .'. These included the remarks cited earlier by William Alliston, pointing out that what the commissioners were doing was unneighbourly, illegal, and liable to be questioned in Parliament. The complaints were borne out by lists of defaulters which the commissioners sent into the Council. Predictably these

[20] Hunt, *The Puritan Moment*, pp. 149, 203, 254–9; Smith, *Ecclesiastical History of Essex*, pp. 21, 26, 39, 41, 49; Shipps, 'Lay Patronage', apps. ix, x, xv; Newcourt, *Repertorium*, ii. 275, 557.

[21] Morant, *Essex*, ii. 297, 302, 325, 335–7, 395, 417–18; *DNB* Vere, Horace Lord; Shipps, 'Lay Patronage', pp. 186, 209, apps. xv; PRO C.219/37, indenture for the Essex shire election (I am grateful to Christopher Thompson for this point).

showed large numbers of subsidymen simply failing to appear; but more significantly they also indicated some twenty-seven resisters who took the trouble to turn up and then refuse the service to the commissioners' faces. This was surely a demonstration of the strength of local feeling. As Table 2 shows, resistance was concentrated largely in the southern and eastern parts of the hundred, from Steeple Bumstead in the north down to Felstead in the south, and this was reflected in the final yields: William Richardson responsible for the south showed the largest deficit, £260. 13*s*. 4*d*. out of £563; Edward Harrington responsible for the north-east a slightly smaller one of £113. 13*s*. 4*d*. out of £322. 19*s*. 0*d*.; and William Bramston dealing with the north-west only £61 out of £406. 13*s*. 4*d*.[22]

TABLE 2. Hinckford defaulters, August 1627

Townships with 3 or more defaulters	1628 subsidymen	Non-appearers and non-payers	Outright refusers	% of resisters
Beauchamp St. Paul	4	3	—	75
Bocking	46	11	6	37
Braintree	44	11	7	39
Felstead	26	20	3	88
Finchingfield	36	6	—	17
Great Yeldham	9	3	—	33
Ridgewell	15	6	—	40
Stanborne Lacy	5	3	—	60
Stebbing	18	5	7	67
Steeple Bumstead	18	3	1	22
Sturmer	13	3	1	31
Topesfield	16	9	—	56
Wethersfield	27	9	2	41

Source: PRO E.179/112/626; PRO SP 16/76/22, 22 ii, 22 iii.

The poor response in Hinckford appears to have had much less to do with failings in the machinery of collection than elsewhere. Although, as usual, the Council failed to provide proper support—on several occasions neglecting to send a messenger who had been promised to help the commissioners—the commissioners themselves appear to have been extremely diligent in the service. Henry Gent of Steeple Bumstead, had a reputation as an active JP

[22] PRO SP 16/76/22, 22ii, 22iii.

and to judge by the abuse he attracted was equally zealous in the service of the loan. He was joined by the two remaining commissioners resident in the hundred, Thomas Heigham of Sible Hedingham and James Heron of Panfield, both of whom were again industrious JPs, and finally by Sir Thomas Wiseman from nearby Witham.[23] There was therefore no lack of local support.

Nor was the service wrecked simply by the example of local landowners, although this certainly played an important role in the south of the hundred. In the area around Felstead and Braintree the lead given by Warwick appears to have elicited a clear response. Eight of the ten subsidymen who can be identified as his tenants were involved in defaulting and they were joined by large numbers of others who must have been his dependants. Presumably they felt that the Earl's stance could be taken to legitimate their own resistance; and anyway according to Warwick himself—commenting in 1637 in the context of ship money—many of them shared his own views on prerogative taxation: 'his tenants or farmers were all old and accustomed to the mild rule of Queen Elizabeth and King James, and could not bring themselves to consent to such notable prejudices as Ship-money. They would consider their fault too grave if they died under the stigma of having at the end of their lives signed away the liberties of the realm.'[24] Elsewhere in the hundred, however—apart from in Finchingfield, where the two principal resident gentry William Kempe and John Meade led the resistance—there was little indication of subsidymen following their landlords. In at least five cases—Great Yeldham, Halstead, Panfield, Topesfield, and Steeple Bumstead—numbers of lesser subsidymen defaulted where their resident landlord had paid up, in the case of Steeple Bumstead defying the example of both Gent and Sir Thomas Bendishe.[25] Furthermore if one looks at the social composition of the group involved in defaulting it is apparent that the initiatives very often came from lower down the social scale. Using the admittedly crude guidelines provided by subsidy assessments one finds that in the townships involved in opposition, a considerably larger

[23] PRO SP 16/76/22; Quintrell, 'Government of Essex', pp. 44–5; ERO Q/SR/253–63.

[24] PRO E.179/112/626; SP 16/76/22ii; Rowe, 'Earl of Warwick and ship money in Essex', 162. A list of Warwick's tenants was kindly supplied by Christopher Thompson, compiled from Hunts. RO dd. M.32, bdle 10 and Alnwick Castle MS XII.7. Box 1.

[25] PRO SP 16/76/22ii; E. 179/112/626; Morant *Essex*, ii. 256, 300–2, 348–54, 360, 406.

proportion of lesser subsidymen (i.e. yeomen and husbandmen) were involved in resistance than £3–9 subsidymen (i.e. middling and lesser gentry), some 36 per cent compared with some 23 per cent. The highest proportion of all, 38 per cent was amongst the more substantial gentry; but here the figures were inflated by the two defaulters from Finchingfield (see Table 3).

TABLE 3. Subsidy ratings of Hinckford defaulters

Subsidy rating	1628 subsidymen (within villages where there was opposition)	Defaulters	%
£10+ in lands	8	3	38
£3–9 in lands £4. 13*s*. 4*d*.+ in goods	52	12	23
£1–2 in lands £2–4 in goods	313	112	36

Source: PRO SP 16/76/22, 22 ii, 22 iii; E. 179/112/626.

All this suggests a distance between the wealthier landowners and lesser subsidymen which is again apparent if we consider the dealings of the loan commissioners. As we have seen, they faced a good deal of abuse and several overt challenges to their authority which were surely indicative of social cleavage and a collapse of deference. And just as revealing was their own response, which involved complaining to the Council in terms which invited harsh coercive measures against their neighbours. They appeared to feel that they were being confronted by an upsurge of popular hostility which they were no longer able to control, and that in the circumstances the only way to reimpose their authority was to call on the powers of central government, however disruptive and unneighbourly this might be.[26] Two principal factors can be suggested to account for this situation.

First of all there was the geographical and social structure of the area. This was a large hundred, comprising a variety of farming regions and occupational structures. The northernmost fringe, alongside the River Stour, contained a number of open field villages practising a mixed agriculture; the south western segment of the hundred, from Halstead down to Braintree was the centre of the local clothing industry; and the remainder was largely given over to stock-rearing in small enclosed fields. It was these two

[26] PRO SP 16/76/22.

latter areas which predominated, and by and large shaped the character of the whole. For, with the opportunities for small-scale husbandry and employment in the clothing industry, this was one of the most densely populated divisions of the county, with a relatively high proportion of landholdings between 5 and 50 acres, the ideal size to support yeomen and husbandmen. In addition there is less evidence here than elsewhere of a large landless labour force or extremes of wealth and poverty. In short Hinckford hundred provided perhaps the best example in Essex of an area fulfilling the characteristics which Dr Thirsk and others have ascribed to wood-pasture/clothing regions.[27] The influence of Warwick apart, it provided a relatively egalitarian social structure, within which independent and competitive attitudes could flourish and considerations of social status and deference were often in abeyance.

These characteristics were doubtless reinforced by the influence of puritanism. As Dr Hunt has shown the yeomen and middling sort of this area were very much to the fore in the godly campaign for the reformation of manners, and individual congregations sometimes displayed a fiercely committed and independent attitude. At Finchingfield, for example, Warwick's friend Stephen Marshall who had been introduced to the living by the lord of the manor and loan refuser, William Kempe, was being supported in his efforts at godly reformation by a select vestry consisting largely of local subsidymen. At nearby Wethersfield the local congregation maintained a lecturer at their own expense and had chosen first Marshall and then Daniel Rogers, son of their Elizabethan minister, the famous puritan diarist Richard Rogers. And in Braintree the zeal of the congregation was such as to make life extremely uncomfortable for the moderate puritan incumbent Samuel Collins. In the early 1630s he lamented that

> it is no easy matter to reduce a numerous congregation into order that hath been disorderly these fifty years and that for the seven years last past hath bin encouraged in that way by the refractory ministers in the county, with whom they have had acquaintance in their private meetings and conferences, who have left divers schismatical books among them, and during their continuance here laboured to make my person and ministry contemptible and odious because I would not hold conversation with

[27] Hull, 'Agriculture of Essex', pp. 5–9, 13, 72–83, 554; Thirsk, *Agrarian History*, iv. 2–15; D. Underdown, 'Community and class: theories of local politics in the English Revolution', in B. C. Malament, ed., *After The Reformation* (Manchester, 1980), pp. 159–62.

them. If I had suddenly and hastily fallen upon the whole parte of conformity I had undone myself. For upon the first notice of alteration many were resolved to goe to New England and others to remove elsewhere.[28]

This combination of religious and economic independence suggests that the southern and western segments of the hundred harboured large numbers of the godly middling sort and that it was they who were to the fore in the resisting the loan. As in Lexden and Witham there was a close correspondence between parishes with signs of puritan sympathies and those with loan defaulters. This was the case with seven of the thirteen parishes involved most heavily in resistance—Bocking, Braintree, Felstead, Finchingfield, Stebbing, Steeple Bumstead, and Wethersfield; and only two parishes with puritan ministers showed no signs of opposition at all—Foxearth and Gestingthorpe—both of them well to the north, away from the main focus of resistance. Given the parallels between their response on religious matters and their particularly forthright response to the loan it seems not unreasonable to suggest that the mixture of social and cultural influences which gave rise to the former also helped to shape the latter.

The next adjoining hundred of Dunmow provided a complete contrast with Hinckford. Apart from two ministers who were nonconformists—at Great Dunmow and Berners Roding—it showed little evidence of puritanism; and its economic and social structure was markedly different. Much of the hundred was located on the chalk soils which stretched down from the north-western corner of the shire towards Chelmsford. The predominant pattern of farming therefore resembled that of the classical open field areas of the Midlands and Home Counties rather than the mixure of wood-pasture, forest, and marshland which predominated over much of Essex. The villages of this region still held their manorial courts which helped to regulate village life, whilst the distribution of wealth showed a sharp incline, with a large body of smallholders and virtually landless labourers and most of the property concentrated in the hands of a few large farmers. These provided the ideal conditions for maintaining a settled, hierarchical pattern of social relations in which the sense of deference and the

[28] Hunt, *The Puritan Moment*, pp. 82–3, 142–3; 253–6; Shipps, 'Lay Patronage', pp. 111, 125 n., 127–8, 150; *Early Essex Town Meetings*, pp. vii, xii–xiv, 107–36.

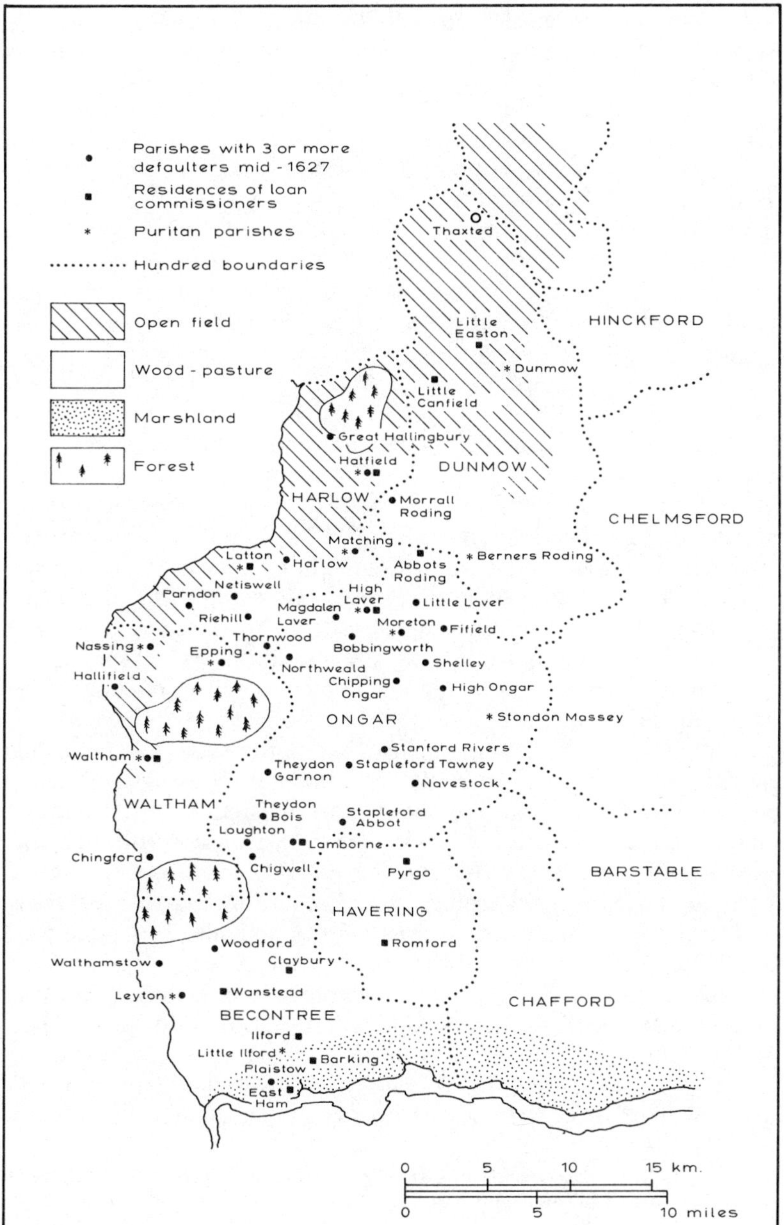

MAP 2: South-eastern Essex and the Loan

authority of the gentry were liable to predominate; and this appears to have made an important contribution to the success of the loan.[29]

The other main influence in this direction was the presence of William Lord Maynard. Of the commissioners residing within the hundred he was the only one who was obviously active: Sir William Fitch of Little Easton appears to have been mainly involved further south, in Becontree and Havering, and Sir Robert Wiseman of Little Canfield was a resister. However this probably mattered little since it was Maynard who in territorial and political terms dominated the hundred. He held a compact block of estates stretching across the middle between the two principal market towns of Dunmow and Thaxted, and he played to the full the role of a paternalistic local magnate. He was generally in residence at his house at Little Easton and looked to protect the interests of local inhabitants; he was continually active as a JP and Deputy Lieutenant; and he used his patronage of local livings to secure the presence of men who shared his own Laudian leanings, such as the aggressive conformist John Browning, a former chaplain to Lancelot Andrewes.[30] Maynard's approach to dealing with the loan was to make full use of this local standing.

Evidence of precisely what happened in Dunmow is scanty; but it appears that—as with the benevolence—after encountering some initial resistance because of heavy opposition in the adjacent hundred of Hinckford and Harlow, Maynard was able to win his neighbours round. Significantly he did so not by using the heavy-handed coercion of the Hinckford commissioners, but by more subtle persuasions and 'by faire meanes without troublinge the Board with complaints'. In this way he was working very much with the grain of local society, drawing on its sense of deference and reciprocal obligation towards its principal landowner. He was in effect utilizing the same 'creditt and power' that he had employed in dealing with the benevolence, and again it proved largely successful. By the end of July 1627 he could claim that within the four northern hundreds of Dunmow, Freshwell, Uttlesford, and Clavering all but twenty of the subsidymen had paid up 'and those persons of noe greate noate, exceptinge Sir

[29] Shipps, 'Lay Patronage', app. ix; Newcourt, *Repertorium*, ii. 226, 509; Hull, 'Agriculture of Essex', pp. 11–37, 50–2, 72–83; Thirsk, *Agrarian History*, iv. 2–15.

[30] PRO SP 16/72/44; Bodl.L. Firth MS c.4, p. 373; Morant, *Essex*, ii. 432–48, 463; Hunt, *The Puritan Moment*, p. 256; *DNB*, Browning, John.

Robert Wiseman, and very few of them that doe absolutely refuse.'[31]

With the next division, the adjoining hundred of Ongar, and half-hundreds of Harlow and Waltham, the pattern changes yet again. This was a largely rural area with a mixture of open-field farming along the western side of Harlow, forest in Harlow and Waltham and wood-pasture over much of Ongar. The predominant social structure was probably closer to the relative egalitarianism of Hinckford than the graduated hierarchy of Dunmow;[32] however there were still several landowners in a position to exercise a dominating influence. The wealthiest of these was Edward Earl of Norwich, who held a block of five manors around Waltham Cross. He was a natural ally of the Council, having enjoyed a long career at Court and finally receiving an earldom in November 1626 when the Duke was rewarding his supporters. However his usefulness was reduced by the fact that he rarely involved himself in local government, and in the event he did not attend the service of the loan.[33] In his absence the most powerful local landowner was Sir Francis Barrington, owner of several manors around his seat at Hatfield Broadoak. Barrington's influence here compared not unfavourably with that of Warwick or Maynard elsewhere and it was based on similar foundations. He generally remained in residence in the area and together with his son was continually active as a JP and Deputy Lieutenant. He had a considerable reputation as a patron of puritan ministers, with his household long established as a resort for the godly. And he was closely linked with other prominent gentry in the vicinity: Richard Franke of Hatfield, one of the loan commissioners, was his tenant; Sir Edward Altham of Latton, another commissioner, was his brother-in-law; and Sir William Masham of High Laver, a third, was his son-in-law and close friend.[34] The only other local

[31] PRO SP 16/72/44.

[32] Hull, 'Agriculture of Essex', pp. 11–37, 72–83; Thirsk, *Agrarian History*, iv. 53–5.

[33] VCH *Essex*, 8 vols. (1903–83), v. 157–60; GEC ix. 768; ERO Q/SR/249–64; PRO SP 16/74/48.

[34] Morant, *Essex*, ii. 487–8, 497, 505–8; Quintrell, 'Government of Essex', pp. 44–5, 121–31; Shipps, 'Lay Patronage', pp. 107–15. The Earl of Warwick, another close friend of Barrington, also held several manors in Ongar hundred; however these were detached from the main landholdings in Chelmsford, south Hinckford, and Rochford hundreds and thus his direct influence in the area was probably not great: VCH *Essex*, iv. 47, 181, 287. Sir Nathaniel Rich, Warwick's cousin and man-of-affairs held the right of presentment at Stondon

commissioner was Sir Gamaliel Capell who, although a hard-working JP and Deputy Lieutenant, lacked the wealth and prestige to challenge Barrington's pre-eminence.[35]

Another feature of this area was again the presence of godly ministers and congregations. It is possible to identify at least eight nonconformists amongst the parish clergy—at Epping, Hatfield Broadoak, High Laver, Latton, Matching, Moreton, Nassing, and Stondon Massey—and at least two of these served notably Puritan congregations: Edward Jude's parishioners at Nassing included several who were to emigrate for religious reasons in the 1630s, most notably John Eliot, 'the Apostle to the Indians'; and James Harrison's congregation at Hatfield had entered into a religious covenant when he had taken up his duties as lecturer in 1625. Most of these parishes were concentrated in the area where both Barrington and Masham lived and were accustomed to taking a cue from these two renowned, godly magistrates.[36]

Most of the detailed information relating to the service in this area unfortunately covers only the latter stages, when opposition was causing it to break down almost completely. Nevertheless there is enough evidence early on to indicate that this had been building up for some time. Up to the end of February 1627 the Exchequer had received only £100 from the local collectors, so in July the Council dispatched a messenger, Daniel Bucock, to deal with the defaulters. Bucock's failure—either to bring refusers before the commissioners or make them appear in front of the Council—was both a measure of the strength of opposition and a further encouragement to it. Returns from about this date indicate that the service was on the verge of collapse: in Ongar more people were defaulting than had actually paid; many who had initially promised payment were now holding back; and those who still owed money included John Feltham and Thomas Bennett, the two collectors, and Sir Gamaliel Capell, one of the only two active commissioners. By August he and Sir Edward Altham had more or less given up, conceding to the Council that 'our endeavours have not suseeded to our desiers, noe appearance being now

Massey, but again his influence within Ongar appears to have been limited: Shipps, 'Lay Patronage', app. ix.

[35] VCH *Essex*, iv. 190–2; ERO Q/SR/253–63.

[36] Shipps, 'Lay Patronage', p. 111, apps. ix, x, xv; Newcourt, *Repertorium*, ii. 208, 248, 352, 367, 432, 545; *DNB* Eliot, John; N. C. P. Tyacke, 'Migration from East Anglia to New England before 1660' (University of London, Ph.D. thesis, 1951), pp. 26, 29, app. i; Hunt, *The Puritan Moment*, pp. 104, 107–9, 141, 166, 230–1.

made before us'.[37] As Table 4 shows their task had become almost impossible.

TABLE 4. Harlow, Waltham, and Ongar defaulters, July 1627

Township	1628 subsidymen	Defaulters	Refusers and non-appearers	% of resisters
Harlow				
Hatfield	28	15	1	57
Harlow	20	5	—	25
Great Hallingbury	11	3	—	27
Little Hallingbury	8	1	—	13
Hastingwood Hamlet	3	1	—	33
Latton	6	1	—	17
Matching	10	2	1	33
Netiswell	7	5	—	71
Parndon	20	11	—	55
Roydon	18	1	1	11
Riehill Hamlet	5	2	1	60
Shearing	8	—	1	13
Thornwood Hamlet	4	3	1	100
TOTAL	148	49	7	38
Waltham				
Chingford	11	5	3	73
Epping	16	9	2	69
Nassing	21	11	5	76
Roydon Hamlet	4	1	—	25
Sewardstone	9	—	—	—
Upshire and Hallifield	24	6	4	42
Waltham	20	4	1	25
TOTAL	105	36	15	49
Ongar				
Abbots Roding	2	2	—	100
Bobbingworth	6	3	—	50
Beauchamp Roding	3	2	—	66
Chigwell	15	8	3	73
Chipping Ongar	6	3	1	66
Fifield	9	3	—	33
Greenstead	4	1	—	25
High Laver	7	5	1	86
High Ongar	9	6	—	66
Kelvedon	4	—	1	25
Lambourne	12	10	—	83
Little Laver	4	3	—	75
Loughton	6	3	3	100

[37] *APC 1627*, pp. 425–6; PRO SP 16/52/63, 66; 74/48.

TABLE 4. (*cont.*):

Township	1628 subsidymen	Defaulters	Refusers and non-appearers	% of resisters
Magdalen Laver	5	5	—	100
Moreton	5	5	—	100
Morrall Roding	4	4	—	100
Navestock	20	11	—	55
Northweald Bassett	5	3	—	60
Norton Mandevill	3	2	—	66
Shelley	6	3	2	83
Stanford Rivers	12	5	3	66
Stapleford Abbot	9	6	1	78
Stapleford Tawney	4	4	—	100
Stondon Massey	6	2	—	33
Theydon Bois	5	4	—	80
Theydon Garnon	15	12	3	100
Theydon Mount	3	2	—	66
TOTAL	189	117	18	71

Source: PRO E.179/112/620; SP 16/52/63, 65–6.

So widespread was resistance in this area that it is hard to distinguish any real pattern to it. The refusal by Barrington and Masham at the very start must have had a considerable impact, given their local influence; and their example probably made a particular impression on some of the godly congregations. Harrison's letters at this time indicate that he was very much in sympathy with their stand and regarded it as an aspect of their religious commitment. It was therefore surely no coincidence that Hatfield provided the highest number of defaulters in Harlow Hundred and that elsewhere puritan parishes such as Epping, High Laver, and Nassing were well to the fore in resistance. However what probably damaged the service more than anything was the growing sense that the commissioners could be defied with impunity. The clearest indication of this was in the large number of Ongar subsidymen who, having promised to pay up—in November or December 1626—were by the summer of 1627 withholding their contributions. Presumably in the intervening months widespread and successful defiance in the area had destroyed any respect they might have felt for the machinery of enforcement. The end result was that only £90 out of £556. 13*s*. 4*d*. was ever received by the Exchequer.[38]

[38] PRO E.401/2322–4, 2444.

Problems with this machinery again loomed large in the final area to be covered, the hundred of Becontree and the Liberty of Havering. This was again a mixture of farming regions, with the predominant wood pasture changing to marshland and sometimes open field villages along the banks of the Thames.[39] However, unlike its neighbours this area showed no real evidence of puritanism, apart from the presence of the nonconformist Daniel Cawdry at Little Ilford and a godly congregation at Leyton.[40] There was also a good deal of support for the service from the leading landowners in the area. Six of the ten commissioners living here were active during the loan, all of them substantial and influential gentry: Sir Thomas Fanshawe of Jenkins, Surveyor of Crown Lands and owner of five manors around Barking; Sir Thomas Cheeke of Pyrgo, former knight of the shire and a friend of the Earl of Warwick; Sir Nicholas Coote of Ilford, one of the most conscientious JPs in the county: his close friend, Francis Fuller, another substantial landowner around Ilford; another friend Sir William Fitch of Barking; and finally Sir Richard Heigham of East Ham. These men provided a solid foundation on which collection was based and compensated for the four remaining local commissioners—Sir Henry Mildmay of Wanstead, Master of the Jewels, Sir Robert Quarles and John Wright of Romford, and Richard Hales of Claybury—refraining from involvement.[41]

In the Liberty of Havering the problem facing commissioners was not so much entrenched opposition as simple obstructionism. This was revealed in an unusually detailed set of returns which show the process of collection at three stages and indicate the large numbers who initially either pleaded poverty or simply avoided being at home when the collector called. In November 1626, when he went his rounds for the first time, sixty-nine out of 114 made some sort of excuse; however by the following January—aided no doubt by the fact that one of the leading local refusers, Thomas Legatt of Hornchurch, had appeared before the Council and agreed to pay up—the commissioners had sorted their way through these defaulters, established which had genuine excuses and persuaded the remaining fifty-five to pay up. In August there were only three actual refusers left in the hundred

[39] Hull, 'Agriculture of Essex', pp. 5–9, 11–37.

[40] Shipps, 'Lay Patronage', app. ix; VCH *Essex*, vi. 216.

[41] PRO SP 16/52/62, 64–5; 67/49; PCC Wills, 15 Seagar; VCH *Essex*, v. 192, 200–1, 212–13; vi. 25; vii. 16, 32, 65; ERO Q/SR/253–63; Quintrell, 'Government of Essex', pp. 44–5.

TABLE 5. Havering defaulters, November 1626–August 1627

Townships	1625–6 subsidymen	Those pleading poverty or not at home c.November 1626	Those giving excuses who had paid by January 1627	Those released for poverty by January 1627	Those refusing c.August 1627
Colliers Row	16	8	5	3	—
Harolds Wood	16	12	9	1	2
Havering Ward	8	3	1	2	—
Hornchurch	9	3	3	—	—
Nokehill Ward	8	6	4	2	—
Northend Ward	14	8	8	—	—
Romford	26	16	12	3	1
Southend Ward	17	13	13	—	—
TOTAL	114	69	55	11	3

Source: PRO E.179/112/616B; SP 16/44/8; 52/64.

and the arrears of £66. 6*s*. 8*d*. on the final account was accounted for by the death or removal of six of the leading subsidymen.[42] (See Table 5.)

In Becontree the commissioners were rather less successful and again the principal problems were excuses and absenteeism. It had long been the practice of the local subsidy assessors to fill up their rolls with individuals who were in fact London residents, and therefore liable to pay in the capital. Some sixty-seven of the 270 local subsidymen came into this category and their absence accounted for a large part of the £928. 6*s*. 8*d*. still owing in the summer.[43] But it did not account for all of it. As Table 6 shows, there were still forty-eight defaulters who had either not paid or refused outright. The main centres of resistance were Leyton, Plaistow, and Walthamstow and this may have had something to do with the presence of a godly congregation in the former and defaulting landlords in the two latter. In more general terms opposition was probably also a response to the proximity and

TABLE 6. Becontree defaulters, *c*.July 1627

Townships	1625–6 subsidymen	Those resident elsewhere	Non-payers and non-appearers	Refusers	% Resisters
Barking	21	2	2	—	9
Chadwell	16	4	1	—	6
Church Street	18	11	2	—	11
Dagenham Town	22	5	2	—	8
East Ham	21	5	2	—	9
Great Ilford	35	11	1	—	2
Leyton Ward	17	4	6	2	47
Little Ilford	2	1	—	—	—
Plaistow	27	2	9	1	37
Ripple Ward	13	1	—	1	8
Stratford Langthorne	21	7	2	—	9
Upton Ward	9	1	2	—	22
Walthamstow	20	4	8	2	50
Wanstead	11	3	1	—	9
Woodford	17	6	4	—	24
TOTAL	270	67	42	6	18

Source: PRO E.179/112/616A; SP 16/52/62, 65; 73/71.

[42] PRO SP 16/44/8; 52/64; 73/71; *APC 1626*, p. 328.
[43] Quintrell, 'Government of Essex', p. 315; PRO SP 16/52/62.

influence of the City, which throughout the loan was obstructive to the Council.[44] However the pattern in this area is less clear than it is almost anywhere else and it would be unwise to try to draw any firm conclusions.

III. SUBSIDYMEN AND POLITICS

From this survey of about half the shire it should be evident that variations in response within Essex were considerable. Each division exhibited a different mix of social, political, and religious characteristics and each reacted in its own distinctive way. Because of this it is possible to treat Essex as a microcosm of the country as a whole and use its experience to explore a whole variety of factors influencing political behaviour at the level of the subsidymen. This is not, of course, to say that it was typical. As has been stressed, in many respects it was extremely untypical, presenting a heightened and exaggerated perspective in comparison with events elsewhere. Its significance derives rather from the fact that local taxpayers were presented with an unusually open choice which makes the considerations shaping their response a good deal more visible than in many areas. It is in this sense, then, that the conclusions drawn from Essex can be regarded as having a wider and more general influence.

Perhaps the clearest of these is that there appears to be no straightforward link between resistance to the loan and the other financial burdens of the period. In this respect Essex provides an excellent test case since it was one of the counties bearing the brunt of costs from the war. Its clothing industry was heavily dependent on the export trade which suffered considerable disruption, and its position as a coastal shire ensured that it had to spend heavily on local defence. To add to this it failed to receive any substantial concessions over the loan. Like other shires it was allowed to recoup coat and conduct charges, but it was given no real compensation for the expenditure of over £4,000 during the Harwich emergency of 1625.[1] The local taxpayers, then, were

[44] PRO SP 16/52/62, 65; 73/71; VCH *Essex*, vi. 216, 256, 263; Pearl, *London and the Puritan Revolution*, pp. 72–8.

[1] Quintrell, 'Government of Essex', pp. 249–62, 326–30; Bodl. L. Firth MS c.4, p. 277–83. The county had been released from the privy seal loan of 1625 in partial compensation for the expenditure at Harwich; but since much of the money due from other shires was never collected, this was not particularly helpful: Firth MS c.4, p. 192.

certainly more heavily burdened than most; however this does not appear to explain their opposition.

If one examines the pattern of resistance from hundred to hundred it soon becomes clear that this bore little relation to the distribution of financial burdens. Tendring, which paid out more in contributions to the war than any other area, was also the readiest and the quickest to pay the loan. The area around Witham was also described as 'most conformable', in spite of being loaded with more than its fair share of taxation. On the other hand those hundreds which local governors noted as having consistently avoided paying military rates, Ongar, Harlow, and Waltham, were also amongst the main centres of opposition.[2]

Similarly there is little evidence of a link between the trade recession and loan resistance. Several of the big clothing centres—notably Bocking, Braintree, Boxted, Coggeshall, Dedham, and Langham—were also centres of resistance, but this does not appear to have been directly related to their economic situation. It has to be remembered that during 1626 and 1627 they were enjoying something of a respite in between the troughs of unemployment and hardship which they experienced in 1624–5 and 1628–9. We should also allow for the fact that those individuals suffering financial difficulties could appeal to the commissioners to be discharged on the grounds of poverty; so there was often no need for them to run the risks incurred by opposition. Had there been a direct link between the prosperity of local industry and the readiness of subsidymen to pay national taxes we might perhaps have expected it to show itself during the subsidy payments of 1624–6 or 1628–9. However there is no indication of extensive defaults on either levy. The two surviving exchequer lists of defaulters—from Hinckford in 1626 and Becontree in 1629—show three and sixteen names respectively which was no more than a small fraction of the defaults over the loan.[3]

All this is not to deny any sort of connection between ability to meet the Crown's mounting demands and the incidence of opposition: the two were self-evidently linked. The point, rather, is to suggest that this relationship was mediated by an awareness of the legal status and intentions behind the loan. As with other levies—such as the rate for local muster masters—the response of taxpayers was shaped by a whole variety of influences, ranging from narrow, explicitly local, considerations, to wider issues of

[2] PRO SP 16/71/29; BL Add. MS 34,679, fo. 61.

[3] PRO E.179/112/609; 276/77.

legitimacy and ideology.[4] It is to some of these that we can now turn, still using Essex as the basic example.

At an immediate local level, an obvious influence on the extent of resistance was the efficiency of the machinery for enforcement. As we have seen from the situation in Havering, face-to-face contact between commissioners and subsidymen played an extremely significant part in collection. A willingness to knock on doors, to harry non-payers and investigate pleas of poverty could make a marked impression on the numbers of defaulters. This seems to have been just as true elsewhere. Although we do not have such detailed returns from other areas it is fairly clear that commissioners such as Sir Thomas Jervoise and Lord St John in Hampshire and Sir John Hare and Owen Sheppard in Norfolk made a considerable impact through their industry and application.[5] Conversely where support from commissioners was lacking, or where the coercive machinery was weak, this was often a direct encouragement to resist. This has been observed in parts of Lexden hundred, and in the area of Ongar, Harlow and Waltham, where large numbers joined in the resistance once it appeared they were unlikely to be punished. It is something which can also be seen elsewhere, perhaps best illustrated in the south Lincolnshire wapentake of Elloe.

By July 1627 the commissioners for this area were on the verge of admitting defeat, informing the Council that the service had virtually collapsed and the subsidymen of 'these parts were in great revolt'. This, however, was not a situation which had developed overnight; it had been building up for several months as the credibility of the service was steadily eroded. Initial opposition had come from fifteen local subsidymen who in March 1627 had travelled to Lincoln to make their stand before the Privy Councillors. At least eight of these were men of some substance—rated at £3–8 in the subsidy roll—drawn from the ranks of the lesser gentry and yeomen farmers who were accustomed to leading local protests over matters such as fen drainage. Their example certainly encouraged wider resistance and helped to deter the two most active local governors—Sir William Welby of

[4] Boynton, *The Elizabethan Militia*, pp. 287–91; R. Ashton, *The English Civil War* (1978), pp. 55–9; Barnes, *Somerset*, pp. 262–4; Hassell Smith, *County and Court*, pp. 336–7.

[5] See above, pp. 138, 140–2.

Gedney and Bevill Wymberley of Pinchbeck—from involving themselves in the business. This left it in the hands of one resident commissioner who had not previously served as a JP—Nicholas Evington of Spalding—and one outsider—Sir Edward Heron of Surfleet.[6]

These two set about their task diligently enough, in spite of the fact that in dealing with the insular and comparatively egalitarian fenland parishes they lacked some of the authority which would probably have been accorded to them elsewhere;[7] however, they were crucially hampered by the Council's failure to punish refusers. In spite of being presented with a detailed list after the March meeting at Lincoln it summoned only one local defaulter to answer in London. The remaining fourteen escaped without even a reprimand, and twelve of them were still withholding payment in the summer. Their example appears to have been infectious. Once the local subsidymen saw how easy it was to get away with resisting they joined in large numbers. In the two townships of Holbech and Holbechthurne—where one of the early refusers had continued to defy the collector—a further eight out of twenty subsidymen were resisting by the summer. In nearby Fleet—where eight of the subsidymen had refused at the start—a further six later defaulted. And in the area as a whole 101 out of 300 subsidymen were reported as non-payers in July: twenty-two of them were refusing absolutely, seventeen pleading poverty or some other excuse, twenty-six withholding further payment, having already promised or paid in part, and thirty-six refusing to pay without 'bearers'. This last group, in particular, illustrated the way in which the machinery of collection was falling apart. 'Bearers' had been allowed by the Privy Councillors in March, as a concession to persuade the poorer subsidymen to make their contributions; but such a concession required careful handling if it was not to be abused, and it soon became clear that the commissioners lacked either the local knowledge or the authority to provide this. They seem to have been incapable of sorting out who should or should not be allowed a 'bearer' and in consequence provided subsidymen with a ready made means of evasion: as the commissioners reported, 'at tyme of their payment [they] would debet over those bearers or absolutely pay nothing'. The end result seems to have been near chaos. After their report in July no more

[6] PRO SP 16/56/39; 71/50; E. 179/139/722; C. 193/12/2; E. 163/18/12.

[7] J. Thirsk, *English Peasant Farming* (1957), pp. 13–17, 20–1, 120–6.

money was paid into the Exchequer and arrears of £321. 16*s*. 8*d*. out of £698. 16*s*. 8*d*. remained outstanding.[8]

In this case the hard core of absolute refusers was relatively small; but once they had made a breach in the credibility of the service, those who were less forthright or less adventurous were only too willing to take advantage and bring it to a standstill. The processes of collection and enforcement were thus linked very closely to the pattern of opposition. Having said this, however, it should again be emphasized that they only partially account for this. They doubtless did much to determine the eventual extent of resistance, but they do not explain how it got started or why it was strong in the early months when threats of punishment still retained much of their deterrent force. To understand this we need to look at those influences which fostered political awareness and a conviction that the loan was something to be opposed.

One of the more obvious of these was the example of local magnates. As we have seen in the case of Essex, when a powerful landowner gave a positive lead in the service local subsidymen generally followed. Warwick's tenants and dependants in the area around Braintree and Felstead were very much to the fore in resistance within Hinckford hundred—and significantly considerable opposition was also reported from Chelmsford and Rochford hundreds where most of his other estates were situated.[9] Similarly the neighbours of Barrington and Masham around Hatfield Broadoak and High Laver proved extremely obstructive. On the other side of the coin the strongest support for the loan came from areas dominated by the magnates supporting the levy: from around the Rivers estates in Tendring, Thurstable, and Winstree; from Maynard's sphere of influence in Dunmow; and from the neighbours of Wiseman and Smythe in the northern part of Witham.

It was much the same story elsewhere. Opposition amongst the Northamptonshire subsidymen, for example, was concentrated in the western half of the shire, where fifteen of the twenty-two gentry refusers lived.[10] At the time of March meeting in Lincoln some ten of the seventeen refusers in the divisions of Kesteven

[8] PRO SP 16/56/39; 58/110; 71/50; E. 401/2322–4; *APC 1627*, pp. 253, 395, 430.

[9] *APC 1627*, p. 102; Morant, *Essex*, i. 271–325; ii. 75–102.

[10] *APC 1627*, pp. 25, 33, 54, 62; J. H. Gleason, *The Justices of the Peace in England, 1558–1640* (1969), pp. 172–4.

and Lindsey came from the Earl of Lincoln's estates.[11] In Gloucestershire the most stubborn resistance was concentrated in the hundreds of Cirencester, Whitston, and Bisley in, or near, which lived eight of the twelve commissioners refusing at the initial meeting.[12] Within the East Riding most of the forty-five defaulters reported to the Council were said to have come from those parts where Sir William Constable and Sir John Hotham 'doe eyther dwell or have their greatest frends and kyndred'.[13] And opposition in the two hundreds of North Oxfordshire, was ascribed by Banbury and Carelton, the visiting Council representatives to the 'ill example of a neighbouring lord [i.e. Saye and Sele] which some were so unadvised as to alleadge unto us here as an escuse for themselves'.[14] Conversely, within these same shires it was the areas presided over by magnates supporting the loan which tended to pay up. In the eastern division of Northamptonshire the influence of Lord Montague, Lord Mordaunt, and the Earl of Westmoreland was thrown fully behind the service and the Council was able to congratulate local subsidymen on the alacrity of their payments.[15] The south Lincolnshire wapentake of Wevebridge reported only two defaulters and this was presumably related to the presence there of three influential landowners supporting the levy—Sir Edward Hussey of Honington, Sir Clement Cotterell of Wilford and Thomas Harrington of Boothby Pagnell.[16] And during a campaign of resistance to billeting charges in north Oxfordshire early in 1628—which the Earl of Banbury regarded as a continuation of the resistance to the loan—the only villages which paid up were those containing tenants of Sir William Pope, a Deputy Lieutenant and consistently loyal servant of the Crown.[17] There was, then, evidently a link between the influence of landowners and the behaviour of subsidymen. The question is how did this operate?

At a crude level it could undoubtedly work through the material controls which landlords exercised over their tenants. Sir John Jackson, a Yorkshire refuser was reported to have vowed that 'iff any of his men had given anie they should never hold land of him, and iff anie of my tenants shall give, Gods wounds I could or would hange them with my owne hands'. Such threats may well

[11] PRO SP 16/56/39; J. L. Sanford, *The Great Governing Families of England*, 2 vols. (Edinburgh, 1865), i. 207–8.

[12] PRO SP 16/54/28, 28ii–xiii; 58/1.

[13] PRO SP 16/68/51.

[14] PRO SP 16/50/36.

[15] PRO SP 16/49/8; *APC 1627*, p. 51.

[16] PRO SP 16/73/45; 78/32.

[17] PRO SP 16/94/73, 73i; 95/91.

have been repeated elsewhere; however in general the connection probably operated rather more subtly, either through the 'powers, favours and creditts' envisaged by the Privy Council and employed by someone like Maynard, or through more complex notions of deference and legitimacy.[18]

This can be illustrated by recalling the success of the Nottinghamshire commissioners at their initial meeting. They had talked a body of largely unwilling subsidymen into accepting the levy by stressing the King's promise to repay the money and not to use it to avoid a Parliament. Presumably what was convincing was not so much the quality of their arguments—since these had been put at the time of the benevolence with little success—as the fact that they were being put by several of the shire's leading landowners, including Mansfield and Sir Gervase Clifton. The view of these men undoubtedly carried considerable weight. As we have seen Mansfield was highly regarded as an honest broker in the affairs of the county and Clifton, who sat as first Knight of the Shire throughout the 1620s, enjoyed a similar esteem.[19] It was this as much as anything which appears to have carried the day. For by pledging their credit on the King's assurances these local governors were putting the subsidymen in a position where to disbelieve them would be to imply at the very least ingratitude and distrust, and could have been taken as a gross breach of deference and respect. Few of the audience could have wished for this—any more than the local governors—since their own position as often as not rested on similar sets of notions relating to order and obligation; and thus it provided a highly effective form of psychological leverage.

The nature of this was complex and varied, and could just as easily be brought to bear against the service. As we have seen, the example of social superiors was sometimes cited before Privy Councillors as a reason for non-payment. The reference to Lord Saye and Sele in north Oxfordshire can be matched with a plea from one of the subsidymen from the Earl of Lincoln's estates, that he would not pay 'bycawse he saw so many eminent men refuse'.[20] This suggests that the actions of 'eminent men' were seen as in some sense legitimating opposition. Precisely why this should have been so is not explicitly stated. Perhaps it was because copying the example of social superiors was taken to

[18] PRO SP 16/36/43; 51/35; 524/100.
[19] PRO SP 16/36/34; 55/1; see above, pp. 118–9; *Returns of M.P.s*, i. 450–79.
[20] PRO SP 16/56/39.

indicate continuing respect for authority and thereby to remove any taint of 'rebelliousness' or 'disobedience' from the subsidymen's actions; or more probably it was because the judgement of these particular 'eminent men' was regarded as an authoritative assessment of the best interests of 'the Country'. Either way this indicates that the influence of landowners often worked in quite a subtle and intricate fashion, serving to shift the grounds of discussion and undermine the appearance of consensus and unity on which the success of the service to a considerable extent depended.

All this should not, of course, be taken to argue that subsidymen were mere ciphers, responding automatically to promptings from above. Their relationship to local magnates was basically reciprocal, implying obligations and expectations on both sides. This seems to have been the case more and more as the pattern for such relationships, altered from one founded on notions of 'good lordship', in which lineage and seigneurial ties formed the basis of the bond, to a more explicitly 'political' relationship, in which the magnate was expected to serve the interests of 'the Country', and show himself to be 'a good Patriot'.[21] Something of this was reflected in the identity of outlook which Warwick was to claim between himself and his tenants in 1637. More particularly it emerged from the way in which local governors were coming to pledge their credit, discuss notions of legitimacy and frame their arguments in the overtly political terms used by someone like the Earl of Lincoln, all of which inevitably gave rise to expectations on the part of the subsidymen which the local governors were then under an obligation to fulfil.[22] The effects of this were apparent in the cases of Phelips, Wentworth and Lord Montague who, as we have seen, felt themselves to be under considerable pressure to resist the loan in order to maintain their credit with their neighbours.[23] In short it is evident that local governors were influenced by subsidymen just as surely as subsidymen were influenced by their local governors. Indeed it was around this reciprocity that the fate of the service frequently hinged.

[21] James, *A Tudor Magnate and the Tudor State*, pp. 5–9; Barnes, *Somerset* pp. 286–7; Cust and Lake, 'Sir Richard Grosvenor', 50–3; A. L. Hughes, 'Thomas Dugard and his circle in the 1630s—a "Parliamentary–Puritan" connection?', *HJ* xxix (1986).

[22] Rowe, 'Earl of Warwick and ship money in Essex', 161–3 Hunt, *The Puritan Moment*, pp. 163–6, 265; see above, pp. 172–5.

[23] See above, pp. 107–8, 110–11, 222–3.

One of the most crucial factors affecting this relationship was the geographical and social structure of a particular area; and this also appears to have been another influence on the pattern of opposition. The connection between these factors has recently been examined by civil war historians studying patterns of popular allegiance, and their findings indicate some of the ways in which it worked. Professor Underdown's study of three south-western shires has demonstrated that the Clubmen of the 1640s were clearly divided in their aims: those from the wood-pasture/clothing areas tended to support Parliament, whilst those in the open-field parishes largely sided with the Crown. He argues that this pattern was related to basic differences in social structure and religious attitudes. The large, open parishes of the wood-pasture tended to foster a relatively egalitarian society, with a wealthy and conspicuous 'middling sort' giving strong support to puritanism. The open-field areas on the other hand provided a more settled and hierarchical society, with greater inequalities of wealth, a higher degree of subordination to the gentry and a strong attachment to the established church.[24] This model has been refined in Dr Hughes's study of Warwickshire. She has shown that the same basic distinction between wood-pasture and open-field can be discerned at the outbreak of the Civil War, but has also demonstrated that the gentry of the wood-pasture tended to side with the King, which she attributes to their greater awareness of the dangers of social insubordination.[25] Following these conclusions therefore one might expect to find that the areas of heaviest opposition to the loan were the wood-pasture and clothing regions which—during the 1640s at any rate—appear to have been more receptive to the ideals embraced by Parliament.

If we apply this to Essex the fit is rather uneven. Some of the most committed opposition came from the wood-pasture/clothing regions of northern Lexden and southern Hinckford, which exhibited several of the features apparent in civil war studies, such as a strong attachment to puritanism and a relative lack of social deference. Conversely the conformity in Dunmow appears to have stemmed from the strength of hierarchy and respect for authority within an open-field society. However elsewhere the situation accords less closely with the basic model. Ongar, Harlow, and

[24] Underdown, 'Community and class', pp. 154–62; D. Underdown 'The Chalk and the cheese: contrasts amongst the English Clubmen', *P. and P.* 85 (1979), 25–48.

[25] Hughes, 'Warwickshire: a "County Community"?', 44–5, 63–5.

Waltham, which resisted strongly, was a division containing both sorts of farming regions, and some of the most obstructive parishes, running down from Hatfield Broadoak along the western fringe, were situated in the open-field. Similarly Becontree and Havering was again a mixed area with no particular tie-up between resistance and farming regions. And Tendring and northern Witham, both of which readily conformed, were largely located in the wood-pasture.[26]

It is much the same story in other shires. A county like Northamptonshire clearly does not fit the basic model. Here most of the resistance was concentrated in the open field areas stretching across much of the western division and into north Oxfordshire; and the more conformable parts of the shire were in the wood-pasture and fenland country of the east.[27] On the other hand the model might help to explain the fierce resistance amongst the Cotswold clothing parishes of Gloucestershire where there was a long tradition of independence and resistance to established authority.[28] Perhaps the clearest example of a match between the pattern of responses and the geography and social structure is provided in southern Lincolnshire. It is therefore worth investigating this area in more detail.

As Dr Thirsk has demonstrated, it was very clearly divided into three regions, each with a distinctive pattern of farming. The eastern half was dominated by fenland, characterized by similar features to the wood-pasture, but in a more accentuated form. Husbandry here consisted predominantly of rearing cattle in enclosed pasture reclaimed from the sea or the floods; villages tended to have large areas of common and were therefore able to support a substantial, and rapidly growing, population; whilst the long-standing practice of partible inheritance ensured a relatively egalitarian structure of landholding, as a result of which there was a notorious shortage of substantial resident gentry. This all helped to develop a strong sense of self-reliance and communal solidarity which revealed itself particularly in the resistance of the 'middling sort' to schemes for fen drainage. The area immediately adjacent consisted of a clayland vale in which the local economy was based on a mixture of grazing and arable. This gave it a character more

26 Hull, 'Agriculture of Essex', pp. 5–9, 11–37, 72–83.

27 *APC 1627*, p. 51; Thirsk, *Agrarian History*, iv. 5, 89–99.

28 PRO SP 16/58/1; I. Roy, 'The English Civil War and local society' in B. Bond and I. Roy eds., *War and Society: a Yearbook of Military History* (1975), pp. 35–6.

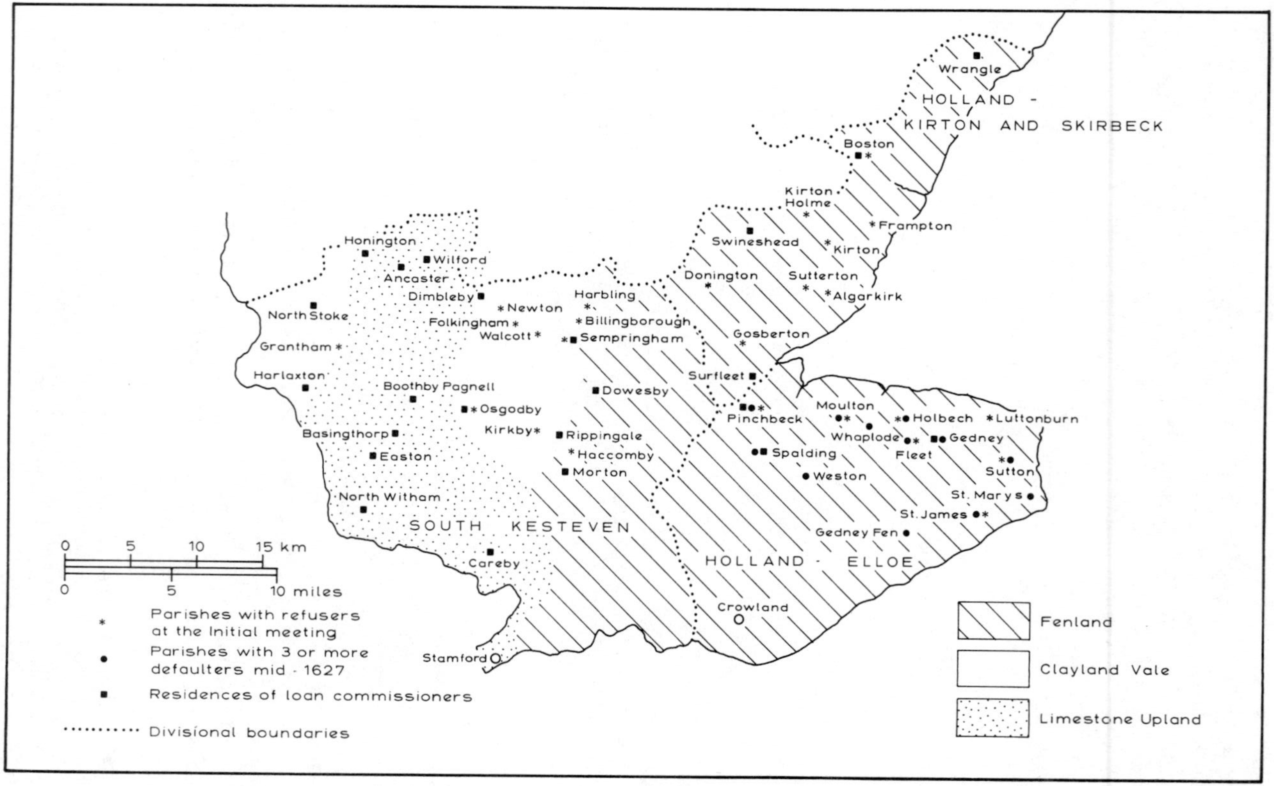

MAP 3. Southern Lincolnshire and the Loan

akin to the open-field. Villages tended to be smaller than in the fenland and the pyramid of wealth sloped more steeply. Husbandmen and yeoman farmers were less in evidence and a good deal more authority was exercised by magnates such as the Earl of Lincoln and Sir William Armine of Osgodby. However it was the third region which showed the sharpest distinctions in status and wealth. This was the limestone upland which was given over almost exclusively to sheep-corn husbandry. The social pattern here was typical of the classical open field, comprising small, closed villages, generally dominated by a resident squire and containing a large proportion of landless labourers. It was a relatively settled, hierarchical society in which the authority of the big landowners—men such as Sir Edward Hussey and Sir John Hatcher of Careby—went largely unchallenged; and the conservative and paternalistic values which predominated can be seen illustrated in the works of Robert Sanderson, the conformist rector of Boothby Pagnell.[29]

Each of these regions responded differently to the loan. The bulk of opposition came from the fenland where, as Professor Holmes has shown, leading villagers had developed a sophisticated sense of legal customs and privileges and had long been used to maintaining their rights by collective action. The protests at the time of the loan drew on this tradition. The town of Boston and some twelve villages stretching to the south sent what were in effect deputations of leading subsidymen to present their protests at Lincoln; and it was proposed that they should establish a common-purse 'to contribute to the charge and expense of theyre late Mayor and Edward Tillson and anye else that suffer trouble in the cause of the loane . . .'[30] In the months following the March meeting the local inhabitants obstructed the service relentlessly. As we have seen they employed every sort of excuse and evasion and the two local commissioners were eventually forced to appeal for help from the centre in much the same terms as those employed by the Hinckford commissioners.[31] This was not the only parallel between the two areas. A breakdown of defaulters in

[29] Thirsk, *English Peasant Farming*, pp. 13–21, 79–88, 92–100, 120–6; J. Thirsk, 'Farming in Kesteven 1540–1640' *Rural Economy in England* (1984), pp. 129–47; Hajzyk, 'Church in Lincolnshire', pp. 357–60; Holmes, *Seventeenth Century Lincolnshire*, pp. 22–3, 42–3, 52, 61, 72–3, 81–3, 97, 112, 178; *Works of Robert Sanderson*, iii. 89–90; vi. 289–95.

[30] Holmes, 'Fenland disturbances in the seventeenth century', pp. 186–94; PRO SP 16/56/39; 72/36.

[31] See above, p. 269.

terms of their subsidy assessments, provided in Table 7, also indicates that in face-to-face dealings with the commissioners the lesser subsidymen were just an obstructive as the village leaders—although there was less evidence of a cleavage between yeomen and lesser gentry.

TABLE 7. Subsidy ratings of Elloe defaulters

Subsidy	1628 subsidymen[a]	Defaulters	
		No.	%
£10+ in lands	2	—	—
£3–9 in lands £4. 13*s*. 4*d*.+ in goods	54	16	30
£1–2 in lands £2–4 in goods	230	67	29

[a] Within villages where there was opposition.
Source: PRO E.179/139/722; SP 16/56/39; 58/110.

In the adjacent clayland vales the service was altogether more successful. Initially it had been impeded by the example of the Earl of Lincoln, who evidently encouraged his neighbours and tenants to refuse in March. However by the early summer, with Lincoln out of the way and the two resident commissioners—John Brownlow of Rippingale and John Thorold of Morton—taking an active part assisted by four of their near neighbours—Hussey, Cotterell, Harrington, and John Bluett—collection appears to have been proceeding relatively smoothly. Regular payments were made into the Exchequer and there are no obvious signs of resistance.[32]

The most conformable area, however, was the limestone upland. This was particularly well stocked with resident gentry and there was no problem in finding enough active commissioners. It therefore hardly mattered that Sir John Hatcher and Sir Alexander Pell declined to involve themselves. A positive lead was provided by the largest of the local landowners, Sir Edward Hussey, the courtier and office-holder Sir Clement Cotterell, and the most experienced and reputable of the local governors, Robert Sanderson's patron, Thomas Harrington; and they were able to

[32] SP 16/56/39; 73/45, 45i–ii; E.401/2322–4.

draw on the relatively strong traditions of deference within this society.[33]

The pattern in southern Lincolnshire fits closely enough with the model provided by civil war historians to suggest that their conclusions can usefully be applied to loan resistance. Of course even in this area the fit is not perfect: the fenland of south Kesteven for example, appears by and large to have co-operated, perhaps in response to the example of Stamford, the main urban centre in the area.[34] However this should not be a cause for surprise, or for discarding the basic model. What we are dealing with, after all, is not a simple geographical and social determinism; rather it is a complex network of influences operating at different levels and with varying weight. Farming practices and the hierarchy of property owning established certain basic features in local society—what might be described as the 'deep structures'—but on top of these were layered a whole series of other determinants, ranging from accustomed patterns of authority and the impact of individual landowners, to the effects of cultural attitudes, religious opinions, and political awareness. To some degree the development of the latter was shaped by the former, but the precise pattern could show enormous variation. The direction given by a forceful landowner or an influential minister might easily cut across that of social structure or occupation. Thus without discarding the basic model we can conclude that it needs to be applied with caution. Much the same could be said as we approach the final area of discussion, the links between loan resistance and puritanism.

It has already been stressed that within Essex there was a considerable overlap between the two, and this is equally evident elsewhere. It can be seen, for example, in the resistance of the southern half of Northamptonshire and the northern part of Oxfordshire. Unfortunately the reports from this area are too brief to allow for anything more than a general impression; but even from this the connection is clear enough. The two godly strongholds of Banbury and Northampton were both exceptionally obstructive. Refusers from Banbury were summoned before the Council immediately after the initial meeting early in February and defaulters were still being hounded in June: these included Sir

[33] PRO SP 16/73/45; 78/32; Thirsk, 'Farming in Kesteven'; Holmes, *Seventeenth Century Lincolnshire*, pp. 84, 160, 180; HMC *Rutland*, i. 481.

[34] PRO SP 16/73/45, 45i–ii; 78/32; E.401, 2322–4.

William Knight, and his son Belaziel, and Thomas Hallhead, members of the two leading godly families in the town.[35] From Northampton the Mayor was reporting continued resistance as late as July, complaining that those 'which ever have been as yet backward to yield to any, for the most part they so continue', and naming amongst others, Christopher Sherland, the town's MP and Recorder, and Thomas Ball, minister of All Saints, both of whom were involved in the circle around John Preston.[36] The villages immediately adjacent to these two centres, which shared in their strong tradition of nonconformity, appear to have responded in a similar fashion; and the list of local gentry involved in resistance was virtually a roll call of leading puritan families in the area: Lord Saye and Sele and Sir William Cope in Oxfordshire and Richard Knightley, Erasmus Dryden, Sir William and Sir Richard Samwell, Sir John Pickering, George Catesby, Francis Nicolls, and Richard Lane in Northamptonshire.[37]

Similar connections can be seen in the Holland division of Lincolnshire. Again this was an area noted for its attachment to puritanism. It was the main centre of lay nonconformity in the shire—with parishioners frequently being reported for wearing hats during divine service, remaining seated during communion and 'gadding' to sermons—and also provided livings for some of its most reputable godly ministers: William Worship and Samuel Whiting at Skirbeck, John Ramshaw at Sutton St James, Edmund Diggle at Sutterton and, of course, John Cotton, whose preaching at Boston provided a focus for the life of the godly in surrounding parishes. Cotton and his friends have already appeared in this account because of their involvement in drafting and distributing the Lincolnshire pamphlet; but it is equally clear that they were heavily implicated in open resistance. They formed an influential nucleus amongst the Aldermen and Common Councilmen in Boston and appear to have been largely responsible for pressing ahead with making a protest at Lincoln, in spite of the corporation's decision to co-operate with the levy. The three aldermen who actually appeared in Lincoln were all closely connected with Cotton: John Whiting, the Mayor, was the brother of Samuel Whiting, a minister who accompanied Cotton to American in the

[35] PRO SP 16/52/74; *APC 1627*, pp. 51, 59; VCH *Oxfordshire*, x, 8, 74, 97–100; Fiennes and Gibson, 'Providence and Henry Hallhead', 199–208.

[36] PRO SP 16/75/27, 27i; Morgan, *Prince Charles' Puritan Chaplain*, pp. 31, 178; Sheils, *Puritans in the Diocese of Peterborough*, pp. 119–30.

[37] VCH *Oxfordshire* ix. 98, 119–20; x. 8, 98; Sheils, op. cit., pp. 102–18.

1630s; Atherton Hough also emigrated at the same time; and Edward Tillson was prosecuted for nonconformity in 1634, in what was apparently a retrospective drive against Cotton's friends. In addition four of the remaining nine protesters were linked with Cotton: Thomas Leverett, a Common Councilman, was another who emigrated; William Cony, again a Common Councilman, helped to finance the Massachusetts Bay Company: and Edmund Jackson and Richard Westland were both prosecuted alongside Tillson for nonconformity. The overlap between puritans and opponents of the loan here, then, is clear enough. Elsewhere in Lincolnshire it is less easy to identify, largely because of a lack of detailed evidence for religion in the area. However there is the striking instance in Sutterton of a group of leading parishioners who were involved both in sending a deputation to protest before the Councillors at Lincoln and in holding conventicles at Diggle's house; and in other parishes there is enough evidence of a general nature to suggest that puritanism reinforced the traditional independence of the fenland communities.[38]

Other shires showed similar connections, although generally less marked. In Norfolk, which by and large conformed, the main centres of resistance were the godly towns of Norwich and Yarmouth.[39] In Gloucestershire resistance was concentrated around the clothing centres of Stroud and Painswick, which again had strong puritan traditions.[40] And in the East Riding four of the leading resisters—Sir William Constable, Sir Matthew Boynton, Henry Alured, and Walter Strickland—had a reputation for godliness.[41] The links amongst the laity, then, are clear enough. If we turn to the clergy, however, they become rather less visible.

On the face of it this is perhaps surprising. If the godly laity were coming to the fore in resistance one might normally have expected puritan ministers to be equally prominent, acting as their spokesmen and urging their cause. However the situation in late 1626 was by no means normal. In the aftermath of the York House Conference the godly were faced with an increasingly aggressive group of conformist and arminian bishops, backed by the king and the Duke. They were also losing much of the support

[38] PRO SP 16/56/39; 72/36; Hajzyk, 'Church in Lincolnshire', 344, 357–60, 364, 462–6; Spurrell, *The Puritan Town of Boston*, pp. 1–23; F. Rose Troup, *The Massachusetts Bay Company* (1930), p. 40.

[39] Evans, *Seventeenth Century Norwich*, pp. 84–104; P. Collinson, *The Religion of Protestants* (1983), pp. 153 n., 160 n., 274.

[40] VCH, *Gloucestershire*, 11 vols. (1903–76), xi. 34, 81–3, 136–40.

[41] Cliffe, *The Yorkshire Gentry*, pp. 256–81.

they had previously enjoyed at Court, as spokesmen such as Warwick, Saye and Sele, and Pembroke were pushed out of favour. And in these circumstances they were confronted with measures such as the 'Instructions to the Clergy' of November 1626, which were calculated to put those with misgivings over the loan in an even more uncomfortable position.[42] All this meant that any attempt to block the levy openly was liable to be counterproductive. Given the King's commitment it would probably provoke a new campaign to enforce conformity. Hugh Peter had attempted to question it from the pulpit, but had been quickly warned off by the Bishop of London; and this must have brought home the tactical need for the godly to be unobtrusive. As a result—apart from Peter and John Preston—there is no obvious evidence of the public protests which might have been anticipated.[43] Warwick's allies in Essex, men such as Thomas Hooker and Stephen Marshall, who were not normally noted for their discretion, were nevertheless careful not to draw attention to themselves. Preston's friends amongst the London ministers, Richard Sibbes, John Davenport, and Henry Burton, avoided making an issue of the loan, in spite of the fact that Burton was willing to go into print to denounce the Duke during 1627. And, most significantly of all, John Cotton, who, as we have seen, stood at the centre of a network of resisters, was sufficiently discreet to escape being reported to the Council, in spite of the presence of the hostile local informer Sir Edward Heron.[44] This apparently deliberate silence ensured that in public the puritan case went largely unstated. In private, however, it seems to have been a very different story.

It was one of the principal complaints of conformist clergy such as Bargrave and Wren that godly ministers were active behind the scenes stirring up opposition to the loan.[45] Some allowance has to be made for their ideological standpoint, which presumed a link between puritanism and rebellion; but, even so, there is ample evidence to support their contention. James Harrison and Ezekiel Rogers both wrote to Barrington in the Fleet, encouraging him to

[42] Tyacke, 'Puritanism, arminianism and counter-revolution', pp. 132–4; Morgan, *Prince Charles' Puritan Chaplain*, pp. 157–96; see above, pp. 49–50.

[43] Stearns, *The Strenuous Puritan*, pp. 29–30, 41; Hill, *Puritanism and Revolution*, pp. 251–7.

[44] Hunt, *The Puritan Moment*, pp. 164, 199–200; Morgan, *Prince Charles' Puritan Chaplain*, pp. 174–83; H. Burton, *The Baiting of the Pope's Bull* (1627), epistle dedicatory to King Charles (I am grateful to Tom Cogswell for this reference).

[45] Bargrave, *A Sermon*, pp. 18–19; Wren, *A Sermon*, pp. 34–8.

stand by his principles, whilst John Dod preached to him in a similar vein; and John Rogers of Dedham and Thomas Ball of Northampton both resisted the loan in their localities and presumably encouraged a similar response from their parishioners.[46] There are also several examples of encouragement to resist from clergy whose religious stance is unknown but who came from puritan areas or had puritan connections and therefore may well have been affected by godly attitudes. William Alliston of Sturmer in north Essex, for example, openly denounced the local commissioners and threatened them with a Parliament; John Burgoyne of Cirencester sent letters to several local gentry urging them to resist; and Benjamin Tomkins of Harpole, just outside Northampton, who was a close friend of the godly loan resisters Sir Edmund Hampden and Sir Richard Samwell, was said to be a 'great encourager of his friends to contradiction'. In addition to these there is the case of Ezekiel Jackson of Powick, in Worcestershire, who was summoned before the Council and required to sign a declaration '1. That hee did not choose the text which hee then handled for that present occasion . . . 2. That hee did nott ayme or intend thereby to hinder His Majestie's royall intencions in the matter of the loane. 3. That hee did not at any time diswade any of His Majestie's subjects from assenting to the said loane.'[47] Whatever the precise nature of Jackson's fault, it is clear that the Council suspected some clergy of stirring up opposition to the loan and, as we have seen, they had good reason. The problem is finding out how it was done. What arguments did ministers use against the levy and how do these help explain the apparent connection between puritanism and opposition?

Unfortunately—because of the difficulties involved in arguing against the loan publicly—the evidence available to answer these questions is extremely thin. Scott's treatise provides a very full and impressive demonstration of this connection in the case of one individual; but, as we have seen, his viewpoint was, in some respects, an extreme one and the statements from other sources which might be used to balance it are in general too abbreviated to properly convey the connections between ideas.[48] A good deal has

[46] ERO D/Ba/F.43; BL Eg. MS 2644, fos. 250–1: *C. and T.* i. 188; PRO SP 16/39/31; 75/27, 271.

[47] PRO SP 16/71/46; 76/22i; 458/106; PCC Wills 53 Barrington and 23 Coke (I am grateful to John Fielding for these references); *APC 1627*, pp. 130, 144, 200; *APC 1627–8*, pp. 17, 83–4, 239, 241; *C. and T.* i. 212.

[48] See above, pp. 176–85.

to be based on inference, and because of this it must be stressed that the conclusions offered here are necessarily tentative and provisional.

In approaching these questions we should recognize, first of all, that puritanism itself was far from being a precise or rigid set of attitudes. One of the principal conclusions to emerge from recent discussion of the term is that it represented a relatively loosely defined series of responses, covering a broad spectrum of opinions. Dr Lake has identified at the core of these responses a basic evangelical impulse, 'an intense vision of the reality and mutuality of the community of the godly and of the way in which that community would and should be called together through the word . . .'; but he has also stressed that the way in which this vision was applied to events varied a good deal, according to the circumstances and perspective of a particular individual.[49] This implies, then, that what one is looking for, in the links between puritanism and opposition, is not a single and unchanging response, but rather a whole range of reactions, varying with a person's situation, but still reflecting sets of shared assumptions which tended to lead in a particular direction. Hence the fact that a godly gentleman, such as Sir Richard Grosvenor, could support the collection of the levy, or that a nonconformist clergyman, such as John Viccars of Stamford, felt able to preach in favour of it, should not be taken to negate the idea of a distinctively puritan response.[50]

One of the most obvious connections between the responses which went to make up puritanism was a constant concern with the threat of popery, and this appears to provide a key to the way in which the godly viewed the loan. Popery was seen as existing in a variety of guises, both spiritual and secular. These covered an enormously wide range, from the activities of popish college tutors and arminian divines who wished to destroy the unity of protestant doctrine, to the local recusant, who in a time of crisis might prove disloyal to his country, and to the evil counsellor, who sought to undermine the godly resolutions of his monarch. In the eyes of puritans these were all bound together by the fact that they represented manifestations of the Antichrist working within the world. The existence of this Antichrist acted as a constant spur to action. It recalled the continuing existence of sin and the

[49] Lake, *Moderate Puritans*, pp. 1–15, 279–92.

[50] PRO SP 16/56/72; Cust and Lake, 'Sir Richard Grosvenor', 40–53; *Cases in the Courts of Star Chamber and High Commission*, pp. 209–10; Holmes, *Seventeenth Century Lincolnshire*, pp. 42–3, 62–3.

precarious hold of protestantism in England, and at the same time stirred them to a continual vigilance in countering its evil influence. This vigilance has been described by Lake as an ideal of 'active citizenship', and the description neatly illustrates the way in which it created obligations not just in religious matters, but also in the sphere of secular life and politics. Hence the local freeholder involved in electing the 'wisest, stoutest and most religious men' to Parliament, the local governor who was active in preserving social order and the political pamphleteer who tried to open the eyes of the King to the evils around him could all be seen as engaged in fighting the same antichristian foe.[51] It is this view which perhaps does most to explain the relationship between godliness and loan resistance. For within the framework which puritans had established for analysing contemporary politics, the dangers presented by the loan could be assimilated to the threat from popery.

This framework was most commonly based on the idea of a polarization between 'Court' and 'Country' which, as has been observed, was increasingly influential during the early seventeenth century. Each term described a series of images which combined the spiritual and the secular. 'The Court' had come to represent a pervasive mixture of popery, moral degeneration, arbitrary government, and appeasement; 'the Country' was its direct antithesis, standing for everything which was pure and protestant and in accord with the liberties of the subject. Within the framework as a whole a prominent place was accorded to Parliament, which was seen as representing the point at which the people became involved with national politics whilst at the same time providing a practical means of removing the evil influences of the 'Court' and maintaining the purity of protestant religion.[52] Thus, in threatening Parliament and the values represented by the 'Country', the loan struck at the root of the political concerns of the godly.

Recognition of this was reinforced by other aspects publicized by opponents of the levy. For example the fact that the loan would help to safeguard the position of the Duke, a theme constantly

[51] Lake, 'Constitutional consensus and puritan opposition', 805–25; P. G. Lake, 'The significance of the Elizabethan identification of the Pope as Antichrist', *JEH* xxxi (1980), 161–78; Cust and Lake, 'Sir Richard Grosvenor', 40–53 (I am grateful to Ann Hughes and Peter Lake for many valuable suggestions on this subject).

[52] Zagorin, *Court and Country*, pp. 33–9; Stone, *Causes of the English Revolution*, pp. 105–8; Lake, 'Constitutional consensus and puritan opposition', 805–25.

harped on by 'Canterbury' Scott and the Lincolnshire pamphleteer, meant that it could be seen as helping to perpetuate the evil system of 'Court' favourites. And this concern was given an additional, spiritual, twist in *The Baiting of the Pope's Bull*—published by Henry Burton during 1627 and said to have caused 'much ado' in London—which pointed to the growing number of papists insinuating themselves into the King's presence via Buckingham's household.[53] Related to this there was also the worry that Catholics had won their way into royal favour through their forwardness in promoting prerogative taxation. William Whyteway, a Dorchester merchant with godly sympathies, noted in his diary that at the time of the benevolence 'little was given, but that by papists and popish persons'; and in the course of the 1628 Parliament Sir Richard Grosvenor expressed alarm at those individuals, 'some papists, some mad men of a more pliable disposition, ready . . . to act whatsoever shall be commanded them'. This was even alluded to by Roger Manwaring during his sermon, *Religion and Allegiance*. In a reference which must have been peculiarly offensive to the godly he contrasted what he called their 'recusancy in temporalls' with the loyalty to the King displayed by many Catholics.[54]

These were important elements in the threat which the loan was seen to present in both secular and spiritual terms; however, if the tone parliamentary debates of 1628 is any guide, the most alarming development was the combination of high church divinity and arbitrary government outlined in the sermons by Sibthorpe and Manwaring. According to Pym these brought together all the most repugnant aspects of the 'Court': popery, arminianism, evil counsel, and arbitrary government. He accused Manwaring of harbouring 'a wicked intention to avert His Majesty's mind from the calling of Parliaments' and acting 'the part of the Romish Jesuits: they labour our destruction by dissolving the Oath of allegiance taken by the people, he doth the same work by dissolving the oath of protection and justice taken by the King'.[55] Because of the inhibitions on denouncing royal policy it is more difficult to discover such statements outside

[53] See above, pp. 173, 179–82; Burton, *The Baiting of the Pope's Bull*, epistle dedicatory; *C. and T.* i. 227–9.

[54] BL Eg. MS 784, p. 116; *CD 1628*, iv. 76; Manwaring, *Religion and Obedience*, p. 31.

[55] Cited in Russell, 'John Pym', 162–4; Russell, *Parliaments and English Politics*, p. 375, 404–5, 407.

Parliament; but there seems little doubt that such sentiments were widely shared, and brought home to many for the first time, the dangers inherent in the new theology. William Whyteway, for example, denigrated the sermons as works of 'Catholike Obedience'; 'Canterbury' Scott bracketed them with Bargraves' sermon as a product of 'that Branded Clergy'; and the Earl of Clare, although by no means a puritan, denounced them in terms which clearly anticipated the charges made by Pym. Discussing the prospects for a Parliament in the aftermath of the Windsor council meeting of August 1627, he lamented that

> the King [is] so advers as it is laesa maiestas to name it, so tastefully hath Sibthorp and suche like court sectaries fueled the palate of absolute power . . . I must confess that those who have more deepely drunke of the cleere fountayn of God's word have left a meum and tuum in the world, wittnes the commandment in that behalf; and untill this new doctrrine, styled by the forgers thereof apostolicall obedience be out of fashion, and detested by King and people as a fyrebrand of discord and a quencher of that paternall and filiall love that might be betweene them, lett no man dreame of Parliament, of legall and regular proceedings.[56]

This was an excellent illustration of the way in which the loan was seen as offering both a religious and a political threat in ways which particularly concerned the godly. However it will not quite do as a general explanation for puritan resistance, since this particular danger only emerged relatively late in the service. Instead it is necessary to take a broader perspective and focus on the general threat to Parliament, which throughout was the main source of concern to opponents of the levy. Of course, this concern was not restricted to the godly; others acknowledged it as well, and no doubt assimilated it to the interference of evil counsellors and the pernicious influence of 'the Court'. The significant difference was that where the godly perceived this sort of grievance they were under a peculiarly strong obligation to do something about it. It was not enough for them to temporize and wait for things to change; the onus was on them to act.

This is something which emerges very clearly from their assorted discussions of various aspects of the loan. From 'Canterbury' Scott's exposition of the duties of 'the conscientious Puritan', to Harrison's references to 'providence' and 'divine ordination', to the Lincolnshire pamphleteer's exhortation to all 'good men', the same ideal of 'active citizenship' was constantly

[56] BL Eg. MS 784, p. 128; KAO U.951/Z.10, p. 13; *Holles*, ii. 366.

invoked. This last piece, although framed in deliberately secular terms, provides perhaps the best illustration of the spirit in which many of the godly—not least amongst them some of the subsidymen who defied the councillors at Lincoln—must have entered into opposition to the levy: 'shall we to avoyd a little present feare, or danger of being impressoned or the like, plunge ourselves into an irrecoverable mischiefe. Now let us unite ourselves to stand for our own liberties, whatsoever comes of it . . . the commissioners may threaten you, but they cannot hurt you, for they have no law in their side . . . honest men and wise men will shew themselves either now or never.'[57]

This examination of the factors influencing responses to the loan has concentrated largely on those individuals involved in opposition and those shires where resistance was strongest. In the process it has perhaps created the impression that resistance was more widespread than was in fact the case; it therefore needs to be stressed once again that over most of the country the majority of subsidymen co-operated and paid up. However it should also have highlighted the way in which the actions of those below the gentry could have a significant impact on both local and national politics, and this is something worth emphasizing. The effects of their actions were often completely out of proportion to their numbers. Small groups of committed refusers, such as 'the Chelmsford seven' or those Westminster men who allowed themselves to be pressed rather than accept the Council's let-out of pleading poverty, exerted a crucial influence on the service.[58] By standing out openly against the levy they reminded contemporaries of the issues at stake; by challenging and obstructing the commissioners they exposed weaknesses in the machinery of enforcement; by their example they put pressure on local governors to oppose the levy and reverse the policies behind it; and by their suffering they provided martyrs to nourish the ideal of 'the Country'. The motives which inspired them were varied and complex, often involving notions of legitimacy and a sense of the obligations of the godly, which can be only dimly perceived. At the last, however, they furnish an important corrective to those who might assume that ordinary English men and women were unconcerned at the broad issues of contemporary politics or incapable of action to affect these.

[57] KAO U.951/Z.10, pp. 7–8; ERO D/Ba/F.43; PRO SP 16/54/82i.

[58] *C. and T.* i. 207–8; PRO SP 16/60/10; *APC 1626*, pp. 313, 388.

IV. THE 1628 ELECTIONS

It used to be argued that the 1628 elections were basically a display of support for those who had resisted the loan. John Rushworth, in editing his collection of historical documents during the 1650s, recalled that 'as fast as the writs came to the counties and boroughs to choose members for Parliament, those gentlemen who suffered for the loan were chiefly in the people's eyes to be elected to serve for them in the ensuing Parliament'; and S. R. Gardiner endorsed this opinion in the nineteenth century, with the verdict that 'the elections . . . with a few rare exceptions . . . went against the Crown. Those who had refused the loan were sure of seats. The House when it met would be as stern in its opposition to illegal measures as the parliament of 1626.'[1] More recently however this view has been challenged. In 'A survey of the parliamentary elections of 1625–8', J. D. Thomas has pointed out that most of the loan refusers returned were in any case men who had sat regularly in Parliament before and that where those who had supported the loan chose to stand they generally had little difficulty in getting elected. He therefore concluded that opposition to the levy was a much less decisive issue than Rushworth or Gardiner had supposed, although he still acknowledged that 'it was an aid to nomination'. This view has been pushed considerably further by Professor Hirst who argues that the evidence for 1628 shows that ordinary electors were little concerned with anything other than local issues. After an exhaustive study of parliamentary contests throughout the 1620s, he has concluded that 'nowhere prior to 1630 was there a consistent record of political arousal on the part of the electorate; the most trenchant anti-Court warnings seem to have had no more than momentary effect'; and that 'there is little sign of this most obvious aspect of national politics having a direct electoral repercussion except insofar as it might condition the attitude of the local gentry towards an individual'.[2]

In the light of Hirst's verdict it is clearly necessary to make some assessment of the mood of the electorate in 1628. If, as has been argued, the loan raised issues which were of fundamental

[1] *Rushworth*, i. 472; Gardiner, *History of England*, vi. 229.

[2] J. D. Thomas, 'A Survey of Parliamentary Elections 1625–1628' (University of London, MA thesis, 1952), pp. 48–50; Hirst, *Representative of the People?*, pp. 140, 145.

concern to freeholders, we would have expected this to leave some impression during the elections. In the county seats in particular —in spite of the continuing influence of local landowners—these probably represented the best opportunity for individuals below the leading gentry to express their political opinions.[3] We might therefore have anticipated a backlash against the Crown and those associated with its policies similar to that which is apparent in 1640. The main difficulty in testing for this is that because the number of contested elections in 1628 was relatively small—thirty-three compared with sixty-two for the Short Parliament and eighty-six for the Long Parliament—there is much less evidence to indicate how electors arrived at their choice. Hirst takes this paucity of contests as itself a sign of the lack of political excitement; but as we shall see it can be read more than one way and along with his other conclusions seems open to question.[4]

A number of initial points can be made. First of all Hirst's case is based very heavily on the absence of evidence, and such arguments from silence need to be treated with caution. As we have seen, over the loan there were all sorts of reasons why evidence of principled opposition tended to be played down and suppressed in the sources; and it is much the same over elections. We should take account of this and make some allowance.[5] Secondly we have to be careful in comparing 1628 with 1640. The elections of the latter year were exceptionally fiercely fought, with issues being aired which had built up over five years or more and the Crown making a particularly concerted effort to get its candidates returned. Neither of these pre-conditions applied to 1628; so to use 1640 as a yardstick of political arousal is rather artificial.[6] And, thirdly, the relative lack of contests in 1628 can be variously interpreted. It might be taken to indicate lack of excitement; but it might just as easily suggest that feelings were running so high that some prospective candidates were deterred

[3] Hirst, *Representative of the People?*, pp. 29–43, 109–53.

[4] These figures are drawn from the work of Professor Hirst who has tended to assume the existence of a contest wherever there is evidence of competition before an election: ibid., pp. 139–40, app. iv. This may well overestimate the number of seats actually contested on polling day; however it can be argued that for the purposes of investigating political arousal it is relevant to study contests in their broadest sense. I will therefore employ this wider usage of the term (I am grateful to Mark Kishlansky for many suggestions about election contests, although it will be apparent that our views on this subject differ).

[5] See above, pp. 150, 165–7.

[6] J. K. Gruenfelder, 'The election to the Short Parliament' in H. S. Reinmuth, ed., *Early Stuart Studies* (Minneapolis, 1970), pp. 180–230.

from standing—particularly those who had made themselves unpopular over the loan—in which case the appearance of consensus would be preserved. If we bear these points in mind it is possible to construct an account of the elections which goes some way towards confirming the picture presented by Rushworth and Gardiner.

The clearest evidence for this comes from the comments of two of the best informed newsletter writers of the period. Joseph Mead described the reports which were reaching him in Cambridge at the end of February:

> You heare what work the Londoners have made in choosing their 4 burgesses, that they passed by their Recorder and all their Knights and have chose 2 Aldermen who were never Mayors, Moulson and Clethro, and 2 of their Commons, one Captain Waller and Bunce a linnen draper lately in prison for the loane. They were very unruly, not onely passing by their Recorder and others, but disgracing them with publick outcrye . . . They are generally of this strange humour in their elections. In Lyncolnshire they have chosen Sir John Wray and Sir William Ermin, both loan recusants. In Yorkshire they are about to chuse Sir Thomas Wentworth . . . At Coventry they have done as at London, admitted 2 gentlemen recusants to the country to be of their Corporation that they might chuse them and passe by against their custom all their owne, as being not that way qualified. They were I heard in the like fury in Northampton, refusing Sir Richard Spenser to whom they have bin much beholding onely because he came off to the loane, and would chuse Sir Erasmus Dryden whether he would or no . . .

A few days later he reported a similar mood in the capital's other seat:

> There was a turbulent election of burgesses at Westminster, whereof the Duke, being steward, made account he should be his authority and vicinity, have put in Sir Robert Pye. It continued three days, and when Sir Robert Pye's party cried 'A Pye! a Pye! a Pye!' the adverse party would cry 'A pudding! a pudding! a pudding!' and others 'A lie! a lie! a lie!' In fine, Bradshaw, a brewer, and Maurice a grocer, carried it from him by above a thousand voices, they passing by also Sir Robert Cotton and besides Mr. Man and Mr. Hayward who were their last burgesses, because as is said they had discontented their neighbours in urging the payment of the loan. It is feared saith mine author becaws such patriots are chosen every where, the parliament will not last above eight days . . .

The Earl of Clare in London during February and March picked up a similar impression and explained to his old friend, Lord Vere, how

Essex they say will chuse Sir Francis Barrington and Sir Harbottle Grimstone, both refusers. The same pathe the rest of the shyres (notwithstanding great labor and interpretation to the contrary) ar supposed to treade: for as a playn cuntriman sayd to Mr. Treasurer [i.e. Sir Thomas Edmondes] going to the election, asking him for whom he was answered for whom should he be but for those who have suffered for their country. Of these pieces the House of Commons is like to consist . . .[7]

We should bear in mind that these two writers were picking up the headline material and were tending to base their reports on those areas where opposition to the loan had been heaviest. Their view of the extent of opposition was therefore prone to exaggeration.[8] However if we examine the returns for the county seats there is at least some evidence to support their description.

Each of the four counties where resistance was heaviest—Essex, Gloucestershire, Lincolnshire, and Northamptonshire—returned two loan refusers as their candidates; and, although some of these were regular shire MPs, others—such as Nathaniel Stephens in Gloucestershire or Francis Nicolls in Northamptonshire—had not sat before. Other counties where there had been less evidence of resistance also selected loan refusers who had not previously served as knights of the shires: Sir John Eliot in Cornwall, Sir John Heveningham in Norfolk, and Sir Nathaniel Barnardiston in Suffolk. Just as significantly in those shires where there was no loan refuser suitable to stand, the county often plumped for men who had deliberately refrained from involving themselves in the service. Buckinghamshire, Hampshire, Hertfordshire, and Warwickshire all responded in this way, and elsewhere Sir Robert Phelips and Sir Roger Townsend gained county seats after distancing themselves from the service in a particularly calculating way. In fact out of forty-two county MPs whose response to the loan is known, eighteen were refusers, thirteen either abstained or were uninvolved in the service and only eleven were active as commissioners.[9] These returns, then, suggest that over quite a wide range of shires gentry and freeholders were conscious of the way in which parliamentary candidates had responded to the loan.

[7] BL Harl. MS 390, fo. 356^{v}; *C. and T.* i. 327; *Holles*, ii. 376–7.

[8] However it is worth noting that a similar impression was formed by the keeper of the vestry minutes at Weedon Bec, Northamptonshire. He recorded that 'this yeare the 17th of March began the desired Parliament . . . The Commons in divers shires chose divers of those gent that were refusers of the . . . [one word illegible]': NRO 344P/501.

[9] *Returns of M.P.s*, i. 450–79. These returns are analysed more fully in Cust, 'The Forced Loan and English Politics', app. iv.

The implications of this were illustrated in three of the elections which were contested.

The first of these was at Boston, which, although not a county seat, had a sufficiently wide franchise to allow the subsidymen to express their opinions. When this election was questioned before the House of Commons it was presented as a local struggle over the rights of the freemen; however there were also strong undertones of support for the loan refusers. Excitement over the levy had been running high for several months during 1627. In March Boston had sent its contingent of twelve subsidymen to protest before the commissioners at Lincoln; in April several local men were imprisoned by the Council, including the Mayor and a leading Alderman; and in July there was discussion of the proposal for a common-purse to pay their expenses. This concern appears to have carried over into the election of the following year. All those involved were agreed on the selection of Richard Bellingham for the first seat. He was the town's recorder and a godly ally of Cotton. But over the second they were divided. Amongst the Aldermen and Common Councilmen fourteen supported the renowned local loan refuser, Sir Anthony Irby; but fifteen voted in favour of Bishop Williams's nominee, Mr Okely. This probably reflected the split of a year earlier when the merchant majority had apparently pushed through a resolution in favour of paying the loan which several of their godly colleagues had immediately defied. It looked as if this situation might arise again; however on this occasion the freemen intervened decisively and showed their support for opposition to the loan by electing Irby by sixty-seven votes to none.[10]

It was much the same story in Essex where the local freeholders again declared in favour of loan refusers. The contest here had arisen because of an ill-judged attempt by Rivers and his friends, Wiseman, Smythe, and Maxey to block the election of Barrington and Grimstone. This appears to have been arranged in concert with Sir Thomas Fanshawe, the Surveyor General of Crown Lands, and two of the moderate Privy Councillors with local connections, Sir Richard Weston and Sir Thomas Edmondes. Letters were composed in the name of Wiseman and Smythe giving instructions to the high constables and claiming that 'we have received a command from the King's Majestie and the Lords of his highness' privie counsell to give our attendance at

[10] *CD 1628*, iii. 325–6; PRO SP 16/56/39; 72/36; *APC 1627* pp. 139, 252.

Chelmsford on Tuesday 4th March . . . to entreat the freeholders to give their voices for such gentlemen to be Knights as shall bee agreed upon by the more part of the Justices of the Peace of this countrie there assembled for the good of the Countrie . . .' The whole scheme seems to have been an attempt at 'undertaking', to exclude those MPs who might be troublesome in the following Parliament;[11] however it was blocked by the Earl of Warwick and his allies, drawing on their support amongst local freeholders.

To start with, Rivers and his allies attempted to secure their ends by springing a snap election at Stratford before the electorate could assemble; but this was thwarted when news leaked out and 'upon a jealousy conceived by those of Essex that the sherrif . . . had a purpose there to make a secret election for the parliament of some persons that they did not like, all the freeholders, to a number of 1000 or 1200, repaired presently thither to have hindred that choice and to have named Sir Francis Barrington and Sir Harbottle Grimstone in their places'. The speed with which this assembly gathered suggests some organization on behalf of these two gentlemen, and there are reports elsewhere of temporary freeholds being created to maximize their support. This, however, should not be taken to diminish the significance of sympathy for loan refusers. In the last analysis it is obviously difficult to distinguish this sort of concern with principle from the influence exerted by territorial power—the more so because for someone like Warwick the effects of each reinforced the other—but it should surely be included somewhere in the equation. Given their recent experiences, Essex freeholders could hardly help but take notice of how their candidates had responded to the loan, and this surely helps to explain their willingness to turn out in relatively large numbers. At the final poll it was reported that Barrington and Grimstone had 'all the voyces of 15,000 men, those who say least and were there, 10,000 freeholders, with more passages than I have time to tell . . .'[12]

In Cornwall the turnout was less sizeable, but the response was equally emphatic, which was particularly significant in view of the fact that there had been little resistance from ordinary subsidymen during the service.[13] The campaign here was long and

[11] Quintrell, 'Gentry Faction', 122–3; HMC *Buccleuch*, iii. 324; ERO D/DY2/4, p. 67; BL Add. MS 34,679, fo. 61; see above p. 80.

[12] *C. and T.* i. 323, 329, ERO D/DY2/4; p. 85; PRO SP 16/95/35; C.219/41B/103.

[13] PRO SP 16/56/31; 73/103.

hard-fought and provided the opportunity for a thorough airing of views on both sides. It began on 8 February—virtually as soon as the news of an impending Parliament reached the county—with William Coryton moving 'Sir Reginald Mohun, Sir Bernard Grenville and Sir William Wray at a meeting at Liskeard . . . for their voices to make him a Knight of our shire to serve in this parliament, saying unto them that he had suffered for his country, yet he knew nothing by himself which might make him unworthy of the place . . .' In doing this Coryton was following the local practice of seeking approval of the JPs and Deputy Lieutenants before pressing ahead with his candidature. However, given the fact that all three of these men were friends of Bagg, there was probably also an element of deliberate provocation on his part, perhaps in order to gain added publicity.

Predictably his enemies rose to the bait and after convening the customary meeting they decided to send out a series of letters to local landowners and officials. In these it was stressed that Eliot and Coryton were 'unquiet spirits' and that any attempt to elect them would be regarded by His Majesty as 'an affront to his service; and so we shall draw the displeasure of the King on us'. They were also reported to have obtained letters from Pembroke, the Lord Lieutenant 'requiring them . . . to call the colonels, lieutenant colonels, captains and the trained bands, all armed, to be present at the election'.[14] These were apparently part of the Earl's efforts to distance himself from his former clients and demonstrate the sincerity of his assurances that he would not attack the Duke. They also suggest that Bagg's men were again combining with those elements in the Council engaged in illicit 'undertaking'.

Meanwhile Coryton was pursuing a more popular route to election. As we have seen, both he and Eliot had made their views on the loan widely known through the circulation of 'separates', and Coryton proceeded to make this the focus of his campaign. First of all 'he laboured over the whole country, by means of himself and his friends, divulging amongst the vulgar that he had suffered for his country'. Then he had notes sent around to the local clergy, reminding forty-shilling freeholders of their right to vote and the date of the election. And finally 'it was proclaimed in parish churches that Sir John Eliot and Mr Coryton desired all the

[14] PRO SP 16/106/14; 471/69; *CD 1628*, ii. 33; HMC *First Report* (1874), p. 62; *C. and T.* i. 332.

freeholders to give their voices at the county court to make them Knights of the shire'.[15]

There was never much doubt who was going to win this campaign. When the day of the election came Bagg's friends were conspicuous by their absence. Those local governors who signed the indenture were largely drawn from Eliot and Coryton's allies—such as Sir Bevil Grenville, Charles Trevanion, and John Arundel—or those commissioners who had distanced themselves from the loan—such as William Rous, Thomas St Aubin, John Moyle, and Humfrey Nicolls; and they were supported by large contingents of local freeholders. Grenville, Trevanion, and Arundel arrived at the election 'with five hundred men at each of their heels'; and when it came to the return 'neither did any man appear that gave his voice against Sir John Elliott and Mr. Coryton; but by report there were 4,000 to 5,000 persons present that gave their voices for them; their pretence of suffering for their country had stolen away the harts of the people . . .'.[16]

This sort of unambiguous display of popular support suggests that where freeholders were presented with a clear choice, and issues were widely aired, there was little doubt about which side they supported. However, as has been observed, in many cases such a clear presentation did not occur. Only five of the county seats—Cheshire, Cornwall, Essex, Somerset, and Yorkshire—show evidence of having been contested, and where there was no contest there was less opportunity for the sort of discussion which could focus and refine popular opinion.[17] Inevitably therefore some counties showed little sign of considering the loan as an election issue. Nottinghamshire, which had returned the future refuser Sir Thomas Hutchinson in 1626, reverted to a more conservative choice, selecting its regular Knight, Sir Gervase Clifton, in spite of the fact that he had been one of the most active loan commissioners in the shire. This may well have reflected the dominating influence of the leading county families which was again apparent in 1640.[18] In Westmoreland the freeholders returned Sir John Lowther, even though he was closely associated with the Duke and had played a leading part in the

[15] See above, pp. 168–70; PRO SP 16/96/48; 106/14i.

[16] PRO C.219/41A/135; SP 16/73/103; 96/36; 106/14i.

[17] Hirst, *Representative of the People?*, app. iv.

[18] *Returns of M.P.s*, i. 470, 477; P. R. Seddon, 'The Nottinghamshire election for the Short Parliament of 1640', *Transactions of the Thoroton Soc.* xxxi (1977), 63–8.

collection of loan money.[19] The Suffolk freeholders around Ipswich were said to have been unenthusiastic about the return of Sir Nathaniel Barnardiston, which was reflected in a low turnout at the final poll.[20] And in parts of Yorkshire—where Wentworth had resisted in the belief that this would improve his election prospects—there were some freeholders who showed little concern at anything other than local issues. Christopher Wandesford's statement that there was 'no man I mete with more sensible of the ryght we have then my neybor was when he only enquired for the quota pars of Richmondshyre' has perhaps been made too much of, since James Howell, who eventually sat for the local seat, showed every awareness of broader issues, expressing the hope just before Parliament convened that 'God send me fair weather in the House of Commons for there is much murmuring about the restraint of those that would not conform to the Loan Moneys.' Nevertheless the initial point stands. Wentworth clearly encountered difficulties in his campaign, and, far from finding that his status as a refuser carried all before it, he was obliged to enter into some unsavoury bargains with North Riding recusants.[21]

These cases are a salutary reminder that local issues and gentry patronage still counted for a good deal in shire elections. However this is perhaps not very surprising. What is surely more significant is the evidence demonstrating that the loan was often an issue which transcended localism and that for many freeholders it offered a touchstone by which to judge the fitness of candidates to serve 'the Country'.

[19] *Returns of M.P.s*, i. 478; *Lowther Family Estate Book*, p. 229; PRO SP 16/53/43; 75/6.

[20] PRO SP 16/95/35.

[21] Russell, *Parliaments and English Politics*, p. 334, Howell, *Familiar Letters*, pp. 249–50; *Wentworth Papers*, pp. 4–5.

Conclusion

WITH the 1628 elections events had come more or less full circle from the starting-point of this study. Beginning with the decision to abandon the pursuit of supply through Parliament and adopt 'new counsels', the Crown had successfully collected the forced loan and then been forced to reconsider, because of changing circumstances and the widespread reaction amongst the governing classes. This brought the prospect of a re-summons of Parliament and a return to the status quo. However, the divisions opened up in the meantime had revealed a considerable potential for conflict within the English political system. The opposition to the loan mounted by local governors and subsidymen marked the first outbreak of large scale disobedience since the sixteenth century, all the more significant because it occurred over an issue on which the King had staked so much of his credit; and the protests in Parliament which followed from it have been described by Professor Russell as belonging 'to a world which was much closer to 1640 than to 1621'.[1] An examination of this period, then, ought to teach us something of wider and more general importance. By analysing the onset of crisis, and examining the system under stress, it should be possible to draw conclusions about the nature of political relationships and the assumptions which underpinned the political order.

The first, and perhaps the most straightforward, of these relates to the importance of events outside Parliament. This study was originally conceived in response to Russell's plea for treating the history of Parliaments in the period as the history of men 'reacting to events taking place elsewhere'.[2] An analysis of the origins and consequences of the loan amply bears out his insistence that crucial developments tended to take place not within Parliament but at Court, in Council and out in the shires. It also indicates that the involvement of the political nation in national politics was, for much of the time, a continuous process. This was greatly facilitated by recent developments in the communication of political news. The main beneficiaries at the time of the loan were its opponents, whose success in drawing attention to the basic

[1] Russell, *Parliaments and English Politics*, p. 420.
[2] Ibid., pp. 1–2, 417–19.

issues parallelled that of opponents of the Spanish Match earlier in the decade. However they were not alone. Councillors and courtiers were also capable of using the news to their advantage as they demonstrated during the Council's discussions about re-summoning of Parliament. By the 1620s, to a much greater extent than before, news provided the means for publishing broad political issues and mobilizing political opinion, whether or not there was a Parliament in session.[3] This is not to argue, however, that Parliament was becoming irrelevant, or powerless to shape the course of events. The politics of the period show precisely the opposite, demonstrating that even when it was not sitting the prospects for a Parliament crucially influenced the balance of power and range of options, both nationally and locally.[4] Rather it is to suggest that in seeking explanations for breakdown and conflict, we should look beyond the traditional preoccupation with parliamentary set pieces and explore the tensions existing within the more permanent structures of the day.

If we adopt this approach then the obvious place to start is with the Court, which was the central focus for both the formal and informal processes of government. The period was characterized by a narrowing of access to the Court, and restrictions in the range of royal patronage, as the Duke sought to punish his enemies and reward his friends. This was not the first time he had implemented such a policy. After the return from Madrid in 1623, when the loyalty of supporters of a Spanish alliance such as Middlesex and Williams, had become suspect, he had begun the processes which were to lead to their removal from office.[5] However, the measures of 1626 were much broader in scope and scale, and reached well beyond the Court into the shires. For most of those who opposed the Duke there was no longer much prospect of securing a hearing at the centre and they had either to keep their heads down or turn elsewhere. This produced a situation which resembled that of earlier periods when royal favourites had sought to assert their dominance. A part of the political nation became divided between 'ins' and 'outs' and there was imbalance at Court and instability in the counties. The consequences were disruptive, particularly when the Crown was imposing heavier burdens on local inhabitants

[3] Cust, 'News and politics', 60–90.

[4] See also Cogswell, 'Foreign policy and Parliament: the case of La Rochelle', 241–67.

[5] R. E. Ruigh *The Parliament of 1624* (Cambridge, Mass., 1971), pp. 303–44; Russell, *Parliaments and English politics*, pp. 156, 160.

and depending on their acquiescence for the success of the war effort; however their impact should not be exaggerated. The Stuart regime was much less susceptible than its predecessors to the dangers of aristocratic rebellion or a court coup. Channels of communication between centre and localities continued to function, even for an apparent outcast such as Sir Robert Phelips. And the Duke's determination to punish his enemies was by no means fixed or permanent. In the aftermath of the 1628 Parliament, he made his peace with Williams and two of his leading antagonists in 1626, Arundel and Bristol, and even recruited as 'his creature' Sir Thomas Wentworth—perhaps with an eye to a future Parliament.[6] The political character of the Court, whilst the Duke remained favourite, tended to shift to and fro, in a series of relatively short cycles. Those who were out of favour one day might be in the next, and a summons of Parliament could alter everything. This meant that leading politicians—certainly the more flexible amongst them—were rarely alienated for long even if, like Wentworth, their temporary despair had led them to oppose the regime openly.

Where the narrowing of the Court was much more damaging was in its effect on attitudes in the shires. The temporary change in climate led to less restrained behaviour on the part of some local governors, as one faction sought to identify itself more closely with the regime at the centre and another responded by criticizing it. This was potentially very disruptive as Dr Hassell Smith has shown, for an earlier period, in his study of Elizabethan Norfolk. Here the activities of a group of patentees, purveyors and Deputy-Lieutenants, with backing at Court, provoked opponents into appealing for support from the quarter sessions and local freeholders. JPs sponsored a series of complaints and investigations which helped to influence the course of county elections and ultimately encouraged criticism of the Crown within Parliament.[7] Much the same thing was happening in the 1620s, this time over a wide range of shires. As demands from the centre grew, grand juries and subsidymen were drawn more and more into discussing the legitimacy of benevolences, ship money and militia charges. This increased local awareness of broad political issues, which, coupled with the unpopularity of the Duke and some of those local governors with whom he was associated, helped to promote a growing hostility to 'the Court'. The main focus for this became

[6] Lockyer, *Buckingham*, p. 448; Zagorin, 'Did Stafford change sides?', 161.
[7] Hassell Smith, *County and Court*, pp. 246–333.

parliamentary elections—where such concerns could often be expressed relatively openly—and this created pressure for those seeking election to adopt an anti-Court stance. Eventually it reached into Parliament itself and helped to generate, for example, the bitter criticisms of Deputy Lieutenants voiced in 1628.[8] Such developments, however, were not simply a result of Buckingham's purge and the character of the Court. A good deal depended on the broader climate of political opinion, which was tending to polarize and encourage more extreme responses from local governors. And even more rested on the fact that, as at the end of Elizabeth's reign, the country was at war.

War was mainly responsible for the financial pressures which so preoccupied Charles and his advisers and which had led to the adoption of the loan in the first place. It also imposed a considerable strain on the system of government and tended to generate friction at one of its most sensitive points, the link between the centre and the localities. These circumstances have been seen by Russell, Hirst, and others as a principal cause of political conflict, both in this period and again from 1639 to 1640.[9] A study of the loan amply supports their views. The most serious conflicts generated by it tended to occur at the point at which central government demanded money from the taxpayers; and these were then fed back into the system, opening up new areas of disagreement, such as the Five Knights' Case. Moreover many of the weaknesses in the service, which sometimes caused central government to overreact, can be traced back to faults within the system stressed by Russell and others: the Council's inability to cope with a large volume of wartime business, the strains placed on local governors by an accumulation of demands and the backsliding of taxpayers once the credibility of enforcement had been breached. The very fact of a war tended to raise the political temperature, introducing pressures and problems which did not exist in peacetime; however it was also significant that this was a war which was going badly.

Military failure was inevitably damaging to the Crown, the more so because, as Dr Cogswell has shown, there had been

[8] Hirst, 'Court, country and politics', pp. 133–7; Barnes, *Somerset*, pp. 244–71; *CD 1628*, ii. 79–90, 168–74, 254–64.

[9] Russell, *Parliaments and English Politics*, pp. 70–85, 323–40; C. S. R. Russell, 'Monarchies, wars and estates in England, France and Spain, c.1580–1640', *Legislative Studies Quarterly*, vii (1982), 205–19; Hirst, 'Privy Council and enforcement', 46–66; Morrill, *Revolt of the Provinces*, pp. 24–31.

considerable optimism about the prospects for the war back in 1624.[10] The political consequences, however, are not always easy to discern because of the general reticence about discussing such matters openly. There was certainly some loss of confidence in the government's handling of policy which manifested itself in criticism in Parliament, or the general scepticism about the reality of invasion threats, and generally hampered the war effort. Less obviously there also appears to have been an important shift in the political climate, which widened divisions within the political nation. It seems likely that many Englishmen shared the views of the Earl of Clare—one of the few letter-writers to cast aside contemporary inhibitions—and saw the lack of military success as a result of the harmful influence of the Duke.[11] This encouraged a tendency, which was already pronounced amongst the godly, to turn inwards when seeking the causes of defeat and disharmony. Whereas earlier in the 1620s, blame had normally been laid at the door of external enemies, such as the papist and the Spaniard, now it was more usual to locate shortcomings within the Court and to trace the origins of these to the Duke and his adherents or, sometimes, even to the King. This is apparent from some of the 'news-diaries' of the period, which often recorded views too sensitive to be set down elsewhere.[12] It was also reflected in the attacks on the loan made by 'Canterbury' Scott and the Lincolnshire pamphleteer. Both were considerably influenced by the concerns of the godly, and yet both tended to gloss over evidence of popish involvement in the loan and concentrate instead on the role of Buckingham and Charles. Such a turning inwards was, of course, not due simply to the war. It also had to do with ideological developments which will be discussed in due course. However, failure in war clearly made a contribution to this process; and it did so not only because of its impact on the Crown's critics, but also because of the response it evoked from the King.

During this period Charles became almost obsessively concerned with the loyalty of his subjects. This had to do, in part at least, with his experience of military defeat. He was always acutely

[10] T. E. Cogswell, 'Crown, Parliament and War, 1623–1625' (Washington University, St Louis, Ph.D., 1983); Cogswell, 'Foreign Policy and Parliament': the case of La Rochelle', 241–67.

[11] *Holles*, i, pp. lvi–lxviii; ii, *passim*. There is evidence for this at a popular level in *Rous*, pp. 3–4, 11–22.

[12] Lake, 'Constitutional consensus and puritan opposition', 805–25; Cust, 'News and politics', 79–87.

sensitive about matters which involved his personal honour and the war gave rise to a number of these: his commitment to restoring the patrimony of his brother-in-law, his pledges to the French Huguenots and his promises of assistance to his uncle, Christian of Denmark. In each case, Charles seems to have laid the blame for his inability to fulfil his obligations on his own subjects, whom he saw as having reneged on their 'ingagements' to provide adequate supply for the war through Parliament.[13] This helps to explain the character of his involvement with the loan. His drive and determination to see it through during the early weeks, his personal oversight of the process of enforcement, his willingness to resort to the extremes of the prerogative and, above all, his vindictive attitude towards those who resisted—as if they had affronted him personally—were all in some degree a reflection of his sense of shame at having allowed Christian's defeat at Lutter. Later evidence from the period of the Bishops' Wars suggests that Charles was at his most aggressive and inflexible in wartime and that this in itself could be divisive.[14] However, once more it is important not to lose a sense of perspective. War placed a severe strain on political relationships; but it alone cannot account for the level of conflict generated in the late 1620s.

In the first place it should be recognized that even in wartime the political system retained considerable scope for flexibility and constructive interaction. Some recent work has tended to imply that, although the links between centre and locality were often very close and extremely sophisticated, the relationship was nevertheless largely based on confrontation, with central government constantly trying to break down local particularism. This emphasis, however, has been questioned in the work of Dr Lake and Dr Hughes. They have pointed to some of the more 'functional' aspects of the relationship and demonstrated how, in spite of—indeed in many respects because of—the strength of localism, the system frequently operated in an effective fashion.[15] It is this side of the picture which is most visible when examining the mechanics of the loan. We have to remember that in financial terms the levy did actually succeed, which was remarkable, given the failure of the benevolence a few months earlier. Setting aside the obvious importance of coercion, this seems largely explicable

[13] Russell, *Parliaments and English Politics*, pp. 323, 391, 397–8.

[14] Russell, 'Why did Charles I summon the Long Parliament', 375–83.

[15] Lake, 'Ship money in Cheshire', 44–71; Hughes, 'The King, the Parliament and the localities during the English Civil War', 236–63.

on two levels. In straightforward administrative terms the fact that the Council had considerable resources at its disposal, particularly in wartime, enabled it to operate through a process of bargaining and negotiation, in which benefits were traded off for local co-operation and support. At a subtler, and more political level, the existence of division, both at Court and within the shires, often encouraged competing parties to outbid each other in expressions of loyalty and demonstrations of fitness to receive favour. The effect of this was demonstrated in different ways by the willingness of corporations to co-operate with the loan in order to receive release from ship money and the efforts of individuals to qualify for preferment through personal pledges to the King. Of course for such a system to function effectively required that both Court and Council be accessible to all comers, and clearly this did not always happen. However the extent of the obstacles should not be exaggerated. Buckingham's purge was certainly disruptive in this respect, but it still allowed the likes of Phelips and Wentworth to find 'friends at Court' in this period. For most local governors a greater problem was simply the difficulty of securing a hearing when channels of communication were clogged with wartime business. In the case of the loan, however, a remedy was provided by the councillors' initial meetings in the shires. Thus, in spite of the war, there remained considerable scope for meeting the expectations of those involved in the process of government; and because of this local governors, for the most part, continued to co-operate with the Council.

There also appears to have been plenty of room for extracting additional resources from local inhabitants. Comparisons with continental states or with the period of the Civil War suggest that Englishmen in the 1620s were still relatively lightly taxed. Indeed in a coastal shire such as Kent, the amounts raised probably did not reach the totals for the 1590s.[16] This should give us pause before assuming that resistance to levies like the loan was somehow inevitable, given the general weight of taxation. In Essex those areas which had borne the brunt of wartime levies were also amongst the readiest to contribute to the loan and opposition was based on a whole series of variables, of which general tax levels and ability to pay were only two. It would seem, from the experience of both the 1590s and the 1640s, that most shires were capable of sustaining the burdens of war for at least as

[16] Aylmer, *The King's Servants*, pp. 439–53; Fletcher, *A County Community*, pp. 202–17, 336–9; Clark, *English Provincial Society*, pp. 226–8.

long as they had to during the 1620s. The real issue was whether or not they had the will to do so; and this was largely related to political considerations.

Much the same point can be made about the Council's decision to raise extra-parliamentary supply. This was not by any means the only way of meeting their wartime needs. Charles's basic argument—that there was no real alternative—evidently did not convince his own Council since there remained a large group of moderates who favoured a summons of Parliament and strove to create the conditions in which this would become practicable. Their approach was founded largely on an assessment of the political benefits which would accrue, in terms of reassuring the subject about the Crown's intentions and demonstrating unity and strength of purpose to allies abroad; but it also had a financial basis. The crucial question of whether or not Parliament would actually deliver a supply was still very much open to debate. Its recent record was not impressive, as opponents of a re-summons were quick to emphasize; however the Council moderates recognized that for a Parliament to work they had to make realistic concessions which previously had not always been forthcoming. If an acceptable package could be devised it should still be possible to persuade the Commons to grant subsidies; and in the circumstances this would be particularly valuable. What was needed, after all, in wartime was the means to raise large lump sums on the money market for financing foreign expeditions. This parliamentary subsidies provided. Unlike most other sources of income they were not pledged in advance and their yield was reasonably predictable.This made them the ideal security for the Crown's financiers and allowed loans to be raised within a few days of a grant being approved, as happened in 1628.[17] By comparison extra-parliamentary supply had considerable drawbacks. Its yield was unpredictable and it was therefore not acceptable as a pledge to the financiers. It was slow to come in—with only just over £5,000 being raised from the counties in the first three months of the loan—and much of the money had to be traded away in concessions to make possible the collection of the rest. And the loan was not a levy which could be repeated. Charles had given assurances that it would be a one-off and, as the reaction against raising ship money in 1628 indicated, there were many, both inside and outside the Council, who were determined

[17] PRO SP 16/8/26: Ashton, *The Crown and the Money Market*, p. 32.

to hold him to this. The choice between parliamentary and extra-parliamentary supply, then, was not simply a financial one since either course carried with it a high degree of risk. Ultimately it had to be political, with Charles and his advisers weighing the problems which might arise from a summons of Parliament and deciding whether they could allow the concessions needed in order for it to succeed.

This brings us to what, in many respects, was the root of the particular difficulties experienced in these years, the decision to delay a summons of Parliament for over eighteen months. This is not the place to re-examine the debates in Council, which reveal that a majority of Charles's advisers favoured a re-summons sooner than this. However, it is worth trying to shed a little more light on one of the murkier, but more crucial, aspects of this period, the attitude of the King.

Many contemporaries—and some later historians—attributed this to a 'crisis of counsel', believing that Charles was led astray by the harmful influence of the Duke.[18] There is clearly some truth in this. Buckingham had everything to lose from Parliament and, where it is possible to find evidence, it seems that he and some of his most intimate adherents opposed it. However he was a shrewd enough politician to recognize that circumstances might make a summons inevitable, and that he should therefore keep his options open and, in appearance at least, be ready to support it. This deliberate ambiguity seems to have been characteristic of his role as a royal counsellor. His first priority, which took precedence over any attachment to a particular policy, was his own political survival; and this largely determined the nature of his relationship with Charles. Often the two men worked so closely together that it is impossible to identify who had initiated a particular course of action. This often allowed contemporaries—who were predisposed anyway towards believing in 'evil counsellors'—to shift any blame away from the King; however, where one can discern the origins of a policy it was generally Charles who was making the decisive move, certainly during this period. The Duke's main concern seems to have been to try to anticipate his wishes and move to meet them. Given this, we should perhaps consider dating the start of the 'personal rule' not from 1629 or, as has recently been suggested, from the death of the Duke in August 1628,[19] but rather

[18] K. Sharpe, 'Parliamentary history 1603–29; in or out of perspective?' in Sharpe, ed., *Faction and Parliament*, pp. 37–42.

[19] D. M. Hirst, *Authority and Conflict: England 1603–58* (1986), p. 155.

from mid-1626, when Charles was instrumental in shifting the basic direction of domestic policy and persuading his ministers to pursue 'new counsels'.

Having established the importance of the King's role, however, we need to try to explain his motives; and here there are difficulties. In contrast to his father, Charles was generally reticent about expounding his own ideas. He was not given to writing political treatises, he rarely committed his thoughts to paper and he was renowned for the brevity of his public pronouncements. He also displayed a continuing capacity to surprise those closest to him, as the Duke discovered when he suddenly approved the summoning of Parliament in January 1628. However, we would be unwise to conclude from this that Charles's motives were irrational or inexplicable. On the face of it his actions can appear inconsistent; but if one looks closely at these, and also takes account of such public statements as were made in his name—notably Proclamations and the declarations on the dissolution of Parliaments—it is possible to identify some persistent themes which characterized his approach to politics.

Amongst these was a respect for tradition and what he took to be legal and proper. This accounts for his willingness to pay more than lip-service to the principle that a monarch should consult his Privy Council. On several occasions he followed its advice even though he had given every indication of committing himself in a contrary direction. It also helps to explain his concern to seek judicial sanctions for his actions even when, as with the Five Knights' Case, there was risk involved in doing so. Above all it seems to explain why, in January 1628, after months of putting the case against it, he finally agreed to meet a Parliament. In terms of immediate practicalities this decision was obviously taken because of the Crown's financial needs and—once the Parliament was in session and the scale of opposition to royal policies became apparent—it was this more than anything which kept it in being. However, when assessing Charles it is important to remember that he saw himself as a man of honour and principle. This meant that concrete matters, such as supply, were rarely treated just as ends in themselves; they tended to be endowed with a broader symbolic significance which reflected the King's perception of the relationship between himself and his people. Thus parliamentary subsidies, as he explained in his 1626 *Declaration*, were important not just because of their financial value, but even more as a 'pledge' of the people's 'most bounden duty and thankfulness and as the 'fruits of their most dutifull affections'.[20] Similarly Parliament itself was much more than just an assembly to transact business. If successful it represented the loyalty and mutual affection which should bind together monarch and subjects. 'These meetings and assemblies' he was to declare in 1640, 'were in their first originall and in the practise of all succeeding ages ordained and held as pledges and testimonies of affection between the King and his people, the King for his part graciously hearing and reddressing such grievances as his people in humble and dutifull manner shall represent unto him, and the subjects on their part . . . supplying His Majesty upon all extraordinary occasions'.[21] This vision was very close to being a general ideal amongst early seventeenth-century Englishmen and—if the various declarations issued in Charles's name are any guide—it was something the King wished for as sincerely as the next man. But if this was the case why did he hesitate so long before meeting Parliaments?

The basic reason was a difference of perspective which separated the King from the majority of his people. When a Parliament met Charles expected it to be docile and submissive, and to fulfil its obligations in accord with the 'ingagements' of 1624. If it failed he was largely unable to appreciate that this might be because of the activities of his favourite or other grievances which seemed so pressing to MPs. Instead he interpreted it as evidence for the disruptive influence of an element within the Commons, bent on undermining monarchy.The basis for such a view was already well established. Charles, however, was to go much further than previous monarchs in integrating it into his approach to government; and the most decisive stage in this process was the period from 1626 to 1628.

The existence of a disruptive element was discussed publicly in the *Declaration* of June 1626, and in other royal statements which appeared at this time; but it was not yet clear how far their disloyalty had spread beyond Parliament to the nation as a whole. Charles was apparently still prepared to believe that the damage was limited to a 'few members', seeking 'private and personal ends'.[22] This seems to have changed, however, with the opposition

[20] *A Declaration*, pp. 7–8.

[21] *His Majesties' Declaration to all his Loving Subjects on the Causes which moved him to dissolve the last Parliament* (1640), printed in Rushworth, iii. 1160–7.

[22] *A Declaration*, pp. 19–20.

to the summer benevolence. The initial royal letters accompanying this implied that the King expected loyal co-operation. When this was not forthcoming the tone altered and the equivalent letters sent out at the time of the loan suggested that opposition was being anticipated and prepared for. The extent of the shift was revealed in the sermons by royalist divines in 1627, of which Charles evidently approved. He had apparently come to share their view that opposition to the loan was the symptom of a much deeper disloyalty. As a result he was becoming extremely distrustful of his people's intentions. At the time of the ship money levy in 1628 he sent out letters which implied that Parliament could only be allowed to meet if the taxpayer had first given some proof of his loyalty and affection. And when Parliament did actually convene he interpreted the Commons obstructiveness as the manifestation of a far-reaching conspiracy. In the draft of a declaration, which Attorney-General Heath drew up in the King's name—to be issued in the event of his carrying out the threatened dissolution in early May—opposition was identified with certain MPs who, 'blinded with a popular applause have, under the specious shewe of redeeminge the libertye of the subject, indeavoured to destroy our just power of sovereignty . . .'.[23] This was a measure of the development in royal thinking in this period. Popular expectations were now seen as part of a general threat to the Crown; and the draft as a whole implied that the disruptive element was now capable of overriding any loyal majority in the Commons. In such circumstances it was perhaps hardly surprising that Parliaments were coming to appear unpalatable.

But how much of this was a consequence of the immediate circumstances facing the Crown, in particular the pressures and frustrations engendered by the war? Here it is worth noting that none of the statements made by the King or others who advocated rule without Parliament specified whether such a policy was to be temporary or permanent. It might be expected therefore that once the war had ended Charles's perspective would alter. However this does not seem to have happened, at least not between 1629 and 1632. Dr Reeve's study of this period has shown that the King remained profoundly suspicious about his people's loyalty. The possibility of calling a Parliament was discussed in Council on several occasions, and was still supported by a group of moderates —now led by Pembroke, Holland and Secretary Dorchester—

[23] PRO SP 16/138/45; For a fuller discussion of this important document see Cust, 'Charles I and a draft declaration'.

however each time a summons was deferred, ultimately, it seems, because Charles decided against it. A series of domestic emergencies and the misbehaviour of those MPs imprisoned in 1629 combined to persuade him that his people could still not be trusted.[24] It would appear then, that, although war created the conditions in which the King's concern with disloyalty came to the fore, it alone was not responsible for this. A more profound cause was the ideological division which explains his difference of perspective.

The extent of this has been underplayed in some of the recent accounts of the period. In particular the marked stress on the need for consensus and harmony—itself often a measure of the uncertainty as to whether this could be achieved—has been taken to imply an absence of division or concern with matters of principle.[25] To judge by the loan this would be a mistake. It forced into the open a distinction between what Dr Sommerville has identified as two separate and conflicting themes within the political thought of the early seventeenth century. One emphasized the absolute and unlimited extent of royal power, whilst the other stressed that this was bounded by common law and the law of nature. These themes were normally able to coexist because of the general desire for unity and the readiness of a contemporaries to paper over their differences. However when a crisis arose which touched on basic liberties, then, inevitably, the conflicts were brought to the surface; and in the circumstances of the loan they were exacerbated because they came to be identified with differing views of the nature of true religion.[26] This produced what in their crudest, and most immediately intelligible, form were presented as alternative conspiracy theories, each indicating a different analysis of the ills of the day and a different means of restoring balance and harmony. On one side there was what can best be described as the ideology of 'the Country' in which deliverance from the evils of popery and the corruption emanating from 'the Court' was seen as depending on the beneficial effects of a freely elected Parliament; on the other was the sort of view which tended to go with support for 'new counsels' and prerogative rule, in which the main threat was seen as 'popularity' and the remedy depended on teaching obedience and denying 'the multitude'

[24] L. J. Reeve, 'The Secretaryship of State of Viscount Dorchester 1628–1632' (University of Cambridge, Ph.D., 1983), pp. 73–214.

[25] Rabb and Hirst, 'Revisionism revised', 58–60, 79–81.

[26] Somerville, *Politics and Ideology*, pp. 9–111, 145–88: Russell, *Parliaments and English Politics*, pp. 419–20.

opportunities to concert their action, in Parliament or elsewhere. Each of these sets of ideas contained the potential for achieving harmony; but each envisaged this as possible only after a period of struggle, in which various evils were exorcised through a process of dynamic tension. Ultimately, then, both allowed for—indeed to some extent presumed—the existence of ideological conflict.[27] Of course by no means everyone subscribed to these notions. The middle ground in English politics lay somewhere between the two—perhaps rather closer to the former than the latter—in a broad identity of interest which embraced moderate Privy Councillors, as well as the majority of local governors and subsidymen. The problem in this period was that, under the pressure of events, this middle ground had been substantially eroded.

For Charles and Buckingham and some of those who identified most closely with their interests, both at Court and in the Shires, this led to an increasing stress on loyalty and obedience and a concern to defend royal authority against the assaults of 'popularity'. Amongst those critical of the Crown it produced a less coherent, but, in some cases, equally hard-edged response. The loan had created a situation in which the gentler measures evolved for securing consensus were coming to appear less and less adequate. As Phelips discovered, when he sought the advice of Nathaniel Tomkins, the issues which it raised were such that there was little scope for compromise and little to be gained from pursuing a moderate course. The loan's significance for the future of Parliament, coupled with the nature of the King's intervention and the sufferings of the refusers, tended to mean that it was regarded in a highly emotional—and emotive—fashion as a test of fundamental loyalties and fitness to serve either King or 'Country'. In these circumstances positions hardened, attitudes became more polarized and individuals were drawn to extremes, even to the point of doubting the integrity of the King himself. This was perhaps the most divisive aspect of the whole process, and it was this distrust of Charles which often distinguished the Crown's most radical critics.

The majority still adhered to the view that the best way to deal with the King was to assume that his intentions were of the best and strive to foster a spirit of unity and co-operation. It is sometimes forgotten how young and immature Charles still

[27] Cust, 'News and Politics', 75–90. The internal dynamics of 'Country' ideology have been explained more fully in Lake, 'Constitutional consensus and puritan opposition', 805–25.

appeared to contemporaries, and many were prepared to give him the benefit of the doubt. As Tomkins remarked, in November 1626, he was widely regarded as 'a most virtuous young prince, only thought misguided by his affections, which time, exprience, good counsel and sundry accidents may rectifie; and god forbid he should now be so exasperated and embittered as that there should settle in him any disaffection to his people'.[28] These sorts of consideration must have weighed heavily with the likes of Wentworth and Wandesford as they discussed ways of re-uniting Crown and subject; but not everyone was prepared to make such allowances. Amongst the godly John Pym and Henry Burton were probably not untypical in coming to harbour subversive doubts about Charles, because he was unwilling to rid himself of Arminian advisers.[29] And others were deeply concerned at his refusal to disown the Duke and his personal involvement with the loan. The Earl of Clare was certainly not alone in being taken aback at evidence of this; and—although he himself continued to blame Buckingham—there were those who drew the logical conclusion: if the King was so directly involved in a challenge to the subjects' liberties then he could no longer be trusted. Evidence for this is understandably limited since it was a matter of great sensitivity. However there is enough in the treatises of 'Canterbury' Scott and the Lincolnshire pamphleteer to suggest that some of the Crown's critics now believed the King would only be deterred by a forceful display or opposition. And it is significant that during the 1628 Parliament there was a threat that the whole issue of trust might be publicly debated when William Coryton persisted with attempts to legislate, against Charles's express wishes.[30]

These responses were a measure of how far some had moved towards an open confrontation with the Crown. They also illustrated the way in which the loan exposed fundamental issues to public or semi-public debate; and in many respects this was even more significant. The campaign of opposition took a relatively novel form, using the opportunities provided by the news network to appeal directly to public opinion and mobilise support amongst ordinary subsidymen as well as gentry and local governors. This enhanced general awareness of the implications of the levy and ensured that, in many cases, the individual taxpayer

[28] SRO Phelips, MSS 219/35.

[29] Russell, 'John Pym', pp. 160–4; *A Narration of the Life of Mr. Henry Burton* (1643), p. 3.

[30] Guy, 'Origins of the Petition of Right', 307–11.

faced the most direct test of his ultimate political loyalties prior to 1642. As a result the effects of the loan were not simply confined to an élite; in one respect or another it touched the major part of the political nation.

Hitherto the analysis has concentrated largely on the origins and nature of the crisis between 1626 and 1628; but in a sense this is only half the story. There remains the task of assessing its legacy, and in particular establishing how far the divisions exposed by the loan contributed to the conflicts of the 1630s and 1640s. This is by no means straightforward. Apart from the obvious difficulties in summarizing such an eventful period and balancing the loan against other influences, there has been little agreement amongst historians writing on the subject. It used to be argued—most notably by Gardiner—that the loan represented one of the constitutional milestones of the early seventeenth century; but more recently Russell and Hirst, amongst others, have tended to play down its impact and stress the rapidity with which it was superseded by other concerns.[31] The significance attached to the loan has tended to vary according to a historian's view of the period as a whole. It is therefore very hard to reach a set of conclusions likely to meet with universal acceptance, and what is attempted here is something rather more modest: a series of suggestions, based largely on the work of others, about ways in which the experience of the loan helped to shape later events.

Its immediate impact was apparent in the Parliament of 1628. Although the loan itself attracted little discussion—largely because the Council conceded at an early stage that it was indefensible[32]—the main focus of debate became the issue of imprisonment without showing cause, which had surfaced because of the stand taken by loan resisters. And the way in which this was handled reflected earlier anxieties. The revelation that Attorney-General Heath, acting at Charles's behest, had sought to tamper with the controlment roll relating to the Five Knights' Case seems to have confirmed any distrust MPs may have felt towards the King; and this served to strengthen their determination not to settle for verbal assurances, but to press for some sort of binding legislation.[33]

[31] Gardiner, *History*, vi. 122–33, 156–7; Russell, *Parliaments and English Politics*, pp. 330–4, 337–40, 394–6; Hirst, *Representative of the People?*, p. 140.

[32] Russell, *Parliaments and English Politics*, pp. 346–7.

[33] Guy, 'Origins of the Petition and Right', 289–312; L. J. Reeve, 'The Legal Status of the Petition of Right', *HJ* xxix (1986), 257–77.

Charles, for his part, seems to have been influenced by the suspicions he already harboured about his people's intentions. During the early stages in the Parliament he was kept very much in the background whilst the Council moderates—represented by Coke, May, and Pembroke's client, Sir Benjamin Rudyard—offered concessions and secured an agreement in principle that the Commons would grant supply. But once imprisonment without showing a cause came to the fore he became fully involved and firmly opposed any compromise. By early May he was threatening to bring the session to an end and the full extent of his fears was revealed in Heath's draft declaration. In the event the Parliament continued and the Commons' principal demands were met—largely it seems because of the desperate need for money to re-equip the Rochelle fleet—but Charles's sense of grievance did not really abate. In the latter stages of the Parliament he warned the Commons on several occasions not to interfere with Tonnage and Poundage or further undermine his royal power. And as soon as the session was over he called in the first printing of the Petition of Right—'to be made waste paper'—and ordered a second, which included his unsatisfactory first answer and a series of qualifications made on 26 June.[34] This was the clearest possible demonstration of the extent of the mutual distrust developing out of the loan, and it finally destroyed any prospects that the Parliament might provide a lasting settlement.

Events after 1628 continued to be overshadowed by what had gone before. In particular a fear of disobedience and 'popular rebellion' remained to influence the deliberations of the Council and create an atmosphere in which 'new counsels' still seemed the most appropriate course. The assassination of Buckingham in August 1628 helped persuade Charles to postpone the second session of the Parliament planned for October, and when this finally met the unruly behaviour of the Commons' served to confirm earlier warnings about faction and disorder.[35] Thereafter, as Dr Reeve has demonstrated, the Council drifted from one emergency to the next in an atmosphere of almost perpetual crisis. There remained a group of moderates who struggled to create the conditions in which a re-summons of Parliament would once more become possible; but the King remained firmly opposed and he had the support of an influential lobby led by Lord Treasurer

[34] E. R. Foster, 'Printing the Petition of Right', *HLQ* xxviii (1974), 81–3.

[35] Russell, *Parliaments and English Politics*, p. 392; Gardiner, *History of England*, vii. 77–8.

Weston, who, after being attacked in the Parliament of 1629, had come to adopt the attitude of the Duke. By 1632 conciliar politics were entering a new phase with the deaths of Pembroke and Dorchester and a foreign policy based on non-intervention in Europe.[36] For the time being the prospect of a Parliament diminished and conciliar divisions over domestic policy became less apparent; but neither disappeared altogether and, with the crisis of 1639–40, resulting from the war with Scotland, the King was once more to be at odds with many of his closest advisers.[37]

In the meantime just as conciliar politics continued to follow a pattern established between 1626 and 1628 so too did the actions of local governors and taxpayers. In some cases attitudes developing out of the loan were transferred to other services which had previously been allowed to operate without political controversy. This helps, to explain, for example, the growing opposition to billeting during 1628. Thomas Scott, the Canterbury radical, described this as linked with the stand of those 'wise men and honest men' who had refused the loan; and others may well have regarded it in the same way. Some of the most militant resistance to billeting came from areas which had experienced the service only briefly, but which less than a year before had been involved in opposing the loan. These included the western division of Northamptonshire, parts of Essex and the Banbury and Bloxham hundreds in Oxfordshire—where the Lord Lieutenant evidently regarded the refusal to pay billeting charges as a continuation of their earlier resistance.[38] Of course the loan was not the only influence operating in this direction. A more important factor was the meeting of the 1628 Parliament, where the debates taking place about the liberties of the subject and the reports relayed back to constituents served to legitimate resistance and trigger hostility towards the soldiers.[39] None the less there can be little doubt that the memories of opposing and defying the Crown's servants in 1626 and 1627 carried into the later period and helped to undermine billeting, the collection of knighthood fines and ship money, as well as less obviously political services such as fen drainage.[40]

[36] Reeve, 'The Secretaryship of Dorchester', pp. 73–214.

[37] Russell, 'Why did Charles I call the Long Parliament?', 375–83.

[38] *P. in P. 1628*, p. 220; G. E. Aylmer, 'St. Patrick's day 1628 in Witham, Essex'. *P. and P.*, 61 (1973), 139–48; PRO SP 16/94/73, 73i; 100/87; 110/56.

[39] Barnes, *Somerset*, pp. 256–8; Fletcher, *A County Community*, pp. 197–8.

[40] H. H. Leonard, 'Distraint of Knighthood: the last phase 1625–41', *Hist.*

There were also important tactical developments emerging out of the resistance to the loan. A pattern was established whereby—in the absence of a Parliament—the Crown's opponents first of all tried to obstruct the process of raising money in the shires and then, if this failed to dissuade the Council, sought to bring about a political trial which would mobilize public opinion. This approach was evident in the proceedings over distraint of knighthood, where early opposition led to the former loan refuser Nathaniel Stephens being given an extended hearing in the Exchequer. And it was even more apparent with regard to ship money where the initial efforts of Warwick—to obstruct the service and persuade the King to summon a Parliament—gave way to attempts by Saye and Sele and John Hampden to secure a trial, which was calculated to have the same sort of effect as the Five Knights' Case.[41] The progression which has already been noted, whereby opponents of the Crown moved away from the Council and the Court towards stirring up dissent amongst the wider public, was maintained and extended; and this was to lead to the methods employed by Pym and his allies during the Long Parliament, culminating in the Grand Remonstrance.[42]

There is a further striking continuity in the behaviour of individuals when the loan is compared with later events. As Dr Hughes and Dr Holmes have noted many of those who came to the fore as loan resisters also took a leading part in opposing Crown levies of the 1630s and actively supported Parliament during the Civil War. This is apparent, for example, in Lincolnshire where the Earl of Lincoln, Sir John Wray, and Sir Anthony Irby—all prominent loan refusers—obstructed the ship money sheriff in 1635 and, together with the former loan refusers, Sir William Armyne and Sir Edward Ayscough, loyally supported Pym and the Parliament in 1641 and 1642. It is also evident in Essex where Warwick and his supporters, Sir William Masham and Sir Thomas Barrington (son of Sir Francis) again opposed the first ship money writ and later organized support for Parliament.

lxiii (1978), 23–37; Holmes, *Seventeenth Century Lincolnshire*, pp. 105–8, 121–40.

[41] Leonard, 'Distraint of Knighthood', 29–31; Keeler, *Long Parliament*, p. 351; Rowe, 'Warwick and the payment of ship money in Essex', 161–3; Bard, 'The ship money case of Saye and Sele', 177–84. For another example of this approach see the efforts by Eliot and the other MPs imprisoned in 1629 to secure a trial which would test the strength of the Petition of Right: Reeve, 'The Secretaryship of Dorchester', pp. 158–64, 171–3.

[42] Fletcher, *Outbreak of the English Civil War*, pp. 81–90, 145–51.

Whilst in Warwickshire several less prominent loan refusers, such as William Purefoy and John Temple, were openly opposed to distraint of knighthood and became leading parliamentarians after 1642.[43] Further research would probably reveal similar correlations elsewhere and there also appears to be a less widely noted overlap between those who were active in supporting the loan and those who enforced the Crown's levies during the 1630s and later raised forces for the King. Lord Montague and Viscount Mansfield (after 1628 the Earl of Newcastle) both went to considerable trouble in collecting knighthood fines and sided decisively with Charles at the outbreak of Civil War. Sir Edward Heron in Lincolnshire remained a committed royal servant throughout the 1630s and appears to have begun hostilities within the shire almost single-handed when he set about seizing the arms of parliamentarians in September 1642. And in Somerset Poulett, Stawell, and Rodney provided staunch support for the early royalist musters.[44] There were, of course, exceptions to this general pattern. Former loan refusers such as Sir Marmaduke Langdale, Sir John Strangeways, and even William Coryton were to support the King's side during the Civil War.[45] But given the vagaries of personal circumstance and the rapid shifts in national politics after 1640—which enabled the King to present himself as the defender of traditional liberties—this is perhaps hardly surprising. What is surely more striking is the extent of continuity with the earlier period. In those shires where the issues were clearly perceived and loyalties were not distorted by factionalism, the response to the loan often provided the best indication of ultimate political allegiance prior to the Civil War, especially amongst those who had no aspirations for royal office. This is a measure of the extent to which the later lines were already drawn. Although there were not yet, or perhaps ever, two clearly defined 'sides', many of the basic principles had

[43] Holmes, 'The County Community in Stuart historiography', 66; Holmes, *Seventeenth Century Lincolnshire*, 139–44, 165, 187, 204; Rowe, 'Warwick and the payment of ship money in Essex', 160–3; C. Holmes, *The Eastern Association in the English Civil War* (Cambridge, 1974), pp. 34–48; Hughes, 'Politics Society and Civil War in Warwickshire', pp. 168–9, 174–5.

[44] Cope, *Life of a Public Man*, pp. 134–7, 193–6; Dias, 'Politics and administration in Nottinghamshire and Derbyshire', pp. 347–56, 392–3: Holmes, *Seventeenth Century Lincolnshire*, pp. 150–60. D. Underdown, *Somerset in the Civil War and Interregnum* (Newton Abbott, 1973), p. 32.

[45] Cliffe, *The Yorkshire Gentry*, pp. 293, 334, 346; A. R. Bayley, *The Great Civil War in Dorset*, 1642–60 (Taunton, 1910), p. 30; M. Coate, *Cornwall in the Great Civil War and Interregnum*, (Oxford, 1933), pp. 20–2, 24–6, 31, 58–9.

emerged and some had been obliged to declare where they stood in relation to these.

These principles related to the broad issues which had been brought to the fore between 1626 and 1628. For the Crown the main concern was with preserving royal authority against what were seen as the assaults of the 'ill-affected' and the 'popular'. Amongst its critics there was distrust of the King's intentions, anxiety about the future of Parliaments and unease at the influence of 'evil counsellors', particularly those with Arminian or popish leanings. The continuity of these concerns was illustrated in later statements. For example, Charles's declarations on the dissolution of Parliaments in 1629 and 1640, and his declaration of the reasons for going to war in August 1642, picked up and developed themes established in 1626 and 1628. The 1629 *Declaration* traced the designs of a group of 'malevolent persons' who, through their attacks on the Duke, had sought 'to abate the powers of the Crown and bring our government into obloquy and confusion'. They had also succeeded in infusing 'their spirit' into merchants who opposed Tonnage and Poundage, lawyers who sought to question royal officials and even subsidy assessors who failed to take sufficient account of the King's needs.[46] That of 1640 continued the story, recalling how the King's efforts to offer satisfaction and reassurance over matters such as ship money had been ignored by the 'ill affected' who sought to make a grant of supply conditional on the King 'quitting somewhat of his Royal Prerogative' and 'would quickly bring ruine and confusion to the State, and render contemptible this glorious Monarchy',[47] And the 1642 *Declaration* provided a clear summary of the ultimate scope of the threat. A 'faction of discontented seditious persons' was seeking to bring a 'horrid . . . confusion' in religion and 'a thorough alteration' in the state: 'Can any thing be more evident than that the end of these men is to introduce a paritie and confusion of all degrees and conditions. Are not several papers published by their direction, at least under their contenance, against monarchy itself.' It was this direct challenge which, the King claimed, had finally left him with no alternative but to attempt to arrest the five members and, when this failed, to contemplate the use of armed force against his own subjects.[48]

46 Rushworth, i, app., pp. 1–11.

47 Ibid., iii. 1166.

48 *His Majesties' Declaration to all his Loving Subjects* (York, 1642), pp. 7, 12, 22, 33, 36–40, 72–3, 78–9.

Amongst Charles's critics the Grand Remonstrance of 1641 indicated similar links with an earlier period. It traced the emergence of 'a corrupt and ill-affected party' during the late 1620s and showed how its influence had gradually been extended to disrupt government and undermine true doctrine and the liberties of the subject. Much of the emphasis in the Remonstrance was on the religious aspects of this process; but the authors never lost sight of the fact that a principal 'root of those evils' had been the repeated efforts 'to disaffect the King to Parliaments by slander and false imputations and by putting him upon other ways of supply.'[49] This point might just as easily have been in the Parliament of 1628—or even, perhaps, those of 1610 and 1614—which was a measure of the continuity and thematic unity in much of the ideological conflict of the early seventeenth century. The same issues re-emerged time and again and were still causing division on the eve of the Civil War. Indeed in this sense the causes of the Civil War can be said to have extended back beyond the immediate situation out of which it arose. This is not to argue that earlier conflicts of principle made it inevitable; but they did ensure that where differences arose it was much harder to find common ground and reach a mutually acceptable settlement. And it was the particular contribution of the loan to bring these principles out into the open, promote discussion of them before a wide public audience, and require many of those involved in politics, down to the lowliest subsidymen, to decide between them.

[49] *Constitutional Documents of the Puritan Revolution*, pp. 207, 209, 222.

Bibliography

I. MANUSCRIPT SOURCES

BRITISH LIBRARY

Additional MSS:

11,044	Papers of Sir John Scudamore, Deputy Lieutenant, Herefordshire
12,946	Notes on Star Chamber proceedings.
21,922	Lieutenancy Book of Sir Richard Norton, Deputy Lieutenant, Hampshire.
28,032	Diary of Walter Yonge of Colyton, Devon, 1604–27.
30,926	Miscellaneous 'separates'.
34,218	Papers of Sir Francis Fane, JP, Kent and Northamptonshire.
34,239	Papers of Sir Edward Rodney, Deputy Lieutenant, Somerset.
34,324	Papers of Sir Julius Caesar, Master of the Rolls.
34,599	Papers of Sir Henry Spelman, antiquarian and JP in Norfolk.
34,679	Papers of the Smythe family of Cressing Temple, Essex.
35,331	Diary of Walter Yonge of Colyton, Devon, 1627–42.
39,948	Miscellaneous letters.
40,838	Miscellaneous 'separates'.
44,848	Miscellaneous 'separates'.
46,188	Papers of Robert, Earl of Essex.

Cotton MSS:

Julius C. III	Papers of Sir Robert Cotton, antiquarian.

Egerton MSS:

784	Diary of William Whyteway of Dorchester.
2644	Papers of the Barrington family of Hatfield Broadoak, Essex.
2715	Papers of the Gawdy family of East Harling, Norfolk.
2978, 2982	Papers of Sir Robert Heath, Attorney-General.

Hargrave MSS:

226	Miscellaneous 'separates'.
321	Book of legal precedents, notes on council meetings, etc.

Harleian MSS:

39	Miscellaneous 'separates'.
286	Miscellaneous state papers.
383	Papers of Sir Simonds D'Ewes of Milden, Suffolk.
390	Newsletters of Joseph Mead of Cambridge University.
737	Miscellaneous 'separates'.
7010	Newsletters of John Beaulieu of London.

Loan MSS:

23/1	Papers of Robert, Earl of Essex.

Sloane MSS:

1775	Miscellaneous 'separates'.
1856	Miscellaneous 'separates'.

Spencer of Althorpe MSS:

A2	Papers of the Spencer Family of Althorpe, Northamptonshire.

PUBLIC RECORD OFFICE

C.66	Patent Rolls.
C.115/M.21–37, N.1–8	Newsletter collection of Sir John Scudamore, Deputy Lieutenant, Herefordshire.
C.193/12/2	List of commissioners for the forced loan, 1626–7.
C.219	Returns into Chancery of MPs.
C.231/4	Crown office docquet book, for Commissions of the Peace.
E.163/18/12	Liber Pacis, *c.*September 1626.
E.179	Subsidy rolls and rolls of lenders of the loan.
E.401/1913–5	Pells receipt books.
E401/2322–5	Abbreviates of receipt books.
E.401/2442–4	Auditors' receipts.
E.401/2586	Book relating to privy seal loans of 1625–6.
PROB 11	Prerogative Court of Canterbury, wills.
S.P.14	State papers, James I.
S.P.16	State papers, Charles I.
S.P.78	State papers, France.
S.P. 104/167	Letter book of Lord Conway, Secretary of State, 1625–7.
STAC 8	Star chamber cases, James I.
30/26/59	Roll of loan payments in Devon.
31/3/63	Transcripts of the French ambassador's dispatches.

HOUSE OF LORDS RECORD OFFICE

Main papers series, 1628	Items relating to the 1628 Parliament.
Lords Proxy Book, 1626.	

NATIONAL LIBRARY OF WALES

Wynn of Gwydir MSS	Papers of the Wynn family of Gwydir, county Carnarvon.

BODLEIAN LIBRARY, OXFORD

MS Carte 103	Miscellaneous state papers.
MS Clarendon no. 4	Miscellaneous state papers.
MS Firth c.4	Lieutenancy book of William Lord Maynard, Deputy Lieutenant, Essex.

TRINITY COLLEGE, CAMBRIDGE

MS 0.7.3	Anonymous news diary, 1625–7.

TRINITY COLLEGE, DUBLIN

MS 708, vol. 1	Papers of Sir Thomas Roe.

GRAY'S INN, LONDON

Gray's Inn MS, no. 31	Miscellaneous 'separates'.

FOLGER SHAKESPEARE LIBRARY, WASHINGTON DC

V.b.70	Notes of Star Chamber Proceedings.

MINNESOTA UNIVERSITY LIBRARY

MS 435	Letter Book of the Suffolk Lieutenancy.

ALNWICK CASTLE, NORTHUMBERLAND

Alnwick Castle MSS.XII.7. Box. 1, unnumbered MS	Accounts for estates belonging to Robert, Earl of Warwick.

BEDFORDSHIRE RECORD OFFICE

St John MSS	Papers of Sir Rowland St John, Deputy Lieutenant, Northamptonshire.

BERKSHIRE RECORD OFFICE

Trumbull Additional MSS, bdle. 48	Minutes of the Council of War, May–June 1626.
Trumbull Misc. MSS XVIII	Papers of William Trumbull, Clerk to the Council.

BIRMINGHAM CENTRAL REFERENCE LIBRARY

Coventry MSS, Commissions of the Peace and Commissions for the loan	Docquets of Lord Keeper Coventry.

BOSTON GUILDHALL, LINCOLNSHIRE

Boston Council Minute Book, no. 2, 1608–38.

CHESTER CITY RECORD OFFICE

C.R. 63/2/19	Commonplace book of William Davenport of Bramhall, Cheshire.

DEVON RECORD OFFICE

Exeter Corpn. MS 60D	Corporation letters for the 1620s.

EATON HALL, CHESHIRE

Grosvenor MSS, nos. 25, 26, 31A, 45	Speeches and charges of Sir Richard Grosvenor, JP, Cheshire.

ESSEX RECORD OFFICE

D/Ba	Papers of the Barrington family of Hatfield Broadoak, Essex.
Q/SR 249–264	Essex quarter session rolls, 1620s.
Morant MSS, D/DY2	Letters relating to Colchester Corporation

GLOUCESTERSHIRE RECORD OFFICE

G.B.R., B.8/13	Gloucester Corporation letters.

HAMPSHIRE RECORD OFFICE

Daly MSS, 5M50/1954	Letter book of Sir Henry Whitehead, JP, Hampshire.
Jervoise of Herriard MSS, 44M 69	Papers of Sir Thomas Jervoise, Deputy Lieutenant, Hampshire.
QO/1, 1607–28	Hampshire quarter sessions order book.

HULL CITY RECORD OFFICE

Hull Corporation Minute Book, no. 5, 1609–50.

HUNTINGDONSHIRE RECORD OFFICE

d.d.M. 32, bdle. 10	Accounts for estates of Robert, Earl of Warwick.

ISLE OF WIGHT RECORD OFFICE

Oglander MSS, Box 17	Papers of Sir John Oglander, Deputy Lieutenant, Isle of Wight.

KENT ARCHIVES OFFICE

U.951	Papers of the Knatchbull family of Mersham, Kent, including the papers of Thomas Scott of Canterbury.

LINCOLNSHIRE ARCHIVES OFFICE

A.1.	Lindsey division quarter session rolls, 1625–30.

LONGLEAT HOUSE, WILTSHIRE

Thynne papers, vol. 8	Papers of Sir John Thynne, JP, Wiltshire.

MELBOURNE HALL, DERBYSHIRE

Papers of Sir John Coke, Secretary of State.

NORFOLK AND NORWICH RECORD OFFICE

Norwich A.B. 1613–42	Assembly book of the Common Council of Norwich.
Norwich M.C.B. 1624–34	Norwich Mayor's Court book.
Rye MS, No. 72	Transcripts from the papers of Thomas Knyvett of Ashwellthorpe, Norfolk.

NORTHAMPTONSHIRE RECORD OFFICE

I.L. and I.C.	Papers of the Isham family of Lamport, Northamptonshire.
Montague MSS	Papers of the Montague family of Boughton, Northamptonshire (on temporary deposit).
344P/501	Weedon Bec Vestry Minutes.

NOTTINGHAM UNIVERSITY LIBRARY

Ne.C. 15404	Letters of John, Earl of Clare to his son.
Ne.C. 15405	Letters of John, Earl of Clare to various persons.

SHEFFIELD CITY LIBRARY

Elmhirst MSS 1352–61	Papers of Sir Robert Pye, auditor of the Exchequer.

SOMERSET RECORD OFFICE

Phelips MSS, DD/Ph	Papers of Sir Robert Phelips, Deputy Lieutenant, Somerset.

STAFFORDSHIRE RECORD OFFICE

Leveson MSS, D. 593/S/4	Papers of Sir John Leveson, Deputy Lieutenant, Kent.

YARMOUTH RECORD OFFICE, NORFOLK

Yarmouth, C.18/6	Letter Book of Yarmouth Corporation.
Yarmouth, C.19/6	Assembly Book of Yarmouth Corporation, 1625–42.

YORKSHIRE ARCHAEOLOGICAL SOCIETY, LEEDS

Fairfax MSS, no. 38	Precedent Book of Sir Thomas Fairfax, JP, Yorkshire.

II. PRINTED PRIMARY SOURCES

Acts of the Privy Council.

Bargrave, I., *A sermon preached before King Charles, 27 March 1627: being the anniversary of His Majestie's Inauguration* (1627).

Barrington Family Letters 1628–32, ed. A. Searle (Camden. Soc. 4th Ser. xxviii, 1983).

Burton, H., *The Baiting of the Pope's Bull* (1627).

Cabala Sive Scrinia Sacra (3rd edn., 1691).

A Calendar of Chester City Council Minutes, 1603–42, ed. M. G. Groombridge (Lancs. and Cheshire Record Soc. cvi, 1966).

Calendar of State Papers Domestic.

Calendar of State Papers, Venetian.

Cases in the Courts of Star Chamber and High Commission, ed. S. R. Gardiner (Camden Soc. New Ser. xxxix, 1886).

Clarendon's History of the Rebellion and Civil Wars in England, 6 vols., ed. W. D. Macray (Oxford, 1888).

Clarke, S., *Lives of Sundry Eminent Persons* (1683 edn.).

Commons Debates for 1629, ed. W. Notestein and F. H. Relf (Minneapolis, 1921).

Commons Journals.

The Constitutional Documents of the Puritan Revolution, 1625–1660, ed. S. R. Gardiner (3rd edn., 1936).

The Court and Times of Charles I, 2 vols., ed. T. Birch (1848).

The Court and Times of James I, 2 vols., ed. T. Birch (1848).

Debates in the House of Commons in 1625, ed. S. R. Gardiner (Camden Soc. New Ser. vi. 1873).

A declaration of the true causes which moved His Majestie to assemble and after forced him to dissolve the two last meetings in Parliament (1626).

Deputy Keeper of the Public Records, 47th Report (1886).

The Diary of John Rous, ed. M. A. Everett Green (Camden Soc. 1st Ser. lxvi, 1856).

The Diary of Walter Yonge, ed. G. Roberts (Camden Soc. 1st Ser. xli. 1848).

The Earl of Strafforde's Letters and Dispatches, 2 vols., ed. W. Knowler (1729).

Early Essex Town Meetings, ed. F. G. Emmison (1970).

Eliot, Sir John, *Negotium Posterorum, or An Apology to Socrates*, ed. A. B. Grosart (1881).

The Fairfax Correspondence, Memoirs of the Reign of Charles 1, 2 vols., ed. G. W. Johnson (1848).

Hacket, J., *Scrinia Reserata: a memorial offered to the great deservings of John Williams, D.D.* (1693).

The Harleian Miscellany, 10 vols. (1808–13).

Heylyn, P., *Cyprianus Anglicus or the history of the life and death of William, by divine providence Lord Archbishop of Canterbury* (1671).

Historical Manuscript Commission: *Eleventh Report Appendix I* (1887), H. D. Skrine MSS; *Twelfth Report Appendix I* (1888), Earl Cowper MSS; *Twelfth Report Appendix IV* (1888), Earl of Rutland MSS; *Duke of Portland MSS, III* (1894); *Duke of Buccleuch and Queensberry MSS, I and III* (1899, 1926); *Lord Montague of Beaulieu MSS* (1900); *Various Collections IV* (1907), F. H. T. Jervoise and the Corporation of Aldeburgh MSS; *Marquess of Salisbury MSS, XXI and XXII* (1907–1).

Howell, J., *Epistolae Ho Elianae: Familiar Letters*, ed. J. Jacobs (1890).

Hutchinson, Lucy, *Memoirs of the Life of Colonel Hutchinson*, ed. J. Sunderland (1973).

Instructions directed from the King's most excellent majestie unto all the Bishops of this kingdom and fit to be put in execution agreeable to the necessitie of the time (1626).

The Knyvett Letters 1620–44, ed. B. Schofield (1949).

Laud, W., *The Works*, 6 vols. (1853).

Lesley, Henry, *A Sermon Preached Before His Majestie at Wokin, 28 August 1627* (1627).

The Letters of John Chamberlain, 2 vols., ed. N. E. McClure (Philadelphia, 1939).

The Letters of John Holles 1587–1637, 2 vols., ed. P. R. Seddon (Thoroton Soc. Rec. Ser. xxxi, xxxv, 1975–83).

Letters and Papers of the Verney Family, ed. J. Bruce (Camden Soc. 1st Ser. lvi, 1852).

The Life and Original Correspondence of Sir George Radcliffe, ed. T. D. Whitaker (1810).

The Life of the Renowned Dr. Preston Writ by his Pupil, Thomas Ball, ed. E. W. Harcourt (1885).

The Life of William Cavendish, Earl of Newcastle, ed. C. H. Firth (1907).

Lords Journals

The Lowther Family Estate Book 1617–75, ed. C. B. Phillips (Surtees Soc. cxci, 1979).

Manwaring, R., *Religion and Allegiance* (1627).

'Minute book of the Sussex Deputy Lieutenantship', ed. E. S. Cunliffe, *Sussex Arch. Collections*, xl (1896).

A Narration of the Life of Mr. Henry Burton (1643).

'The Papers of Richard Taylor of Clapham', ed. G. D. Gilmore, *Bedfordshire Historical Record Society*, xxv (1947).

Parentalia or Memoirs of the Family of the Wrens, ed. S. Wren (1760).

Poems and Songs Relating to George Villiers, Duke of Buckingham, ed. F. W. Fairholt (Percy Soc. xxix, 1850).

The Port Books of Boston 1610–60, ed. R. W. K. Hinton (Lincs. Rec. Soc. 1, 1956).

Proceedings in Parliament, 1610, 2 vols., ed. E. R. Foster (New Haven, 1966).

Proceedings in Parliament 1628, 6 vols., ed. R. C. Johnson, M. F. Keeler, M. J. Cole, and W. B. Bidwell (New Haven, 1977–83).

Records of an English Village: Earls Colne 1400–1750, 3 vols., ed. A. MacFarlane, S. Harrison, C. Jardine, T. King, and J. King (Cambridge 1980).

Rural economy in Yorkshire in 1641, being the farming and account books of Henry Best of Elmeswell in the East Riding, ed. C. B. Robinson (Surtees Soc. xxxiii, 1857).

Rushworth, J., *Historical Collections*, 7 vols. (1659–1701).

Rymer, T., *Foedera*, 20 vols. (1704–35).

Sibthorpe, R., *Apostolike Obedience* (1627).

State Papers relating to Musters, Beacons, Shipmoney etc. in Norfolk, ed. W. Rye (Norwich, 1907).

Stuart Royal Proclamations, 2 vols., ed. P. L. Hughes and J. F. Larkin (Oxford, 1973–83).

The Visitation of Essex, ed. W. C. Metcalfe (Harleian Soc., vols. 13–14, 1878–9).

The Wentworth Papers 1597–1628, J. P. Cooper (Camden Soc. 4th Ser. xii, 1973).

Winthrop Papers, 4 vols. (Massachusetts Historical Soc., 1929–43).

The Works of Francis Bacon, 14 vols., ed. J. J. Spedding, R. L. Ellis, and D. D. Heath (1857–74).

The Works of Joseph Hall, 12 vols. (Oxford, 1837).

The Works of Robert Sanderson, 6 vols., ed. W. Jacobson (Oxford, 1854).

Wren, Matthew, *A Sermon Preached Before the King's Majestie on Sunday 17 February Last, at Whitehall* (Cambridge, 1627).

Index